Econometrics Informing Natural Resources Management

NEW HORIZONS IN ENVIRONMENTAL ECONOMICS

Series Editors: Wallace E. Oates, *Professor of Economics, University of Maryland, USA* and Henk Folmer, *Professor of General Economics, Wageningen University and Professor of Environmental Economics, Tilburg University, The Netherlands*

This important series is designed to make a significant contribution to the development of the principles and practices of environmental economics. It includes both theoretical and empirical work. International in scope, it addresses issues of current and future concern in both East and West and in developed and developing countries.

The main purpose of the series is to create a forum for the publication of high quality work and to show how economic analysis can make a contribution to understanding and resolving the environmental problems confronting the world in the twenty-first century.

Recent titles in the series include:

The Economic Valuation of the Environment and Public Policy
A Hedonic Approach
Noboru Hidano

Global Climate Change
The Science, Economics and Politics
James M. Griffin

Global Environmental Change in Alpine Regions
Recognition, Impact, Adaptation and Mitigation
Edited by Karl W. Steininger and Hannelore Weck-Hannemann

Environmental Management and the Competitiveness of Nature-Based Tourism Destinations
Twan Huybers and Jeff Bennett

The International Yearbook of Environmental and Resource Economics 2003/2004
A Survey of Current Issues
Edited by Henk Folmer and Tom Tietenberg

The Economics of Hydroelectric Power
Brian K. Edwards

Does Environmental Policy Work?
The Theory and Practice of Outcomes Assessment
Edited by David E. Ervin, James R. Kahn and Marie Leigh Livingston

The International Yearbook of Environmental and Resource Economics 2004/2005
A Survey of Current Issues
Edited by Tom Tietenberg and Henk Folmer

Voluntary Approaches in Climate Policy
Edited by Andrea Baranzini and Philippe Thalmann

Welfare Measurement in Imperfect Markets
A Growth Theoretical Approach
Thomas Aronsson, Karl-Gustaf Löfgren and Kenneth Backland

Econometrics Informing Natural Resources Management
Selected Empirical Analyses
Phoebe Koundouri

Econometrics Informing Natural Resources Management

Selected Empirical Analyses

Edited by

Phoebe Koundouri

Senior Lecturer, Department of Economics, University of Reading, UK; Senior Research Fellow, Department of Economics, University College London, UK; Member of The World Bank Groundwater Management Advisory Team (GWMATE)

NEW HORIZONS IN ENVIRONMENTAL ECONOMICS

Edward Elgar

Cheltenham, UK • Northampton, MA, USA

Published by
Edward Elgar Publishing Limited
Glensanda House
Montpellier Parade
Cheltenham
Glos GL50 1UA
UK

Edward Elgar Publishing, Inc.
136 West Street
Suite 202
Northampton
Massachusetts 01060
USA

A catalogue record for this book
is available from the British Library

ISBN 1 84376 922 0 (cased)

Printed and bound in Great Britain by MPG Books Ltd, Bodmin, Cornwall

Dedication

To Nikitas, my inspiration and rock, hopefully throughout this fascinating journey.

Contents

Contributors

Melinda Acutt, Revenue and Economic Policy Unit, Yorkshire Water.

Arief Anshory Yusuf, Lecturer, Department of Economics and Development Studies, Faculty of Economics, Padjadjaran University, Bandung, Indonesia.
anshory@bdg.centrin.net.id

Ian Bateman, Professor, Centre for Social and Economic Research on the Global Environment (CSERGE) and Zuckerman Institute for Connective Environmental Research (ZICER), School of Environmental Sciences, University of East Anglia, UK. Managing Editor, *Journal of Environmental and Resource Economics.*
I.Bateman@uea.ac.uk

Christophe Bontemps, Senior Research Fellow, INRA, Department of Economics, University of Toulouse, France.
bontemps@toulouse.inra.fr

Matthew Cole, Senior Lecturer, Department of Economics, University of Birmingham, UK.
m.a.cole.1@bham.ac.uk

Stéphane Couture, Senior Research Fellow, LEF-ENGREF/INRA, Department of Economics, University of Toulouse, France.
couture@nancy-engref.inra.fr

Laurent Dalmas, Research Fellow, Faculty of Law, Political Science, Economics and Business, CEMAFI, University of Nice-Sophia Antipolis, Nice, France.
laudalm@aol.com

Salvatore Di Falco, Visiting Scholar, Agricultural and Resource Economics Department, University of Maryland, College Park, USA and Research Fellow, Department of Economics, National University of Ireland, Galway, Ireland.
s.difalco@nuigalway.ie

Pascal Favard, Professor of Economics, University of La Rochelle, France.
pfavard@cict.fr

María A. García-Valiñas, Research Fellow, Department of Economics, University of Oviedo, Spain.
mariangv@uniovi.es

Stavros Georgiou, Senior Research Fellow, Centre for Social and Economic Research on the Global Environment (CSERGE), School of Environmental Sciences, University of East Anglia, UK.
s.georgiou@uea.ac.uk

Ben Groom, Research Fellow, Department of Economics and Centre for Socio-Economic Research on the Global Environment (CSERGE), Department of Economics, University College London, UK.
b.groom@ucl.ac.uk

Hilda Guerrero Garcia Rojas, Research Fellow, LEERNA-INRA, University of the Social Sciences, Toulouse, France.
Hilda.guerrero@univ-tlsel.fr

David Hadley, Research Fellow, Programme on Environmental Decision-Making, Centre for Social and Economic Research on the Global Environment (CSERGE), School of Environmental Sciences, University of East Anglia, UK.
d.hadley@uea.ac.uk

A.P. Jones, Research Fellow, Programme on Environmental Decision-Making, Centre for Social and Economic Research on the Global Environment (CSERGE), School of Environmental Sciences, University of East Anglia, UK.
a.p.jones@uea.ac.uk

Andreas Kontoleon, Lecturer, Department of Land Economics, University of Cambridge, UK.
a.kontoleon@ucl.ac.uk

Phoebe Koundouri, Senior Lecturer in Economics (B), Department of Economics, University of Reading, UK; Senior Research Fellow, Department of Economics University College London, UK and Member of World Bank Groundwater Management Advisory Team (GW-MATE), The World Bank, US.
p.koundouri@reading.ac.uk

Marita Laukkanen, MTT Agrifood Research Finland, Economic Research, Helsinki, Finland.
marita.laukkanen@mtt.fi

Charles Perrings, Professor of Environmental Economics and Environmental Management, Department of Environment, University of York, UK. Managing Editor, *Environment and Development Economics*.
cap 8@york.ac.uk

Arnaud Reynaud, Senior Research Fellow, LEERNA-INRA, University of Toulouse 1, France.
areynaud@toulouse.inra.fr

Riccardo Scarpa, Lecturer in Environmental and Applied Economics, Environment Department, University of York, UK.
rs 24@york.ac.uk

Timothy Swanson, Professor of Economics and Law, Department of Economics, University College London, UK.
tim.swanson@ucl.ac.uk

Alban Thomas, Professor of Environmental Economics and Econometrics, LEERNA-INRA, University of the Social Sciences, Toulouse, France.
thomas@toulouse.inra.fr

Kenneth G. Willis, Professor of Environmental Economics, School of Architecture, Planning and Landscape (SAPL), Centre for Research in Environmental Appraisal and Management (CREAM), University of Newcastle, UK.
Ken.willis@ncl.ac.uk

Acknowledgements

My overwhelming debt is to all the contributing authors of this book, for their devotion to the completion of their chapters in a relatively short time period and their participation in the reviewing process of the included chapters. I owe a special intellectual debt to all of them, for providing me with a stimulating and challenging environment, not only throughout the period of editing this book, but also throughout my years in academia. I am also grateful to all my colleagues from the Department of Economics at the University of Reading and the Department of Economics and CSERGE/Economics at University College London, for insightful comments and suggestions that have improved the original draft of the book a great deal. Special thanks to Ben Groom for refereeing and proofreading a number of the included chapters.

I am also indebted to two interdisciplinary research teams that I work with. My thanks go, firstly, to every one of the 80 researchers working for the ARID Cluster of European projects that I co-ordinate under the Fifth Framework Program of the European Commission, as well as DG Research for funding this clustering initiative. Secondly, I am indebted to my GW-MATEs from the Groundwater Management Advisory Team of the World Bank, for widening my understanding of the needs and challenges faced by the developing world. Both of these teams have provided me with feedback from other scientific disciplines, as well as field experiences, that enriched my way of thinking about the economics of resource management and broadened my understanding of the scientific and policy issues involved.

I also wish to thank my publisher, Edward Elgar Publishing, whose staff were enthusiastic about this project from the beginning. I owe special thanks to Dymphna Evans, my commissioning editor.

Finally a special debt is owed to my partner, family and friends, who put up with me in such a discreet and endearing manner and who sustain a healthy suspicion about all the writings of economists.

The publishers wish to thank the following who have kindly given permission for the use of copyright material.

Kluwer Academic Publishers for the article: 'Applying Geographical Information Systems (GIS) to Environmental and Resource Economics' by

I.J. Bateman, A.P. Jones, A.A. Lovett, I. Lake and B.H. Day, *Environmental and Resource Economics*, **22** (1), 219–69, 2002.

Every effort has been made to trace all the copyright holders but if any have been inadvertently overlooked the publishers will be pleased to make the necessary arrangements at the first opportunity.

INTRODUCTION

1. Econometrics informing natural resources management: introducing the book

Phoebe Koundouri

The increasing scarcity of natural resources (in terms of quantity and quality) is one of the most pervasive allocation issues facing development planners throughout the world. The need for sustainable management of these valuable resources has become a critical policy concern. Econometrics is a tool that can inform and facilitate such management. However, it is only recently that natural resource management has attracted the attention and interest of a critical mass of applied econometricians.

This volume outlines the fundamental principles and difficulties that characterize the challenging task of using econometrics to inform natural resource management policies and illustrates them through a number of case studies from all over the world. The book aims to be a comprehensive sketch of the broader picture of the state of the art in the area of Econometrics applied to Environmental and Natural Resource Management. The selection of contributions and referee process opted for a wide range of econometric techniques that can be used to inform natural resource management, while keeping a balance between methods and applications. Applications concern atmospheric carbon reduction, water resource management, wildlife, crop and aquatic biodiversity conservation, fisheries management, as well as broader issues on the relationship between growth, sustainability and the environment. The case studies have been carefully chosen as being of major concern in the arena of environmental policy, mainly in Europe (both EU member states and accessing countries), but also in the US and some developing countries.

The volume begins with a review of the arguments for and the implications of employing Declining Discount Rates (DDRs) in cost benefit analysis (CBA) and in the analysis of economic growth and sustainability. Groom and Koundouri show that there exist several growth models in which a relationship has been found between the long-run equilibrium under DDRs and equilibrium when a zero discount rate is employed. This can have the effect of pushing the optimum under DDRs away from the conventional utilitarian outcome towards the Green Golden Rule (GGR) level of capital or environmental stocks. Furthermore, in response to worries that the GGR places weight on the future at too great a cost to the present, Groom and Koundouri highlight the result of Li and Löfgren (2000): DDRs can evoke a solution to resource management problems in which the objective function explicitly takes into account the preferences of present and future generations. Neither zero nor conventional discounting achieves this solution. It is in these senses that DDRs can be seen to encourage a more equal treatment of generations and to promote sustainable outcomes.

Groom and Koundouri also provide a methodology for the estimation of a working schedule of DDRs assuming that future discount rates and the past provide information about the future. The implications of this are that a correctly specified model of discount rates provides a schedule of DDRs which values atmospheric carbon reduction 150% higher than conventional exponential discounting, and almost 90% higher than incorrectly specified models. In this sense sustainable outcomes are more likely to emerge from project appraisal with DDRs, but given that the theory of DDRs for CBA reviewed relates to the socially efficient discount rate, such outcomes can also be thought of as efficient.

The rest of the book is divided into four parts. Part I, focuses on the static and dynamic estimations of the demand function for natural resources. The applications concern water resources management and allocation in the industrial and residential sectors. In particular, the first application concerns water pricing reforms in the manufacturing sector of a developing country, Mexico. The second application focuses on residential demand estimation in an EU (European Union) accessor, the Slovak Republic. Finally, the third application concerns estimation of the dynamic demand for urban residential and industrial water in an EU member state.

Given the public good characteristics and externalities inherent in the nature and allocation of most natural resources and environmental services, quite often their demand needs to be retrieved in the absence of an underlying market where these resources are traded. Part II of the book focuses on methods that can be employed to measure willingness to pay (WTP) for flows and stocks of environmental goods and services. In particular, this part of the book introduces policy-oriented applications of valuation methods, as well as applications of advances in the methodology of valuation methods. In brief, these are the hedonic pricing technique, the contingent valuation method, the contingent ranking technique, and Delphi experiments (consultation/consensus of experts).

Parts I and II of the book have addressed problems in which agents are assumed to function under certainty. However, stochasticity and resulting risk are inherent in most problems of natural resource and environmental management. Part III of the book focuses on the challenges that face econometricians when faced with the difficult task of assessing demand and supply attributes of stocks and flows of natural resources when these are used as inputs in a stochastic production process. Applications concern the role of risk and risk preferences in crop diversity conservation and fisheries management, as well as characterization of irrigation water demand under uncertainty.

Finally, Part IV of the book introduces recent advances in the use of econometrics applied to natural resource management. These include advances relevant to the valuation literature, as well as to the more general environmental management literature. In particular, this final part of the book includes a chapter that presents a variety of meta-analysis models, contrasting conventionally estimated models with those provided by novel, multi-level modelling techniques, as well as a chapter on the evaluation of new estimation techniques for valuing taste heterogeneity. A third chapter introduces a new econometric methodology for examining whether regulations imposed by a management authority comply with the economic objective of discounted rent maximization. Finally, the last chapter of the book uses non-parametric econometric techniques to evaluate the relationship between economic development and environmental quality, the so-called Environmental Kuznets Curve.

PART I: STATIC AND DYNAMIC ESTIMATION OF NATURAL RESOURCE DEMAND

The chapter by Guerrero and Thomas deals with the effects of water pricing on the manufacturing sector in Mexico. In particular, the authors investigate the responsiveness of water demand in the Mexican manufacturing section and hence the efficiency of pricing as an economic tool for water demand management. Estimation is performed on a translog cost function, using a sample of 500 Mexican firms distributed in eight industries (mining, food, sugar, beverages, textiles, paper, chemicals, and steel) for the year 1994. Empirical results demonstrate that industrial water demand is not very sensitive to water price, and that water is a substitute for both labour and materials in the sense of the 'Morishima Elasticity of Substitution' (see Blackorby and Russell, 1989). Finally, another important finding of the application with regard to water resource management is that, conditional on water availability zone, average water productivity is highly and positively correlated with water price.

Moving from demand estimation applied to a cross-section to one applied to a panel data-set, the chapter by Dalmas and Reynaud focuses on the estimation of residential water demand in the Slovak Republic, using a sample of 71 municipalities observed from 1999 to 2001. Three different functional forms for the demand curve are estimated and compared: a lin-lin specification, a log-log form and a Stone-Geary function. Results indicate an inelastic but price-responsive water demand, with slightly higher elasticity than that of EU member states. These results suggest the potential importance of price as a policy tool to manage water scarcity.

The chapter by María García-Valiñas, makes the move from static to dynamic demand estimation. In particular, it focuses on the characterization of water demand in an urban context by estimating water demand for domestic and commercial/industrial levels in a Spanish municipality. Estimation of two dynamic demand models is performed on a microeconomic intra-annual panel of households and firms, using Blundell and Bond's (1998) econometric methodology. That is, estimation of the dynamic error components model is considered using two alternative linear estimators that are designed to improve the properties of the standard first-differenced Generalized Method of Moments (GMM) estimator. Both estimators require restrictions on the initial conditions process. Results on the different degrees of response of the two specified groups of users inform the design of optimal tariffs for the service.

PART II: VALUATION METHODS

The first chapter of the second part of the book is set out to derive willingness to pay for different water sources in Indonesia, in an attempt to access the potential of the Demand Driven Approach (DDA) to water provision. The DDA has been one important aspect of the new paradigm in water provision as opposed to the 'old' paradigm of the Supply Driven Approach (SDA). The proponents of the DDA argue that water is an economic not a social good and its efficient provision has to be directed to those who are willing to pay for it. Many case studies using the Contingent Valuation Method (CVM) suggest that people in poor rural areas of the developing world are willing to pay a significant portion of their income for water and reject the so-called 3–5% rule (which holds that water charges should not exceed 3–5% of consumers' income). Using hedonic analysis on a nation-wide microeconomic data-set from Indonesia, Anshory and Koundouri provide evidence that, in urban areas, people do value the services derived from existing improved domestic water sources (piped and pump water). However, the same is not true in rural areas. Moreover, they find that people in both urban and rural areas do not seem to reveal any valuation of communal water sources, probably due to free-rider problems deriving from the public good nature of these water sources. In general, Anshory and Koundouri's results imply that people in rural Indonesia are not willing to pay for improved domestic water sources. This may indicate that existing services are of very low quality in rural areas or else that there are severe income constraints in these areas. In either case, the results constitute a challenge to the DDA. If the first argument is correct, then the DDA can be implemented only if the supply-side provision is of acceptable quality. If the second argument is correct, then the demand-side approach is not easily implementable and subsidization of water provision is still called for.

Moving from the case where valuation can be inferred from transactions in a related market, Swanson and Kontoleon contemplate biodiversity valuation when no market behaviour exists, on which valuation can be based. Total economic values for endangered species have been stated to be the sum of the range of potential use and non-use values corresponding to a given species; however, it is clear that these values do not aggregate in such a straightforward fashion. This is so since the utilization of wildlife from one constituent affects the production or utility functions of another, leading in essence to various forms of production and consumption externalities between these parties. These types of conflicts between values are at the heart of most disagreements over the direction of conservation witnessed in international wildlife institutions such as CITES. The chapter by Swanson and Kontoleon examines the extent and nature of these conflicts within the context of a case study on the Namibian black rhinoceros. The study consists of a contingent valuation survey that ascertained the willingness of the UK public to pay to support various forms of conservation programmes for the black rhinoceros, ranging from the least intensive (eco-tourism) to the most intensive and intrusive (trophy hunting). The authors find that the strongest conflict between UK-based conservationists is not between animal welfare supporters and animal users (both of which support broad-based conservation measures); rather, they find that the greatest conflict exists between those who receive utility from the use of animals and those who receive disutility from others' use of animals. That is, there is a substantial vicarious disutility motive (akin to a consumption externality) imbedded within the aggregate willingness to pay for non-use of this species. This discussion demonstrates that the fundamental nature of the conflict within a forum such as CITES is not between animal welfare lobbies and general conservationists; rather, the fundamental conflict is between those who enjoy specific uses of a species and those who receive vicarious disutility from this activity by others. This implies that some countries may be able to maximize the total economic value of a particular species by the proscription of specific uses provided that mechanisms are instituted to tap the willingness to pay for such proscriptions.

The chapter by Georgiou et al. also focuses on valuation of natural resources through survey methods and follows naturally on from Swanson and Kontoleon's work. In particular, the method used is contingent ranking (Smith and Desvousges, 1986), which is a survey-based technique designed to isolate the value of individual product characteristics (attributes), which are typically supplied in combination with one another. In this chapter, Georgiou et al. provide us with the first study in the UK to estimate the benefits of river water quality improvements in terms of objective water quality indices. In particular, the authors assess the benefits of water quality improvements in the River Tame with regard to recreational and biodiversity improvements. The results of the study come at a timely moment for the authorities responsible for UK water management. Recent interest in the use of stated preference methods has been expressed by bodies such as the Environment Agency, who are in the process of developing guidelines for the assessment of river water quality improvements. This study hopes to provide useful input into the debate over the use of monetary valuation techniques in this context and should serve to show some of the relative merits and limitations associated with the techniques discussed.

The NOAA guidelines for the implementation of stated preference techniques for economic valuation of environmental resources (Arrow et al., 1993) suggest that the outcomes of stated preference techniques should be compared to the opinions and rankings of experts as a test of their validity. Theoretical and empirical studies have indicated that the reliability of stated preference responses may be called into question when the level of information or knowledgeability that respondents bring to a survey is low, where there is a low level of familiarity with the good being valued, or the 'relevance' of the good to the individual is in question (Ajzen, et al., 1996; Bergstrom et al., 1989). In such cases, the value of expert opinion as a validation of stated preference techniques may be amplified. Despite this, only a few studies have addressed the reasoning behind the use of expert opinion in this way or have compared the preferences of experts and members of the public over the same goods (Boyle et al., 1995; Kenyon and Edwards-Jones, 1998). To our knowledge no comparison has been made between the preference orderings of experts and members of the public for goods with a large non-use value component, the very class of resource values where the aforementioned problems are most likely to arise. Groom et al address the NOAA recommendation through comparing the outcomes of a Delphi experiment (consultation/consensus of experts) and a CVM survey, both of which address decisions concerning the same environmental resource. The comparison is broadened by the use of different levels of information for subsets of respondents to assess the informational effects, and hence different levels of knowledgeability, on willingness to pay bids. This is undertaken for an environmental good for which non-use value is the predominant class of economic values, and with which public familiarity is low, that is, remote mountain lakes.

PART III: ESTIMATION UNDER UNCERTAINTY

The chapter by Di Falco and Perrings assesses the potential role of risk properties in crop diversity conservation. It has been found that the impact of biodiversity on the variance of farm profits, along with farmers' risk aversion, has a pivotal role in determining agro-biodiversity. The authors show that if diversity is negatively related to production variance, the agro-ecosystem will have more diversity. The adoption of a Just and Pope specification provides a straightforward way of modelling farmers' crop diversity choices when uncertainty takes place, and estimating the impact of agro-biodiversity on the mean and the variance of farm income. An application example, based on data from the south of Italy, is presented. This geographical area has been classified as a *Vavilon megadiversity* area for cereals. It has been found that diversity is negatively related to the variance of production. Hence, at least in the long run, keeping crop diversity is a risk-reducing activity.

As indicated in the previous paragraph, Di Falco and Perrings use Just and Pope's (1978) methodology for estimating a stochastic production function. Just and Pope have identified the restrictiveness of the traditional approach (theoretical and empirical) to evaluating the impact of the choice of inputs on production risk, which amounted to making implicit, if not explicit, assumptions to the effect that inputs increase production risk. For this reason, they have proposed a more general stochastic specification of the production function which includes two general functions: one which specifies the effects of inputs on the mean of output and another on its variance, thus allowing inputs to be either risk-increasing or risk-decreasing. The methodology is applied to crop diversity conservation.

While Just and Pope's model is a generalization of the traditional model, as it does not restrict the effects of inputs on the variance to be related to the mean, Antle (1983, 1987) has shown that their model does restrict the effects of inputs across the second and higher moments in exactly the way traditional econometric models do across all moments. Thus Antle's departure point was to establish a set of general conditions under which standard econometric techniques may be used to identify and estimate risk attitude parameters as part of a structural econometric model, under less restrictive conditions. More specifically, Antle's moment-based approach begins with a general parameterization of the moments of the probability distribution of output, which allows more flexible representations of output distributions and allows the identification of risk parameters.

Koundouri and Laukkanen, in the second chapter of Part III of the book, employ Antle's specification to estimate the stochastic production technology and risk preferences of fishermen in the North Sea Fishery. Their results show that fishermen are risk averse and that failure to include risk-averse behaviour in the characterization of the production function may bias parameter estimates and give wrong results with regard to technological parameters. Risk-averse behaviour is translated into a risk premium, which is viewed as the implicit cost of private risk bearing. Risk premium as a percentage of mean profit is found to differ between mobile and static gears, with mobile gears exhibiting higher premia by 10% and 8% of profit, for capital and days at sea inputs, respectively. The authors conclude that neglecting risk considerations when assessing impacts of regulation policies on input choices and expected profit could provide misleading guidance to policy makers. This serves as a significant warning to all policy makers contemplating regulation of stochastic production processes in general, and fisheries in particular.

The third chapter of Part III of the book proposes an approach to modelling irrigation demand under uncertainty. Despite rising concern over the economic regulation of irrigation water demand, no general approach to modelling this demand under uncertainty has been developed. Bontemps, Couture and Favard develop a framework in which such modelling can be carried out and demonstrate the characterization of the demand function for irrigation water. In particular, they use the programming model framework to derive an inverse demand for water under uncertainty. The resolution procedure of the model is numerical and is composed of the agronomic model, EPIC-Phase, the economic model, and an algorithm of search for the solution. In their application, they find the presence of inflexion points in the irrigation water demand curve and analyse the effects of this result in terms of policy analysis.

PART IV: RECENT ADVANCES IN ECONOMETRICS METHODS APPLIED TO NATURAL RESOURCE MANAGEMENT

Part IV of the book is introduced by Bateman and Jones, who present a variety of meta analysis[1] models of woodland recreation benefit estimates, contrasting conventionally estimated models (i.e., expressed preference methods such as contingent valuation (CV) and conjoint analysis (CA), together with revealed preference techniques such as hedonic pricing (HP) and individual and zonal travel cost (TC)) with those provided by novel, multi-level modelling (MLM) techniques. The authors find that while both sets of results generally conform well to expectations derived from their theoretical considerations or empirical regularities, conventional regression findings suggest that certain authors and forests are associated with larger recreation value residuals. However, the more sophisticated and conservative MLM approach shows that these residuals are not large enough to be differentiated from variation that might be expected by chance. Moreover, allowing for the fact that the MLM approach explicitly incorporates the hierarchical nature of meta-analysis data with estimates nested within study sites and authors, leads to the conclusion that these residuals are not a significant determinant upon values. This suggests that, at least in this aspect, estimates may be more robust than indicated by less sophisticated models.

The next chapter is also relevant to recent advances in valuation literature. In particular, Scarpa, Willis and Acutt use multi-attribute stated preference data derived from choice experiments to investigate the presence of a finite number of preference groups in a sample of Yorkshire Water residential customers. The chapter explores alternative ways of modelling heterogeneity of tastes for attributes of a composite public good via choice experiments. The authors focus on public good values and retrieve the implicit customer-specific welfare measures conditional on a sequence of four observed choices. They assess and contrast the sample evidence for the presence of two, three and four latent classes of separate preference profiles, and show the non-parametric kernel densities of the implicit marginal values for river quality, area flooding, presence of odour and flies, water-related amenities and other externalities produced by water and waste treatment companies. With regard to the econometric methodology used in the analysis, they depart from the conventional way of analysing multinomial discrete choice responses via multinomial logit models and mixed logit models. The analysis employs an alternative characterization of preference heterogeneity via finite mixing (Provencher et al., 2002) or latent class analysis (Boxall and Adamovicz, 2002). Their approach, perhaps less elegant and flexible than the continuous mixing allowed by mixed logit (Train, 2003), is shown to have some appeal on the basis of ease of interpretation of the utility functions of each preference group identified in the sample, as well as ease of computation. The main feature of the method used is that, instead of a continuum of taste intensities for each attribute of choice, it provides the preference structure for each of a small number of groups in the sample. Group identification is endogenous, although the number of groups is exogenously imposed, albeit statistically tested for.

The chapter by Marita Laukkanen introduces a new econometric methodology in order to examine how regulations imposed by a fishery management authority comply with the economic objective of discounted rent maximization. The parameters of a dynamic bioeconomic model are estimated using maximum empirical likelihood and time series observations on quota targets, biomass levels and prices of landed fish. The discount rate that is implicit in historical regulatory decisions provides an index of regulatory behaviour. The empirical likelihood method of estimation uses the information in the first order conditions that define the solution to a dynamic resource management problem. In addition to parameter estimates, the procedure yields optimal weights for the instrumental variables included in the estimation. The results indicate that a fishery manager discounting the future at a rate of 15 per cent would set target harvests at about historical levels, which implies that historical harvest levels have been relatively close to the socially optimal policy.

The last chapter of the book uses non-parametric econometric techniques to evaluate the relationship between economic development and environmental quality in the last ten years. This relationship has captured a lot of attention in the scientific community, while today it is one of the most lively research lines in Environmental Economics. After the seminal paper of Grossman and Krueger (1995), an increasing amount of literature has appeared on the so-called Environmental Kuznets Curve (EKC) and testing the existence of an inverted U shape between an environmental quality indicator (e.g. carbon dioxide concentration) and levels of per capita income. Surprisingly, less attention has been paid to the econometrics of the EKC. Recently, Taskin and Zaim (2000) suggested the use of non-parametric estimation techniques to assess the existence of such a parabolic form in the data. The chapter by Di Falco applies possible non-parametric estimators on the EKC hypothesis and compares results between parametric and non-parametric estimators.

NOTE

1. Meta-analysis is the statistical analysis of the summary of findings of prior empirical studies for the purpose of their integration. This kind of analysis offers a transparent structure with which to understand underlying patterns of assumptions, relations and causalities, so permitting the derivation of useful generalizations.

REFERENCES

Ajzen, I., Brown, T.C., and Rosenthal, L.H. (1996), 'Information Bias in Contingent Valuation: Effect of Personal Relevance, Quality of Information and Motivational Orientation', *Journal of Environmental Economics and Management*, **30**, 43–57.

Antle, J. (1983), 'Testing the Stochastic Structure of Production: A Flexible Moment-based Approach', *Journal of Business and Economic Statistics*, **1**, 192–201.

Antle, J. (1987), 'Econometric Estimation of Producers' Risk Attitudes', *American Journal of Agricultural Economics*, 509–22.

Arrow, K., Solow, R., Portney P.R., Learner, R.E.E., and Schuman, H. (1993), 'Report of the NOAA Panel on Contingent Valuation', *Federal Register*, **58** (10), 4601–14.

Bergstrom, J.C., Stoll, J.R., and Randall, A. (1989), 'Information Effects in Contingent Markets', *American Journal of Agricultural Economics*, **71** (3), 685–91.

Blackorby, C., and Russell, R.R. (1989), 'Will the Real Elasticity of Substitution Please Stand Up? (A Comparison of the Allen/Uzawa and Morishima Elasticities)', *American Economic Review*, **79** (4), 882–8.

Blundell, R., and Bond, S. (1998), 'Initial Conditions and Moment Restrictions in Dynamic Panel Data Models', *Journal of Econometrics*, **87**, 115–43.

Boxall, P.C., and Adamovicz, V.L. (2002), 'Understanding Heterogeneous Preferences in Random Utility Models: The Use of Latent Class Analysis', *Environmental and Resources Economics*, **23** (4), 421–46.

Boyle, K.J., Welsh, M.P., Bishop, R.C., and Baumgartner, R.M. (1995), 'Validating Contingent Valuation with Surveys of Experts', *Agricultural and Resource Economics Review*, October, 247–54.

Grossman, G.M., and Krueger, A.B. (1995), 'Economic Growth and the Environment', *Quarterly Journal of Economics*, **110** (2).

Just, R., and Pope, R. (1978), 'Stochastic Representation of Production Functions and Econometric Implications', *Journal of Econometrics*, **7**, 67–86.

Kenyon, W., and Edward-Jones, G. (1998), 'What Level of Information Enables the Public to Act like Experts when Evaluating Ecological Goods?', *Journal of Environmental Planning and Management*, **41** (4), 463–75.

Li, C.Z., and Lofgren, K.G. (2000), 'Renewable Resources and Economic Sustainability: A Dynamic Analysis with Heterogeneous Time Preferences', *Journal of Environmental Economics and Management*, **40**, 236–50.

Provencher, B., Barenklau, K.A., and Bishop, R.C. (2002), 'A Finite Mixture Logit Model of Recreational Angling with Serially Correlated Ransom Utility', *American Journal of Agricultural Economics*, **84**, 1066–76.

Smith, V.K., and Desvousges, W.H. (1986), 'The Value of Avoiding a LULU: Hazardous Waste Disposal Sites', *Review of Economics and Statistics*, **68**, 93–9.

Taskin, F., and Zaim, O. (2000), 'Searching for a Kuznets Curve in Environmental Efficiency using Kernel Estimation', *Economic Letters*, **68**, 217–23.

Train, K. (2003), *Discrete Choice Methods with Simulation*, Cambridge: Cambridge University Press.

2. Sustainability informed by econometrics: the dynamics of the long-run discount rate

Ben Groom and Phoebe Koundouri

1. INTRODUCTION

Discounting is an issue that continues to receive much attention in the analysis of economic growth and sustainability, Cost Benefit Analysis (CBA) and in the study of microeconomic behaviour. With the advent of a distinct long-term policy arena however, in which long-term decisions must be made concerning climate change, biodiversity loss and nuclear build-up for example, attention has necessarily turned towards alternative methods of determining intertemporal values rather than exponential discounting. In particular, the use of discount rates that decline with the time horizon, that is, Declining Discount Rates (DDRs), has received much attention as a useful alternative and the reasons for this attention are numerous.

Firstly, the use of conventional constant exponential discounting over long time horizons ensures that the welfare of generations in the distant future is discounted back to a negligible sum. As Weitzman (1998) states, 'to think about the distant future in terms of standard discounting is to have an uneasy intuitive feeling that something is wrong, somewhere'. Chichilnisky (1996) referred to this as the 'tyranny' of exponential discounting, in that it makes the current generation a dictator over future generations. Such unequal treatment of generations caused Ramsey (1928) to label discounting of future utilities as 'ethically indefensible'. Secondly, not only does this trouble our intuition and sense of fairness, it is also clearly contrary to the widely supported goal of sustainable development. Sustainable development requires that policies and investments now have due regard for the need to secure sustained increases in per capita welfare over longer time horizons than might normally be considered in policy-making (Atkinson et al., 1997). In this regard, the use of DDRs has been found to offer solutions to resource management problems that adhere to desirable axioms of intergenerational choice, such that neither the present nor the future generation holds a dictatorship over the other in determining optimal management. That is, in many cases DDRs can ensure intergenerational equity and sustainability. Lastly, there is a wide body of experimental and empirical evidence associated with the 'hyperbolic' discounting literature (for example, Loewenstein and Elster, 1992; Frederick, Loewenstein and O'Donoghue, 2002), suggesting that individuals actually employ discount rates that decline over time in evaluating projects or scenarios. For this reason, it seems sensible to incorporate such preferences into CBA and the analysis of economic growth and sustainability.

So, on the one hand, the use of DDRs is often seen as a resolution of what Pigou called the 'defective telescopic faculty' of conventional exponential discounting (Pigou, 1932), in that greater weight is placed upon the consequences of projects that occur in the far distant future and the preferences of future generations are more clearly registered. On the other hand, it appears on occasion to reflect how people actually behave. However, despite these arguments, questions remain for the practitioner of CBA: what formal justifications exist for using a DDR in CBA? And, if we accept the theoretical arguments for DDRs, what is the optimal trajectory of the decline? In this chapter we discuss the implications of DDRs for sustainability and intergenerational equity and review the various arguments for the use of DDRs in CBA. Beyond this, we posit a methodology for estimating a schedule of DDRs following the work of Newell and Pizer (2003). This allows a demonstration of the implications resulting from DDRs for the analysis of climate change.

2. A REVIEW OF DISCOUNT RATES

Project Appraisal or Cost Benefit Analysis (CBA) and the Net Present Value (NPV) criterion with which it is associated are rooted in the tradition of discounted utilitarianism. The utilitarian objective is to maximize the sum of net welfare changes for generations within the prescribed time horizon. CBA can be thought of as consisting of two stages in determining the NPV. Firstly, the impacts and the costs and benefits of particular projects or policy interventions must be assessed in terms of their incidence in time and their economic value. Secondly, a judgement must be made concerning the relative value of costs and benefits that accrue in different time periods, that is, a discount function needs to be selected. The discount function employed reflects the manner in which the numeraire changes in value depending upon its incidence in time, and hence the discount rate will usually depend upon the numeraire. However, whatever the numeraire, a decision must also be made concerning the behaviour of the discount rate over time. Koopmans (1965), for example, provides an axiomatic approach to the selection of the discount function which provides a rationale for conventional constant rate exponential discounting. Following the tradition of Little and Mirlees (1974) and Lind (1982), for example, it is usual in CBA to evaluate all costs and benefits using consumption as the numeraire and employing exponential discounting. In this sense, the NPV of a public project with time horizon T can be evaluated as follows:

$$\int_0^T (b_t - c_t)\exp(-at)dt \tag{2.1}$$

where b_t and c_t represent the costs and benefits at time t and a represents the chosen Social Discount Rate (SDR). Where consumption is the numeraire, the social rate of discount is commonly called the consumption rate of interest/discount or the social rate of time preference. We denote this by δ. This discount rate reflects how the contribution of increments of consumption to the underlying utilitarian welfare function changes over time. It also reflects the economic arguments for discounting in CBA.

Firstly, individuals discount consumption in the future because they are impatient. This is reflected by the pure rate of time preference or utility discount rate, ρ.[1] Secondly, utility-maximizing individuals discount the future in accordance with how they expect their wealth to change in the future. There are two important effects here, the *wealth effect* and the *prudence effect* (see for example, Gollier, 2002a). Put simply, if individuals expect their wealth to increase in the future, they value current consumption more highly and as a result discount the future more heavily. Inversely, if individuals are 'prudent', that is, they increase savings in response to greater uncertainty about future consumption, then they will value consumption in the future more, and hence discount the future at a lower rate. These effects and the consumption decisions of utility-maximizing individuals are commonly represented by the Ramsey equation (Ramsey, 1928):

$$r = \delta = \rho + \mu g \tag{2.2}$$

where r is the risk-free rate of return or marginal opportunity cost of capital, μ represents the elasticity of marginal utility of consumption, a measure of the curvature of the utility function and hence the desire to smooth consumption over time, and g represents the growth rate of consumption.[2] Equation (2.2) shows, with reasonable assumptions concerning preferences ($\mu > 0$), that positive growth will raise δ.[3] The equivalent of (2.2) when growth is uncertain is (Gollier, 2002a):

$$r = \delta \approx \rho + \mu E[\tilde{g}_{t+1}] - \frac{\mu}{2}\mathrm{var}(\tilde{g}_{t+1})P(C) \tag{2.3}$$

where $P(C)$ is a measure of an individual's relative prudence as a function of consumption C, $E[\tilde{g}_{t+1}]$ is today's expectation of growth in period $t + 1$ and $\mathrm{var}(\tilde{g}_{t+1})$ is the variance. Kimball (1990) shows that if individuals are prudent then $P(C) > 0$ and hence the associated value of δ decreases with the variance.[4] Equation (2.3) shows that the overall effect on δ depends upon the balance between the prudence effect (the third element) and the wealth effect (the second element). Under uncertainty, the term μ represents another element of individuals' preferences for risk: it is the coefficient of relative risk aversion, and together with the measure of prudence $P(C)$, equation (2.3) shows how the discount rate is dependent upon such preferences.

In a competitive economy, δ will be equal to the social (risk-free) rate of return on capital, r, which, in the absence of distortions such as taxes and externalities, will equal the private rate of return on capital, i. However, under the (realistic) assumption of imperfect markets, these rates are unlikely to be equal and thus the appropriate discount rate is not immediately obvious (Lind, 1982). For this reason, economists and others have argued over which of these several discount rates should be used as the SDR, r, i, or δ. In a competitive economy, these rates are equal, reflecting the interaction of utility-maximizing consumption decisions and profit-maximizing production decisions. Nevertheless, a consensus in recent literature appears to have been reached that the SDR should equal the opportunity cost of capital, r (Portney and Weyant, 1999).

A number of additional arguments have been advanced in favour of once and for all adjustments to the level of the discount rate in particular circumstances. For example, Krutilla and Fisher (1975) suggested that the discount rate should be reduced for projects that have a significant environmental component, since if environmental goods are increasing in scarcity and incomes are growing, future generations will harbour a greater willingness to pay for such goods. Gravelle and Smith (2000) used a similar argument for the case of health benefits. Such an approach implies a composite discount rate for the evaluation of these particular benefits and costs, which is reduced by the inclusion of the growth rate of willingness to pay.[5] However, Horowitz (2002) rightly highlights the importance of separating out contemporaneous and intertemporal valuation issues from the discounting issues. Weitzman (1994) also called for a reduction in the level of the discount rate applied for CBA in order to account for the increased diversion of consumption required in order to meet environmental standards in the face of greater output. He showed that consumption externalities lead to such 'environmental drag' and can cause a divergence between the social and private rates of return to capital, particularly where environmental damage is not easily reversed. A number of other arguments exist for this once and for all reduction in the level of the discount rate.[6]

In the analysis of economic growth and sustainability, the tradition of discounted utilitarianism has also received much attention. The objective function in such models is frequently concerned with the maximization of welfare over time by a representative social planner. In other words, it is utility rather than consumption that is the important value. The objective function in such cases is commonly:

$$\max_{\{C_t\}} W = \int_0^T u(C_t) \exp(-\rho t) dt \tag{2.4}$$

subject to the constraints of the particular model in hand, where $u(C_t)$ represents the utility at time t. The appropriate discount rate in this case, and for all cases where utility is the numeraire, is the utility discount rate ρ.

Clearly, there is a correspondence between the two discount rates described thus far: ρ and δ. Both of these concepts arise in the discounted utilitarian framework, respectively for valuing changes in utility and consumption that occur at different points in time. However, the correspondence between the two will depend upon the assumptions contained in the underlying welfare function. For example, equation (2.2) reflects the assumptions contained in the Ramsey model, that is, that utility depends solely on consumption. The two rates will differ in general and we should be aware that it is quite possible to have positive discounting of consumption and zero discounting of utility, or vice versa, occurring simultaneously.[7]

Economic growth theorists differ in their opinions with regard to the discounting of utility in this way. For example, Chichilnisky (1996) framed the discussion in the language of social choice in her analysis of sustainable growth, by noting that the utilitarian objective function for which $\rho > 0$ places an effective *dictatorship* of the present over the future: positive discounting reduces to zero the importance of future generations' welfare in the calculus of economic growth. Indeed, due to this unequal treatment of generations, many of the early growth theorists were strongly opposed to discounting utility. For example, Ramsey (1928) stated that such a practice is 'ethically indefensible' while Harrod (1948) stated that it represented a 'triumph of reason over passion'. As a result, there are many examples of growth models in which the objective function in equation (2.4) has been evaluated using a zero utility discount rate.

The implications of using zero discount rates are numerous and of great interest in the analysis of growth and sustainability, starting with the analysis of Ramsey (1928) and culminating more recently with the analysis of, among others, Li and Löfgren (2001). Of particular importance is the analysis of alternative growth paths, or interventions, in which benefits or costs occur over an infinite horizon, since when the welfare effects are positive over such a horizon, the integral in (2.4) is unbounded, making comparisons between different alternatives on this basis impossible. This is coupled with problems in the analysis of the long-run equilibrium (Barro, 1999). However, since there is general agreement that the essence of sustainability and the analysis thereof is generally thought to lie in a 'treatment of the present and the future that places a positive value on the very long-run' (Heal, 1998), the choice of discount rate and/or the use of zero discount rates has remained a matter of great importance. As a result, this choice has received much attention in the literature.

This chapter is concerned with an alternative approach to discounting which is relevant to and has been extensively studied with regard to both CBA and models of optimal growth and sustainability. In addition to calls for once and for all reductions in or zero discount rates for the sake of intergenerational equity, environmental or other reasons, discount rates that decline with time, or DDRs, have arisen as an alternative way in which to incorporate these efficiency and equity goals. We now turn to these issues.

3. DECLINING DISCOUNT RATES

In this section we review the use of DDRs in the analysis of economic growth and sustainability and show how current work views the role of DDRs in considering intergenerational equity. This discussion concerns the utility discount rate ρ. We then go on to review the theoretical justifications that have emerged for the use of the declining consumption rate of interest, δ, in CBA.

3.1 Growth, Sustainable Resource Management, Intergenerational Equity and Declining Utility Discount Rates, ρ

3.1.1 DDRs, growth and environment

A number of authors have discussed the implications of DDRs for optimal and sustainable growth in the context of economic growth models. Important contributions in this area include Heal (1998), Barro (1999),

Chichilnisky (1996) and Li and Löfgren (2000, 2001). In many of these cases the analysis is undertaken in the context of the stylized discounted utilitarian for whom the objective is to maximize the intertemporal sum of discounted utility. In this sense, where DDRs are employed, they refer to the pure rate of time preference, that is ρ, which in general will differ from the consumption rate of interest, δ, commonly used in CBA, as described in Section 2. The motivation for the use of such DDRs comes from the empirical and experimental evidence that has been discussed at length in the 'hyperbolic' discounting literature.[8] This is true of Li and Löfgren (2000, 2001) and Barro (1999), for example. The hyperbolic discounting literature provides empirical evidence suggesting that the discount rates that individuals actually apply vary and decline with the time horizon involved. For example, there is evidence to show that individuals discount the short run at rates of up to 15%, whilst the discount rate applied to the long run falls to close to 2% for horizons beyond 100 years (Loewenstein and Elster, 1992).

The implications for the utilitarian social planner's decisions of employing DDRs have been addressed by several authors in different contexts. Perhaps the simplest analysis of these implications is the analysis of an economy dependent upon an exhaustible resource by Heal (1998, ch. 2). He develops a model of resource exploitation à la Hotelling (1931) and shows that if the social planner employs DDRs, the path of consumption declines far slower than in the presence of conventional exponential discounting. Naturally, although consumption eventually falls to zero, the decline is much slower and so certain future generations enjoy higher levels of consumption. This illustrates one way in which intergenerational equity is partially addressed by DDRs: inequality increases at a slower rate here (Heal, 1998).

With regard to renewable resources it is a common result that, where utility depends upon the amenity value of environmental stocks, the optimal stationary solution as the discount rate goes to zero coincides with that of the so-called Green Golden Rule (GGR), a variant of Phelps' golden rule in the context of environmental resources (Phelps, 1961; Heal, 1998; Li and Löfgren, 2000). The GGR is an important concept in the analysis of sustainability and is characterized by the highest sustainable or long-run level of utility. In this sense the GGR equilibrium treats each generation more equally and leads to a level of the resource stock that is higher than that under conventional utilitarianism.[9] Interestingly, Heal (1998) shows that a solution to the renewable resource problem involving the use of DDRs that are asymptotic to zero as $t \to \infty$ is asymptotically equivalent to the solution in the presence of zero discount rates, since the dynamic equations are asymptotically equivalent. That is, when DDRs are used, the long-run stationary solution tends towards the GGR. This represents a more concrete example of the relation between the use of DDRs and the concepts of sustainability and intergenerational equity.

Barro (1999) looked at the implications for the Ramsey model of using DDRs. Motivated by the work of Laibson (1997) he analysed what is widely recognized as a thorny problem in the application of DDRs, namely time inconsistency.[10] He showed that where there is non-commitment, such that time-inconsistent policies can be implemented, the optimal path may mimic that observed under conventional discounting. He concludes that the 'introduction of variable rates of time preference leaves the basic properties of the Ramsey model intact'. However, Barro (1999) assumed that the discount rate declined asymptotically to some positive constant and was not interested in environmental sustainability.

Li and Löfgren (2001) address this issue in the context of the Ramsey and Brock (Brock 1977) growth models, the latter incorporates environmental quality into the Ramsey model. They also assume that the DDR declines asymptotically to zero. In comparing optimal growth paths for the discounted utilitarian for whom $\rho > 0$, zero discounting ($\rho = 0$) and for DDRs, they find that in the Ramsey model the stable arm of the saddle growth path of consumption under DDRs is bounded by those arising under utilitarianism and zero discounting. Specifically, the consumption path starts off in the region of the discounted path and converges in the long run to that of the zero discounting case. The stationary solution in the zero discounting Ramsey case is equivalent to Phelps' (1961) golden rule where the capital stock is held at the maximum sustainable yield (MSY) stock. Just as in the renewable resource case with amenity value described above, the introduction of DDRs leads to a steady state at the golden rule level of utility and takes more account of long-run sustainability.[11] However, where stock pollution is introduced in the Brock model, these results do not hold in general, due mainly to the interaction of capital and pollution stocks, and it becomes unclear whether or not environmental quality increases or decreases when DDRs are employed.

These are just some of the impacts that DDRs have upon the traditional analysis of optimal economic growth, environmental resource management and sustainability. In many cases, the use of DDRs leads to optimal long-run steady states which mimic the sustainable outcomes that arise under zero discounting: the GGR. However, it is widely thought that such outcomes place too much weight upon far-distant future generations, at some considerable cost to the present or near future. Further contributions have attempted to move away from the pure utilitarian or sustainability maximands towards a more general formulation balancing the objectives of the present and the future more satisfactorily. In the examples that follow, this balance is defined in terms of axioms of social/intergenerational choice.

3.1.2 Intergenerational equity vs dictatorship

Perhaps the most interesting contributions in this area are those which endeavour to tackle the issue of intergenerational equity axiomatically. Chichilnisky (1996) sets out a series of desirable axioms of sustainability and derives objective functions that adhere to them. Beyond this, Heal (1995) and Li and Löfgren (2000) show the importance of using DDRs to solve renewable resource allocation problems that also adhere to these axioms. Perhaps the most important of these from the perspective of intergenerational equity is the axiom of non-dictatorship, which states that there should neither be a dictatorship of the present over the future nor vice versa in evaluating long-run economic growth. Chichilnisky (1996) notes that a utilitarian social planner who employs conventional discounting implies a dictatorship of the present over the future. That is, in such a representation, there always exists a point at which the costs and benefits that accrue to the future generations do not enter into the calculus of the current utilitarian. In order to overcome the dictatorship of either generation over the other, Chilchilnisky proposes an augmented objective function that explicitly incorporates, or is 'sensitive' to, the welfare of current and future generations. Chichilnisky's criterion is:

$$\max_{c,s} \alpha \int_0^{\infty} u(c_t,q_t)\Delta(t)dt + (1-\alpha)\lim_{t\to\infty} u(c_t,q_t) \tag{2.5}$$

where utility (u) is a time-invariant function of consumption (c) and the resource stock (q) at each time period (t) and $\Delta(t)$ is the discount factor which could be the conventional exponential factor. Intuitively, the *lim* term reflects the sustainable utility level attained by a particular policy decision regarding c_t and q_t. This can be interpreted as the well-being of generations in the far distant future and is the term that, if maximized alone, is associated with the GGR. Chichilnisky's approach is therefore a mixture of the discounted utilitarian approach, allowing for DDRs or constant exponential discounting, and an approach that ranks paths of consumption and natural resource use according to their long-run characteristics, or sustainable utility levels. Notice that $\alpha \llcorner(0,1)$, represents the weights the social planner applies to each of the components of the objective function, respectively current and future generations. Chichilnisky shows that the maximization of (2.5) avoids the dictatorship of one generation over another. However, while Heal (1995) shows that the maximization of (2.5) in the presence of non-renewables does not exhaust the resource stock, leading to a positive long-run level of utility, the solution in the presence of renewable resources requires the use of DDRs. In the latter case however, the dictatorship axiom is violated: the present is implicitly a dictator over the future.[12]

In response to these issues, Li and Löfgren (2000) treat the future slightly differently. They assume society consists of two individuals, a utilitarian and a conservationist, each of whom makes decisions over the intertemporal allocation of resources. However, the former discounts the future at the constant rate $\rho_U > 0$ and the latter discounts at the rate $\rho_C = 0$. The utility functions of these two individuals are identical, and again have consumption (c), and the resource stock (q), as their arguments:

$$\max U = \alpha U_1 + (\alpha - 1) U_2 = \int_0^{\infty} u(c_t, q_t)\Delta(t)dt \tag{2.6}$$

$$U_1 = \int_0^{\infty} u(c_t, q_t)\exp(-\rho_U t)dt$$

$$U_2 = \lim_{\delta \to 0} \int_0^{\infty} u(c_t, q_t)\exp(-\rho_C t)dt$$

where $\Delta(t)$ is the effective discount factor. The overall societal objective is to maximize a weighted sum of well-being for both members of the society, given their different respective weights upon future generations and subject to a renewable resource constraint. As in the case of Heal (1995), Li and Löfgren show that the use of a DDR which declines asymptotically to zero generates a solution to this problem where the DDR in this case is:

$$a(t) = -\frac{1}{t}\left[\ln\{(1-\alpha)\exp(-\rho_C t) + \alpha \exp(-\rho_U t)\}\right] \tag{2.7}$$

For $\rho_C = 0$, this gives a discount factor equal to $\Delta(t) = (1-\alpha) + \alpha \exp(-\rho_U t)$, which has a minimum value of $(1 - \alpha)$, the weight attached to the conservationist or future generations. This ensures that the effective discount *rate* declines to zero. Thus, unlike the utilitarian discount function, which tends to zero as time approaches infinity, the weighted discount function of Li and Löfgren's model results in a positive welfare weight for the conservationist. For this reason, there is no dictatorship of present over future generations. As the utilitarian's welfare level is explicitly considered, neither will there be a dictatorship of the future over the present. Thus, the axiom of non-dictatorship is adhered to.

Both Chichilnisky and Li and Löfgren show that a declining *utility* discount rate is consistent with non-dictatorship of one generation over another. In this way the 'tyranny of the present over the future' associated with constant rate discounting is overcome. However, whereas Chichilnisky allows the use of DDRs, the axioms of sustainability employed say nothing about the need for DDRs to generate sustainable and equitable solutions to resource allocation problems. Heal and Li and Löfgren show the importance of employing DDRs for this purpose, but only Li and Löfgren's formulation achieves intergenerational equity in the sense of avoiding dictatorship. Perhaps equally important here is the fact that the dual objective function also provides clearer guidance as to the best path towards the sustainable solution, something that is absent from the definition of the GGR. One interpretation of this is that the absence of dictatorship also represents a reasonable efficiency-equity trade-off.

3.2 Cost Benefit Analysis (CBA) and Declining Social Rate of Time Preference, δ

3.2.1 Discount rates determined

In our discussion above of the determination of the correct discount rate for CBA, we have reviewed several arguments for once and for all reductions in the *level* of the discount rate in particular circumstances. Both Fisher and Krutilla (1975) and Weitzman (1994) provide separate rationales for a lower 'environmental discount rate' and although the arguments are not rooted in consideration of intergenerational equity per se, this lower discount rate would naturally place greater weight upon the far-distant future. However, as we have described above, such a reduction would still entail a dictatorship of the present over the future if the discount rate remained positive. Perhaps for this reason, the issue of DDRs for CBA has emerged, motivated less by the experimental evidence that has given rise to the notion of hyperbolic discounting, but more by the analysis of the socially efficient discount rate captured by the Ramsey equation, versions of which are seen in equations (2.2) and (2.3).

Two important contributions in this area are those of Weitzman (1998) and Gollier (2002a, 2002b), each of whom analyses the impact of uncertainty upon the determination of the social rate of time preference, δ, in a competitive economy. This is not to say that the issue of DDRs in a deterministic world has not been the subject of discussion. Weitzman (1994), for example, showed that the divergence between the social and private rates of return on capital, r and i respectively, is captured by the following equation:

$$r = i\left[1 - Z\left(1 + \frac{1}{E}\right)\right] \tag{2.8}$$

where Z represents the proportion of national income spent on environmental goods and projects (for instance, clean-ups), while E represents the elasticity of environmental improvement with respect to expenditure on environmental goods (such as preservation, mitigation), and $E > 0$. This reflects the tension in his model between investments in environmental protection and the production of consumption goods and the associated 'environmental drag': the fraction of extra consumption arising from a marginal investment that would have to be diverted to maintain the environmental standard. Notice that the social rate of discount, r, is lower than the private rate, i, for all positive levels of Z and E.[13] The important implication here is that the socially efficient discount rate will be *declining over time* if the proportion of income spent on environmental goods, E, is increasing over time. With positive growth this is guaranteed if environmental resources are luxury goods. A similar result holds if the elasticity of environmental improvement is declining over time. This analysis, summarized by equation (2.8), shows that even in a deterministic world consideration of preferences for the environment alone can provide an argument for DDRs.[14]

3.2.2 Declining discount rates and uncertainty

Clearly, the one thing that can be said with certainty about the far-distant future is that future states of the world are uncertain. Recent work by Weitzman (1998, 2001) and Gollier (2002a, 2002b, 2002c) has investigated the impact of uncertainty upon the determination of the social discount rate for CBA and found that the arguments for DDRs are compelling. Their analysis of uncertainty concerning future states of the world has focussed respectively upon the opportunity cost of capital, r, and growth, g. Furthermore, just as Weitzman (1994) introduced preferences for environmental goods as a determinant of the SDR in a structural model, Gollier (2002a, 2002b) shows that in an uncertain world it is preference for risk that becomes important.

Uncertain marginal productivity of capital (r) and DDRs

In an interesting paper, Weitzman (1998) develops ideas first formalized by Dybvig et al. (1996) and shows how uncertainty regarding the marginal productivity of capital, r, leads to a DDR. He argues that there are good reasons to expect that in the long run r is uncertain: there is uncertainty concerning capital accumulation, the degree of diminishing returns, the state of the environment, the state of international relations, and the level and pace of technological progress and so on.

Weitzman (1998) shows the relationship between the socially efficient discount rates and the time horizon when it is assumed that r is uncertain and agents are risk-neutral.[15] He shows that, when these agents wish to maximize the NPV of investment either at an uncertain per-period risk-free interest rate, $\tilde{R}$, or in a project that yields a sure benefit in period T, the socially efficient discount rate (before the realization of the uncertain risk-free rate) is declining with time. In other words, the yield curve is declining.

This result comes from the observation that we should average over discount factors rather than because rates and discounted values are a convex function of the discount rate. In discrete time, recall that the discount factor (A_t) for a time period t is given by:

$$A_t = \frac{1}{1+r_1} \times \frac{1}{1+r_2} \times \frac{1}{1+r_3} \times \cdots \times \frac{1}{1+r_t} \tag{2.9}$$

With conventional discounting $r_t = r$. When the social rate of return is uncertain, however, there are several potential states of the world, each with an associated discount rate and probability of realization. For simplicity, imagine there are two potential future states of the world, states 1 and 2, each with an associated interest rate, $R_1$and R_2, and probability of being realized, p_1 and p_2, where $p_1 + p_2 = 1$. Assuming that R_1 and R_2 are constant across time in each scenario, the associated discount factors for each scenario are:

$$A_{1t} = \frac{1}{(1+R_1)^t} \text{ and, } A_{2t} = \frac{1}{(1+R_2)^t}$$

In the face of uncertain r, agents are unsure as to how to evaluate the opportunity cost of the project, and hence which discount factor to employ in determining the NPV. Agents must make some judgement about the discount factor and will use the expected, or *certainty equivalent discount factor*. Weitzman defines the certainty equivalent discount factor for risk-neutral agents as the expected value:

$$E[(1+\tilde{R}_t)^{-t}] = p_1(1+R_1)^{-t} + p_2(1+R_2)^{-t} \tag{2.10}$$

Gollier (2002a) notes that, given the assumption of risk neutrality, there would be arbitrage were it not the case that:

$$E[(1+\tilde{R}_t)^{-t}]^{1/t} = 1 + r_t \tag{2.11}$$

where r_t is the equilibrium rate of interest for risk-neutral agents prior to the realization of $\tilde{R}$, and is defined by the point at which the expected cost of purchasing the claim of \$1 at time t is equal to the present value of the benefit. Equation (2.11) shows that r_t is the appropriate socially efficient discount *rate* for use in CBA, and this is the *certainty equivalent discount rate* (CER).[16] It is easy to show that the CER is a declining function of time and a formal proof of this result can be sketched by noting that equation (2.8) is simply a re-statement of Jenson's inequality: $(1 + r_t)$ is a harmonic mean of $(1 + \tilde{R})$ over time, which is less than the arithmetic mean and tends to its lowest possible value, R_{min}, as $t \rightarrow \infty$.[17] This is a well-known result which can be derived from Pratt's theorem (Gollier, 2002c).[18]

Table 2.1 Numerical example of Weitzman's declining certainty equivalent discount rate

Interest rate scenarios	Discount factors in period t				
	10	50	100	200	500
2% (p_1 = 0.5)	0.82	0.37	0.14	0.02	0.00
5% (p_2 = 0.5)	0.61	0.09	0.01	0.00	0.00
Certainty equivalent discount factor, $E[(1+\tilde{R}_t)^{-t}]$	0.72	0.23	0.07	0.01	0.00
Average CER, r_t	3.38%	2.99%	2.65%	2.35%	2.14%
Marginal CER, $\tilde{r}_t$	3.28%	2.57%	2.16%	2.01%	2.00%

A numerical example is useful to see how these results are borne out. Table 2.1 assumes there are two potential scenarios (j =2) the probabilities of which are distributed uniformly ($p_1 = p_2 = 0.5$). The intuition behind this result is that calculating the CER rate requires taking a weighted average of several discount rate scenarios, where the weights are the discount *factors*. The discount factors in each scenario decrease exponentially over time in the way we observe when using conventional constant discount rates. In scenarios with higher discount rates, the discount factors decline more rapidly to zero. As such, the weight placed on scenarios with high discount rates itself declines with time, until the only relevant scenario is that with the lowest conceivable interest rate. In effect, the power of exponential discounting reduces the importance of future scenarios with high discount rates to zero, since the discount factor in these scenarios goes to zero. Since in the *ex ante* equilibrium the certainty equivalent rate of discount must equal the socially efficient discount rate in all periods of time, this results in an SDR which declines over time. This behaviour is exhibited in Table 2.1: the CER approaches the lowest discount rate of the two scenarios considered, 2%. In year 200 the marginal CER has fallen to 2.01%, and by year 500 this rate has fallen to 2.0%.

Weitzman's argument seems very convincing: uncertainty in the discount rate itself leads to an arbitrage in which the socially efficient discount rate is a declining function of time. In addition, the apparent ease of application renders it appealing to the practitioner. However, Gollier (2002c) argues that Weitzman's logic relies critically upon a tacit assumption that we are maximizing the Expected Net Present Value (ENPV) of a project, such that it is the current generation that bears the risk of variation in the SDR. He illustrates this point by analysing the socially optimal discount rate that arises when we use an alternative criterion for project appraisal, the Expected Net Future Value (ENFV).

ENPV vs ENFV

In order to find the ENPV of a project that costs \$1 today and yields \$*Z* at time *T* when the discount rate, $\tilde{R}$, is uncertain, the planner will evaluate:

$$\text{ENPV:}\ -1 + ZEe^{-\tilde{R}t} \geq 0$$

If this condition holds, then the agent should proceed with the project. The certainty equivalent per period discount rate in this environment, $r_w(t)$, is that which satisfies $Ee^{-\tilde{R}t} = e^{-r_u(t)t}$, and this is declining over time as described above.

Alternatively, Gollier asks us to imagine that we want to maximize the ENFV, that is, we wish to rank our projects on the basis of maximizing the value of assets that accumulate to future generations. The ENFV rule can be thought of as:

$$\text{ENFV:}\ -Ee^{\tilde{x}t} + Z \geq 0$$

in which case the certainty equivalent per period *interest* rate, $r(t)$ is that which satisfies $Ee^{\tilde{x}t} = e^{r(t)t}$. Noting that $r_w(t) \neq r(t)$, Gollier suggests that, when we rank projects by ENFV, the socially efficient discount rate, $r(t)$ is in fact *increasing* over time, and converges to the highest possible value of r as $t \to \infty$, the precise mirror image of Weitzman's (1998) result. Gollier argues that both of these criteria cannot be correct and that since the two only differ in the location of the residual risk – when we use ENPV, agents in the present are bearing the risk and under the ENFV it is the future generations that are bearing the risk – we need some method of choosing how to allocate risk in order to choose between them.[19]

In many ways this seems like a bizarre result: the location of risk affects the decision of risk-neutral agents. Indeed, Hepburn and Groom (2004) show that this particular conundrum has an altogether different interpretation which has nothing to do with the location in time of risk. They show that ENPV and ENFV are special cases of a more general Expected Net Value (ENV) criterion which is dependent upon the base year chosen for project evaluation. In this light they show that the certainty equivalent discount rate is increasing in the base year chosen for CBA (the temporal numeraire) but decreasing with the passage of time in the manner of Weitzman (1998). This aside, as shown by equation (2.3), when we are considering uncertainty, it is eminently sensible to understand the role of risk preferences, the extent of risk aversion, the level of prudence, in determining the discount rate. This is the approach taken by Gollier (2002a, 2002b).

The effect of uncertain growth, g, *on the social time preference rate,* δ
In the absence of currently existing financial markets which extend to the far-distant future, Gollier analyses the economic arguments for discounting the long run contained in δ. As described in Section 2 above, there are two underlying characteristics of individual preferences which determine δ, (i) pure impatience, represented by the utility discount rate, ρ, and (ii) the desire to smooth growing wealth over time reflected by the term μg. Under certainty μ reflects the degree of aversion to fluctuations in consumption; however, in the environment of uncertain growth that is the focus of Gollier, this term represents the coefficient of relative risk aversion. This captures individuals' preferences for risk and how these preferences vary with income. The effect of individual preferences for risk upon the *level* of the discount rate has already been described: the wealth effect increases the discount rate and prudent individuals facing uncertain growth reduce the discount rate. These effects can be understood with reference to equations (2.2) and (2.3) above. What is also clear from equation (2.3) is that changes over time in individuals' preferences for risk.

Gollier analyses the yield curve in the context of a Lucas (1977) tree economy.[20] Simply put, Gollier (2002a, 2002b) shows that where growth is uncertain but definitely positive, that is there is no prospect of recession, and individuals exhibit Decreasing Relative Risk Aversion (DRRA) (μ decreases with income), the socially efficient discount rate will also be decreasing over time. In other words, as incomes grow over time, the prudence effect outweighs the wealth effect and the yield curve is downward sloping. The corollary of this is that, under conditions where individuals display Constant Relative Risk Aversion (CRRA), μ remains constant and the socially efficient discount rate remains flat: that is, the prudence and wealth effects exactly compensate one another and the yield curve is flat.

The complexity of the analysis is dependent upon the assumptions concerning the probability distribution of growth.[21] When the prospect of recession is introduced, the conditions for a declining yield curve become highly specialized. For example, if there is a risk of recession in the long run, the yield curve is declining only if individuals display both DRRA and Increasing Absolute Prudence (IAP): $P'(c) > 0$.[22] This represents a distinct class of utility functions with restrictions upon fourth derivatives. Furthermore, if the risk of recession is extended to all future periods, short run and long run, a declining yield curve requires restrictions on the fifth derivatives of the utility function. As Gollier himself states, there is little hope that such conditions can be tested in the near future.

So, despite the apparent resolution that Gollier provides in response to the conundrum arising from Weitzman's analysis regarding the intergenerational allocation of risk, the necessary conditions for DDRs to be theoretically justified become highly restrictive. This is particularly so when one makes realistic assumptions concerning the probability distribution of growth (that is, there is a positive probability of negative growth). Nevertheless, these conditions are testable in theory.

3.2.3 Summary

So far we have reviewed the current rationales for the use of DDRs in CBA and the effect that the use of DDRs will have upon models of economic growth and sustainability. We have found with regard to the second that the use of a utility discount rate (ρ) that declines over time is frequently justified by reference to the hyperbolic discount rate literature and can also result from objective functions that combine traditional utilitarian objectives with those of a conservationist interested in long-term sustainability. We have also noted the correspondence of the steady state of some these models with those employing zero discount rates. This has made clearer the relation between the justification for hyperbolic discounting from the perspective of experimental evidence and calls for the use of DDRs in order to address issues of sustainability and intergenerational equity.

The use of DDRs in CBA has been advocated for similar reasons: the consideration of intergenerational equity and sustainability. However, in the case of CBA, where the discount rate employed is commonly the consumption rate of interest, δ, the theoretical justification for the use of DDRs has recently emerged from the analysis of economic behaviour under uncertainty. The theoretical contributions of Weitzman and Gollier appear to be compelling in this sense. For the practitioner, however, one important question emerges from the theoretical literature: how are we to generate a schedule of workable DDRs for day-to-day use in the long-term policy arena? In the following section we provide a brief review of some of the approaches taken in this area and provide our own methodology for the estimation of the schedule of DDRs. Beyond this, we show a practical example of the impact of employing DDRs in CBA in the long-term policy arena.

4. DETERMINING A SCHEDULE OF DECLINING DISCOUNT RATES FOR CBA

One of the practical steps involved in undertaking CBA is to determine the appropriate level of the discount rate. As described above, CBA usually uses units of consumption as the numeraire and thus the appropriate discount rate is the so-called consumption rate of interest or Social Rate of Time Preference, δ, which in a competitive economy is equal to the marginal opportunity cost of capital or risk-free rate, r. For example, the UK government uses $\delta = 3.5\%$ as the discount rate for CBA where the decomposition is $\rho = 1\%$, $\mu = 1\%$ and $g = 2.5\%$ (see, for example, Pearce and Ulph, 1999 for a discussion). Similarly, if the practitioner wishes to implement DDRs for CBA, a methodology is required to determine the appropriate schedule over time, based upon the theoretical contributions outlined above.

The two most compelling arguments for declining δ come from Weitzman and Gollier. The rationale for declining discount rates provided by Gollier (2002a, 2002b) is perhaps the most theoretically rigorous of these contributions. But determination of the trajectory requires very specific information concerning the preferences of current generations at the very least, and, in the long run, the preferences of future generations. (With the infinitely lived representative agent approach, there is effectively only one agent, and thus one generation. The reference to current and future generations is therefore an intuitive interpretation of the long run.) These parameters include the aversion to consumption fluctuations over time, the pure time preference rate, and the degree of relative risk aversion. For the case with zero recession, restrictions on the fourth and fifth derivatives of the utility function become necessary. In addition, the probability distribution of growth needs to be characterized in some way. Clearly, the informational requirements of the Gollier approach could be daunting.

In order to implement the approach suggested by Weitzman (1998), it is necessary to characterize the uncertainty of the interest rate. In general terms, this characterization amounts to defining a probability distribution for the future discount rate, and its behaviour over time. In this sense there are two ways in which we can interpret the example in Table 2.1. Firstly, it could represent the thought experiment of Weitzman (1998), in which we are currently uncertain about interest rates, and yet the interest rates will persist indefinitely *ex post* realization. In this sense, we have a probability distribution for the current uncertainty, which assumes that interest rates of 2% and 5% are equally likely, and we employ this distribution for all future periods. Uncertainty is therefore regarded as existing from day one, and all that is required is the current probability distribution of the discount rate.

In a further article, Weitzman (2001) takes precisely this approach. In order to establish the probability distribution for the socially optimal discount rate he undertakes a survey of over 2000 academic economists, and a so-called 'blue ribbon' selection of 50, as to their opinion on the constant rate of discount to use for CBA. The responses were distributed with a gamma distribution with mean 4%, and standard deviation 3%, providing an ad hoc working assumption to determine the schedule of DDRs. The assumption implicit in the use of the gamma distribution is that there is uncertainty in the present about the interest rate in the future and that when uncertainty is resolved the realized interest rate will persist forever.

Newell and Pizer (2003) (N&P) take an alternative view. Rather than assuming uncertainty in the present, they state that we are currently fairly certain about the discount rate but uncertainty increases in the future. From this standpoint, they characterize the uncertainty of the discount rate by econometric modelling of the time series process of interest rates. The estimated model is used to forecast future rates based upon their behaviour in the past. From these forecasts, they derive numerical solutions for the CER. In doing so, they are also able to provide a (weak) test of another assumption important to the Weitzman (1998) result, namely the persistence of discount rates over time. They compare the discount rates modelled as a mean reversion process to a random walk model, and find support for the latter. The practical implications of implementing the declining discount rates that result are significant. When applied to global warming damage, the present value of damage from carbon emissions increases by 82%, compared with the same damage evaluated at the constant treasury rate of 4%. In monetary terms, this translates into an increase in the benefits of carbon mitigation from $5.7 per ton of carbon, to $10.4 per ton of carbon.

4.1 Estimation Issues

These applications bring to light some interesting issues concerning the characterization of interest rate uncertainty. Firstly, it is interesting to note that the decline in discount rates in both of these approaches depends upon the persistence of interest rates over time. The theoretical model of Weitzman (2001) has this persistence in-built, the assumption being that each individual discounts the future at their preferred constant rate. That is, each of the responses that make up the probability distribution remains constant over time. In N&P, however, the existence of persistence is an empirical question, and the existence or otherwise of a unit root in the series determines the rate of decline of the CER. Secondly, beyond choosing a different sample of humanity, it is not immediately clear how one might improve upon the empirical approach taken by Weitzman (2001). However, in the case of N&P, there are several additional avenues available for the characterization of interest rate uncertainty and the resulting definition of the CER.

These empirical issues are the main concern of the paper by Groom, Koundouri, Panopoulou and Pantelidis (2004). In particular, this paper builds upon the following two points. Firstly, it is clear that, if we believe that the past is informative about the future, it is important to characterize the past as accurately as possible. Indeed, the selection of the econometric model is of considerable moment in operationalizing a theory of DDRs that depends upon uncertainty and defines the CER in statistical terms, since each specification differs in the assumptions made concerning the time series process. This will affect the attributes of the resulting schedule of CER. Secondly, selection among these models is also an empirical question. Tests for stationarity, model misspecification and comparisons among models based upon efficiency criteria should guide model selection for the practitioner. N&P, for example, specify a simple AR(p) model of interest rate uncertainty, which limits the characterization of uncertainty to a process in which the distribution of the permanent and temporary stochastic components is constant for all time.[23] Such a process guarantees declining CERs whilst ignoring the possibility of structural breaks.

Groom et al. (2004) revisit these issues for US and UK interest rate data and, by building on N&P's approach in determining DDRs, they make the following points concerning model selection and, the use of DDRs in general. Firstly, N&P's approach is predicated upon the assumption that the past is informative about the future. Therefore, characterizing uncertainty in the past can assist in forecasting the future and determining the path of CERs. If one subscribes to this view, it is important to characterize the past as well as possible by correctly specifying the model of the time series process. This is particularly so when dealing with lengthy time horizons where the accuracy of forecasts is important. Indeed, the selection of the econometric model is of considerable moment in operationalizing a theory of DDRs that depends upon uncertainty, because econometric models contain different assumptions concerning the probability distribution of the object of interest. Groom et al. have shown for US and UK interest rate data that the econometric specification should allow the data generating process to change over time, and that State Space and Regime Switching models are likely to be appropriate. Secondly, selection between well-specified models can and should be undertaken by reference to measures of efficiency such as coefficients of variation, confidence bounds and out-of-sample forecast Mean Squared Errors (MSEs).

4.2 Characterizing the Alternative Models

The AR(p)–GARCH(l,m) model is often used in empirical studies to describe processes that exhibit heteroscedasticity. Using such a model to describe the real interest rates gives us:

$$r_t = \eta + e_t$$

$$\sum_{i=1}^{P} a_i e_{t-i} + \xi_t$$

$$\xi_t = h_t^{0.5} z_t$$

$$h_t = c + \sum_{i=1}^{m} \beta_i \xi_{t-i}^2 + \sum_{i=1}^{l} \gamma_i h_{t-i}$$

where $\xi_t \sim N(0,\sigma_\xi^2)$, $\eta \sim N(\eta,\sigma_\eta^2)$ and z_t is an i.i.d. zero-mean distribution random variable with unit variance. l and m represent the lags on the terms which make up h_t. This is a more flexible representation of $r\{t\}$ than the AR(p) model. Above all the AR(p)–GARCH(l,m) model allows more efficient estimation in the presence of (conditionally) heteroscedastic errors and is often thought to better reflect the processes of financial variables (Harvey, 1993).

Both the AR(p) and AR(p)–GARCH(l,m) models assume that the parameters driving the stochastic process are constant over the sample period. This is likely to be an unrealistic assumption for the period for which we have data and certainly for forecasting the CER over the long-term policy horizon in hand which, following N&P, Groom et al. assume extends for 400 years. For example, the behaviour of interest rates is strongly affected by economic cycles as well as shocks destabilizing them, that is, periods of economic crisis. For this reason a more appropriate econometric model might be one that allows for changes in the behaviour of interest rates. Moreover, the strong persistence in the volatility of the estimated GARCH model is an indication of a regime-switching mechanism, as it can be an artefact of changes in the rate-generating mechanism (see for example Gray, 1996). Estimation results are presented in the following sections.

Groom et al. use two possible models to account for the possibility of time-varying parameters and regime changes. Firstly, a Regime-Switching (RS) model with two regimes is used. This model provides a more flexible characterization of uncertainty than the simple, single regime, AR(p) model. Each regime incorporates a different speed of mean reversion, along with a different permanent component and error variance. Specifically, the model is as follows:

$$r_t = \eta_k + e_t$$

$$\sum_{i=1}^{P} a_i^k e_{t-i} + \xi_t$$

where ξ_t is an i.i.d. zero-mean normally distributed random variable with variance σ_k^2, $k = 1, 2$ for the first and second regimes respectively. At any particular point in time, there is uncertainty as to which regime we are in. The probability of being in each regime at time t is specified as a Markov 1 process, that is, it depends only on the regime at time $t-1$. The probability that the process remains at the first regime is defined as P, while the probability that the process remains at the second regime is Q. The matrix with the transition probabilities is assumed to be constant.

Secondly, time-varying parameters using a State Space (SS) (autoregressive random coefficient) model is used. This is given by the following system of equations:

$$r_t = \eta + \alpha_t r_{t-1} + e_t$$

$$\sum_{i=1}^{P} \eta_i \alpha_{t-i} + u_t$$

where e_t and u_t are serially independent, zero-mean normal disturbances such that:

$$\begin{pmatrix} e_t \\ u_t \end{pmatrix} \sim N\left(\begin{bmatrix} 0 \\ 0 \end{bmatrix}, \begin{bmatrix} \sigma_e^2 & \\ & \sigma_u^2 \end{bmatrix} \right)$$

In other words, the interest rate is modelled as an AR(1) model with an AR(p) coefficient. This model represents a more flexible representation of the stochastic process than the 'constant parameter' models.

Finally, Groom et al. allow for the possibility of multivariate models in order to exploit covariation between UK and US interest rates. They estimate a VAR model with real UK and US interest rates as endogenous variables. The specification of the model is typically the following:

$$\begin{pmatrix} r_t^{uk} \\ r_t^{us} \end{pmatrix} = \begin{pmatrix} n_1 \\ n_2 \end{pmatrix} + \sum_{i=1}^{p} A_i \times \begin{pmatrix} r_{t-1}^{uk} \\ r_{t-1}^{us} \end{pmatrix} + \begin{pmatrix} e_{1t} \\ e_{2t} \end{pmatrix}$$

where $E_t = (e_{1t}, e_{2t})'$ follows a bivariate normal distribution and A_i are (2×2) matrices of coefficients. The VAR models incorporate interactions between the endogenous variables which is important from the perspective of forecasting.

In sum, Groom et al.'s estimations indicate that selecting models on the basis of their ability to characterize the past and their accuracy concerning forecasts of the future points to the superiority of the SS model, with the RS model ranking as second-best for both US and UK interest rate data.

4.3 Valuing the Benefits from Climate Change Mitigation using DDRs

In this section, We highlight the policy implications of declining discount rates and the impact of model misspecification by looking at a case study

Table 2.2 Value of carbon damage according to model selection (1989$ per ton of carbon, base year 1995)

Model	Carbon values ($/tc 400 years)	Relative to constant rate (%)	Relative to mean reverting (%)	Relative to random walk (%)
Regime Switch	5.22	−9.0	−18.7	−31.7
Conventional (4.0%)	5.74		−10.7	−25.0
IGARCH	6.37	+10.9	−1.0	−16.8
N&P (MR)	6.43	+12.0		−16.0
MR 55	7.23	+26.0	+12.5	−5.5
VAR	7.41	+29.1	+15.2	−3.2
N&P (RW)	7.65	+33.3	+19.0	
State Space	14.44	+151.7	+124.7	+88.8

on climate change, which is particularly relevant to the long-term policy arena. See N&P for the assumptions concerning the modelling of carbon emissions damages. We establish the present values of the removal of 1 ton of carbon from the atmosphere, and hence the present value of the benefits of the avoidance of climate change damage for each of the specified models. The analysis uses the US data. Table 2.2 shows the present value per ton of carbon emissions with respect to the SS and other models.

The only noticeable difference in values occurs in the case of SS. In this case, the value of carbon emissions reduction is over 150% larger than that under constant discounting at 4%. In addition, the RW model values carbon reduction 33.3% higher than under constant discounting. Similarly, employing the mean reverting model, we find an increase in value of only 12% compared to the 14% difference noted by N&P under their mean reverting equivalent. The preceding discussion has argued that the RS and SS models are to be preferred over the others, since they allow for changes in the interest-rate generating process and have desirable efficiency qualities. From the policy perspective, we have established that both of these models provide well-specified representations of the interest rate series. However, on the one hand, the RS model provides roughly equivalent values of carbon to the constant discounting rate values (there is a 9% difference), while on the other, the SS produces values up to 150% higher. Comparing the performance of our models to the RW model used by N&P, we find that RW produces larger values of carbon than all models other than the SS model, which exceeds the RW model by about 88.8%. In our case, this represents an 88.8% increase compared to the methodology employed by N&P.

The disparity between the RS and the SS models, and the proximity of the carbon values generated by the former to those generated by conventional constant discounting, represents a clear signal of the policy relevance of model selection in determining the CER. It is crucial from a policy perspective to make a clear judgement as to which of the two models is most appropriate to the case in hand. It also highlights the importance of the presence of persistence in this estimation, recalling that the autoregressive process of the SS model parameters was effectively an RW model. In this case, we have found that in addition to the lower coefficient of variation, the SS model is also preferable to the RS model owing to its lower MSE for the 30-year horizon. Hence, we suggest it is reasonable to assume that the SS model is preferable in this case. This means that the carbon values are increased by 150% compared to conventional discounting and 88% compared to N&P's approach.

Given that the value of carbon depends upon model selection for discount rates, it is interesting to examine the implications of this for climate change prevention projects and/or the appraisal of investments in carbon-intensive sectors of the economy. For this reason, we look at the implications of using the regime switching and state space models in the appraisal of nuclear power investments in the UK (Groom et al., 2004).

In conclusion, one could assert that the path of the CER differs considerably from one model to another and therefore each places a different weight upon the future. The policy implications of these estimates is revealed in the estimation of the value of carbon emissions reduction, with values which are up to 150% higher than when using constant discount rates, and up to 88% higher than the Random Walk model employed by N&P.

5. CONCLUSION

This chapter has reviewed the arguments for and the implications of employing Declining Discount Rates in CBA and in the analysis of economic growth and sustainability. The review shows that there are several growth models in which a relationship has been found between the long-run equilibrium under DDRs and that in which a zero discount rate is employed. This can have the effect of pushing the optimum under DDRs away from the conventional utilitarian outcome towards the Green Golden Rule (GGR) level of capital or environmental stocks. Furthermore, in response to worries that the GGR places weight on the future at too great a cost to the present, we highlight the result of Li and Löfgren (2000): DDRs can evoke a solution to resource management problems in which the objective function explicitly takes into account the preferences of present and future generations, such as those posited by Li and Löfgren (2000). That is, the use of DDRs can balance the preferences of current and future generations such that neither is a dictator over the other. This solution is not achieved by either zero or conventional discounting. It is in these senses that DDRs can be seen to encourage a more equal treatment of generations and promote sustainable outcomes.

In the application of CBA, in which consumption is generally the numeraire, we have shown that there exists a body of theoretical work justifying the use of DDRs based upon the analysis of decisions under uncertainty. Not only this, but we have provided a methodology à la Newell and Pizer (2003) for the estimation of a working schedule of DDRs assuming that future discount rates are uncertain and the past provides information about the future. The implications of this are that a correctly specified model of discount rates provides a schedule of DDRs which values atmospheric carbon reduction 150% higher than conventional exponential discounting, and almost 90% higher than incorrectly specified models. In this sense, sustainable outcomes are more likely to emerge from project appraisal with DDRs, but given that the theory of DDRs for CBA reviewed relates to the socially efficient discount rate, such outcomes can also be thought of as efficient.

NOTES

1. Some authors have suggested that ρ reflects impatience arising from the instantaneous risk, or hazard rate of death at a particular point in time. See for example Pearce and Ulph (1992).
2. $\mu = [-u''(C)/u'(C)]C$, where $u(C)$ is the individual's utility function and $u'(.)$ is the first derivative of the utility function and $u''(.)$ is the second derivative and so on.
3. With certain knowledge of each of the parameters on the right-hand side (RHS) of (2.2), the level of the SDR is known with certainty. For example, the UK government employs δ as the test rate for project and policy appraisal. They assume that $\rho = 1\%$, $\mu = 1$ and $g = 2.5\%$, making the social time preference rate equal to 3.5% (HM Treasury, 2003).
4. Precisely, individuals are defined as prudent where $u''' > 0$. Noting that relative prudence is defined as $P(C) = [-u'''/u'']C$, and that $u'' < 0$, where individuals are prudent $P(C) > 0$.
5. If willingness to pay (WTP) for environment evolves at some pre-determined rate, say α, the rationale for this increase in WTP being that preferences for environmental resources are changing over time due to income growth or increased scarcity (Fisher and Krutilla, 1975), then WTP for a unit of environmental goods at time t can be written as: $WTP_t = WTP_0(1 + \alpha)^t$, where WTP_0 is willingness to pay at $t = 0$. In a deterministic world this means that we can derive an 'environmental' discount rate, w, such that the present value of benefits (costs) that accrue at time t can be written as: $WTP_0/(1 + w)^t$, where $w = (r - \alpha)/(1 + \alpha)$, where r is the conventional discount rate and $r > w$.
6. See Pearce et al. (2003), for a review.
7. For example, if utility depends upon the amenity value of environmental stock, q, as well as consumption, then the relation between δ and ρ will reflect the changes in these stocks. The relation under certainty then becomes $\delta = \rho + \mu_{C,C}g_C + \mu_{C,S}g_S$, where the μ terms represent the elasticity of marginal utility with respect to consumption and q, and the

g terms represent the growth of consumption and q respectively. Note that in steady states $g_C = g_S = 0$ and the two concepts coincide.

8. Useful references in this area include Laibson (1997), Loewenstein (2000), and Loewenstein and Prelec (1992).
9. Where both consumption and environmental stocks (amenity value) enter into the utility function, this is achieved where the marginal rate of substitution between consumption and the stock are equal to the marginal rate of transformation of the stock of renewable resources.
10. For more on the issue of time inconsistency, see Heal (1998, ch. 7) and Pearce et al. (2003).
11. The MSY level of the capital stock reflects the point at which the marginal productivity of capital equals zero. Li and Löfgren (2001) assume that the production function is increasing up to this stock level and decreasing thereafter.
12. However, Dasgupta (2001) highlights a criticism (attributed to Kenneth Judd) of this approach to the effect that there is a way in which all generations can have their cake and eat it too. Suppose the current generation devises a plan that maximizes only the integral part of the maximand in equation (2.12). It simultaneously announces its intention to abandon that plan at some date in the distant future, at which point it will switch to a plan that then maximizes only the asymptotic part of the maximand. The farther this switching date, the more nearly the integral part will be maximized. But there will always be an infinite number of dates after the currently planned switching date, and hence it will always be possible to increase welfare by postponing the switching date.
13. For a given level of Z, when the elasticity is low, and environmental expenditures are ineffective at cleaning up environmental damage, this divergence is increased. Weitzman's interpretation, from the perspective of optimal growth, is that this is a signal that the economy is finding prior environmental damage difficult to undo, and one solution is to reduce growth (if this is a feasible policy option). Alternatively, where the elasticity is high, a better solution might be to increase environmental expenditures (Weitzman, 1994).
14. Other more ad hoc proposals for DDRs exist. Rabl (1996), for example, suggests that utility should not be discounted in the long term, and hence not included in the calculation of the SDR for CBA, not because of the 'ethical indefensibility' suggested by Ramsey, but rather because of the inadequacy of financial markets in performing long-term redistribution of resources. The implication here is that ρ represents the desire of the current generation to redistribute wealth, which is constrained by the time horizon covered by current financial markets – usually about 30 years. His proposal implies a stepped schedule of discount rates for CBA, that is, with ρ set to zero after a period of 30 years or so.
15. This is not crucial for this particular result to hold, but is important for ease of exposition. The certainty equivalent could be defined to incorporate higher moments of the distribution of discount rates to reflect risk aversion, with a loss of tractability.
16. It is important to note here that equation (2.8) reflects the discount rate that should be used to discount costs and benefits that occur at time t back to the present. However, Weitzman (1998) defines the CER as the rate of change of the certainty equivalent discount factor over time, thus his CER represents the period-to-period discount rate. The former can be thought of as the average CER, while the latter can be thought of as the marginal CER. Weitzman shows that the marginal CER declines over time, while Gollier (2002a) shows how the average CER declines over time.
17. It is worth noting once more the distinction between the *average* CER and the *marginal* CER. The discount rate discussed above, following Gollier (2002a), is the *average* CER. It is the per-period discount rate that would need to apply over the entire time horizon under consideration to ensure there are no opportunities for costless arbitrage. In contrast, Weitzman (1998) discusses the marginal CER, defined in continuous time by $\tilde{r}_t = (-d\tilde{A}_t/dt)/\tilde{A}_t$ rather than the solution to (2.6) above. Both the certainty equivalent average and marginal discount rates are declining over time in equilibrium; the marginal discount rate declines more rapidly. However, Weitzman notes that at the limit, as $t \to \infty$, both are the same.

18. A rough sketch of the proof is as follows: r_t can be thought of as the certainty equivalent of a random payoff. $\tilde{x}$ for an agent with a constant degree of absolute risk aversion t. As risk aversion increases, that is, t increases, it is well known that the certainty equivalent r_t will decrease (Pratt, 1964). Furthermore, as $t \to \infty$, r_t will tend to the lower bound of $\tilde{x}$.
19. Under ENPV, after the realization of the uncertain discount rate, the NPV may or may not be positive, and since the payoff in the future is certain, any residual losses are borne by the present generation. However, when we use the ENFV criterion it is future generations that are bearing the risk. The present generation makes a certain contribution to the project, but the rate at which the fund accumulates, and hence the outcome in the future, is uncertain before the realization of $\tilde{R}$.
20. The yield curve describes the term structure of financial assets.
21. It is also dependent upon the intertemporal relationships. For the purpose of the analysis Gollier (2002a) assumes that the growth shocks are independently and identically distributed. Although this is unrealistic, it avoids the complications associated with the analysis of serially correlated shocks.
22. There are a number of additional necessary conditions for this to hold – for details see Gollier (2002b).
23. The AR(1) model that they describe provides the following expression for the certainty equivalent discount rate: $\tilde{r} = \eta - t\sigma_\eta^2 - \sigma_\xi^2\Omega(\alpha,t)$. Since $\Omega(.) > 0$ and the variance of the permanent and temporary components is positive and constant over time, $\tilde{r}$ is constant over time.

REFERENCES

Atkinson, G., Dubourg, R., Hamilton, K., Munasinghe, M., Pearce, D.W., and Young, C. (1997), *Measuring Sustainable Development: Macroeconomics and the Environment*, Cheltenham, UK and Lyme, USA: Edward Elgar.

Barro, R.J. (1999), 'Ramsey Meets Laibson in the Neoclassical Growth Model', *Quarterly Journal of Economics*, **114** (4), 1125–52.

Brock, W.A. (1977), 'A Polluted Golden Age', in V. Smith (ed.), *Economics of Natural Resources*, New York: Gordan and Breach.

Chichilnisky, G. (1996), 'An Axiomatic Approach to Sustainable Development', *Social Choice and Welfare*, **13**, 231–57.

Dasgupta, P. (2001), *Human Wellbeing and the Natural Environment*, Oxford: Oxford University Press.

Dybvig, P., Ingersoll, J., and Ross, S. (1996), 'Long Forward and Zero-Coupon Rates Can Never Fall', *Journal of Business*, **69** (1), 1–25.

Fisher, A.C., and Krutilla, J. (1975), 'Resource Conservation, Environmental Preservation, and the Rate of Discount', *Quarterly Journal of Economics*, **89** (3), 358–70.

Gollier, C. (2002a), 'Time Horizon and the Discount Rate', *Journal of Economic Theory*, **107** (2), 463–73.

Gollier, C. (2002b), 'Discounting an Uncertain Future', *Journal of Public Economics*, **85**, 149–66.

Gollier, C. (2002c), 'Maximising Expected Net Future Value as an Alternative to Gamma Discounting', Working Paper, Toulouse University.

Gravelle, H., and Smith, D. (2000), 'Discounting for Health Effects in Cost Benefit and Cost Effectiveness Analysis', *Centre for Health Economics Technical Paper Series 20*, University of York.

Gray, F.S. (1996), 'Modeling the Conditional Distribution of Interest Rates as a Regime-Switching Process', *Journal of Financial Economics*, **42**, 27–62.

Groom, B., Koundouri, P., Panopoulou, K., and Pantelides, T. (2004), 'Model Selection in Discounting the Distant Future', University College London, Economics Working Paper Series, No 04-02. Downloadable from http//: www.econ.ucl.ac.uk.

Harrod, R. (1948), *Toward a Dynamic Economics*, London: Macmillan.

Harvey, A.C. (1993), 'Long Memory in Stochastic Volatility', Mimeo, London School of Economics.

Heal, G. (1995), Lecture Notes on Sustainability, Memorandum 16, Department of Economics, University of Oslo, Norway.

Heal, G. (1998), *Valuing the Future: Economic Theory and Sustainability*, New York: Columbia University Press.

Hepburn, C., and Groom, B. (2004), 'Uncertain Discount Rates Increase with the Temporal Numeraire', Mimeo, Nuffield College Oxford.

HM Treasury (2003), *The Green Book: Appraisal and Evaluation in Central Government,* London: HM Treasury.

Horowitz, J. (2002), 'Preferences in the Future', *Environmental and Resource Economics*, **21**, 241–59.

Hotelling H. (1931), 'The Economics of Exhaustible Resources', *Journal of Political Economy*, **39**, 137–75.

Kimball, M.S. (1990), 'Precautionary Saving in the Small and in the Large', *Econometrica*, **58**, 53–73.

Koopmans, T.C. (1965), 'On the Concept of Optimal Economic Growth', *Pontificae Academiae Scientiarum Scripta Varia*, **28**, 225–300.

Krutilla, J., and Fisher, A.C. (1975), *The Economics of Natural Environments*, Baltimore: Johns Hopkins University Press.

Laibson R. (1997), 'Golden Eggs and Hyperbolic Discounting', *Quarterly Journal of Economics*, **112**, 443–77.

Li, C.Z., and Löfgren, K.G. (2000), 'Renewable Resources and Economic Sustainability: A Dynamic Analysis with Heterogeneous Time Preferences', *Journal of Environmental Economics and Management*, **40**, 236–50.

Li, C.Z., and Löfgren, K.G. (2001), 'Economic Growth, Environmental Quality and Hyperbolic Discounting', Mimeo.

Lind, R. (1982), 'A Primer on the Major Issues Relating to the Discount Rate for Evaluating National Energy Options', in R. Lind (ed.), *Discounting for Time and Risk in Energy Policy*, Washington: Resources for the Future, pp. 21–114.

Little, I.M.D. and Mirlees, J.A. (1974), *Project Appraisal and Planning for Development Countries*, New York: Basic Books.

Loewenstein, G., and Elster, J. (eds.) (1992), *Choice over Time*, New York: Russell Sage Foundation.

Loewenstein, G., and Prelec, D. (1992), 'Anomalies in Intertemporal Choice: Evidence and an Interpretation', *Quarterly Journal of Economics*, **107**, 573–97.

Lucas, R.E. (1977), 'Asset Prices in an Exchange Economy', *Econometrica*, **46**, 1429–45.

Newell, R., and Pizer, W. (2003), 'Discounting the Benefits of Climate Change Mitigation: How Much do Uncertain Rates Increase Valuations?', *Journal of Environmental Economics and Management*, **46** (1), 52–71.

Pearce, D., Groom, B., Hepburn, C., and Koundouri, P. (2003), 'Valuing the Future: Recent Advances in Social Discounting', *World Economics*, **4** (2), 121–41.

Pearce, D.W., and Ulph, D. (1992), 'A Social Discount Rate for the United Kingdom', in D.W. Pearce, *Environmental Economics: Essays in Ecological Economics and Sustainable Development*, Aldershot, UK and Brookfield, US: Edward Elgar, 268–85.

Phelps, E.S. (1961), 'The Golden Rule of Accumulation: A Fable for Growthmen', *American Economic Review*, 638–43.

Pigou, A. (1932), *The Economics of Welfare*, 4th edition, London: Macmillan.

Portney, P. and Weyant, J. (eds) (1999), *Discounting and Intergenerational Equity*, Washington, DC: Resources for the Future.

Pratt, J. (1964), 'Risk Aversion in the Small and the Large', *Econometrica*, **32**, 122–36.

Rabl, A. (1996), 'Discounting of Long Term Costs: What Would Future Generations Prefer Us to Do?', *Ecological Economics*, **17**, 137–45.

Ramsey, F.P. (1928), 'A Mathematical Theory of Saving', *Economic Journal*, **38**, 543–59.

Weitzman, M. (1994), 'On the "Environmental" Discount Rate', *Journal of Environmental Economics and Management*, **26** (1), 200–209.

Weitzman, M. (1998), 'Why the Far Distant Future should be Discounted at its Lowest Possible Rate', *Journal of Environmental Economics and Management*, **36**, 201–08.

Weitzman, M. (2001), 'Gamma Discounting', *American Economic Review*, **91** (1) March, 261–71.

PART I

Static and dynamic estimation of natural resource demand

3. Water pricing reforms in Mexico: the case of the manufacturing sector

Hilda Guerrero Garcia Rojas and Alban Thomas

1. INTRODUCTION

It is well documented that water is becoming a resource with increasing scarcity for a majority of semi-arid countries. In order to promote efficient water management, policymakers are trying to find the best policy tools to allocate existing water reserves and persuade users to adopt conservation practices. Dinar and Subramanian (1997) document country experiences on water pricing, and identify water pricing as a key to improving water allocation and encourage resource conservation. Hence, reforms on water pricing have come to play an important role in encouraging efficient use of water. Dinar (2000) addresses this issue and presents a framework for comparing water pricing reforms, as well as selected experiences of reforms in different sectors and countries.

In Mexico, water management rests on a delicate balance between government regulation and market mechanisms. Rather than going into a complicated scheme of calculating, if possible, opportunity costs or long-term marginal costs, Mexico's approach to pricing water has been pragmatic in nature, considering the political resistance associated with the introduction of any kind of new fiscal burden. That is why the introduction of water levies in 1986 was less for the purpose of assigning the 'right' price than to introduce the concept of water as an economic good with a specific value.

Industrial water use in Mexico is 6.6 km^3 per year, with 5 km^3 surface water and 1.6 km^3 from a groundwater source,[1] representing about 9% of total water withdrawals (72.5 km^3).[2] Fifty per cent of total industrial water consumption is used in cooling systems, 35% in production processes, 5% in heating systems and 10% in cleaning facilities and services.[3] Eighty-six per cent of industrial water demand originates from eight industries: sugar, chemicals, mining, paper, steel, textiles, food and beverages.

It is important to note that industrial water comes mainly from self-supplied water sources, either surface or groundwater. Privately managed water outlets are under a concession – that is, water right – or licence granted by the National Water Commission, and the industry is under the obligation to pay a federal charge for the use of water, as well as for effluent emissions. These payments are unique (once and for all), and are made when the firm starts operating. In addition, self-supplied industrial water users have to pay quarterly extraction levies per cubic metre, depending on their geographical location, which is determined according to relative water scarcity. For effluent emissions, industrial users also have to pay for pollutant concentration, as well as for the volumes discharged. With respect to the extraction charge, a system of public subsidies has been rapidly installed, to partially compensate for the fiscal burden of water-intensive industries. For example in 1993, the sugar industry was allowed to pay only 60% of the charge per cubic metre, depending on the available water zone corresponding to the industrial plant location. For the first quarter of 2003, this amount was lowered to 50%. Additionally, some municipalities are also compensated for a given proportion of their water charges, resulting in an implicit subsidy scheme. The amount of these subsidy payments are set up in Federal Law (Ley Federal de Derechos en Materia de Agua), and are updated each year.

The interesting aspect of the Mexican water policy in its current orientation is the direct and explicit relationship between industry location and the water charge paid for extraction (and effluent emission). By directly indexing these charges on resource scarcity, the water authority sends a signal to industrialists, who can then integrate this factor into the plant location decision. Hence, all other things being equal, one could expect water-intensive plants to be situated in regions where water charges are lowest (and where the resource is more abundant). Of course, significant differences in unit water charges are unlikely to be a major determinant of plant location decisions if the share of water expenditures in total cost is limited. Moreover, where a plant was initially located in a region before the water price reform of the 1980s, the cost of moving out to another area may be prohibitive if specific investments are important. Keeping these words of caution in mind, it would still be useful to compare average production costs among regions for different industries, as a function of input prices, including water. This cost comparison would help to determine if water charges are efficiently designed, that is, if they match more or less the distribution of firms across regions.

Nevertheless, providing a selection of empirical facts and evidence on industrial water use should be a prerequisite for a sound assessment of any water policy reform. In this chapter, our objective is not to determine whether water price in Mexico already represents the relevant value for water.[4] Rather, we deal here with the effects water pricing reform in Mexico have produced inside the manufacturing sector. For that, we try to answer the following questions: Is water price working as a good economical tool to support the efficient use of water within Mexican manufacturing sector? If this is the case, then what is the level of responsiveness of the demand for water by Mexican industry? And finally, what can be said about the geographical distribution of the manufacturing sector in Mexico?

In order to address these issues, we first estimate a production cost system using data on 500 firms from eight industries for the year 1994. Cost estimates allow us to compute price and (Morishima) substitution elasticities, which are necessary tools for determining whether industries are indeed responsive to water prices. An associated empirical question is whether or not water price, as defined by scarcity zones, is pushing industrialists towards efficient use of water.

A previous study (IMTA, 1998) and its associated paper (Guerrero et al., 1998) assume a given price elasticity, and claim that water tariffs in Mexico can achieve water savings without lowering the profitability of some of the industries considered. In the former, water price elasticity was not the target but rather, the issue was how rises in water tariff would affect industry benefits.

This chapter reports the results of a first attempt, to our knowledge, of this kind of approach, in which we estimate the elasticity of substitution between water and other productive inputs for the Mexican manufacturing and mining industries (even if, strictly speaking, mining is not manufacturing industry, we include it in the present study because it is considered one of the main water users in Mexico).[5]

The outline of the chapter is as follows. In Section 2, we give a brief survey of the literature on industrial water demand. The cost model is presented in Section 3, together with available measures of the elasticity of substitution between inputs. Section 4 presents the data used in the empirical part of the chapter, and a first statistical analysis is presented in Section 5. Estimation results are discussed in Section 6, and Section 7 presents the results of a firm location experiment, by water availability zone. Based on our cost estimates, we predict cost differentials for firms in different water pricing zones, conditional on the industry. Section 8 is the conclusion.

2. A BRIEF SURVEY ON INDUSTRIAL WATER DEMAND

The literature concerning econometric estimation of industrial water demands is quite limited compared to other water uses. Renzetti (2002) in his introduction to *The Economics of Industrial Water Use* pointed out that an

ECONLIT search for 'Industrial Water' for the period 1982–98 returned only five bibliographical items, compared with 63 citations for 'Residential/ Urban Water' and 105 references for 'Agriculture/Irrigation Water'.

Table 3.1 highlights the main features and results of the econometric studies of industrial water demand documented so far. Renzetti's works are the first referenced studies in which industrial water use is analysed, not just as one more input for industry together with capital, labour and other inputs, but by considering the different uses water may have within industrial production processes. That is, he takes account of different production steps involving water from a technical point of view: intake water, recirculation, water treatment prior to use and water treatment prior to discharges (Renzetti, 1988); or intake and recirculation (Dupont and Renzetti, 2001). Reynaud (2003) considers the origin of water source, each being treated as a different input: water supplied by the water utility (municipality network), autonomous water (self-supplied) and water treated before use. Apart from these studies, all the others consider intake water only.

In general, these studies deal with the problem of defining the price of water. The authors propose different methods and techniques to address this issue, but it is often stressed that working with non-market natural resources, like water, is problematic. As an example, Halvorsen and Smith (1986) use a restricted cost function (Translog) to estimate substitution possibilities for unpriced natural resources for the Canadian metal mining industry (metallic ore). The elasticity of substitution between reproducible inputs and natural resources is equal to unity, and water is treated as a quasi-fixed input.

There also exist other econometric studies where water is viewed as an output. Teeples and Glyer (1987) present a production function model of water delivery which can be estimated from a multiproduct, dual cost function (Translog). They measure the price of purchased water as an average cost (the sum of amounts paid by a firm to its suppliers divided by total units received). Data are for 1980 in Southern California for 119 water distribution firms. Their results show that purchased and own-water inputs are strong direct substitutes (elasticity of substitution equal to 4.14), but the interactions of each with other inputs are different. Own water is a substitute for the capital-materials input and complementary to energy. For purchased water, these relationships are reversed. Garcia and Thomas (2001) model the structure of production for municipal water utilities with two outputs: water sold to final customer and water network losses. They estimate the cost structure of water utilities via a Generalized Method of Moments procedure with a Translog cost function and panel data, using 55 water utilities (53 privately operated) located in the Bordeaux region (France) for the years 1995 to 1997. They compute economies of density,

Table 3.1 Econometric applications to analyse industrial water demand[a]

Authors / Country[b]	Functional form (method) / Inputs	Principal results[c] (price elasticities)
(1) Reess (1969) / England (Southeast)	Variety of forms (OLS) / Intake water	Chemical (−0.958); food (3.28); drink (1.3); non-metallic (2.5); paper (1.44) at lowest price
(2) Turnovsky (1969) / USA (Massachusetts towns)(n = 19, years 1962 & 1965)	Linear equation (OLS) / Industrial and Domestic	From (−0.473) to (−0.836)
(3) De Rooy (1974) / USA (New Jersey) (n = 30, year 1965)	Cobb-Douglas (OLS) / Water Intake for chemical industry	Cooling (−0.894); Processing (−0.354); Steam generation (−0.590)
(4) Grebenstein and Field (1979) / USA (year 1973)	Translog (SUR) / K, L and Water Intake	AWWA series (−0.326) MM series (−0.801). L & W substitutes; K & W complements
(5) Babin, Willis and Allen (1982) / USA (year 1973)	Translog (SUR) / K, L and Water Intake	Pooled (−0.56): food (0.14) to paper (−0.66). Labour substitutes for K and W
(6) Ziegler and Bell (1984) / USA (Arkansas) (n = 23)	Cobb-Douglas (OLS) paper and chemical / Intake water	Average cost better estimates than marginal cost
(7) Renzetti (1988) / Canada (British Columbia) (n = 372; year 1981)	Cobb-Douglas (2SLS) / Intake water; Treatment prior use; Recirculation; Discharge	Intake: petrochemical (−0.12) to light industry (−0.54). Intake & discharge complement. Intake & recirculation substitutes
(8) Renzetti (1992) / Canada (n = 1068, year 1985)	Translog (I3SLS) / Intake water; Treatment prior use; Recirculation; Discharge	Intake manufacturing (−0.3817): plastic (−0.1534) to paper (−0.5885). Recirculation substitute for Intake & Discharge

Table 3.1 (continued)

Authors / Country[b]	Functional form (method) / Inputs	Principal results[c] (price elasticities)
(9) Renzetti (1993) / Canada (n = 1068, year 1985)	Probit and Regression Model (ML) / public and private supply. External and internal water price	Intake external: self (−0.308) public (−0.755). Internal: self (−0.090) public (−0.068). So, public supply intake more sensitive to external price
(10) Dupont and Renzetti (2001) / Canada (n = 58 for each year 1981, 1986 & 1991)	Translog (SUR) / Intake and Recirculation and KLEM	Intake and recirculation subs. Intake substitute for K, L & E, but complement to M. Recirculation substitute to L
(11) Wang and Lall (2002) / China (n = 2000, year 1993)	Translog Production (SUR) / KLEM and Water Intake	Elasticity (−1.0) Mean Marginal Productivity 2.5 yuan/m[c]
(12) Reynaud (2003) / France (n = 51 for each year from 1994 to 1996)	Translog (SUR & FGLS) / Water Network; Autonomous and treated prior use	Network (−0.29): alcohol (−0.10) to (0.79) for various. Treated (−1.42): alcohol (−0.9) to (−2.21) for chemical. Autonomous & Treatment Complements. Network & Treatment substitutes
(13) Renzetti and Dupont (2003) / Canada (n = 58 for each year 1981, 1986 & 1991)	Translog (SUR) / Recirculation, Treatment and KLEM. Intake quasi-fixed	Intake: elasticity (−0.1308) and Shadow value 0.046CAN$/m[c]

Notes:
[a] These studies are briefly commented in Appendix 3.1.
[b] Database information (n = number of observations and year) when available.
[c] K, L, E, M, W stand for Capital, Labour, Energy, Materials and Water, respectively.

scale and scope in the water industry. Concerning substitution elasticities, they found that all inputs (labour, electricity and materials) are significant substitutes in the Morishima sense.

3. THE MODEL

In the empirical literature, the production technology is typically represented either by the production function (primal approach) or by the profit or cost function (dual approach). Input demand levels can thus be seen as the result of one of the following approaches: profit maximization or cost minimization. To characterize the technology of Mexican industry, we adopt the dual approach and consider a cost function which relates (short-run) variable cost of production to input prices and output level.

The Translog flexible form offers several advantages including the ease of modelling production relationships without restrictive assumptions about elasticities of substitution. The three-input model used in this chapter includes labour (L), Water (W) and other input materials (M). We take capital as a quasi-fixed input; in this sense, we consider a short-run cost function from the minimization of variable cost, subject to K and, from now on, we contemplate the variable cost function.

Following Berndt and Wood (1979), the non-homothetic Translog cost function in our case reads:

$$\begin{aligned}\ln VC = {} & \alpha_0 + \alpha_L \ln P_L + \alpha_W \ln P_W + \alpha_M \ln P_M + \alpha_q \ln Q + \frac{1}{2}\beta_{LL}(\ln P_L)^2 \\ & + \frac{1}{2}\beta_{WW}(\ln P_W)^2 + \frac{1}{2}\beta_{MM}(\ln P_M)^2 + \frac{1}{2}\beta_{qq}(\ln Q)^2 \\ & + \beta_{LW}\ln P_L \ln P_W + \beta_{WM}\ln P_W \ln P_M + \beta_{LM}\ln P_L \ln P_M \\ & + \beta_{LQ}\ln P_L \ln Q + \beta_{WQ}\ln P_W \ln Q + \beta_{MQ}\ln P_M \ln Q, \qquad (3.1)\end{aligned}$$

where VC is total variable cost, Q is output, P_i are input prices. α_i, α_q, β_{ij}, β_{qq} and β_{iq} are the parameters to be estimated for $i, j = L, W, M$. Each one of the variables is divided by its sample mean, to centre the local logarithmic approximation of the variable cost around zero. The restriction of symmetry is imposed, that is, $\beta_{ij} = \beta_{ji}$ *for* $i \neq j$.

The cost function (3.1) is well behaved if it is positive and homogeneous of degree one with respect to input prices. This implies the following restrictions on the parameters of:

$$\textstyle\sum_i \alpha_i = 1, \quad \sum_i \beta_{ij} = \sum_j \beta_{ij} = \sum_i \beta_i Q = 0; \; i, j = L, W, M.$$

Berndt and Wood (1979) point out that efficiency can be gained by estimating the optimal, cost-minimizing input demand equations, transformed into cost share equations, applying Shepard's lemma. Representing cost share by S_i for input i, we have, with our specification:

$$S_i = \alpha_i + \sum_j \beta_{ij} \ln P_j + \beta_{iq} \ln Q \quad i = L, W, M. \tag{3.2}$$

Symmetry and homogeneity of degree one are imposed via constraints on cost parameters. Simultaneous estimation of the cost function (3.1) and input share equations (3.2) can be performed by iterating Zellner's two-step procedure for estimating seemingly unrelated regressions. As input shares sum to 1, one of the cost share equations has to be dropped to obtain a non-singular covariance matrix (unless full-information techniques such as FIML are considered).

One objective of the empirical analysis is to determine the existence and magnitude of substitution possibilities between labour, water and materials. In particular, we focus first on own-price elasticity of input demands. The elasticities for the Translog cost function are expressed following Berndt and Wood (1979), and own and cross-price elasticities of factor demand are calculated as:

$$\varepsilon_{ii} = \frac{\beta_{ii} + S_i^2 - S_i}{S_i}; \quad i = L, W, M,$$

and

$$\varepsilon_{ij} = \frac{\beta_{ij} + S_i S_j}{S_i}; \quad i, j = L, W, M, \ i \neq j. \tag{3.3}$$

Thus, ε_{ij} is the percentage change in the quantity of the ith input resulting from a 1% change in the price of the jth input, output being constant.

The Allen Elasticities of Substitution (AES) are:

$$\sigma_{ii} = \frac{\beta_{ii} + S_i^2 - S_i}{S_i^2}; \quad i = L, W, M$$

and

$$\sigma_{ij} = \frac{\beta_{ij} + S_i S_j}{S_i S_j} = 1 + \frac{\beta_{ij}}{S_i S_j}; \quad i, j = L, W, M, \ i \neq j. \tag{3.4}$$

AES turns out to be a simple function of the cross-price elasticities, ε_{ij} and factor shares, S_j. Positive (respectively negative) σ_{ij}'s indicates that factor inputs i and j are substitutes (respectively complements).

For our analysis of elasticities of substitution we also consider the Morishima Elasticities of Substitution (MES; see Blackorby and Russell, 1989):

$$M_{ij} = \varepsilon_{ji} - \varepsilon_{ii} \quad \text{and} \quad M_{ji} = \varepsilon_{ij} - \varepsilon_{jj}. \tag{3.5}$$

Morishima elasticities measure input adjustment relative to single-factor price change. Thus, asymmetry of partial elasticities of substitution is natural. Blackorby and Russell (1989) showed that AES is an appropriate measure of substitution only in specific cases and provide no additional information relative to the cross-price elasticities and the factor shares. They showed that the MES has several advantages over the AES, concluding that MES is a more natural extension to the multi-input case.

4. DATA DESCRIPTION

The National Water Commission in Mexico (CNA – Comision Nacional del Agua) is the federal agency in charge of defining water policy. CNA defined 13 administrative regions in 1998, according to hydrological, not administrative, criteria.[6]

For this research, our principal data source is the National Institute of Statistics, Geography and Informatics (INEGI – Instituto Nacional de Estadistica, Geografia e Informatica). The source for water data is the Mexican Institute of Water Technology (IMTA – Instituto Mexicano de Tecnologia del Agua). Information on water use allows us to compute the amount of pesos per cubic metre paid by each firm. The total number of observations is 500 (cross-sections). The initial dataset consists of 14 variables for the year 1994, out of which eight are related to production factors and output. The other six are associated with reference codes which allow us to classify the sample by water availability zones, administrative regions as well as by kind of industry.

With the first eight variables, output supply level and input prices (Q, P_L, P_W and P_M) are computed. Table 3.2 presents the unit, description and source of each one of the variables used. The symbol used refers to 1994 Mexican pesos, except for water expenses, where it refers to 1996 Mexican pesos, as the observation year is different (see below).

Inputs

- *Labour (L)*: Labour (L) is defined as the average number of (equivalent) full-time workers. Labour expenditure (C_L) represents the total

Table 3.2 Data description (500 observations)

Variable	Unit	Description (mean in Spanish)	Source:
Y	Thousand Mexican pesos	VBP (Produccion Bruta Total)	INEGI, XIV Censo Industrial 1994
P_y	Thousand $/ton	Market price of output	INEGI, Encuesta Industrial Mensual
Q	Ton	Physical production	= Y / Py
K	Thousand $	Fix assets (activos fijos netos dic. 1993)	INEGI, XIV Censo Industrial 1994
L	Workers	Labour (personal ocupado total promedio)	INEGI, XIV Censo Industrial 1994
C_L	Thousand $	Labour expenditure (Remuneraciones totales al personal remunerado)	INEGI, XIV Censo Industrial 1994
P_L	$/worker	Price of labour	= CL / L
W	m^3	Water consumption (Volumen asociado al uso superficial y subterraneo)	IMTA, Sisefa – Red de Agua 1996
C_W	Thousand $	Water expenses – bill (pago por derecho de uso superficial y subterraneo)	IMTA, Sisefa – Red de Agua 1996
P_w	$\$/m^3$	Price of water	= Cw / W
M	Thousand $	Total expenses in inputs (Insumos totales)	INEGI, XIV Censo Industrial 1994
P_m	$/output	Pesos per unit of output in monetary unit	= M / Y
ENT		State: represent the Mexican political division (32)	INEGI, XIV Censo Industrial 1994
MPO		Municipality: represent the state division	INEGI, XIV Censo Industrial 1994
CODIGO		Code: Inegi classification for kind of industry	INEGI, XIV Censo Industrial 1994

CLV_IND		Industry reference: represent 8 industries	INEGI, XIV Censo Industrial 1994
ZON_98		Availability water zone in 1998: represent 9 zones	IMTA, Sisefa – Red de Agua 1996
REG_AD		Administrative region: represent 13 regions	IMTA, Sisefa – Red de Agua 1996
DZ1 . . . DZ9	Dummy Variable	9 dummy variables for 9 water availability zones	
DR1 . . . DR13	Dummy Variable	13 dummy variables for 13 administrative regions	
Dal, Daz, Dbe, Dmi, Dpa, Dqu, Dsi, Dte	Dummy Variable	8 dummy variables for 8 industries: al (food 126), az (sugar 21), be (beverage 151), mi (mining 43), pa (paper 64), qu (chemistry 32), si (steel 4), te (textile 59)	

remuneration to workers. The unit price of labour (P_L) is obtained by dividing C_L by the number of workers.

- *Water (W)*: As mentioned by a majority of authors, obtaining reliable data on water is difficult, and Mexico is no exception. It has previously been pointed out that Mexican industrialists have the obligation to pay a fixed fee for the use of water, even if the source is self-supplied. The amount of pesos per cubic metre each firm should pay is determined according to the water availability zone where the exploitation is made. There are nine tariff zones: zone 1 is defined as a zone with serious water problems, and zone 9 is a zone where water is in abundance. Consequently, in zone 1 water users pay the highest amount of pesos per cubic metre of water and zone 9 is the cheapest one.

The source for the other variables (other than water) employed in this application is from 1994. The most complete and accurate source for water data is from 1996 and assuming that industrial processes are not likely to change much in a two-year period, we take these data sources as reliable. The unit water price (P_W) is obtained by dividing the annual water expenses of a firm (C_W) by its annual water consumption (W), which exclusively represents water intake. At this point, it is important to note two issues. First, the value of C_W is the payment actually corresponding to water use (withdrawal permit). Second, we did not take as the price of water the official and uniform quotas (fees) fixed by water availability zone for each firm, because we considered that firms' water expenses better represented the payment industrialists actually made for water used. It is not an average price of water since firms pay a proportional fee per cubic metre for withdrawal, and not through a multi-block price scheme.

- *Materials (M)*: Materials (M) is defined as total expenses for other variable inputs. A proxy for the unit price of materials (P_M) is obtained by dividing total expenses in these inputs by the value of output, obtained as a proxy for the unit value of output in monetary unit ($/output).

Output

- *Production (Q)*: The level of production Q corresponds to a physical measure of output (ton as the unit), obtained by dividing total sales (Y) by the market price of output (P_Y). The latter is defined in thousand pesos per ton. In the case of beverages, the original unit is in thousand pesos per cubic metre, but since the beverage output are principally soft carbonated drinks and a few non-alcoholic drinks,

Table 3.3 Sample descriptive statistics

Variable	Unit	Mean	Standard deviation	Minimum	Maximum
Y	1000 pesos	134512.21	235194.67	7	1768017.4
P_Y	1000 pesos/ton	22.041612	115.039745	0.081112	754.432043
K	1000 pesos	95437.43	220727.19	13.5	2537940.9
L	Workers	678.956	1123.89	1	14268
W	m^3	446316.66	1510814.56	90	19908882
C_L	1000 pesos	17642.45	31200.34	4.2	289229.8
C_W	1000 pesos	816.005573	2156.12	0.062	20656.33
M	1000 pesos	89255.32	163970.18	1.1	1496532.5
P_L	Pesos/worker	22045.98	14149.61	247.058824	94438.37
P_W	Pesos/m^3	2.568919	2.032163	0.033690	14.401492
P_M	Pesos / output	0.678666	0.526880	0.058511	10.448505
Q	Ton	100169.87	373627.12	0.204525	6370717.03
Cost	1000 pesos	107713.77	191524.73	10.924	1586639.16
S_L	–	0.206681	0.123812	0.007011	0.878799
S_W	–	0.021745	0.079806	2.10E-05	0.954989
S_M	–	0.771574	0.145855	0.036650	0.987464

Note: 500 observations.

and as the density of this kind of liquid is almost the same as water,[7] then we can say that one cubic metre of beverage output is equal to one ton. Consequently, from now on, the unit for Q is in tons for all kinds of industrial production and its price (P_Y) is in thousand pesos per ton.

Cost

The total cost facing a firm is the sum of labour expenditures (C_L), water expenses (C_W) and total expenses in other inputs – materials (M). Therefore, cost = $C_L + C_W + M$. The cost unit is in thousand Mexican pesos.

Table 3.3 presents descriptive statistics for variables used. At the mean of the sample, material cost share is equal to 77.2%, labour cost share is equal to 20.6%, and for water the mean cost share is scarcely 2.2%.

5. PRELIMINARY DATA ANALYSIS

The sample consists of a random sample of 500 firms throughout the country, which are concentrated in eight industrial sectors for the year

Table 3.4 Average water productivity for industry

Type of industry	Number of industries	% Water used	Mean water price ($/m^3)	Water av. prod (thous. $/m^3)
Mining	43	15.90	0.81760	0.10735
Food	126	5.86	2.76578	0.93519
Sugar	21	5.27	0.45756	0.25587
Beverage	151	18.74	2.29228	0.48660
Textile	59	5.14	3.61129	0.80299
Paper	64	37.29	3.19733	0.13976
Chemistry	32	7.67	3.56662	0.28709
Steel	4	4.13	3.31115	0.22861
TOTAL	500		2.56892	0.30138

1994. A conditional analysis of characteristics regarding water use can be performed in three different ways: by industry, by water availability zone and by administrative region.

Table 3.4 shows the number of firms by industrial sector. Steel is the sector with the lowest number of observations (less than 1%). The beverage and food industries jointly account for 55% of total observations. This table also displays, by type of industry, average water productivity (that is, the value of output divided by water consumption). For the whole sample, the average productivity of water is about 300 pesos per cubic metre of water. By type of industry, food has the highest average water productivity, 935 pesos per cubic metre of water used. Mining represents the lowest average water productivity, with 107 pesos per cubic metre. With respect to the quantity of water used, the paper industry is the largest user (37.29%) followed by beverages (18.74%) but the latter has a three-time higher average water productivity. Mining is the third highest water user (15.9%). These three industries account for 72% of total water use and represent 51.6% of firms in our sample.

Apparently, average water price is not correlated with average water productivity (a correlation coefficient of 0.3432) when we analyse them only by industry. However, a more significant relationship can be established with respect to the water availability zone.

There are nine water availability zones in Mexico. The zones where water is cheapest are located in the southwest of the country, while water zones where the resource is in poor supply are in the north, where the climatic characteristics are arid and semi-arid. In the central area of the country, excluding the Federal District, where Mexico City is located with its 23 million inhabitants, we find in higher proportion of zones 6 to 9 than in other parts of the country.

Table 3.5 Average water productivity for zone

Availability zone	Number of industries	% Water used	Mean water price ($/m³)	Water av. prod (thous. $/m³)
Zone 1	53	6.15	6.40007	0.86799
Zone 2	47	6.15	5.02263	0.70036
Zone 3	26	4.15	3.91111	0.39519
Zone 4	25	3.39	3.33233	0.64383
Zone 5	116	22.29	2.31898	0.34361
Zone 6	45	8.32	2.05528	0.22726
Zone 7	51	14.08	1.81489	0.13017
Zone 8	66	18.93	0.57940	0.14123
Zone 9	71	16.54	0.44937	0.15776

Table 3.5 shows average water productivity by water availability zone and the average price of water. Consistently with the characteristics of water availability zones, water in zone 1 (the zone with water scarcity problems) has the highest average productivity (868 pesos per m^3) and also the highest average water price (6.40$/m^3). In this table we see that, as one moves from the most expensive to the cheapest water zone, both average water price and average water productivity decrease. This behaviour is corroborated by the high correlation coefficient among them, which is 0.9284. The exception is zone 3, where productivity falls off unexpectedly.

Continuing the analysis regarding water availability zones, the correlation coefficient between the percentage of water used and the percentage concentration of industry is equal to 0.8842, this being due to the fact that the number of firms is almost equally distributed across zones, except for zone 5 which contains the greatest number of industries (23%) as well as the highest water use (22.29%). These two high correlation measures allow us to conclude that water prices, as they are so far defined by water availability zone, have already affected the productivity of industries, at least with respect to water consumption. Table 3.6 shows the distribution of water fees for industrial use between availability zones, for the first quarter of 2003.

The country of Mexico is divided into 13 administrative regions. In the north of Mexico are the regions I, II, III, VI, VII and IX, Central Mexico contains regions IV, VIII, XIII and the north part of region X. Finally, regions V, X, XI and XII are located in the southwest of the country. Table 3.7 presents average water productivity by administrative region and total water used.

Region I has the highest water productivity. This region is located in the northwest of Mexico where the climatic features are similar to those of a

Table 3.6 Average water productivity by administrative region

Administrative region	Number of industries	% Water used	Mean water price ($/m^3)	Water av. prod (thous. $/m^3)
Region I	10	0.21	4.36761	2.18595
Region II	19	6.22	2.23574	0.13088
Region III	24	3.68	1.33074	0.24035
Region IV	64	7.22	1.78686	0.42215
Region V	9	0.34	1.78382	0.92367
Region VI	63	18.20	2.94010	0.25546
Region VII	25	6.57	2.46687	0.24948
Region VIII	114	19.71	2.79716	0.32498
Region IX	26	7.72	1.44043	0.21302
Region X	51	20.59	0.96602	0.16281
Region XI	19	0.81	1.01644	0.46464
Region XII	16	1.50	1.31728	0.33857
Region XIII	60	7.23	5.71786	0.83572

Table 3.7 Water fees – first trimester 2003

Availability zone	$/m^3*
Zone 1	14.1086
Zone 2	11.2865
Zone 3	9.4053
Zone 4	7.7596
Zone 5	6.1133
Zone 6	5.5251
Zone 7	4.1587
Zone 8	1.4776
Zone 9	1.1073

Note: *Reference 10.8213 $/USD, first quarter average.

Source: Comision Nacional del Agua (www.cna.gob.mx); Ley Federal de Derechos en Materia de Agua (LFDMA), 2003.

desert zone. Mexico City is situated in region VIII, where the four most expensive water zones are also located. Hence, this explains why the highest average water price is in this region, followed by region I where high-priced water zones are also located.

We also observe significant correlations between industry and water in administrative regions: first, between industry concentration and water use (0.7943) (recall that the respective correlation regarding water zones is 0.8842), and second, among water average productivity and mean water price (0.5746). This can be explained by the fact that the regions which were indicated with numbers were assigned from northwest to southeast. Therefore, it captures the climatic characteristics from arid and semi-arid to tropical humid, and logically, the more expensive water availability zones are located in the north and the cheapest zones in the south (regions X, XI and XII). These correlations, however, are lower than those in water zones, since the relationship between water and price inside administrative regions is not so linear.

According to this analysis, it would be hazardous to conclude so far that industries are concentrated where water does not represent a real constraint to production. On the other hand, it is certainly possible to conclude that water price is pushing industrialists towards an efficient use of water.

That such a claim mentioned above might be hazardous is confirmed by the fact that there already exist zones with severe water accessibility problems. In IMTA (2001), Ortiz points out that in the regions of Valle de Mexico (XIII), Lerma (VIII), Cuencas Cerradas del Norte (VII) and Baja California (I), economic activities actually lead to more extraction of water than the volume that resource availability would allow. In the Valle de Mexico region alone, extraction represents a level of withdrawal 71% higher than availability. These four regions account for more than 65% of the national industrial product and about 50% of the country's total population.

The 2003 CNA report on water statistics in Mexico mentions that, inside administrative regions, there exists a significant disparity in the source of water (surface or groundwater), regarding self-supplied industries. In Table 3.8 we can see that, in 2001 for example, industries in regions II and XII withdraw 100% from groundwater, while in region VII only one firm extracts from surface water (106 hm^3). On the other hand, in regions IV and X, firms use less than 10% of groundwater. Only five of the 13 regions extract more than 35% from superficial source.

Finally, in Table 3.9, we can see how industrial firms in our sample are distributed across water availability zones and administrative regions.

6. EMPIRICAL RESULTS

Table 3.10 reports parameter estimates for the full Translog system (cost share equations). Overall, the model fits well, with an R^2 statistic of 0.4050, 0.1077 and 0.4302, for the share equations of labour, water and materials,

Table 3.8 Self-supplied industry: source of water

Administrative region		Superficial (hm^3)	Underground (hm^3)	TOTAL (hm^3)
I	Peninsula de Baja California	4	213	217
II	Noroeste	0	32	32
III	Pacifico Norte	47	21	68
IV	Balsas	3264	142	3406
V	Pacifico Sur	5	8	13
VI	Rio Bravo	61	216	277
VII	Cuencas Centrales del Norte	1	105	106
VIII	Lerma-Santiago-Pacifico	74	257	331
IX	Golfo Norte	156	47	203
X	Golfo Centro	1356	90	1446
XI	Frontera Sur	16	68	84
XII	Peninsula de Yucatan	0	152	152
XIII	Valle de Mexico	44	240	284
TOTAL		5028	1591	6619

Source: CNA 'Estadisticas del Agua en Mexico, 2003'. Estimations for 2001.

respectively. All parameters are significantly different from zero, except two (*apw*, the coefficient on water price level, and *aplpw*, the cross-effect of labour and water). Estimated input cost shares are given by the intercept terms (α_i) (Grebenstein and Field, 1979). The estimated share of labour is 15.19% and the estimated share of water is 0.62%, two values notably less than the observed ones. The estimated share for the materials input is 84.26% (variables P_L, P_W and P_M, respectively in Table 3.10).

'The monotonicity requirement is met if the predicted cost shares are positive for all inputs' (Teeples and Glyer, 1987). From Table 3.10 it can be seen that the monotonicity condition holds such that all α_i (*apl*, *apw* and *apm*) are positive and significantly different from zero, except for water.

Table 3.11 presents the Allen Elasticities of Substitution obtained from expression (3.4), in a lower triangular fashion as, by definition, the AES are symmetric.

Table 3.12 contains the own and cross-price elasticities of input demand estimated through expression (3.3) together with their respective *t*-statistics. Each element in the table is the elasticity of demand for the row input after a price change of the column input. These elasticities have been calculated at the mean of the actual input cost shares shown in Table 3.3 (S_L, S_W and S_M, respectively for labour, water and materials), following the suggestion

Table 3.9 Number of industries by water availability zone (500 observations)

Industry	Zone 1	Zone 2	Zone 3	Zone 4	Zone 5	Zone 6	Zone 7	Zone 8	Zone 9	TOTAL
Mining	1	1	1	3	13	8	4	8	4	43
Food	10	12	7	8	36	10	19	13	11	126
Sugar	–	–	–	–	–	2	3	6	10	21
Beverage	15	9	7	6	22	12	15	28	37	151
Textile	10	8	3	3	22	8	2	3	–	59
Paper	11	12	5	3	11	2	5	7	8	64
Chemistry	5	4	3	2	10	3	3	1	1	32
Steel	1	1	–	–	2	–	–	–	–	4
Total	53	47	26	25	116	45	51	66	71	500

Table 3.10 Translog cost function estimation results for Mexican industry

Parameter	Variable	Estimate	Std error	*t* value
apl	P_L	0.1519	0.00577	26.32*
apw	P_W	0.0062	0.00452	1.38
apm	P_M	0.8426	0.00632	133.41*
aplpl	$P_L * P_L$	0.0938	0.00647	14.5*
apwpw	$P_W * P_W$	0.0148	0.00337	4.39*
apmpm	$P_M * P_M$	0.1212	0.00809	14.98*
aplpw	$P_L * P_W$	0.0003	0.00333	0.08
apwpm	$P_W * P_M$	−0.0154	0.00396	−3.9*
aplpm	$P_L * P_M$	−0.0962	0.00607	−15.86*
aplq	$P_L * Q$	−0.0298	0.00186	−16.07*
apwq	$P_W * Q$	−0.0087	0.00133	−6.53*
apmq	$P_M * Q$	0.0387	0.00199	19.44*

Note: * indicates a significant parameter at the 1% level.

Table 3.11 Allen Elasticities of Substitution (AES) = σ_{ij}

	Labour	Water	Material
Labour	−1.6415		
	(−10.83)		
Water	1.0617	−13.6890	
	(1.43)	(−1.92)	
Material	0.3965	0.0801	−0.0924
	(10.41)	(0.33)	(−6.80)

Note: *t*-statistics are in parentheses.

Table 3.12 Own and cross-price elasticities of demand = ε_{ij}

	Labour	Water	Material
Labour	−0.3392	0.0230	0.3059
	(−10.83)	(1.43)	(10.41)
Water	0.2194	−0.2976	0.0618
	(1.43)	(−1.92)	(0.33)
Material	0.0819	0.0017	−0.0713
	(10.41)	(0.33)	(−6.80)

Note: *t*-statistics are in parentheses.

by Anderson and Thursby (1986). Standard errors are estimated from expression (3.6) below, following Binswanger (1974):

$$SE(\varepsilon_{ij}) = \frac{SE(\beta_{ij})}{S_i}; \quad SE(\sigma_{ij}) = \frac{SE(\beta_{ij})}{S_i S_j}. \tag{3.6}$$

Bergström and Panas (1992) point out that concavity requires that the own elasticities of substitution be negative. From Table 3.12 it can be seen that this condition is met. The elasticity of substitution is statistically significant for labour and materials, but not for water.

Table 3.13 reports the Morishima Elasticity of Substitution (MES) obtained from equation (3.5). This table excludes the diagonal because MES is defined as a logarithmic derivative of the optimal input quantity ratio with respect to the input price ratio, and the diagonal contains no information. In the sense of Morishima Elasticities of Substitution, all inputs are significant substitutes (water/material at 10% only), excepting the pair material/water.

All own price elasticities (Table 3.12) have the expected sign, that is, inputs are responding negatively to their own price. As the price elasticity of water is −0.2976, we can conclude that industrial water demand for Mexican manufacturing is inelastic (less than one in absolute value). Also, water demand is not very responsive to changes in water price. Our estimates indicate that a 1% change in the price of water (everything else held constant) will result in a 0.30% reduction in the quantity of water consumed in the Mexican industry.

Continuing with Table 3.12, estimated elasticities (own and cross) for labour and materials are statistically significant at 1%. The own-price elasticity for water is significant at 10% only, while the others are not significant at the 5% level.

Both cross-price elasticities between labour and water have the same signs (0.0230 and 0.2194) but are lower than Morishima measures (0.5587 and

Table 3.13 Morishima Elasticities of Substitution (MES) = M_{ij}

	Labour	Water	Material
Labour		0.5587	0.4212
		(3.40)	(11.17)
Water	0.3207		0.2993
	(2.00)		(1.89)
Material	0.3772	0.1331	
	(10.02)	(0.70)	

Note: *t*-statistics are in parentheses.

0.3207). This indicates that an increase in water price leads to an increase in labour use and conversely, but at the same time, water use become more intense at such a rate that the water/labour ratio rises.

Morishima elasticities measure relative input adjustment to a single-factor price change. In Table 3.13, the first row shows how labour/water and labour/materials ratios respond to a change in the price of labour. According to figures in the second row, after a change in water price, the water/labour ratio changes in a proportion of 0.3207 and the water/materials ratio changes in a proportion of 0.2993. The largest degree of substitution is obtained for changes in the price of labour with respect to water. And its value is half of that in AES in Table 3.11, but this latter is not statistically significant. The main difference between AES and MES concerns the relationship between materials and water, in that these inputs appear as substitutes according to AES (0.0801), but are not significant. Hence, the AES underestimates the elasticity of substitution between water and materials, particularly in response to a change in the price of water, because in Table 3.13, we can see that the elasticity between water and material is significant at 5%.

An important point to notice is that water price does not seem to have a strong impact on the industrial demand for labour. Water is a substitute for labour (1.0617 in Table 3.11, 0.0230 in Table 3.12 for labour/water and 0.2194 for water/labour), but these elasticities are not statistically significant. On the contrary, in Table 3.13 we see that water and labour also happen to be substitutes, in the sense of Morishima, but are statistically significant for both pairs, while the highest elasticity of all the MES (0.5587) is reported for the pair labour/water.

With respect to the relationship between water and other materials, for all cases they are substitutes and not significantly different from zero. The MES pair water/materials has the highest elasticity (0.2993) and is significant at the 10% level.

Regarding labour and other materials, those inputs are statistically significant substitutes, and AES and MES elasticities are nearly the same.

For our analysis, MES appears to be a better tool for determining the effects that water price changes may have on the other production inputs.

As water represents only a small share of total cost in the estimation (less than 1%), it is unlikely that variation in water price will have a significant impact on output price. Hence in our case, the constant output price elasticity of demand for water may not be a poor elasticity approximation.

The value of the price elasticity of demand for water in Mexico (−0.2976) is not very far from those reported in previous studies (see Table 3.1). First, most previous elasticity estimates are also pretty low. Grebenstein and Field (1979) obtain −0.326 for the US manufacturing series, Renzetti reports a water price elasticity of −0.3817 for intake manufacturing (1992) and −0.308 for price of water intake (1993). Reynaud (2003) obtains −0.29 for network water. Only Babin et al. (1982) obtain the highest water price elasticity (in absolute value) on pooled data (−0.56). The lowest elasticity (in absolute value) for intake water (−0.1308) is reported in the last published study of Renzetti and Dupont (2003).

Regarding the relationship of water with other inputs, we find that water is a substitute for both labour and materials. Babin et al. (1982), Grebenstein and Field (1979) and Dupont and Renzetti (2001) all find that water is a substitute for labour, while complementarity of water with respect to materials is reported by Dupont and Renzetti (2001). Concerning these results, it is important to keep in mind that we use Morishima Elasticities of Substitution, while estimates in the literature and reported in Table 3.1 use the standard cross-price elasticity measures instead.

7. WATER ZONE LOCATION EXPERIMENT

In this section, we conduct an experiment whose objective is to evaluate the consistency of the industrial firm distribution regarding water availability zones. Presumably, if a firm faces the same market conditions, and if input prices for labour and materials are uniform across regions, then the firm will be better off by operating in a region where water is cheapest. If, on the other hand, a firm with intensive water use is located in a zone with a high price for water, this would indicate that profit differentials with other water availability zones depend on other factors such as those mentioned above.

In our empirical application, parameter estimates and data on cost shares and output levels allow us to compute average costs for firms in all industries and water availability zones. Given the Translog specification for the cost function, this cost will depend on input prices that are likely to differ across zones but also across industries. Firms with more value-added may require more skilled workers or materials, and local labour market conditions and transportation infrastructures may influence labour cost.

The experiment proceeds as follows. We first compute average input prices by water availability zone and by industry, to control for observed heterogeneity in these cost factors. We then use our cost estimates to construct average cost measures for each firm in the sample, assuming (a) the same output level; (b) no additional investment, *when it faces prices in other zones*. For instance, a firm in the beverage industry and located in zone 1, when 'moving' to zone 2, will now pay the average labour, materials and water unit prices that firms in the beverage industry already face in zone 2.

Finally, we compute for each firm, the relative average-cost differential for being in another zone (actual cost / new cost − 1), and denote this cost differential by *DCi*, where *i* is the index of the zone. For example, for all 15 beverage firms located in zone 1, *DC1* will be equal to zero (as all those firms are actually located in zone 1), but *DC2* could be either greater or less than zero. In the first situation, its actual cost is greater than that in zone 2, so this firm would be better off moving to zone 2. In contrast, when $DC2 < 0$, then we would say that this firm is well located given its actual cost and it would be worse off if it moves to zone 2.

In conjunction with the sign of the cost differential estimate, we also need to check for the significance of the differential *DCi*. This is done by computing a simple Student test statistic for the significance of the empirical mean in the *DCi* measures for each zone and each industry. What should be expected is that, as we move to cheaper water zones, we find positive and possibly higher average cost differentials, meaning that being located in expensive zones for industrial water use is not efficient. Also, we may expect that, as we try to move firms from zone 9 (the cheapest zone), the cost gap is not significantly different from 0, or becomes negative and statistically significant.

The results of this water zone experiment are shown in Table 3.14. Each water zone is examined from 1 to 9 (most expensive to cheapest), for firms in the eight industries. The firms with $DCI = 0$ are obviously excluded, which leaves eight zones in each case. Table 3.14 reports average cost differentials in the form of ratios, $C_i/C_1 - 1$, $C_i/C_2 - 1$, and so on, and *t*-statistics associated with these relative cost differences.

In the beverage industry, for firms already in zone 9, their *DC*s for being in any of the other zones are significantly different from zero except for zone 8, but all of them are negative, meaning that all the 37 firms are actually well located in zone 9 and they will be worse off in any other water pricing zone. We have the same result for beverage firms located in zone 8, with a negative and significant *DC* for zones 1 to 7, and a cost differential that is not significant for zone 9. By inspecting further zones 6 to 1 upward for the beverage industry, we see that this confirms perfectly the prediction regarding water input cost: when the firm moves to a zone with cheaper industrial water (to the 'right' of its actual location in Table 3.14), the relative cost differential is either not significant or is positive and significant. On the other hand, the relative cost ratio is either not significant or negative and significant when the firm in the beverage industry moves to zones with a higher water price (to the 'left' of the actual location). For all firms in this industry located between zone 1 and zone 6, the cost differential with the cheapest water zones 8 and 9 is always positive and significant. This positive and encouraging result can be explained by the fact that this sector is the second highest water user with a rather limited average water productivity (see Table 3.4).

Table 3.14 Water zone location experiment

	DC1 = 0; Firms in zone 1 moving to zone i, i ≠ 1							
	DC2	*DC3*	*DC4*	*DC5*	*DC6*	*DC7*	*DC8*	*DC9*
Mining	−0.93	−0.79	−0.59	−0.81	−0.75	−0.68	−0.77	−0.83
Food	0.26	0.03	0.16	0.33 **	0.13	0.43 **	0.61 **	0.47 **
Sugar								
Beverage	−0.14	−0.09	−0.25 **	−0.03	−0.08	0.05	0.28 **	0.29 **
Textile	0.16 *	0.12	0.04	0.10	0.18 *	0.72 **	0.14 *	
Paper	0.03	−0.18 **	−0.16 **	0.12	0.32 **	−0.32 **	−0.21 **	−0.13 *
Chemistry	0.07	0.56 **	0.02	−0.22 **	−0.14 **	0.52 **	0.31 **	−0.57 **
Steel	2.49			−0.45				
	DC2 = 0; Firms in zone 2 moving to zone i, i ≠ 2							
	DC1	*DC3*	*DC4*	*DC5*	*DC6*	*DC7*	*DC8*	*DC9*
Mining	2.36	1.02	1.65	0.47	0.56	0.86	0.48	0.25
Food	−0.23 **	−0.18 *	−0.08	0.06	−0.10	0.15	0.29 *	0.18
Sugar								
Beverage	0.11	0.04	−0.15 *	0.09	0.04	0.18 *	0.41 **	0.42 **
Textile	−0.15 **	−0.02	−0.10 **	0.00	0.03	0.55 **	0.03	
Paper	−0.11 *	−0.27 **	−0.25 **	0.01	0.19 **	−0.39 **	−0.28 **	−0.20 **
Chemistry	−0.11	0.40	−0.09	−0.30 *	−0.23	0.36	0.17	−0.62 **
Steel	−0.72			−0.84				

Table 3.14 (continued)

	DC3 = 0; Firms in zone 3 moving to zone i, i ≠ 3															
	DC1		*DC2*		*DC4*		*DC5*		*DC6*		*DC7*		*DC8*		*DC9*	
Mining	0.41		−0.47		0.23		−0.30		−0.27		−0.15		−0.31		−0.41	
Food	−0.05		0.23	**	0.13		0.30	**	0.11		0.41	**	0.58	**	0.44	**
Sugar																
Beverage	0.07		−0.06		−0.18	*	0.06		0.01		0.15		0.41	**	0.42	**
Textile	−0.16		−0.01		−0.11		−0.01		0.01		0.53		0.02			
Paper	0.21	**	0.26	**	0.03		0.36	**	0.61	**	−0.17	**	−0.03		0.06	
Chemistry	−0.39	**	−0.34	**	−0.38	**	−0.52	**	−0.47	**	−0.06		−0.17		−0.74	**
Steel																
	DC4 = 0; Firms in zone 4 moving to zone i, i ≠ 4															
	DC1		*DC2*		*DC3*		*DC5*		*DC6*		*DC7*		*DC8*		*DC9*	
Mining	0.62	**	−0.73	**	−0.36	**	−0.50	**	−0.42	**	−0.28	*	−0.45	**	−0.56	**
Food	−0.17	*	0.09		−0.11		0.16		−0.02		0.25	*	0.41	**	0.29	**
Sugar																
Beverage	0.27		0.12		0.19		0.25		0.19		0.36	*	0.64	**	0.65	**
Textile	−0.03		0.13		0.10		0.09		0.15		0.70	**	0.13			
Paper	0.17		0.19	**	−0.03		0.30	**	0.55	**	−0.20	**	−0.08		0.00	
Chemistry	−0.02		0.06		0.53		−0.23		−0.16		0.49		0.28		−0.58	**
Steel																

DC5 = 0; Firms in zone 5 moving to zone i, i ≠ 5

	DC1		*DC2*		*DC3*		*DC4*		*DC6*		*DC7*		*DC8*		*DC9*	
Mining	1.92	**	−0.40	**	0.34	**	0.94	**	0.14		0.40	**	0.08		−0.12	*
Food	−0.29	**	−0.07		−0.24	**	−0.15	**	−0.16	**	0.08		0.22	**	0.11	
Sugar																
Beverage	−0.01		−0.14	**	−0.08		−0.24	**	−0.07		0.07		0.31	**	0.32	**
Textile	−0.24	**	−0.10		−0.12	*	−0.18	**	−0.07		0.43	**	−0.05			
Paper	−0.15		−0.10		−0.29	**	−0.27	**	0.14		−0.41	**	−0.32	**	−0.24	**
Chemistry	0.25	**	0.36	**	0.96	**	0.28	**	0.08		0.91	**	0.64	**	−0.46	**
Steel	0.86	**	4.63	**												

DC6 = 0; Firms in zone 6 moving to zone i, i ≠ 6

	DC1		*DC2*		*DC3*		*DC4*		*DC5*		*DC7*		*DC8*		*DC9*	
Mining	1.21	**	−0.50	**	0.08		0.52	**	−0.19	**	0.09		−0.15	*	−0.30	**
Food	−0.16		0.10		−0.10		0.01		0.17		0.26		0.42	**	0.30	*
Sugar											−0.35	**	−0.22	**	−0.34	**
Beverage	0.01		−0.11		−0.05		−0.22	**	0.01		0.10		0.35	**	0.36	**
Textile	−0.17	**	−0.02		−0.05		−0.12		−0.02		0.52	**	0.01			
Paper	−0.28		−0.22		−0.41		−0.39		−0.17		−0.50	*	−0.41		−0.34	
Chemistry	0.14		0.24	*	0.86	**	0.18		−0.10		0.78	**	0.58	**	−0.50	**
Steel																

Table 3.14 (continued)

	DC1	*DC2*	*DC3*	*DC4*	*DC5*	*DC6*	*DC8*	*DC9*
	DC7 = 0; Firms in zone 7 moving to zone i, i ≠ 7							
Mining	1.00 **	−0.57 **	−0.06	0.34	−0.29	−0.21	−0.25	−0.39 *
Food	−0.36 **	−0.16	−0.32 **	−0.23 *	−0.10	−0.23 *	0.12	0.02
Sugar						0.52 *	0.18	0.00
Beverage	−0.12	−0.23 **	−0.18	−0.33 **	−0.12	−0.16	0.19	0.20
Textile	−0.52	−0.43	−0.43	−0.47	−0.36	−0.40	−0.35	
Paper	0.45	0.50	0.20	0.23	0.62	0.92	0.15	0.26
Chemistry	−0.37	−0.31	0.04	−0.35	−0.50 **	−0.45 **	−0.11	−0.72 **
Steel								
	DC8 = 0; Firms in zone 8 moving to zone i, i ≠ 8							
	DC1	*DC2*	*DC3*	*DC4*	*DC5*	*DC6*	*DC7*	*DC9*
Mining	1.84 **	−0.49 **	0.16	0.75 **	−0.10	0.03	0.28	−0.22
Food	−0.44 **	−0.26 **	−0.40 **	−0.32 **	−0.20 *	−0.32 **	−0.12	−0.09
Sugar						0.28 **	−0.16 *	−0.16 *
Beverage	−0.33 **	−0.41 **	−0.37 **	−0.49 **	−0.32 **	−0.36 **	−0.26 **	−0.05
Textile	−0.13	0.02	−0.01	−0.09	−0.02	0.04	0.53 **	
Paper	0.25	0.29	0.04	0.07	0.40	0.66 *	−0.14	0.08
Chemistry	−0.30	−0.23	0.16	−0.27	−0.44	−0.39	0.11	−0.69
Steel								

DC9 = 0; Firms in zone 9 moving to zone i, i ≠ 9

	DC1	*DC2*	*DC3*	*DC4*	*DC5*	*DC6*	*DC7*	*DC8*
Mining	2.54 **	−0.34	0.49	1.21 *	0.15	0.31	0.61	0.23
Food	−0.41 **	−0.21	−0.36 *	−0.27	−0.13	−0.26	−0.04	0.11
Sugar						0.51 **	−0.01	0.18
Beverage	−0.30 **	−0.39 **	−0.35 **	−0.47 **	−0.30 **	−0.33 **	−0.23 **	−0.04
Textile								
Paper	0.09	0.17	−0.09	−0.07	0.25	0.47	−0.24	−0.11
Chemistry	1.33	1.51	2.56	1.38	0.81	1.00	2.50	1.92
Steel								

Notes: *DCi* is the relative average-cost differential: (actual cost/new cost) − 1, where the new cost is the average cost computed by using input prices from zone *i* . * and ** respectively indicate a relative, average-cost differential significantly different from 0 at the 10% and 5% level.

Hence, in the beverage industry, 61% of the firms are adequately located, while the other 39% would be significantly better off in zones 8 or 9.

According to our water statistics, paper is the largest water user (37.29%) with the second lowest average water productivity (see Table 3.4). This industry seems to be well located in expensive water zones, as *DC*s are not significantly different from zero for all firms located in zones 6 to 9, and are negative and significant for firms in zone 5. With the exception of firms actually located in zones 1 and 2, we find behaviour according to that of the firm (minimize cost), where paper firms would be better off in zone 6. Concerning zones 3 and 4, firms would be better placed in zones 5 or 6, but also in zones 1 and 2, which are more expensive zones. Therefore, 51.5% of paper firms are satisfactory located, 12.5% report unexpected behaviour (those in zones 3 and 4), and 36% would have lower average costs if they moved to zone 6.

Zone 7 seems to be the best option for the textile industry because it reports a positive *DC* which is significantly different from zero for all costs (except *DC3*), even those placed in zone 8. The few others significantly different from zero are negative, indicating a worse situation.

Of food firms, 43.7% are adequately located (firms in zones 2, 7, 8 and 9). Those located in zones 5 and 6 (36.5%) would be better off in zone 8. Firms in zones 1 and 4 would improve if they moved to any of the zones 7 to 9. In contrast, firms in zone 3 would be better off in zone 2, a more expensive zone, and also in cheaper zones (7 to 9).

The chemicals sector displays unusual behaviour for firms placed in zones 5 and 6 (40.6%), because it appears they would do better by moving to any other zone, even the expensive ones (zones 1 to 4), and worse if they go to the cheapest zone. Firms in zone 1 would do better in zones 3, 7 or 8. The other firms seem well situated. A possible explanation is that the unit costs of inputs other than water (labour and materials) are cheaper for chemical plants in precisely those zones where water is more expensive.

Sugar firms in our sample are only located in zones 6 to 9. The best water availability zone for this sector appears to be zone 6, since relative cost differentials associated with being in this zone instead of any other are positive and significantly different from zero.

If we remove the 43 mining firms which by definition cannot be moved from their actual geographical zone to another, as well as the four steel firms, this leaves 453 firms out of the original 500. From these, 44.4% are consistently located regarding the water availability zones. Nineteen of the 21 firms in the sugar industry would be better off in more expensive zones. The same is true for 13 chemicals firms, seven for food, three for textiles, and eight in the paper sector. Hence, 50 firms (11%) show unexpected behaviour regarding water price, leaving 44.6% of firms that would achieve lower production costs in cheaper water availability zones. As pointed out above, this may simply mean that water cost is not a limiting factor for these firms, and that other input costs or different market conditions are more important determinants of actual firm location.

Zones 1 to 5 involve 53.9% of firms, of which 14.3% are adequately located, 6% unexpectely perform well, and the rest (almost 80%) would be better off in cheaper zones for industrial water. Of the other firms located in zones 6 to 9, 85% are well located. An important fact that comes out of this analysis is that 64% of paper firms, the biggest water user, are suitably located, as are 61% of the beverage sector, which is the second highest water user. Indeed, in our sample, these two industries together consume about 56% of total industrial water.

8. CONCLUSION

Peter Rogers (2003) points out that 'in developing countries, water supply and prices are emerging as one of the major constraints in growth of industries'. Considering the case of Mexico, this does not seem to hold for Mexican industry given that, according to our empirical analysis, no matter what effect water price appears to have in pushing industrial firms to use water efficiently, the cost of water only represents a very moderate share of industrial variable cost. It is therefore unlikely that variation in water input price will have a major impact on output price, but in our case, for industrial water use, the constant output price elasticity of input demand might not be a bad approximation for elasticity.

Moreover, from our estimation results, we can conclude that industrial water demand is not very responsive to changes in water price given that the average value for the price elasticity of industrial water demand for Mexican manufacturing is inelastic (−0.2976). The average water productivity for Mexican industry is 0.3013 thousand pesos (Mexican) per cubic metre. Regarding availability of water, the empirical analysis shows two significant correlations: first, between average water productivity and average water price (0.9284); and second, between industry concentration by water zone and water used (0.8842). According to this analysis, we may conclude that water prices, as they are so far defined by water scarcity zones, have already affected the productivity of firms, at least concerning water consumption. It might be premature to conclude that industries are concentrated in regions where water does not represent a real constraint to production. But certainly it is possible to conclude two things: first, water price is pushing industrialists towards the efficient use of water. And second, more than 60% of firms from the two industries with the highest consumption (paper and beverage) are well located as far as water availability zones are concerned.

We also find, like Stiroh (1999), that the Allen Elasticity of Substitution gives a misleading picture of the substitution behaviour between inputs and the Morishima elasticity turns out to be a better tool for determining the effects that changes in industrial water price could have on other production inputs. Water is found to be a substitute for both labour and materials in the sense of the Morishima Elasticity of Substitution.

We find that within the Mexican manufacturing sector, water price is working as a good economic tool to support the efficient use of water, although the responsiveness level of water demand against change in water price is not very strong.

It is nevertheless difficult to determine in an accurate way how much a change in water price would affect the water demanded in industry, in view of the fact that our research considers pooled data for Mexican industry and that we have assumed common parameters for all industries. Thus, it would be difficult to offer guidance for efficient policy in water management on the basis of the estimates obtained so far, since it is important to take into account heterogeneity among consumer groups (industries). Future research on Mexican industry should be able to disaggregate demand, in order to identify the responsiveness (elasticity) of individual groups (type of industry) to a price change (water price).

APPENDIX 3.1: INDUSTRIAL WATER DEMAND STUDIES REPORTED IN TABLE 3.1

(1) *Rees* (1969) uses a variety of functional forms to study water intake demand equations using data for manufacturing firms in southeastern England. Price elasticities of water intake for various sectors are estimated. At the lowest observed price, elasticity results are: chemicals (−0.958), food (3.28), drinks (1.3), non-metallic (2.5), and paper (1.44).

(2) *Turnovsky* (1969) uses two cross-sections, 1962 and 1965, for a sample of 19 Massachusetts towns. A linear equation for industrial water demand is estimated by OLS, with average prices as explanatory variables. The elasticities estimated at the sample mean range from −0.473 to −0.836.

(3) *De Rooy* (1974) uses a Cobb-Douglas functional form to estimate industrial water demand with OLS. His data source consists of 30 New Jersey chemical plants, for 1965. He estimates separate demand equations for cooling, process, steam generation and sanitation. The price of water consists of a weighted average between water intake and water circulation prices. These together with plant output and a technology index are the explanatory

variables. The estimated price elasticities for each water application are: cooling (−0.894), process (−0.354) and steam generation (−0.590).

(4) *Grebenstein and Field* (1979) estimate elasticities of substitution between water and other productive inputs for the aggregate US manufacturing sector for the year 1973, using a Translog cost function. The analysis is carried out for two different series regarding water: one constructed by the American Water Work Association (AWWA) and another by Montanary and Mattern (MM). Cost share of water is respectively 1.2% and 1.9%. The price elasticity of demand for water for the AWWA series is −0.326 and −0.801 for the MM series. Finally, they find that water and capital inputs appear to be complements, not substitutes (as 'normal neoclassical expectations') and that labour and water are substitutes in production.

(5) *Babin, Willis and Allen* (1982) followed Grebenstein and Field's work by examining water use for different US manufacturing industries. Their results show considerable variation in parameter estimates between the individual industry groups and the pooled data set. Whereas price elasticity for the pooled data is −0.56, it varies from 0.14 for food and machinery industries to −0.66 for paper. In the study, capital and labour are substitutes for all industries analysed.

(6) *Ziegler and Bell* (1984) test for the hypothesis that there is no significant difference in the estimates of industrial water demand using either average or marginal costs. They estimate the intake water demand using a Cobb-Douglas functional form for self-supplied industries. They employ cross-section data collected from a sample of 23 high-volume water-using firms (paper and chemical) in Arkansas, USA. They found that considering average cost will result in a better estimate of water demand for self-supplied industries.

(7) *Renzetti* (1988) considers industrial water demand according to four different aspects: water intake, treatment prior to use, recirculation, and treatment prior to discharge. These aspects consider the way water is used inside the production process. The author estimates input demands associated with a Cobb-Douglas cost function, assuming weak separability in water inputs. Four manufacturing subgroups are considered: petrochemicals, heavy industry, forest industry and light industry. The data set is from a survey of water use by Canadian manufacturing firms conducted in 1981 (372 observations for British Columbia, Canada). Results show that the intake price elasticities range from −0.12

(petrochemicals) to −0.54 (light industries). The relative magnitude of these elasticities corresponds to previous expectations: the cost share of water is smallest in the petrochemical industry as well as in heavy industry, whereas water's cost share is largest in light industry. The absolute size of the respective elasticity for intake water follows the same behaviour. With respect to the cross-price elasticity, the results show that for all industries water intake and water discharge are complements; while water intake and recirculation are substitutes.

(8) *Renzetti* (1992) models industrial water use considering the same four components as in Renzetti (1988), but here each of the four components is treated as a separate input and the four demands are estimated as a system of interrelated equations from a water-use cost function (Translog form). Data is from Canadian manufacturing firms (Industrial Water Use Survey and Survey of Municipal Water Prices), for 1985 including 1068 firms. Estimation results show that industrial water use is sensitive to economic factors, and that intake and recirculation are substitutes. Water intake price elasticity varies from −0.1534 (plastic) to −0.5885 (paper). Recirculation and discharge are also substitutes. These results point to the potential for using economic incentives to reduce industrial pollution.

(9) *Renzetti* (1993) In this study, the estimation procedure is based on two stages. The first estimates a Probit model with the firms' selection of either public or private supply as the dependent variable. In a second step, maximum likelihood estimates are derived for network and self-supplied industrial water demands. Renzetti uses the same data set as in Renzetti (1992). Renzetti's estimation considers two types of water price: external price (intake either public or self-supplied) and the internal price of water (treatment, recirculation and discharge). He applied all these for six industry subgroups and a pooled data set for all of the manufacturing firms. Elasticities with respect to external price are −0.3086 for self-supplied firms and −0.7555 for publicly supplied firms. The related elasticities for internal prices are −0.0904 for self-supplied and −0.0686 for network-supplied firms. The author shows that publicly supplied firms' water intake demands are more sensitive to external prices.

(10) *Dupont and Renzetti* (2001) first model water intake and water recirculation as variable factors of production so as to insert them into an econometric KLEM model of Canadian manufacturing industry. The data set is from a cross-sectional survey of water use for 1981, 1986 and 1991. They estimate a Translog cost function, by the SUR procedure, for a total

of 58 cross-sectional observations for each year under study. Their results show that water intake and water recirculation are substitutes. Intake is a substitute for capital, labour and energy; and complements materials. Recirculation is only substitute to labour.

(11) *Wang and Lall* (2002) examine the value of water for industry by estimating, via a SUR procedure, a Translog production function with data for about 2000 Chinese industrial firms for 1993. Water is treated as an input in the production process along with capital, labour, energy and raw materials. They develop a model on the price elasticity of water demand associated with the marginal productivity approach, which is estimated assuming price equal to the marginal cost of water use. Their results show that the average price elasticity of water for the whole of Chinese industry is about −1.0. The marginal productivity of water for industry varies among sectors in China with an industry average of 2.5 yuan/m^3.

(12) *Reynaud* (2003) studies the structure of industrial water in France, by considering three components: the quantity of water brought to a water utility, the quantity of autonomous water, and the quantity of water treated prior to use. Each one is treated as a separate input, and demand for each is estimated within a system of simultaneous equations. The sample consists of 51 firms in the Gironde district observed from 1994 to 1996 using SUR and FGLS in a Translog cost function. Reynaud's results show that industries are sensitive to water price inputs: network water elasticity is −0.29 (it varies from −0.10 for the alcohol industry to −0.79 for various industries); treated water elasticity is −1.42 (it ranges from −0.90 for the alcohol industry to −2.21 for the chemical industry). Autonomous water price elasticity is not significant. Network and treated water are substitutes as production inputs, while autonomous water and treated water are complements. This work constitutes the first econometric estimation of industrial water demand in France.

(13) *Renzetti and Dupont* (2003) examine the value of water in manufacturing processes, by estimating firms' own valuation of their water use. They combine information on water and non-water inputs to estimate a restricted cost function (Translog) for Canadian manufacturing. Their inputs are internal water recirculation, water treatment, and KLEM. Intake water is taking as a quasi-fixed factor. They use the same source data set as in Dupont and Renzetti (2001), and find that the elasticity of cost with respect to the quantity of intake water is −0.1308, and the shadow value of intake water is 0.046 CAN\$/m^3 (1991 CAN\$). This value, although positive, is less than those in preceding studies. An important factor in explaining this result could be the

regulatory environment controlling manufacturing water use, such that, in most provinces, self-supplied water intake is available at almost zero external cost.

NOTES

1. CNA (2003) tables 5A and 5B.
2. Industrial, services and electricity generation (excluding hydroelectric) are included in industrial water use, together with commercial water use.
3. IMTA-CNA (1990).
4. See Guerrero (1995) and Guerrero and Howe (2000) on the water price structure in Mexico.
5. IMTA (2001).
6. CNA (1999), p. 7. 'The number, place and limits of the CNA regional office were published May 18, 1998 and actualized January 18, 1999'.
7. Water has a density of 1 g/ml. The density for the six principal kinds of sodas produced in Mexico goes from 0.978 g/ml to 1.017 which gives an average of 0.9997 g/ml. See Aker (2002).

REFERENCES

Aker, M. (2002), 'The Relationship between Sugar and Soda Density', 7 October; Periods 1, 2, 5, 6. www.fwsd.wednet.edu/staff/laker/downloads/sodareportmrsaker.pdf.

Anderson, R.G., and Thursby, J.G. (1986), 'Confidence Intervals for Elasticity Estimators in Translog Models', *Review of Economics and Statistics*, January, 647–56.

Babin, F., Willis, C.E., and Allen, P.G. (1982), 'Estimation of Substitution Possibilities between Water and Other Production Inputs', *American Journal of Agricultural Economics*, **64** (1), 149–52, reprinted in S. Renzetti (ed.), *The Economics of Industrial Water Use*, Aldershot, UK and Brookfield, US: Edward Elgar.

Bergström, V., and Panas, E. (1992), 'Notes: How Robust is the Capital-Skill Complementarity Hypothesis?', *Review of Economics and Statistics*, 540–6.

Berndt, E.R., and Wood, D.O. (1979), 'Engineering and Econometric Interpretations of Energy – Capital Complementarity', *American Economic Review*, **69**, 342–54.

Binswanger, H.P. (1974), 'A Cost Function Approach to the Measurements of Elasticities of Factor Demand and Elasticities of Substitution', *American Journal of Agricultural Economics*, **56** (1), 377–86.

Blackorby, C., and Russell, R.R. (1989), 'Will the Real Elasticity of Substitution Please Stand Up? (A Comparison of the Allen/Uzawa and Morishima Elasticities)', *American Economic Review*, **79** (4), 882–8.

CNA (1999), 'Compendio Basico del Agua en Mexico', September, Comision Nacional del Agua-Mexico, D.F.

CNA (2003), 'Estadisticas del agua en Mexico', web-pages, http:\\www.cna.gob.mx, Comision Nacional del Agua-Mexico.

De Rooy, J. (1974), 'Price Responsiveness of the Industrial Demand for Water', in S. Renzetti (ed.), *The Economics of Industrial Water Use*, Aldershot, UK and Brookfield, US: Edward Elgar, chapter 5.

Dinar, A. (2000), *The Political Economy of Water Pricing Reforms*, Oxford: Oxford University Press.

Dinar, A., and Subramanian, A. (1997), 'Water Pricing Experiences: An International Perspective', Technical paper no. 386, Washington, DC: World Bank.

Dupont, D., and Renzetti, S. (2001), 'The Role of Water in Manufacturing', *Environmental and Resource Economics*, **18** (4), 411–32.

Garcia, S., and A. Thomas (2001), 'The Structure of Municipal Water Supply Costs: Application to a Panel of French Local Communities', *Journal of Productivity Analysis*, **16**, 5–29.

Grebenstein, C.R., and Field, B.C. (1979), 'Substituting for Water Inputs in U.S. Manufacturing', *Water Resources Research*, **15** (2), 228–32.

Guerrero, H. (1995), 'Water Pricing in Mexico in Principles and in Practice: The Case of Mexico', MA thesis, Department of Economics, University of Colorado, Boulder.

Guerrero, H., Alonso, P., and Ortiz, G. (1998), 'Derechos de agua para uso industrial: El cierre de empresas', XV National Hydraulic Meeting, Oaxaca, Mexico, October.

Guerrero, H., and Howe, C.W. (2000), 'Water Pricing in Mexico: Principles and Reality', Tenth Annual Conference of European Association of Environmental and Resource Economists, University of Crete, Greece, June.

Halvorsen, R., and Smith, T. (1986), 'Substitution Possibilities for Unpriced Natural Resources: Restricted Cost Functions for the Canadian Metal Mining Industry', *Review of Economics and Statistics*, **68** (3), 398–405.

IMTA (1998), 'Aplicacion de Instrumentos de Mercado como mecanismo para regular la demanda de agua para uso industrial', Internal Report No. DP-9728, Instituto Mexicano de Tecnologia del Agua-Mexico.

IMTA (2001), 'Administracion del agua, Aplicacion de Instrumentos de Politica Hidraulica en Escenarios Alternativos', Ortiz, G. November, Instituto Mexicano de Tecnologia del Agua-Mexico, D.F.

IMTA-CNA (1990), 'Programa Nacional de Aprovechamientos de Aguas Residuales', Instituto Mexicano de Tecnologia del Agua-Mexico.

Rees, J.A. (1969), 'Inter-industry Variation in the Demand for Water', reprinted in S. Renzetti (ed.), *The Economics of Industrial Water Use*, Aldershot, UK and Brookfield, US: Edward Elgar, chapter 3.

Renzetti, S. (1988), 'An Econometric Study of Industrial Water Demands in British Columbia, Canada', *Water Resources Research*, October, **24** (10), 1569–73.

Renzetti, S. (1992), 'Estimating the Structure of Industrial Water Demands: The Case of Canadian Manufacturing', *Land Economics*, **68** (4), 396–404.

Renzetti, S. (1993), 'Examining the Differences in Self- and Publicly Supplied Firms' Water Demands', *Land Economics*, May, **69** (2), 181–8.

Renzetti, S. (2002), 'Introduction', in S. Renzetti (ed.), *The Economics of Industrial Water Use*, Cheltenham, UK and Northampton, MA, USA: Edward Elgar.

Renzetti, S., and Dupont, D. (2003), 'The Value of Water in Manufacturing', CSERGE Working Paper ECM 03-03.

Reynaud, A. (2003), 'An Econometric Estimation of Industrial Water Demand in France', *Environmental and Resource Economics*, Forthcoming.

Rogers, P. (2003), 'Should there be an Industrial Water Policy?', Harvard University, www.uwin.siu.edu/ucowr/updates/pdf/V111_A7.pdf, 8 August.

Stiroh, K.J. (1999), 'Measuring Input Substitution in Thrifts: Morishima, Allen-Uzawa, and Cross-Price Elasticities', *Journal of Economics and Business*, **51**, 145–57.

Teeples, R., and Glyer, D. (1987), 'Production Function for Water Delivery Systems: Analysis and Estimation Using Dual Cost Function and Implicit Price Specification', *Water Resources Research*, May, **23** (5), 765–73.

Turnovsky, S.J. (1969), 'The Demand for Water: Some Empirical Evidence on Consumers' Response to a Commodity Uncertain in Supply', reprinted in S. Renzetti (ed.), *The Economics of Industrial Water Use*, Aldershot, UK and Brookfield, US: Edward Elgar, chapter 4.

Wang, Hua and Lall, Somik (2002), 'Valuing Water for Chinese Industries: A Marginal Productivity Analysis', *Applied Economics*, **34** (6), 759–65.

Ziegler, J.A., and Bell, S.E. (1984), 'Estimating Demand for Intake Water by Self-Supplied Firms', reprinted in S. Renzetti (ed.), *The Economics of Industrial Water Use*, Aldershot, UK and Brookfield, US: Edward Elgar, chapter 6.

4. Residential water demand in the Slovak Republic

Laurent Dalmas and Arnaud Reynaud

1. INTRODUCTION

Water resource management requires a reasonable knowledge of water uses. Among the different types of water uses, residential water demand constitutes an essential ingredient in the design of a pricing policy for a water network. This may be why during the last decades numerous studies have been devoted to the estimation of residential water demand functions. Most of them are based on North American data and empirical evidence is still very scarce for European countries. Dalhuisen et al. (2003) have produced a meta-analysis on the variations in price and in income elasticities for residential water demand. Among the 51 articles published in scientific reviews and used by these authors, only ten provide estimates for a European country and none of them deals with Central or Eastern European Countries (CEEC). The lack of data due to the revision of statistical standards since the beginning of the transition process in most of the CEEC is the most likely explanation. This chapter aims at filling this gap by analysing residential water demand in the Slovak Republic.

The Slovak Republic is preparing to join the European Union (EU) in May 2004. One of the basic requirements of accession negotiations for the Slovak Republic was to increase the level of care for the environment so as to comply with EU environmental standards and especially with the EU Water Framework Directive (WFD). Implementation of the WFD in particular will lead the CEEC to review their water pricing practices, especially because current pricing does not allow costs to be recovered. It is likely that households will react and adjust their water consumption to these price increases. Among the CEEC, analysing the sensitivity of Slovak residential water demand is interesting as those consumers may in the future experience the highest price change.[1] Any application of the cost-recovery principle requires being able to predict how households will react to price changes. It follows that estimating residential water demand is a prerequisite for any long-term water management policy.

To our knowledge, this chapter presents the first estimation of the residential water demand in a transition economy. CEEC are more and more considered by large private companies to be a very promising market, and residential water demand in the Slovak Republic is worth analysing.[2] The rest of the chapter is organized as follows. In the next section, we discuss the main issues for the water sector in the Slovak Republic, with a special emphasis on the impact of EU accession and on the characteristics of residential water demand. Next, we present the economic and the econometric model used to estimate residential water demand. We consider different specifications for the demand function, namely lin-lin, log-log and Stone-Geary (SG). The demand model is estimated on a sample of municipalities observed from 1999 to 2001. We show that the price elasticity of the demand for water is high, varying from −0.3 to −0.5. Hence pricing policy could be an effective signal of resource scarcity or of the cost of water supply. In the last section, we provide some simulations and derive policy implications from our estimates.

2. WATER ISSUES IN THE SLOVAK REPUBLIC

2.1 The Impact of EU Accession

Located in the geographical centre of Europe, the Slovak Republic joined the European Union in May 2004 and the country will form the far-eastern border of the new EU. As underlined by the European Commission in its final report towards accession (European Commission, 2003), 'the Slovak Republic is a functioning market economy. The continuation of its current reform path should enable the Slovak Republic to cope with competitive pressure and market forces within the Union'. Nevertheless, the transformation process from a former planned economy to a market economy has not been totally and successfully achieved. Despite the efforts of more liberal governments leading the country since 1998, and despite a higher GDP growth than in the three other Višegrad countries joining the EU,[3] the European Commission has also stressed that 'improvements can be made to the macroeconomic situation, which requires urgent measures to reduce both the fiscal and current account deficits. . . . The unemployment problem[4] necessitates a whole range of structural reforms, including the elimination of disincentive effects in the social protection system and more flexible labour legislation.' The remaining state-owned banks and the insurance companies have been privatized and the restructuring of the financial sector is now almost complete. Bad-debt recovery mechanisms are being better implemented. However, after having decreased to only 3.3 percent in 2002, average annual consumer price inflation has soared to around 8 percent in 2003. This price increase can be seen as a bad but expected effect of the price liberalizations led by the new government in 2003.

Among the requirements of EU accession for the Slovak Republic was the need to improve environmental protection so as to comply with EU environmental standards and with the EU Water Framework Directive (WFD). According to the Association Agreement between the EU and the Slovak Republic in the framework of economic cooperation (Article 72), 'measures of economic cooperation and the other measures leading to economic and social development of the Slovak Republic should be ensured so as to take fully into account aspects of the environment and to link them to harmonic social development'.

The legislation on water quality is in line with the European *acquis* except for the recent *acquis* on water, which needs to be completed by accession. The European Commission has stressed that administrative capacities, which are in place, still need to be strengthened. Monitoring of drinking water needs to be further enhanced and programmes for nitrates and dangerous substances need to be adopted by the date of accession. Transitional arrangements until 31 December 2015 for urban wastewater (and until 31 December 2006 for discharges of certain dangerous substances) have been agreed.

The whole set of measures to be adopted will lead the country to be more involved in the area of water protection. The implementation of the European Directive on Urban Wastewater[5] implies higher wastewater charges (on average around 30 to 50 percent) to cope with new investment and operation costs. Similarly, the implementation of the revised Directive on Drinking Water[6] that sets more stringent limits for lead concentration in drinking water will entail significant investment and increases in prices. As a consequence, all the actors involved in water management in the Slovak Republic will face a substantial rise in investment costs, which needs to be balanced by a growth in financial resources.

Some specific pollution problems have been recently highlighted by an OECD report (OECD, 2002) which shows that the quality of surface water in the Slovak Republic has improved little during the 1990s. Surface water quality has improved in the principal rivers, but is still very poor in small water courses. The introduction of new standards – in compliance with the new EU Directive on Drinking Water – has also demonstrated that groundwater resources were in danger. If the concentrations of industrial and agricultural pollutants have decreased during the 1990s, their levels remain alarming. Lastly, bacteriological pollution is still frequent, proving that the municipal wastewater treatment plants are not efficient enough to cope with this kind of pollution. Adopting more incentive pollution charges may be a way of achieving improvements in water quality more quickly.[7]

2.2 The Structure of Water Utilities

Until 1997 the sole utility was entirely state-owned by the State Water Works Company, Vodárne a Kanalizácie (VaK). In 1997 the government began the process of transforming the sector from a state monopoly into municipal utility companies. However, due to a lack of leadership and because of political divisions, the process was vague and confusing, and as a result only three districts obtained control of a water utility (Beveridge and Guy, 2003). These districts were the Trenčin district (48 municipalities), Komárno district (33 municipalities) and the city of Hlohovec. Only Trenčin has chosen to delegate its water utilities to a private foreign company. After an open-call, the Lyonnaise des Eaux took over the utilities and has been operating them in a joint-stock agreement with the municipal association.

By the year 2000, only 736 of the 1815 municipalities had applied for the transfer of assets and only a small number had actually completed the negotiation process (Thalmeinerova, 2002; Ministry of Agriculture of the Slovak Republic, 2002). Several reasons can be given to explain this low proportion of asset transfer. First, the process itself was slow because the Ministry of Agriculture did not have the technical expertise to adequately deal with asset transfer processes. Second, municipalities where the water and wastewater utility was profitable were reluctant to form companies with unprofitable municipalities. Third, municipalities were unwilling to take on assets which were undergoing redevelopment because the government had made it clear that no additional funds would be made available to complete the work once the transfer process had taken place (Beveridge and Guy, 2003).

In 2000, a new government reformed the process in an attempt to add clarity and to accelerate the pace of change (Thalmeinerova, 2002). It was agreed that VaK had to transfer its control of water utility property – free of charge – to those municipal authorities wishing to establish their own water companies. Once the municipal authority had taken over the utilities, VaK no longer had a role to play. Thus, in theory, the municipal authorities were free to manage utilities in the way most suited to their area and to involve private companies. The state company VaK was then divided into five regional organizations, according to the existing principal water networks. Since May 2003, a new company has been created from the split of the fifth company into two distinct units. There are now

47 separate establishments maintaining local water supply, sewage systems and wastewater treatment plants. A special department in some of the VaK companies is responsible for maintaining the long-distance water supply system and is centrally managed by the Ministry of Agriculture. However, in 2001, 74.9 and 49.2 percent of Slovak inhabitants, respectively, were still connected to public water supply and to the public sewerage system through the VaK Company, a small reduction compared to 1995 (76.3 percent and 51.1 percent for water supply and sewage systems, respectively). This shows that the transfer of property has not yet been achieved.

2.3 Slovak Water Pricing Policy

In the context of EU accession (which implies high costs for compliance with EU environmental legislation) and given limited financial resources, pricing will play a key role in the future water policy of the Slovak Republic. Water pricing policy in the Slovak Republic, as in the other accession countries, does not integrate all economic and environmental objectives. The efficiency role of a price structure is often countered by price levels that are too low to transmit a clear signal on costs to consumers. Accession will certainly lead to important changes in terms of the water policy in the Slovak Republic: Defining efficient water prices based on social, environmental and economic motives is indeed a key recommendation of the EU. But the Slovak Republic cannot be considered as being late in this area, as the other CEEC have not yet fully adopted the WFD. According to a recent EU report (DG Environment, 2000), operation and maintenance costs are generally covered by the charges paid by households in the ten accession countries. Conversely, the coverage of capital costs has either been partially achieved (Hungary, Poland, Romania and Slovenia), or not yet achieved (Lithuania, Bulgaria and the Slovak Republic).

The Slovak Republic constitutes an extreme case in this group. Until the 2001 reform, the price of water was set by the central administration (through maximum prices). All residential users were facing the same price whatever their location. Such a system did not allow the whole burden of actual costs to fall on final users. This administrative price regulation has led to significant discrepancies between the price paid by consumers and the cost of provision of this service, especially for drinking water. As a result, the VaK Company constantly faces a significant deficit after taxation (21.986 million Slovenská Koruna (SKK) in 2001 for instance).

Water pricing in the Slovak Republic is characterized by several forms of cross-subsidies. First, there is an identical maximum permitted water price throughout the territory, although a cost analysis of the VaK companies has shown that there are considerable differences between the costs of drinking water supply in western and eastern regions.[8] As the price is the same everywhere, this means that some VaK units are operating at a loss in some regions and this must be balanced by profits in other regions. Second, the wastewater service is used to subsidize the water service (Dalmas and Farkašová, 2002). Until 1998, both the water and the wastewater services were highly subsidized and the water sector used to run a very significant deficit. In 1996, the average water price for households was 4.00 SKK per cubic metre, well below the estimated average production cost of 7.77 SKK per cubic metre (a deficit of 48.52 percent). The wastewater price for the same year was 4 SKK for an estimated average production cost of 5.21 SKK per cubic metre (a 23.22 percent deficit). From 1998, the wastewater production charges have become higher than the production costs (15.84 percent on average) and the profit generated has been used to balance the deficit of the water service. The recent trend is, however, to limit cross-subsidies by balancing each service separately. For example, in the year 2001, the deficit of the water service represents only 6.32 percent of the total cost whereas the wastewater service generates a profit representing 8.22 percent of total costs.

Finally, cross-subsidization of households by other water users (the industrial sector) is still very common in the region, and the agricultural sector is probably the main beneficiary of cross-subsidization in several CEEC. A study has examined the current practice in agricultural water pricing and has concluded that the price of water for irrigation purposes is supported via the provision of direct subsidies by as much as 70 percent in Slovakia (Regional Environmental Centre for Central and Eastern Europe, 2001). Slovak households used to face very low water prices even in comparison with other CEEC. As mentioned previously, the price per cubic metre for a residential consumer was in 1999 equal to 0.14 euros in the Slovak Republic compared with 0.36, 0.43 and 0.47 euros, respectively, in Bulgaria, Estonia and Hungary. The water bill was almost negligible compared to total household expenditures. Despite the important price increase between 1989 and 2001 (from 0.80 old Czechoslovak Crown to 19 SKK), water expenditures still only represent 0.9 percent of the total expenses of a representative household (OECD, 2003, table 2.2, p. 36). This is significantly lower than in Western EU countries (from 1.1 percent in Denmark, to 1.6 percent in the Netherlands in 1999).

2.4 Residential Water Demand in the Slovak Republic

Whereas the population connected to the public water network has increased from 75 percent in 1990 to 83.6 percent in 2001, the quantity of

Table 4.1 Residential price and water consumption, 1990–2001

Years	1990	1995	1996	1997	1998	1999	2000	2001
Price[a]	0.80	7.0	8.0	10.0	10.0	12.5	15.8	19.0
Annual change	–	0.0%	14.3%	25.0%	0.0%	25.0%	26.4%	20.3%
Water consumption[b]	71.36	57.67	52.01	49.86	48.14	47.96	46.32	45.55
Annual change	–	−9.8%	−4.1%	−3.4%	−0.4%	−3.4%	−1.7%	−0.1%

Notes:
[a] SKK per cubic metre.
[b] cubic metre per year.

Source: Ministry of Agriculture of the Slovak Republic (1998, 2002).

drinking water supplied for residential consumption has paradoxically decreased from 276.4 million cubic metres in 1990 to 172.2 million in 2001. During this decade, the share of residential withdrawals has, however, risen from 52 percent in 1990 to 59 percent in 1999.

The most interesting figures are for changes in water consumption per capita. From 1990 to 2001, the residential consumption of public water has decreased from 71.36 cubic metres by year and per capita (195.5 litres per day) to 45.55 cubic metres (117.1 litres per day), a 40 percent reduction (see Table 4.1). This decrease has been starker between 1990 and 1995 (about 27 percent) than between 1995 and 2001 (about 19 percent).

The OECD (2003) mentioned that as the Slovak economy is expected to grow in the future, it is likely that residential consumption will rise again to reach levels prevalent in the EU (that is, between 50 and 60 cubic metres per year and per capita). An increase could also come, first because of an increasing trend in equipment ownership (washing machines, sanitary equipment, and so on), and second because sections of the population are not yet connected to the public water network (especially the inhabitants of the eastern part of the country). But one should not forget that the residential water price is likely to increase in the future. For the period 1990–2001, the correlation coefficient between price and water consumption per capita is equal to −0.87. This simple evidence suggests that residential users are price sensitive in the Slovak Republic. The net effect of growth and price increases on residential water consumption is a priori ambiguous. The following section helps assess this net effect by estimating residential water demand for the Slovak Republic.

3. ESTIMATING THE SLOVAK RESIDENTIAL WATER DEMAND

3.1 Specifying the Residential Water Demand

3.1.1 A brief survey of the applied literature on residential water demand

Water demand functions have been estimated since the 1950s. For most studies, the primary objective was to derive a measure of the price elasticity of water demand. This may be why the two main econometric issues that have been intensively investigated in the applied literature are the adequate representation of price in the demand function (marginal versus average pricing) and the implications of block rate pricing. Howe and Linaweaver (1967) argued at an early stage that residential consumers are more likely to react to the average price than to the marginal price. Later, Shin (1985) introduced a 'perceived' price which is in fact a combination of the marginal and the average prices. As under block rate pricing, it is difficult to determine the price specification that should be used to estimate the demand function. Most of the models employ a combination of the marginal price and a 'difference' variable which aims to capture the income effect imposed by the block rate structure (Nordin, 1976). But under a block rate tariff, the price is endogenous and specific estimation techniques, such as instrumental variables (two-stage least squares), are required. However, as suggested by Hewitt and Hanemann (1995), the correct specification of the water demand under multiple-block tariffs requires a two-stage model where the block is first selected by the consumer and then the quantity is chosen in a continuous way within that block.

Numerous estimates of price and income elasticities for residential water demand are now available and there is a large consensus among researchers that the residential water demand is inelastic, but not perfectly. Most of the published studies report short-term price elasticities varying from -0.3 to -0.1. However, long-term residential water demand appears to be more price sensitive (see Nauges and Thomas, 2000b, among others). The estimate of income elasticities reveals a more substantial range of values going from 0 to more than 2. In their meta-analysis, Dalhuisen et al. (2003) report that 'the distribution of income elasticities has a mean of 0.46' and that 'water demand appears to be inelastic in terms of income changes'.

3.1.2 Specifying the residential water demand

As described previously, the pricing system implemented in the Slovak Republic is much simpler than in most EU countries since all residential users face a single price whatever their consumption and their location. The main issue here is to correctly specify the functional form that will be used for estimating the water demand function. In their meta-analysis based on 51 published articles, Dalhuisen et al. (2003) report that half of these papers have used a linear specification (lin-lin form) and that 20 articles provide estimates of price and income elasticities based on a logarithmic demand function (either semi or double logarithmic).

In order to easily compare our estimates with those from the previous literature, we also consider lin-lin and log-log specification forms. But it is clear that adjusting water consumption to price requires some time: a fixed quantity of water cannot be adjusted immediately after a price increase. The decision to invest in low water-consumption equipment (washing machines or sanitary fittings) is not an instantaneous reaction of a household. In order to take into account such lag effects, we have considered a Stone-Geary (SG) specification. Such a demand model explicitly supposes that there exists a minimum water consumption level that does not depend on price. This minimum requirement level is estimated as a structural parameter of the model.

Let Y denote the water consumption in cubic metres per year of the representative household in a given local community. The water demand can be written in a very general way as follows:

$$Y = f(P, I, X \mid \beta) \tag{4.1}$$

where P represents the price of water, I the representative household's income and X a vector of exogenous variables influencing water demand (for example, climate variables, demographic characteristics of the representative household). In equation (4.1), β is a vector of parameters to be estimated. A lin-lin specification of (4.1) can be written as:

$$Y = \beta_0 + \beta_p \cdot P + \beta_I \cdot I + X' \cdot \beta \tag{4.2}$$

The resulting price and income elasticities are:

$$E_p = \frac{\partial Y}{\partial p}\frac{P}{Y} = \beta_p \cdot \frac{P}{Y} \text{ and } E_I = \frac{\partial Y}{\partial I}\frac{I}{Y} = \beta_I \cdot \frac{I}{Y} \tag{4.3}$$

Another form often used for estimating residential water demand is a log-log form:

$$\ln(Y) = \beta_0 + \beta_p \cdot \ln(P) + \beta_I \cdot \ln(I) + X' \cdot \ln(\beta) \tag{4.4}$$

and the resulting price and income elasticities are respectively β_p and β_I. The log-log specification is very convenient as the demand elasticities can be directly read from the parameter estimate. However, the price and income elasticities do not vary with household characteristics. The lin-lin and log-log specifications presuppose that total water demand is affected by both economic and behavioural variables. But one part of the residential water demand often serves to satisfy basic human needs like cooking, drinking, and so on. This part, which is not likely to be much affected by price or income levels, corresponds to a minimum water subsistence level. In order to capture such minimum subsistence level effects, we estimate a water demand function derived from a Stone-Geary (SG) specification of consumer's utility. The interested reader may consult Deaton and Muellbauer (1980) for a more complete presentation of the SG utility. This utility specification has been recently used by Gaudin et al. (2001) on a sample of local communities located in Texas, US, and by Martinez-Espiñeira and Nauges (2003) in order to assess the impact of pricing policies on residential water demand in Seville, Spain. Let us assume that the representative consumer can purchase two goods: water, denoted by Y, and another composite good, Y^c. Water is an essential good in the following sense: there exists a minimum water threshold denoted by $\underline{Y}$ such that water consumption does not depend on price below this minimal level. In what follows, $\underline{Y}$ will be called the *price sensitivity threshold.* The SG utility can be written as:

$$U = \beta^w \cdot \ln(Y - \underline{Y}) + \beta^c \cdot \ln(Y^c) \tag{4.5}$$

where β^w and β^c take positive values. These terms respectively represent the fixed proportion of the supernumerary income (the remaining income after having consumed the Y) allocated to each good. The SG water demand can be written:

$$Y = (1 - \beta^w) \cdot \underline{Y} + \beta^w \cdot I/P^w \tag{4.6}$$

where I represents income and P^w the price of water relative to the composite good price. The SG utility function implies that the price-sensitivity threshold $\underline{Y}$ is purchased first, and the remaining income is allocated between the two goods. The SG utility function imposes a set of restrictions. First, utility is strongly separable in the two goods. This assumption is very common in the applied literature on residential water demand. Second, income elasticity is positive for all goods. Third, price and income elasticities have the same magnitude but an opposite sign. This should not be too restrictive an assumption as this is a result often found when estimating residential water demands. With an SG specification of the utility function, the price and income elasticities can be written:

$$\mathrm{E}_p = -\beta^w \cdot \frac{I}{P^w \cdot Y} \text{ and } \mathrm{E}_p = \beta^w \cdot \frac{I}{P^w \cdot Y} \tag{4.7}$$

Finally, the SG specification only allows for inelastic demand functions. This feature should not be a problem given the low price elasticity reported in the empirical literature. An interesting property of the SG specification is that price elasticity is not constrained to increase with price, as is the case with a lin-lin form.

3.2 The Data

Data used for estimating the residential water demand in the Slovak Republic come from various sources including population censuses (1991, 2001, and 1996 micro-census), unpublished Water Management Yearbooks of the Slovak Water Research Institute, unpublished data from the Slovak Hydro Meteorological Institute and regular publications of the Slovak Statistical Office. The dataset covers three years, from 1999 to 2001. The data are aggregated at the city level, for the capitals of the 71 Slovak official districts. The total number of observations is 213. We briefly describe below the main variables used in the econometric application. A more detailed presentation of the database may be found in the Appendix.

Water Price The water price is measured in euros per cubic metres. Based on Act No. 18/96 Dig. on prices and its official decree No. 87/1997 Dig., the State controls the price of drinking and drained water. As mentioned above, this price is one of the lowest in Europe and CEEC. From 1999 to 2001, the regulated residential water price has increased (in real terms) by around 65.3 percent.

Water consumption The endogenous variable used in the demand function is water consumption per year and per capita measured in cubic metres. This endogenous variable is computed by dividing household consumption by the number of persons. Water consumption per capita has decreased from 46.78 cubic metres per year in 1999 to 41.53 in 2001, an 11.22 percent reduction on the whole period. This compares to an annual rate of decrease of residential water use per capita ranging from 1.7 percent in Romania to 15 and 20 percent respectively in Bulgaria and Lithuania during the last decade (DG Environment, 2000). These figures are significantly higher than what has been observed in EU countries (ranging from about 0.6 percent in England and Wales to about 3 percent in Italy; OECD, 1999).

Real income Real income is approximated by employee wages. This variable has increased rapidly from 1999 to 2001 (around 30 percent, compared to a real GDP growth rate of only about 2 percent per year).

Unemployment The unemployment rate has risen from 16.7 percent in 1999 to 19.4 percent in 2001, and is one of the highest in the Višegrad countries (ranging from 5.5 percent in Hungary to 18.5 percent in Poland, both in 2001). There are, however, large regional differences in unemployment levels (ranging from only 4.95% for Bratislava in 2001 to around 30% in more rural areas). The unemployment rate is negatively correlated with real income, with a decreasing trend from 1999 to 2001.

Demographic variables The proportion of inhabitants younger than 15 years has strongly decreased (26.88 percent in 1999 compared to 19.5 percent in 2001) and the proportion of retired inhabitants has risen slightly (from 17.74 percent in 1999 to 18.03 percent in 2001). But the Slovak Republic is still a *young country* in comparison with its close neighbours: the proportion of inhabitants younger than 15 years old ranges from 16.1 percent in the Czech Republic to 18.5 percent in Poland. In 2001 the Slovak Republic was the only European country with a natural population increase.

Climate The year 2000 presents the lowest precipitation level, and is therefore considered as the driest year between 1999 and 2001.

3.3 The Residential Water Demand in the Slovak Republic

3.3.1 Econometric methods

Let Y_{it} denote the water consumption per capita in cubic metres per year for the representative household in the local community *i*. The water demand can be written in a very general way as:

$$Y_{it} = f(P_{it}, I_{it}, X_{it} \mid \beta) + \eta_{it} \tag{4.8}$$

where η_{it} represents the error term. In equation (4.8), *t* indexes time periods (years in the empirical application). As is standard in panel data analysis, we decompose the error term as $\eta_{it} = \alpha_i + \varepsilon_{it}$ where α_i is i.i.d. $N(0, \sigma_\alpha^2)$ and ε_{it} is i.i.d. $N(0, \sigma_\varepsilon^2)$. The term α_i is a community-specific effect and ε_{it} is the usual error term. The equation to be estimated becomes:

$$Y_{it} = f(P_{it}, I_{it}, X_{it} \mid \beta) + \alpha_i + \varepsilon_{it} \tag{4.9}$$

The community-specific effect creates a non-standard covariance structure. The Generalized Least Squares (GLS) estimator is then efficient and improves upon the Ordinary Least Squares (OLS) estimator as long as the fixed effects are not correlated with the regressors.

The interpretation of estimates with panel data crucially depends on the nature of the community-specific effect. We first need to test the presence of the community-specific term, α_i, in equation (4.9). We use a Breusch/Pagan LM test (BP-LM) to discriminate between the pooled model and the random effect model. The basic idea is that, in the model described by (4.9), if $\text{Var}(\alpha_i) = 0$ random effects are not needed. Next, we need to investigate the potential correlation between the community-specific term and the regressors. If some form of correlation is present in the sample, the random effect estimator will be inconsistent. A Hausman specification test can be used to answer this question.

3.3.2 Results

(a) Lin-lin and log-log specification

Table 4.2 gives the estimates of the residential water demand using a lin-lin and a log-log specification. We report estimates both from OLS and GLS. Following previous studies on residential water demand (e.g., Nauges and Thomas, 2000a), some socio-demographic variables aiming at capturing consumer heterogeneity have been introduced in the demand equations (share of households equipped with at least one car, average number of rooms per dwelling, etc.).

First, both for the lin-lin and the log-log specifications, the BP-LM statistics exceeds the tabulated chi-squared value at 1 percent: we reject the null hypothesis ($\text{Var}(\alpha_i) = 0$). The GLS estimator is more appropriate than an OLS estimate on the pooled model. In other words, there are local-community-specific effects in the data. Second, as the Hausman statistics are lower than the tabulated chi-squared value at 1 percent, we keep the null hypothesis: the local-community effect is not correlated with the exogenous variables and GLS estimators are unbiased and efficient.

The explicative power is higher for the log-log specification than for the lin-lin model. With the GLS estimator, the average adjusted R^2 is 0.3 for the log-log specification and less than 0.2 for the lin-lin model. Price and income appear to be important determinants of the Slovak residential water demand. The proportion of cottages designed for recreational purposes (the variable *house*) has a negative impact on water consumption. All other variables are non-significant but their sign makes sense. For example, the level of rainfall (variable *rain*) negatively influences residential water demand. Water consumption increases with the proportion of dwellings equipped with an automatic washing machine (variable *wash*). There is also a positive relationship between the average number of square metres of living floor space and water consumption (variable *surf*). These

Table 4.2 Estimate of the residential water demand with lin-lin and log-log specifications

Variables	Lin-lin				Log-log			
	OLS		GLS		OLS		GLS	
	Coeff.	St. err.	Coeff.	St. err.	Coeff.	St. err.	Coeff.	St. err.
constant	72.471***	18.424	74.259***	20.020	0.957	1.742	1.477	2.031
price	−37.365***	13.642	−35.178**	13.942	−0.303***	0.086	−0.285***	0.090
income	0.004	0.003	0.004	0.003	0.316**	0.151	0.256	0.176
pers	−8.571***	2.628	−8.466***	2.993	−0.752	0.165	−0.739***	0.198
unemp	0.169	0.133	0.130	0.151	0.064	0.045	0.052	0.054
surf	0.113	0.194	0.099	0.222	0.192	0.199	0.158	0.242
wash	0.020	0.125	0.016	0.146	0.077	0.123	0.081	0.151
house	−0.820***	0.258	−0.818***	0.296	−0.098***	0.021	−0.098***	0.026
rain	−0.021	0.040	−0.029	0.037	−0.019	0.043	−0.033	0.039
temp	−0.322	0.547	−0.202	0.516	−0.070	0.129	−0.003	0.117
Adj. R^{2a}	0.163		0.198		0.287		0.315	
F-test	$F(9, 203) = 5.58$ Pr. > F <0.0001				F(9, 203) = 10.49 Pr. > F <0.0001			
BP-LM test			$chi^2(1) = 4.70$ Pr. > $chi^2 = 0.030$				$chi^2(1) = 12.90$ Pr. > $chi^2 = 0.0003$	
Hausman test			$chi^2(7) = 9.54$ Pr. > $chi^2 = 0.2163$				$chi^2(7) = 9.84$ Pr. > $chi^2 = 0.1981$	

Notes:
[a] Adjusted R^2 are reported for OLS regressions. For GLS, a generalized version is used.
*** Significant at 1% or better; ** significant at 5%.

results indicate that water consumption is positively correlated with the living standards of residential consumers. The average number of persons per dwelling has a negative impact on water consumption per capita (variable *pers*). Large families tend to have a lower per capita consumption, on average.

Using the OLS method and the lin-lin specification, we get a price elasticity of water demand varying from −0.50 to −0.16 with a mean equal to −0.30. The range obtained using the GLS approach is very similar, with a minimum of −0.48, a maximum of −0.15 and a mean equal to −0.28. The price elasticities obtained with the log-log specification are also within this range of values: −0.30 for the OLS estimator and −0.29 for the GLS estimator. The Slovak water demand appears to be moderately sensitive to price changes, at least in the short term. A 10 percent price increase will result in a 3 percent reduction of water consumption.

Both the lin-lin and the log-log specifications yield a positive income elasticity estimate. However, the income effect is only significantly different from zero with the log-log specification and the OLS method. Using the OLS method and the lin-lin specification, we get an income elasticity varying between 0.19 to 0.39, with a mean equal to 0.27. The range of values for the GLS approach is similar with a minimum of 0.16, a maximum of 0.33 and a mean equal to 0.22. Income elasticities obtained with the log-log specification are also within this range of values: 0.31 for the OLS estimator and 0.26 for the GLS estimator. A 10 percent real income increase will result in a 3 percent increase of water consumption.

It should be noted that both the price and income elasticities of Slovak residential water demand are similar to what has been found for Western European countries. Price increases have a negative effect on water consumption. However, the expected increase in real income per inhabitant will have the opposite effect on water consumption. The net effect on demand will be studied in detail in the last section of this chapter.

(b) Stone-Geary specification

In this section, we present the results obtained with a demand equation derived from a Stone-Geary utility function. Following equation (4.6), we first estimate a demand function with two exogenous variables: a constant that aims at capturing the price sensitivity threshold and a ratio of real income to water price. This simple model is reported as SG1 in Table 4.3. But the price sensitivity threshold, $\underline{Y}$, may depend on the water-consuming durable equipment of the household, on water pricing and more generally on some characteristics of the household. In order to capture these conditional threshold effects, we will assume that the price sensitivity threshold

$\underline{Y}$ can be written as a function of some exogenous variables (see Gaudin et al., 2001, for a similar model with a varying sensitivity threshold):

$$\underline{Y} = Z' \cdot \gamma \tag{4.10}$$

where Z is a vector of exogenous variables and γ is the associated parameter vector. Substituting $\underline{Y}$ by its form in equation (4.6) gives:

$$Y_{it} = (1 - \beta^w) \cdot Z'_{it} \cdot \gamma + \beta^w \cdot I_{it}/P^w_{it} + \alpha_i + \varepsilon_{it} \tag{4.11}$$

In order to make the estimates with the lin-lin, log-log and SG specifications comparable, the vector Z contains the exogenous variables used in the lin-lin and log-log cases. The SG model with a varying price sensitivity threshold is reported in Table 4.3 in columns SG2.

First, both for SG1 and SG2, the BP-LM calculated statistics exceed the tabulated chi-squared value at 1 percent: we reject the null hypothesis and the GLS estimator is more appropriate than an OLS estimate on the pooled model. Second, as the Hausman statistics are lower than the tabulated chi-squared value at 1 percent, we do not reject the null hypothesis: the local-community effect is not correlated with the exogenous variables and the GLS estimators are unbiased and efficient. Last, explicative power is higher for SG2 than for SG1, as could be expected. The average adjusted R^2 is 0.2 for SG2 and around 0.1 for SG2.

Regarding the sign and the significance of estimated coefficients, the results with the SG specification and those obtained with a lin-lin or a log-log form are very similar. The ratio I/P appears to be an important determinant of the Slovak residential water demand. The proportion of cottages used for recreational purposes and the average number of persons per dwelling have a negative impact on water consumption. No other variables are significant.

As described in equation (4.7), one feature of the SG specification is that the price and income elasticities have the same magnitude but opposite signs. The price and income elasticities we have obtained using lin-lin and log-log specifications indicate that this feature is not too restrictive. The price elasticity obtained with the SG1 specification is higher (in absolute value) than the price elasticity obtained with a log-log or lin-lin model, −0.4 versus −0.3 respectively. When we have the price sensitivity threshold depend on exogenous variables, we get a lower price elasticity, −0.3 on average. The average income elasticity varies from 0.28 to 0.41 according to the demand specification and the econometric method used. These figures are, however, slightly higher than those obtained with a lin-lin or a log-log specification.

Table 4.3 *Estimation of the residential water demand with Stone-Geary specifications*

Variables	SG1				SG2			
	OLS		GLS		OLS		GLS	
	Coeff.	St. err.	Coeff.	St. err.	Coeff.	St. err.	Coeff.	St. err.
Constant	26.369***	3.934	27.539	3.954	60.108***	18.958	60.545***	20.694
I/P	0.002***	0.000	0.002	0.000	0.002***	0.001	0.002***	0.001
pers	–	–	–	–	−8.240***	2.579	−7.928	2.923
unemp	–	–	–	–	0.170	0.131	0.137	0.149
surf	–	–	–	–	0.098	0.190	0.091	0.218
wash	–	–	–	–	0.013	0.114	−0.007	0.131
house	–	–	–	–	−0.815***	0.255	−0.803***	0.293
rain	–	–	–	–	−0.032	0.040	−0.039	0.038
temp	–	–	–	–	−0.371	0.544	−0.255	0.513
Adj. R^{2a}	0.092		0.097		0.167		0.198	
F-test	F(1, 211) = 22.49 Pr. > F <0.0001				F(8, 204) = 6.31 Pr. > F <0.0001			
BP-LM test			$chi^2(1) = 12.69$ Pr. > $chi^2 = 0.0004$				$chi^2(1) = 4.71$ Pr. > $chi^2 = 0.0299$	
Hausman test			$chi^2(1) = 0.72$ Pr. > $chi^2 = 0.3966$				$chi^2(7) = 9.75$ Pr. > $chi^2 = 0.1355$	

Notes:
[a] Adjusted R^2 are reported for OLS regressions. For GLS, a generalized version is used.
*** Significant at 1% or better; ** significant at 5%.

Table 4.4 Price and income elasticity and price sensitivity level with SG specifications

	SG1						SG2					
	OLS			GLS			OLS			GLS		
	Mean	Min	Max	Mean	Min	Max	Mean	Min	Max	Mean	Min	Max
E_p	−0.41	−0.55	−0.32	−0.38	−0.52	−0.30	−0.28	−0.38	−0.20	−0.28	−0.36	−0.20
$\underline{Y}$	26.42	–	–	27.60	–	–	31.97	22.72	39.26	32.28	23.14	39.74

Note: The income elasticity is equal to the price elasticity with an opposite sign.

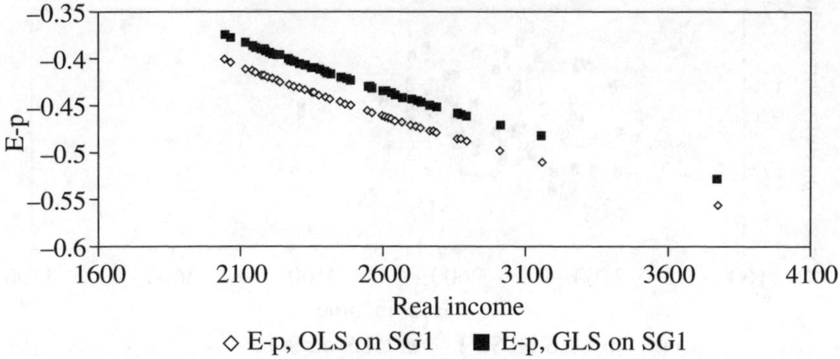

Figure 4.1 Price elasticity with SG1 specification

Figure 4.1 plots the individual price elasticities obtained for year 1999 with an SG1 specification, as a function of real income. Representing elasticities using SG2 is more difficult as the price elasticity also depends on other exogenous variables. However, the pattern of the price elasticity with SG2 as a function of real income is similar to the one represented in Figure 4.1. As expected, price elasticity increases (in absolute value) with real income. For a low real income, water consumption aims at satisfying basic human needs: water demand is very inelastic. For a high real income, water possesses some features of a luxury good (water may serve for air-conditioning or for swimming pools). This part of the demand is much more price sensitive. It follows that any pricing policy aiming at reducing water consumption should take into account that consumers' reaction will depend on their income level. The interpretation of the price sensitivity threshold level $\underline{Y}$ requires caution. This level should be viewed as a threshold below which water demand is no longer price sensitive, rather than as a minimum vital water level. The average price sensitivity threshold is estimated to be between 26 and 32 cubic metres per capita and per year. A substantial part of water consumption appears not to be price sensitive. But this level varies significantly from one observation to another, from a minimum of 22.72 cubic metres to a maximum of 39.74 in our sample. It is interesting to see how this threshold changes with real income. In Figure 4.2, we have plotted the minimum subsistence level $\underline{Y}$ with SG2 specification as a function of real income for the year 1999. As might be expected, the price sensitivity threshold increases with real income. Figures 4.1 and 4.2 reveal that any pricing policy will have a very different impact on households depending on their income.

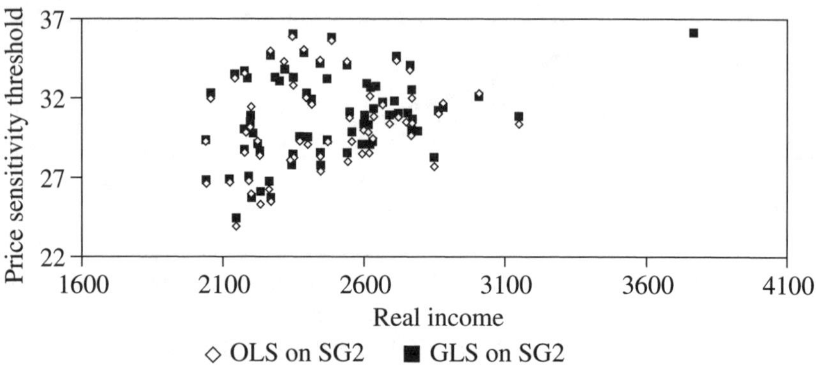

Figure 4.2 Price sensitivity threshold Y *with SG2 specification*

4. POLICY IMPLICATIONS

The water demand function describes the consumption behaviour of Slovak households. The estimated water demand can be used to assess how consumers will react to a modification of their environment. We consider in this section two types of change: a water price increase and economic growth.

4.1 Assessing the Impact of a Price Increase on Water Demand

The substantial water price increase experienced in the past is likely to continue with EU accession. Here we simulate several price increases (+10 percent, +20 percent, +50 percent and +100 percent) and we evaluate the resulting water consumption changes and the modification of consumer surplus. It is clear that, because price elasticity is a local measure of consumer price sensitivity, simulations with a 100 percent price increase should be considered with caution. All these simulations use the SG2 specification and the base year 2001. Similar results have been obtained with lin-lin and log-log specifications and are available from the authors upon request.

A 10 percent price increase will result on average in a 2.34 percent reduction in residential water demand. This figure is consistent with the price elasticity obtained with the SG2 specification. Changes in water consumption differ across consumers: the water consumption change ranges from −2.97 to −1.78 percent. Depending upon their socio-demographic characteristics, Slovak residential consumers will react to a price change in different ways. The 10 percent price increase has a moderate negative

Table 4.5 Assessing the impact of water pricing on Slovak residential consumers

	ΔY (%)			ΔS (%)		
	Mean	Min	Max	Mean	Min	Max
$\Delta P = +10\%$	−2.34	−2.97	−1.78	−4.03	−4.44	−3.33
$\Delta P = +20\%$	−4.30	−5.44	−3.27	−7.70	−8.48	−6.37
$\Delta P = +50\%$	−8.59	−10.88	−6.54	−17.13	−18.87	−14.17
$\Delta P = +100\%$	−12.89	−16.32	−9.80	−29.28	−32.26	−24.23

Notes: Columns ΔY and ΔS respectively give the proportional change in water consumption and in Marshallian consumer surplus. ΔP is the proportional price increase in percent.

impact in terms of consumer surplus, −4 percent on average. This moderate impact results from two effects: a low share of water expenses in the total expenses of the representative household (as discussed in the previous sections) and the possibility of substituting the composite good for water.

Larger price increases result in a lower proportional decrease in water consumption. Multiplying the price by two will only reduce water consumption by 12.89 percent. This would indicate that water pricing may be an efficient tool for indicating water scarcity, up to a certain price level. Notice that important price changes have a much more significant impact on consumer surplus than on water consumption. The loss of utility following a 100 percent price increase is around 2.5 times the reduction of water consumption, −29.28 percent versus −12.89 percent respectively.

Modifying water pricing has, by construction of the model, no effect on the price sensitivity threshold. Behind this property is the idea that, since the price sensitivity threshold mainly depends on household equipment or in a more general way on the structural characteristics of the household, it is likely that any adjustment of this level will take some time and cannot be realized in the short term. A model with a time-varying price sensitivity threshold would allow the dynamic habit effects induced by water price changes to be captured. The limited number of periods available (three years) prevents us from adopting such a model specification.

4.2 Assessing the Impact of Pricing and Economic Growth on Water Demand

Since socio-demographic characteristics may be viewed as fixed in the short term, there are two main factors that determine residential water demand changes. The first determinant is water pricing as emphasized in the previous section. But water consumption will also depend on economic growth. In our very simple water demand model, we will assume that economic growth induces real income growth. Hence, in the following table, we simulate different growth scenarios for income change (recession −10%, stagnation +0%, moderate growth +5% and accelerated growth +15%), together with different pricing scenarios (moderate, important and very important price increase) and we evaluate their impact on average water consumption, the average price sensitivity threshold and the average consumer surplus.

The second row of Table 4.6 corresponds to economic stagnation with no consumer income growth. As these figures have already been discussed in the previous section, we focus our attention on the three remaining rows which correspond to an economic recession, rapid growth and accelerated growth.

In terms of water consumption, a price increase in conjunction with an economic recession will lead the Slovak consumer to reduce their water consumption very significantly. In such a case, both the income and the price changes have a depressing effect on water consumption. The impacts of economic growth and water price appear very important in terms of consumer surplus: for instance, when the price is multiplied by two during an economic recession ($\Delta R = -10\%$), consumer surplus falls by a third.

Because the price and income elasticities have opposite signs, economic growth will mitigate the impact of the price increase on water consumption and consumer surplus (rows 3 and 4 of Table 4.6). The third row of Table 4.6 shows that in a rapid economic growth situation (+5 percent income increase), a 10 percent price increase will have only a limited impact both on water consumption and on surplus. In that case, water consumption

Table 4.6 Assessing the impact of pricing and economic growth on Slovak residential consumers

	$\Delta P = +10\%$		$\Delta P = +20\%$		$\Delta P = +100\%$	
	ΔY	ΔS	ΔY	ΔS	ΔY	ΔS
$\Delta I = -10\%$	−4.68	−8.48	−6.44	−12.15	−14.20	−33.70
$\Delta I = +0\%$	−2.34	−4.03	−8.59	−7.70	−12.89	−29.28
$\Delta I = +5\%$	−1.17	−1.96	−3.22	−5.64	−12.25	−27.21
$\Delta I = +15\%$	+1.17	+1.88	−1.07	−1.80	−10.96	−23.37

Notes: Columns ΔY and ΔS respectively give the proportional change in water consumption and Marshallian consumer surplus. ΔP and ΔI respectively represent the proportional price and income increases in percent.

will again decrease. But it has to be noticed that the 5 percent income increase will attenuate the effect of a 10 percent price increase on water consumption by half (−1.17 percent versus −2.34 percent). Finally, with a very accelerated growth (15 percent increase for domestic income) the income effect dominates the price effect when the water price increase equals 10 percent.

The decreasing trend in water consumption per capita observed during the last decade can be directly related to the water price increase. For instance, the water price from 1999 to 2001 has experienced an average yearly increase higher than 20 percent. But the impact of the pricing policy on water demand has been significantly mitigated by the change in residential income: wages have increased between 5 and 10 percent a year during that period. In a country that is experiencing very important socio-economic changes, predicting the impact of water pricing policy on consumer behaviour therefore requires a careful analysis of income changes.

These findings must be related to the water policy currently being implemented in the Slovak Republic. As has been noted in the first section of this chapter, the price increase aims more at balancing the financial deficits of the Slovak public water utilities than at indicating a resource scarcity. But given that the price elasticity is significantly different from zero, water pricing could also be used as an efficient economic tool by the water authorities. Second, economic growth, is an important determinant of water consumption. The economic situation, and in particular the level of income, has to be taken into account by public authorities when assessing the impact of pricing on residential water consumption. This clearly raises some complex policy issues such as equity across consumers and water access for the poorest households.

5. CONCLUSION

High levels of pollution of water resources and out-of-date infrastructure in water network utilities are the main problems faced by the water authorities in the Slovak Republic. This has resulted in a substantial water price increase over the last decade. If water from the public network could be considered as free by residential consumers under the previous centralized economy, it has now become an economic good. Hence, an efficient management of water resources requires a good knowledge of the water demand function. Identifying the determinants of the Slovak residential water demand and quantifying price and income elasticities have been the central goals of this chapter. To our knowledge, this chapter represents the first estimation of the residential water demand in a transition economy. Such an economic tool is interesting as, with EU accession, the Slovak Republic still needs to complete implementation of the EU Water Framework Directive and, in particular, to review water pricing practices. Moreover, as Central or Eastern European Countries are seen more and more by large private companies as a very promising market, analysing residential water demand in the Slovak Republic is an interesting issue.

The demand model has been estimated for a sample of 71 municipalities observed from 1999 to 2001. Three different functional forms for water demand have been estimated and compared: a lin-lin specification, a log-log form and a Stone-Geary function. First, the price sensitivity threshold using a Stone-Geary specification of the utility function is estimated to be 31.5 cubic metres per person and per year. This level is still significantly lower than the average water consumption per person observed in 2001, 41.5 cubic metres. This result has important policy implications. The average water consumption per person has decreased from 53.6 cubic metres in 1994 to 41.5 cubic metres in 2001. Given the price sensitivity threshold, the decreasing trend for residential water consumption may continue in the future. Second, using the Stone-Geary specification, we get a price elasticity varying from −0.35 to −0.50. Water demand is inelastic but not perfectly inelastic. Slovak consumers are price reactive and the water price can be used to convey to consumers the scarcity of the resource. Last, it should be noted that the price sensitivity for residential water demand is slightly higher in the Slovak Republic than in EU countries.

But considering the pricing policy as the sole determinant of water consumption changes is erroneous, as economic growth will also have an important impact on household decisions. As mentioned by the OECD (2003), the Slovak economy is expected to grow in the future and it is likely that residential consumption will rise again to reach levels prevailing in the EU (that is, between 50 and 60 cubic metres per year and per capita). We have shown that a 5 percent increase in income may compensate the negative impact on water consumption of a 10 percent price increase. Predicting future residential water consumption in the Slovak Republic is clearly a difficult issue as this country is currently experiencing important structural changes. Some more work is required to address the issues we have developed in this chapter more deeply. In particular, a more careful analysis of the links between water consumption and income level would yield interesting insights. But such work requires micro data that are currently not available in the Slovak Republic.

APPENDIX: DATABASE, DEFINITION OF VARIABLES

wat per capita yearly average drinking water consumption in cubic metres. This variable has been computed using the number of connected inhabitants and the daily average consumption in litres. Data have been provided by the Slovak Water Research Institute (V.Ú.V.H.) of Bratislava (http://www.vuvh.sk) and come from their Water Management Yearbooks.

price residential water prices in euros per cubic metre. Data are annually published by the Ministry of Agriculture, Water and Soil Management (yearly Green Reports on Water Management in the Slovak Republic). The price includes a 10 percent VAT on water services. The water charge corresponds to the drinking water supply service (which includes a charge for groundwater used for public water supply since 1996) and the drained water service (which includes a pollution charge paid by municipalities).

income real income in euros. Since data for real income were not available, we have used the average yearly wage for employees by districts as a proxy. The source of data is the Slovak Statistical Office.

unemp official rate of unemployment by district at the end of each year (December), provided by the Slovak Office of Employment.

pers average number of permanently resident persons per permanently occupied dwelling by district, taken from the 2001 census. This variable is constant over the period 1999–2001.

surf average number of square metres of living floor space per permanently occupied dwelling by district, taken from the 2001 census. This variable is constant over the period 1999–2001.

house share (in percent) of cottages designed for recreation as a proportion of total dwellings by district. This variable comes from the 2001 census and the 1996 micro-census.

wash share (in percent) of permanently occupied dwellings equipped with an automatic washing machine, taken from the 2001 census. This variable is constant over the period 1999–2001.

rain average monthly rainfall from April to September by district. Data for autumn and winter periods are not significant owing to the presence of snow on the frozen ground of the whole Slovak Republic territory. The source for this rainfall data is the Slovak Hydro Meteorological Institute of Bratislava.

temp average monthly temperature from March to September by district. Data provided by the Slovak Hydro Meteorological Institute of Bratislava.

NOTES

The authors would like to thank Cécile Aubert, Céline Nauges and Alban Thomas for helpful discussions on a preliminary draft of this chapter. We are also very grateful to Jana Belicová and Zuzana Sekáčová for having provided water consumption and climate data.

1. The price per cubic metre for a residential consumer in 1999 was 0.14 euros in the Slovak Republic versus respectively 0.36, 0.43 and 0.47 euros on average in Bulgaria, Estonia and Hungary. Social aspects have, however, to be kept in mind when revising water prices. Kraav (2000) reports that the application of the full cost recovery principle would lead to a dramatic increase in the costs of water supply and sewerage. As a result, the water bill of an average household would correspond to 8.3 percent of monthly income instead of the current 2.2 percent.
2. Private water companies have recently experienced difficulties with concession contracts in different parts of the world but especially in Latin America. A well-known example is the Aguas del Aconquija dispute. In 1995, the water network for the Province of Tucuman in Argentina was granted to the Aguas del Aconquija consortium led by Vivendi. Three years later, the concession contract was broken and Aguas del Aconquija had to abandon the water utility management. Another particularly well-known case is that of *Aguas del Tunaris* v *Bolivia* where a subsidiary of the US-based company Brechtel Corporation had finally to abandon its concession contract in Cochabamba due to strong protests after a price increase. With more political continuity and stability, CEEC appear to be a promising market for multinational water companies.
3. Real GDP growth accelerated further to 4.4 percent in 2002 (2 percent in the Czech Republic, 3.3 percent in Hungary and 1.4 percent in Poland).
4. Even if the employment rate tends to increase, unemployment remains high (17.7 percent for the first half of 2003 compared with 18.6 percent at the end of 2002).
5. European Directive 91/271/EEC.
6. European Directive 80/778/EEC as amended by Directive 98/83/EC.
7. Current water charges on water pollution were specified in a 1979 regulation, revised in 1989, and have not changed since then.
8. Water costs are higher in the eastern part of the country. Water intakes are of lower quality in the eastern part of the Slovak Republic and therefore require greater treatment expenses.

REFERENCES

Beveridge, R., and Guy, S. (2003), 'Current Status of Water Sector Restructuring in Slovakia', Working Paper, Leibniz Institute for Regional Development and Structural Planning, Germany.

Dalhuisen, J.M., Florax, R.J.G.M., de Groot, H., and Nijkamp, P. (2003), 'Price and Income Elasticities of Residential Water Demand: Why Empirical Estimates Differ', *Land Economics*, **79** (2), 292–308.

Dalmas, L., and Farkašová, E. (2002), 'Present Stage and Future of Pricing Policy within the Water Management in Slovak Republic', *National and Regional Economics IV, 5–7 September 2002, Herl'any, International Conference Proceedings*, Faculty of Economics-Technical University of Košice, Slovak Republic.

Deaton, A., and Muellbauer, J. (1980), *Economics and Consumer Behavior*, Cambridge, MA: Cambridge University Press.

DG Environment (2000), *Water Pricing in Selected Accession Countries to the European Union, Current Policies and Trends. Part I and II*, Final Report produced for the European Commission, Brussels: EC Publisher.

European Commission (2003), *Slovakia's Progress toward Accession*, 97 pages, Brussels: CEC.

Gaudin, S., Griffin, R., and Sickles, R.C. (2001), 'Demand Specification for Municipal Water Management: Evaluation of the Stone-Geary Form', *Land Economics*, **77** (3), 399–422.

Hewitt, J.A., and Hanemann, W.M. (1995), 'A Discrete/Continuous Choice Approach to Residential Water Demand under Block Rate Pricing', *Land Economics*, **71** (2), 173–92.

Howe, C.W., and Linaweaver, F.P. (1967), 'The Impact of Price on Residential Water Demand and its Relation to System Demand and Price Structure', *Water Resources Research*, **3** (1), 13–32.

Kraav, E. (2000), 'SIEI Country Report', Working Paper, Szentendre, Hungary.

Martínez-Espiñeira, R., and Nauges, C. (2003), 'Is Really all Domestic Water Consumption Sensitive to Price Control? An Empirical Analysis', mimeo, University College London.

Ministry of Agriculture of the Slovak Republic (1998), *Report on the Water Management in the Slovak Republic 1998*, Bratislava: Ministry of Agriculture of the Slovak Republic Publisher.

Ministry of Agriculture of the Slovak Republic (2002), *Report on the Water Management in the Slovak Republic 2002*, Bratislava: Ministry of Agriculture of the Slovak Republic Publisher.

Nauges, C., and Thomas, A. (2000), 'Dynamique de la Consommation Domestique d'Eau Potable des Ménages: Une Etude sur un Panel de Communes Françaises', *Economie et Prévision*, 143–4, 175–84.

Nordin, J.A. (1976), 'A Proposed Modification of Taylor's Demand Analysis: Comment', *The Bell Journal of Economics*, **7** (2), 719–21.

OECD (1999), *The Price of Water, Trends in OECD Countries*, Paris: OECD.

OECD (2002), *Environmental Performance Review, Slovak Republic*, Paris: OECD.

OECD (2003), *Social Issues on the Provision and Pricing of Water Service*, Paris: OECD.

Regional Environmental Centre for Central and Eastern Europe (2001), *Agricultural Water Management Policies in Selected CEE Countries*, Budapest: Regional Environmental Centre for Central and Eastern Europe Publisher.

Shin, J.S. (1985), 'Perception of Price When Price Information is Costly: Evidence from Residential Electricity Demand', *Review of Economics and Statistics*, **67** (4), 591–8.

Thalmaneirova, D. (2002), *Water Pricing in Selected Accession Countries to the European Union, Current Policies and Trends, Part II Country Description: Slovakia*, final report produced for the European Commission DG Environment, Brussels: EC Publisher.

5. Estimating urban water demands: a dynamic approach

María A. García-Valiñas

INTRODUCTION

Throughout the ages, water has been considered one of the most important natural resources in making the development of civilization possible, and its availability has conditioned the location of economic activity (Marshall, 1879; Gibbons, 1986). At the same time, water is a scarce good (Winpenny, 1994). Conflicts over this natural resource have caused competition among alternative uses or among regions. In those situations, supplies cannot meet demands, so it is necessary to design policies to allocate water efficiently.

Since the 1970s, a tendency towards using demand-side policies may be observed, at the cost of increasing productive capacity to satisfy growing demands (Herrington, 1995). In this sense, the analysis of the users' preferences constitutes a key element to be considered in water management processes. This study has focused on estimating water demand in an urban context. In spite of the fact that urban water demand is not the most important consumption use, it is the one that has most substantially increased (MMA, 2001). This rising trend is explained by several factors, such as population and income growth or changes in consumption habits. Thus, there is no doubt that urban demands are spreading and urban supply has priority over other uses.

Specifically, the most relevant users in an urban context have been analysed. These are residential and commercial/industrial consumers supplied by the urban network. Studies that have simultaneously produced estimates for both types of users are still scarce (Williams and Suh, 1986; Schneider and Whitlach, 1991; Renzetti, 1992). Additionally, as Arbués et al. (2003, p. 90) showed, 'the use of dynamic panels is still rare and very recent in the field of water demand'. These kinds of dynamic frameworks can help to improve the modelling of users' response, allowing, at the same time, a distinction to be made between long and short-run analysis. In fact, the main contribution of this exercise has been to estimate conjointly residential and commercial/industrial urban water demands, using dynamic panel data methodologies.

We have focused on studying urban water demands in Gijón, a Spanish municipality located in the north of the country. Starting from two micro-data panels, dynamic models for each kind of consumer have been estimated, in order to show the users' response to lagged variables. The chapter has been structured in the following way. In the first section, a general overview of the main contributions of the literature on urban water demand estimation has been provided. Afterwards, the model for demand estimates is outlined. The following section includes a description of the econometric methodology used. After that, the data and the variables that have been considered in the empirical analysis are analysed. Subsequently, the main results are shown. Finally, there is a summary of the study's main findings.

LITERATURE ON URBAN WATER DEMAND: SOME COMMENTS

Although urban water demand is not perfectly price-inelastic, the fact is that the majority of studies that have addressed this issue have obtained low price elasticity values. In regard to residential demands, those values vary from -0.003 to -1.63, but the most usual results are below one (Arbués et al., 2003). However, the sensitivity to price variations is higher for commercial/industrial users. Depending on economic activity and/or the kind of water input, price elasticity values oscillate from -0.08 to -2.21 (Reynaud, 2003). The demand specification, such as variables and functional form, the econometric technique or the data set are some of the factors that have determined these values (Espey et al., 1997; Renzetti, 2002; Arbués et al., 2003; Dalhuisen et al., 2003).

The literature on residential water demand has identified some important influences in this regard,[1] such as prices, climate, demography, meaning household composition, or other socio-economic features such as income, cultural level and housing characteristics (Howe and Linaweaver, 1967; Foster and Beattie, 1979; Billings and Agthe, 1980; Hanke and De Maré, 1984; Renzetti, 1992; Nauges and Thomas, 2003).

The level and kind of economic activity are determining factors to be considered in the specification of commercial/industrial demands.[2] In this sense, it is usual to include some output index in the demand function, and even to consider negative outputs (Reynaud, 2003), and frequently, industrial demand analysis may be found to depend on the industrial sector. Additionally, the modelling of several sources of water is a common topic

(De Rooy, 1974; Ziegler and Bell, 1984; Williams and Suh, 1986; Renzetti, 1992; Reynaud, 2003).

In general, price specification has been a very controversial issue (Arbués et al., 2003). The most frequent alternatives used in the literature concerning this topic are the *average price*,[3] on the one hand, and the *marginal price* on the other (the price of the last block in which the consumer is located), where the latter may be used alone or in conjunction with the difference variable (Nordin, 1976). Additionally, the lack of information regarding the users has led to lagged specifications (Charney and Woodard, 1984; Opaluch, 1984). It has been shown that users are not always aware of current price schedules (Young et al., 1983; Nieswiadomy and Molina, 1991).

Regarding the functional form, the most common for residential demands have been the linear specification (Carver and Boland, 1980; Hanke and De Mare, 1984; Nieswiadomy and Molina, 1989; Dandy et al., 1997; Martínez-Espiñeira, 2002) or the double-log function (Foster and Beattie, 1979; Williams and Suh, 1986; Nieswiadomy, 1992; Hewitt and Haneman, 1995). However, other functional forms have been proposed, such as the translog for industrial demand (Renzetti, 1992; Reynaud, 2003) or the log-linear for residential ones (Al-Quanibet and Johnston, 1985; Gaudin et al., 2001).

Similarly, it is not possible to find a generally accepted econometric technique, though several studies include some type of Instrumental Variables method to solve the simultaneity problems caused by the presence of non-linear prices (Agthe and Billings, 1980; Jones and Morris, 1984; Renzetti, 1992; Martínez-Espiñeira, 2002; Nauges and Thomas, 2003). These kinds of tariffs have generated other problems such as demand discontinuities or unobservable variables, which need specific modelling in order to be solved (Hewitt and Haneman, 1995; Martínez-Espiñeira, 2002).

Finally, it is necessary to mention the importance of data set characteristics. In this sense, the availability of disaggregated information is preferred. For instance, from a temporal point of view, the accessibility of intra-annual data would to specify lag-response of seasonal demand models within a dynamic framework (Lyman, 1992; Martínez-Espiñeira, 2002).

THE MODEL: WATER DEMAND SPECIFICATION

In this chapter, dynamic specifications have been proposed in order to approximate users' response to price variations. The main objective of this exercise consists of obtaining price elasticity values for different kinds of users in order to design optimal water demand policies. Therefore, a basic framework of water demand specification has been proposed, using the same methodology to approximate residential and commercial/industrial users.

Thus, linear demand functions have been specified. The linear functional form has usually been specified in this context. This function implies lower price elasticity values for low-consumption users.[4] Additionally, the linear shape also allows for a level at user satiation at very low prices, which agrees with intuitive expectations in the residential case (Arbués et al., 2003).

Information provided by micro-data panels, which will be described in the next section, has been used. Applied studies that have used appropriate methodologies for the treatment of panel data are still scarce in this context (Moncur, 1987; Höglund, 1999; Pint, 1999; Nauges and Thomas, 2000, 2003; Martínez-Espiñeira, 2002; Reynaud, 2003).

Beginning with residential demands, it was considered that water constitutes a basic resource for households. In this context, it seems especially relevant to model households' consumption habits. Thus, a partial adjustment model has been specified that includes a lagged dependent variable, giving the model a structural character. The following specification of the demand function is proposed:

$$x_{it} = \alpha + \rho x_{it-1} + \beta p_{it-2} + \gamma s_t + \delta f_i + \eta_i + v_{it} \tag{5.1}$$

where x_{it} is the consumption period t of the individual i, including, as an explanatory variable, the consumption of the previous period, x_{it-1}. A two-period price lag is also included. This lag is due to the fact that domestic users observe the price when they receive the bill, an event which occurs in the period following consumption. In consequence, we have opted to incorporate the price corresponding to the period before the preceding period, p_{it-2}. This lagged-price specification has been defended in some studies (Charney and Woodard, 1984; Opaluch, 1984; Lyman, 1992).

Additionally, vector s_t includes variables that present a temporal variation, but not individually, basically reflecting climatic aspects in each period. On the other hand, the f_i vector represents a bundle of socio-economic features that present little or no variability in the period analysed. These include socio-economic aspects which reflect the economic capacity of the households as well as their size and which have a notable influence on water demand (Arbués et al., 2003). Finally, a composite error term has been considered, in which η_i refers to an unobservable individual effect and v_{it} is a conventional error term.

In order to model commercial/industrial demand, the structure of equation (5.1) has been modified. A quicker reaction has been assumed, introducing a price variable with a one-period lag for reasons which are explained below. Also, a lagged dependent variable has been included in the equation but not one related to the immediately preceding bi-monthly period. Instead, we include one related to the same bi-monthly period corresponding to the previous year:

$$x_{it} = \alpha + \rho x_{it-n} + \beta p_{it-1} + \gamma s_t + \zeta r_i + \eta_i + v_{it} \tag{5.2}$$

In equation (5.2), sub-index n refers to the number of intra-annual periods included in a year, and r_i is the vector of variables which are constant over time, which is identified with indicators of activity type and level. As for households, a double-error term has been included.

ECONOMETRIC ISSUES: DYNAMIC PANEL DATA METHODS

Several advantages have been attributed to panel data (Arellano and Bover, 1990; Greene, 2003; Arellano, 2003). These databases allow for higher efficiency and permit unobservable heterogeneity to be controlled. If differences in variables are taken, this error component is eliminated. However, this procedure could generate problems in a dynamic model context. If equation (5.1) is considered in differences, it is possible to observe that there is a correlation between the first-differences lagged dependent variable $(x_{it-1} - x_{it-2})$ and the first-differences error term $(v_{it} - v_{it-1})$, even when the errors are not serially correlated (Baltagi, 1995).

In this context, an estimate by static panel methods would be inconsistent and biased (Nickell, 1981; Kiviet, 1995). A similar problem would appear if there are some endogenous or predetermined variables. In this case, consider the correlation between price increments $(p_{it-1} - p_{it-2})$ and the first-differences error term $(v_{it} - v_{it-1})$ must be thought about if differences in equation (5.2) are taken.

Instrumental Variables methodology is the usual procedure for solving these problems. In general, this method involves finding a variable z_{it} which is not correlated with the error term, but which, at the same time, is correlated with the independent variable that is to be instrumented. In a dynamic modelling context, Anderson and Hsiao (1981) suggested the use of lagged variables as instruments in differences or levels applying Maximum Likelihood techniques for estimation. Arellano and Bond (1991) proposed a generalization of the previous procedure, with a Generalized Moments Method (GMM) estimator. They based this on the orthogonal conditions between the lagged instruments and the error term.

At the same time, and with the objective of making use of non-temporal variability information, the same variables in differences have been considered as additional instruments for the equations in levels (Bhargava and Sargan, 1983; Blundell and Bond, 1998). As will be seen, some socio-economic variables that change individually, but not in time, are included in the analysis. Finally, it would be necessary to test if the instruments have been chosen correctly. In this sense, Sargan (1958) proposed an estimator which, under certain assumptions, approximates to a χ^2. The null hypothesis would be the compatibility among instruments.

DATA AND VARIABLES

First of all it is necessary to describe the main features of the town considered in this study. Gijón is a municipality situated in the north of Spain that has 270,875 inhabitants (INE, 2003). Its population density is close to 1,500 inhabitants per km^2, and the climate is characterized by mild temperatures and rainfall. A public firm (EMA) supplies water in the municipality. Water tariffs are complex, because these include several elements, such as fixed and variable charges and some taxes. Different prices are fixed for residential and industrial/commercial users. Additionally, there are special tariffs for some sub-groups of users. That is the case for households with collective meters, where different rates are charged compared with households with individual meters. The frequency of billing, which is the intra-annual period considered in this study, is bi-monthly.

In order to estimate equations (5.1) and (5.2), we have had two balanced data panels at our disposal. Dimensions such as the individuals (N) as well as the periods (T) appear in Table 5.1. Most of the information related to consumption, tariffs and metering features was provided by the supplier. The remaining socio-economic information was given by other departments of the City Council. The National Institute of Meteorology provided climatic information.

The consumption of the period (CONSUM) has been considered as a dependent variable, expressed by cubic metres per period and user. Regarding households, it is necessary to mention that consumers using both individual and collective meters have been incorporated. Thus, the dependent variable in the demand function has been specified as average

Table 5.1 Data panels: characteristics

User	N	Interval	T	$N \times T$
Residential	1,089	1991(1)–2000(6)	60	65,340
Commercial/industrial	477	1991(1)–2000(6)	60	28,620

consumption per household. The main reason for including households with this kind of metering in the sample is the importance that these have among the population. The independent variables used in the estimates are shown in Table 5.2. While all the variables employed appear in this table, it is necessary to clarify some of the socio-economic aspects.

In respect to the specification of the variable price, we have chosen to use the average price, given the tariff complexity in the majority of these cases. Therefore, in this context, it is difficult for users to have perfect information about tariffs. It is highly probable that they obtain information about prices and consumption when they receive the bill. This fact explains why lags were included in this variable.[5] For commercial/industrial users, information about autonomous water input was not available, so only the price of water bought from water utility has been considered.

With regard to residential demand, a proxy for income has been incorporated. Here, we have used the most frequent choice in household-based studies: the *assessed* property value (Howe and Linaweaver, 1967; Hewitt and Haneman, 1995; Dandy et al., 1997). For industrial/commercial

Table 5.2 Definition of independent variables

	User	
	Residential	Commercial/industrial
Price variables (in 2001 €/m^3) p_{it-s}	P(−2): two-period lagged average price PMETER(−2): interaction of price with METER	P(−1): one-period lagged average price
Lagged dependent variable (in m^3/bim) x_{it-s}	CONSUM (−1): one-period lagged consumption	CONSUM (−6): six-period lagged consumption
Climate variables s_t	TMAX: average of the maximum temperatures recorded in the period (in °C) RAIN: total amount of rainfall (in mm.)	
Socio-economic variables f_i, r_i	INCOME (proxy): assessed value of the property (in 2001 €) NHAB: average number of people per housing	HOTEL, INDUS, COM (dummies): type of business S123 (dummy): proxy of the level of activity
Other variables	METER: dummy; 1 = housing with collective metering	DYEAR: dummies per year

Table 5.3 Descriptive statistics: urban demands

Variable	User			
	Residential		Commercial/industrial	
	Mean	Stan. Dev.	Mean	Stan. Dev.
CONSUM	21.51	31.85	51.32	141.34
P	0.66	1.09	1.14	1.28
TMAX	16.92	2.84	16.92	2.88
RAIN	1,297.15	632.82	1,297.15	632.89
INCOME	4,663.56	2,654.81	–	–
NHAB	1.93	0.70	–	–

demand, information about output could not be obtained from the organizations concerned, although it has been approximated by means of a location index. The indicator used in this case is the fiscal category of the street where the business is located, which could be interpreted as a proxy for the level of economic activity.[6] We have defined a dummy variable (S123) that will be equal to one if the activity is located in a street of the first, second or third category, and zero if otherwise.

Additionally, information related to the type of activity carried out by firms has been used. In this regard, three dummies which are representative of four activity categories have been defined. The first is hotel businesses (HOTEL), including accommodation of various types and restaurant activity (bars, restaurants). Industrial activities and repair services located in the cities come under the second dummy variable[7] (INDUS). Finally, two additional categories have been defined: the commercial activities of the municipality (COM) and the remaining business. Table 5.3 shows the descriptive statistics of the main variables for each type of demand.

RESULTS

The results, which have been obtained by applying the Blundell and Bond (1998) econometric methodology, are shown in Table 5.4. It may be seen how most of the coefficients are significant, and have the expected signs. In general, the presence of second-order serial correlation is rejected because of the errors in differences, whereas first-order auto-regression is confirmed. The significance of the coefficients of lagged consumption may be observed. This feature suggests that consumption habits are

Table 5.4 Estimates of parameters: urban demands

Variables	User			
	Residential		Commercial/industrial	
	Coef.	t-stat	Coef.	t-stat
CONSUM(−1/−6)	0.246***	5578.0	0.432***	1248.0
P(−2/−1)	−1.228***	590.0	−4.911***	542.0
PMETER(−2)	−1.105***	51.1	–	–
TMAX	0.022***	42.7	0.434***	102.0
RAIN	0.00046	0.3	−0.002***	95.7
INCOME	0.001***	640.0	–	–
NHAB	6.445***	338.0	–	–
METER	25.942***	54.7	–	–
HOTEL	–	–	499.016***	41.1
COM	–	–	−71.234***	5.0
INDUS	–	–	621.597***	44.2
S123	–	–	185.307***	34.3
D1993	–	–	−4.142***	81.3
D1994	–	–	−6.280***	92.7
D1995	–	–	−0.282***	6.6
D1996	–	–	1.308***	92.4
D1997	–	–	−0.368***	7.0
D1998	–	–	4.272***	68.4
D1999	–	–	4.084***	54.8
D2000	–	–	10.869***	106.0
Constant	−70.442***	435.0	−281.345***	21.8
Sargan test χ^2_r	986.0 (961)		452.10 (420)	
AR(1) test N (0,1)	−4.232***		−3.166***	
AR(2) test N (0,1)	1.853*		0.265	

Notes: *,*** Significantly different from zero at the 0.10, 0.05, 0.01 significance level, respectively.

strongly established, and, in addition, shows the seasonal trends of firms' water use.

For residential estimates, it is possible to observe the impact of household size (NHAB) on water use. Here, due to the economies of scale in the use of water, the increase in water demand is less than proportional to the increase in household size (Höglund, 1999).

Here, too, price coefficients are significant in all cases. In Table 5.5 it is possible to see that demand is inelastic. Regarding residential demand, the

Table 5.5 Price and income elasticities

		User	
		Residential	Commercial/industrial
ε_p	Collective metering	−0.05 (0.013)	–
	average	−0.04 (0.015)	−0.11 (0.052)
ε_Y		0.27 (0.045)	–

Note: Standard errors are in parentheses.

values of price-elasticity (ε_p) for collective meters are higher than the average for residential demand. That sensitivity may be a little higher because the tariff applicable to these kinds of users has increased greatly during the latest years.

In general, water for residential use is considered as a basic commodity, especially when the amount consumed is small. This could be the reason why low price elasticities have been generated in that context. Income elasticity (ε_Y) is low too, since the total bill represents a low proportion of total income (Chicoine and Ramamurthy, 1986). Additionally, in the obtained results it is easily observable that the industrial users show more sensitivity to price variations.

Certainly, the results of this research confirm those obtained in other studies. As previously mentioned, almost all applications in this field show how water demand responds to price, although not very much (Renzetti, 2002; Arbués et al., 2003). However, very low price elasticity values have been obtained for both kind of users. The explanation can be linked to the water price level in the municipality. In Spain, water tariffs are highly subsidized and do not cover total production costs. In Gijón, prices are low too, and this leads users to consolidate their consumption habits. So their reaction to price changes is not great. Only when a considerable rise in water tariffs is observed, do price elasticity values rise slightly, as happened in the case of households with collective metering.

Regarding commercial/industrial users, it has been pointed out that it was not possible to include large industries in the sample. The focus of this exercise is unusual, in the sense that we have considered several economic activities located in the city, including a significant proportion of commercial activities and other services, which constitute close to 80% of total activities. For this reason, water price elasticity values were, as expected, low, compared to the values obtained in previous studies, which have usually focused on industrial sectors.

CONCLUSIONS

The characterization of water demand is addressed as a first basic step in the designing of water allocation processes. Demand estimates will allow the implementation of pricing policies that improve social welfare. The values of elasticities are important parameters to consider when pricing in order to achieve several objectives such as efficiency, equity or environmental considerations (OECD, 1987, 1999, 2003).

Dynamic panel data models have been proposed, reflecting different reaction speeds for different users in an urban context. Here, the inclusion of lagged variables has allowed for an improvement in water demand specification, within a context of imperfect information about prices. Additionally, following Blundell and Bond's (1998) econometric methodology, use has been made of the information that does not change in time.

In the empirical application, we have obtained price and income elasticities and have found differences between residential and commercial/industrial demands. The results show that it is necessary to implement different price policies depending on the user. So, the findings of this chapter support the application of price discrimination formulas in the context of the water sector.

NOTES

The author would like to thank the Institute of Fiscal Studies and Herrero Bank Foundation for their financial support.

1. See Arbués et al. (2003) for a survey of residential water demand.
2. Some recent studies (Becker et al., 2000; Renzetti, 2002; Reynaud, 2003) have made significant contributions to commercial/industrial water demand estimation.
3. Nordin (1976) suggested the use of another variable instead of average price. This variable, called the *difference variable* D_i, is calculated in the following way:

$$D_i = B_i - p_{ni} x_i$$

D_i is the difference between the total bill B_i and what the user would have paid if all units, x_i, were charged at the marginal price, p_{ni}.
4. This fact has been tested in some empirical studies (Billings and Day, 1989).
5. The moment when the bill is received in the period following consumption is not the same for all users. We do not have information about the exact day of receipt, but the water supplier explained to us that, in general, domestic users receive their bill later than commercial or industrial users.

6. The fiscal category of the streets is fixed depending on several factors, such as the nearness to the city centre or/and the expected level of activity.
7. Here, it was not possible to obtain information about large industries located in industrial estates.

REFERENCES

Agthe, D.E., and Billings, R.B. (1980), 'Dynamic Models of Residential Water Demand', *Water Resources Research*, **16** (3), 476–80.

Al-Quanibet, M.H., and Johnston, R.S. (1985), 'Municipal Demand for Water in Kuwait: Methodological Issues and Empirical Results', *Water Resources Research*, **2** (4), 433–8.

Anderson, T.W., and Hsiao, C. (1981), 'Estimation of Dynamic Models with Error Components', *Journal of the American Statistical Association*, **76**, 598–606.

Arbués, F., García-Valiñas, M.A., and Martínez-Espiñeira, R. (2003), 'Estimation of Residential Water Demand: A State of the Art Review', *The Journal of Socio-Economics*, **32** (1), 81–102.

Arellano, M. (2003), *Panel Data Econometrics*, Advanced Texts in Econometrics, Oxford: Oxford University Press.

Arellano, M., and Bond, S. (1991), 'Some Tests of Specification for Panel Data: Monte Carlo Evidence and an Application to Employment Equations', *Review of Economic Studies*, **58**, 277–97.

Arellano, M., and Bover, O. (1990), 'La Econometría de Datos de Panel', *Investigaciones Económicas*, **14** (1), 3–45.

Baltagi, B.H. (1995), *Econometric Analysis of Panel Data*, Chichester: Wiley and Sons.

Becker, N., Zeitouni, N., and Zilberman, D. (2000), 'Issues in the Economics of Water Resource', in T. Tietenberg and H. Folmer (eds), *The International Yearbook of Environmental and Resource Economics*, Cheltenham, UK and Northampton, MA, USA: Edward Elgar Publishing, pp. 55–99.

Bhargava, A., and Sargan, J.D. (1983), 'Estimating Dynamic Random Effects Models from Panel Data covering Short Time Periods', *Econometrica*, **51** (6), 1635–59.

Billings, R.B., and Agthe, D.E. (1980), 'Price Elasticities for Water: A Case of Increasing Block Rates', *Land Economics*, **56** (1), 73–84.

Billings, R.B., and Day, W.M. (1989), 'Demand Management Factors in Residential Water Use: The Southern Arizona Experience', *Journal of the American Water Works Association*, **81** (3), 58–64.

Blundell, R., and Bond, S. (1998), 'Initial Conditions and Moment Restrictions in Dynamic Panel Data Models', *Journal of Econometrics*, **87**, 115–43.

Carver, P.H., and Boland, J.J. (1980), 'Short-Run and Long-Run Effects of Price on Municipal Water Use', *Water Resources Research*, **16** (4), 609–16.

Charney, A.H., and Woodard, G.C. (1984), 'A Test of Consumer Demand Response to Water Prices: Reply', *Land Economics*, **60** (4), 414–16.

Chicoine, D.L., and Ramamurthy, G. (1986); 'Evidence on the Specification of Price in the Study of Domestic Water Demand', *Land Economics*, **62** (1), 26–32.

Dalhuisen, J.M., De Groot, H.L.F., Florax, R.J.G.M., and Nijkamp, P. (2003), 'Price and Income Elasticities of Residential Water Demand: Why Empirical Estimates Differ', *Land Economics*, **79** (2), 292–308.

Dandy, G., Nguyen, T., and Davies, C. (1997), 'Estimating Residential Water Demand in the Presence of Free Allowances', *Land Economics*, **73** (1), 125–39.
De Rooy, J. (1974), 'Price Responsiveness of the Industrial Demand for Water', *Water Resources Research*, **10** (3), 403–6.
Espey, M., Espey, J., and Shaw, W.D. (1997), 'Price Elasticities of Residential Demand for Water: A Meta-Analysis', *Water Resources Research*, **33** (6), 1369–74.
Foster, H.S., Jr., and Beattie, B.R. (1979), 'Urban Residential Demand for Water in the United States', *Land Economics*, **55** (1), 43–58.
Gaudin, S., Griffin, R.C., and Sickles, R.C. (2001), 'Demand Specification for Municipal Water Management: Evaluation of the Stone-Geary Form', *Land Economics*, **77** (3), 399–422.
Gibbons, D.C. (1986), *The Economic Value of Water*, Washington, DC: Resources for the Future.
Gibbs, K.C. (1978), 'Price Variable in Residential Water Demands Models', *Water Resources Research*, **14** (1), 15–18.
Greene, W.H. (2003), *Econometric Analysis*, 5th edition, London: Prentice Hall International.
Hanke, S.H. and De Maré, L. (1984), 'Municipal Water Demands', in J. Kindler and C.S. Russell (eds), *Modelling Water Demands*, London: Academic Press, pp. 149–70.
Herrington, P. (1995), 'Pricing Water Properly', in T. O'Riordan, *Ecotaxation*, London: Earthscan Publications, pp. 263–86.
Hewitt, J.A., and Hanemann, W.M. (1995), 'A Discrete/continuous Choice Approach to Residential Water Demand under Block Rate Pricing', *Land Economics*, **71** (2), 173–92.
Höglund, L. (1999), 'Household Demand for Water in Sweden with Implications for a Potential Tax on Water Use', *Water Resources Research*, **35** (12), 3853–63.
Howe, C.W., and Linaweaver, F.P. (1967), 'The Impact of Price on Residential Water Demand and its Relationship to System Design and Price Structure', *Water Resources Bulletin*, **3**, 13–32.
Instituto Nacional de Estadística (INE) (2003), 'Cifras de Población Referidas al 1/1/03. Población de Municipios por sexo', http://www.ine.es/pob03/pob03frame.htm.
Jones, C.V., and Morris, J.R. (1984), 'Instrumental Price Estimates and Residential Demand', *Water Resources Research*, **20**, 197–202.
Kiviet, J.F. (1995), 'On Bias, Inconsistency, and Efficiency of Various Estimators in Dynamic Panel Data Models', *Journal of Econometrics*, **68**, 53–78.
Lyman, R.A. (1992), 'Peak and Off-peak Residential Water Demand', *Water Resources Research*, **28**, 2159–67.
Marshall, A. (1879), 'Water as an Element of National Wealth', reprinted in A. Pigou (ed.), *Memorials of Alfred Marshall*, New York: Kelley and Millman, 1956, 134–41.
Martínez-Espiñeira, R. (2002), 'Residential Water Demand in the Northwest of Spain', *Environmental and Resource Economics*, **21** (2), 161–87.
Ministerio de Medio Ambiente (MMA) (2001), 'Evaluación Ambiental Estratégica del Plan Hidrológico Nacional', http:/www.mma.es/rec_hid/pla_hidro/index.htm.
Moncur, J. (1987), 'Urban Water Pricing and Drought Management', *Water Resources Research*, **23**, 393–98.

Nauges, C., and Thomas, A. (2000), 'Privately-operated Water Utilities, Municipal Price Negotiation and Estimation of Residential Demand: The Case of France', *Land Economics*, **76** (1), 68–85.

Nauges, C., and Thomas, A. (2003), 'Long-run Study of Residential Water Consumption', *Environmental and Resource Economics*, **26** (1), 25–43.

Nickell, S. (1981), 'Biases in Dynamic Models with Fixed Effects', *Econometrica*, **49**, 1417–26.

Nieswiadomy, M.L. (1992), 'Estimating Urban Residential Demand: Effect of Price Structure, Conservation and Education', *Water Resources Research*, **28**, 609–15.

Nieswiadomy, M.L., and Molina, D.J. (1989), 'Comparing Residential Water Estimates under Decreasing and Increasing Block Rates using Household Data', *Land Economics*, **65** (3), 280–89.

Nieswiadomy, M.L., and Molina, D.J. (1991), 'A Note on Price Perception in Water Demand Models', *Land Economics*, **67** (3), 352–9.

Nordin, J.A. (1976), 'A Proposed Modification of Taylor's Demand Analysis: Comment', *The Bell Journal of Economics*, **7** (3), 719–21.

OECD (1987), *Pricing of Water Services*, París: OECD.

OECD (1999), *Household Water Pricing in OECD Countries*, Paris: Environment Policy Committee.

OECD (2003), *Social Issues in the Provision and Pricing of Water Services*, Paris: OECD.

Opaluch, J. (1984), 'A Test of Consumer Demand Response to Water Prices: Reply', *Land Economics*, **60** (4), 417–21.

Pint, E.M. (1999), 'Household Responses to Increased Water Rates during the California Drought', *Land Economics*, **75** (2), 246–66.

Renzetti, S. (1992), 'Evaluating the Welfare Effects of Reforming Municipal Water Prices', *Journal of Environmental Economics and Management*, **22**, 147–63.

Renzetti, S. (2002), *The Economics of Industrial Water Use*, Cheltenham, UK and Northampton, MA, USA: Elward Elgar.

Reynaud, A. (2003), 'An Econometric Estimation of Industrial Water Demand in France', *Environmental and Resource Economics*, **25** (1), 213–32.

Sargan, J.D. (1958), 'The Estimation of Econometrics Relationships using Instrumental Variables', *Econometrica*, **26**, 393–415.

Schneider, M.L., and Whitlach, E.E (1991), 'User-specific Water Demand Elasticities', *Journal of Water Resources Planning and Management*, **17** (1), 52–75.

Williams, M., and Suh, B. (1986), 'The Demand for Urban Water by Consumer Class', *Applied Economics*, **18**, 1275–89.

Winpenny, J. (1994), *Managing Water as an Economic Resource*, London: Routledge.

Young, C.E., Kingsley, K.R., and Sharpe, W.E. (1983), 'Impact on Residential Water Consumption of an Increasing Rate Structure', *Water Resources Bulletin*, **19** (1), 81–6.

Ziegler, J.A., and Bell, S.E. (1984), 'Estimating Demand for Intake Water by Self-supplied Firms', *Water Resources Research*, **20** (1), 4–8.

PART II

Valuation methods

6. Households' valuation of domestic water in Indonesia: revisiting the Supply Driven Approach

Arief Anshory Yusuf and Phoebe Koundouri

1. INTRODUCTION

The Demand Driven Approach (DDA) has been one important aspect of the new paradigm of water provision as opposed to the old paradigm of the Supply Driven Approach (SDA). Proponents of the DDA approach argue that water is an economic good and its efficient provision has to be directed to those who are willing to pay for it. Many case studies using the Contingent Valuation Method (CVM) suggest that people in poor rural areas of developing countries are willing to pay a significant portion of their income for water (see, for example, Merret, 2002). This evidence rejects the so-called 3–5% rule (which defines the percentage of income that poor people can afford to pay for water provision), a result that has provided significant support for the DDA and the new paradigm of water management.

We apply the hedonic analysis to a nation-wide microeconomic dataset for Indonesia.[1] Our results indicate that in urban areas, people value having improved domestic water sources (piped and pump water), while this is not true for households in rural areas. Moreover, households in both urban and rural areas do not seem to value communal water sources, probably reflecting the effects of the free-rider problem, when services have characteristics of public goods. On the whole, our results show that households in rural Indonesia are not willing to pay for improved domestic water sources, a finding which represents a major challenge to the DDA. Assuming universal rights for the provision of safe and improved water quantities that cover basic needs, subsidization of water provision is still called for.

2. BRIEF HISTORICAL BACKGROUND

Today, more than one billion people are still vulnerable to deadly health hazard, due to inadequate access to safe drinking water (United Nations, 2003). In response to this situation, in November 2002, United Nations declared that access to adequate amounts of clean water for personal and domestic uses is a fundamental human right of all people. This declaration implies that all people, rich or poor, living in cities or villages, are entitled to sufficient, affordable, physically accessible, safe and acceptable water. The relevant UN Millennium Development Goal is to halve the proportion of people without access to safe drinking water by the year 2015.

In January 1992, the proceedings of the International Conference on Water and the Environment in Dublin, Ireland, declared: 'water has an economic value in all its competing uses and should be recognized as an economic good'. This statement is known as the 'Dublin Principle', which implies that water under scarcity is not a free good, either in quantity or in quality terms, hence its use implies not only benefits to the users, but also costs that they need to incur in order to acquire the relevant quantity. That is, people have to pay for water provision, and thus water should be provided to those who effectively demand it. This principle, however, is contradicted by the principle underlining the Supply Driven Approach to water provision, which emphasizes that water is a basic human right for all people and that it should be treated as a 'social' or 'merit' good, because it is essential to human life. The direct policy implication of this approach is that all people should have access to safe water.

These two lines of thought have sustained a continuing debate, which has been documented in, and has influenced, the evolution of international water and sanitation policies. This debate is usually summarized in the phrase 'demand driven vs. supply driven approaches to water provision' (see Seppälä, 2002, for a review of the past experience of international water policies).

3. SUPPLY DRIVEN VS. DEMAND DRIVEN APPROACH

During the 1980s, which is usually referred to as the International Drinking Water Supply and Sanitation Decade (IDWSSD), a total of US$ 133.9 billion were invested in water supply and sanitation, of which US$ 75 billion (55%) was spent on providing water supply (WRI, 1998). The Supply Driven Approach (SDA) was one of the distinct features that characterized the relationship between donor agencies and developing countries during this decade (Seppälä, 2002). The adoption of this approach was documented in the attempt to provide, not only well-off households, but also poor households, with access to improved safe water, with an emphasis on the public health aspects of water supply and sanitation. The latter was attempted through the introduction of low-cost affordable technologies, which existed at the time. As a result, SDA was driven by a technology-oriented approach that aimed to increase water supply. Technologies that were considered suitable to serve people with low income included hand pumps or community taps. Providing in-house tap water connection was not considered an affordable option.

Another important feature of SDA is the so-called 'affordability rule of thumb'. This refers to the widely used assumption that people are willing to spend 3–5% of their income on water and thus that the design specification of a water system should not require households to pay more than 5% of their income. As Merret (2002) indicates, this 5% rule which is ascribed to van Damme and White (1984 in Merret, 2002) has been documented since 1975 (World Bank, 1975, in Merret, 2002). In short, the basic premise of the SDA is that poor people cannot afford safe drinking water if its provision amounts to more than 3–5% of their income.

The modest achievements of the policies that were adopted during the 'Water Decade' led to disappointment. In their review of relevant evaluation studies, DFID (1999) suggested that it was observed that water and sanitation systems had problems of under-use, poor maintenance and poor cost recovery. Mu, Whittington and Briscoe (1990, in Merret, 2002) mention that there are simply too many leaking taps, abandoned water systems and defunct village water committees for anyone to be sanguine about the current rate of progress. These and many other relevant studies provide evidence that many developing countries have failed in their programme of water provision. Among the various possible causes of this failure, the lack of demand-driven policies and the failure to integrate the economic nature of water into policy-making, are considered to be the most important ones. As Whittington et al. (1990) put it: 'designs for new systems are generally made and projects constructed with little understanding in household water demand behavior' (Whittington, Lauria and Mu, 1991, p. 179 in Merret, 2002).

The need for a shift from the engineering/Supply Driven Approach to the economic/Demand Driven Approach is becoming obvious. Consumers, including households in rural area, may be willing to pay (WTP) substantially more for higher levels (in terms of accessibility, quality and quantity) of water services. Simply relying on the 3–5% rule of thumb could be shown to be erroneous (DFID, 1999). The need for the adoption of the DDA has been formally introduced in 1992 with the Dublin Principle. The DDA and the Demand Responsive Approach (DRA) are central concepts in the post-Water Decade period (Seppälä, 2002). This constitutes one of the most important paradigmatic changes in water and sanitation policy-making.

The Demand Driven Approach (DDA) attracted widespread support as well as opposition. There have been growing concerns that the DDA could lead to inequitable provision of water. For example, the application of the full-cost recovery principle (one of the main implications of DDA) has been heavily criticized because it led to the poor being denied access. In addition, setting an appropriate price for water is also problematic in practice, because not only is water an economic good, but it is also a basic need, a merit good, as well as a social and environmental resource. Moreover, privatization of water provision services, which is supported by the DDA, has also been a disputed solution to the inefficiency inherent in the public provision of water services. Proposals to privatize water provision in developing countries have been strongly resisted, especially by local and international NGOs. In Indonesia, recently, international donor agencies such as the World Bank have been forcefully accused of ignoring issues of social equity in favour of increased efficiency, because they supported privatization in the water sector.

4. THE ROLE OF VALUATION METHODS IN DDA

The bulk of evidence in favour of the argument that households are willing to pay more than just 5% of their income for improved water services derives from willingness to pay studies, most of which use the contingent valuation method (CVM). These studies constitute the backbone of the DDA (see Merret, 2002, for a review of these studies).

CVM, however, is only one of many methods of economic valuation to infer people's preferences. There are basically two broad approaches to valuation, namely the direct and indirect approaches. Straight approaches attempt to elicit preferences directly by the use of survey and experimental techniques in which people are asked openly to state or reveal their willingness to pay for a proposed change in a hypothetical situation. The indirect approaches seek to elicit preferences from actual observed behaviour in markets. Preferences over goods and services are revealed indirectly, when individuals purchase marketed goods which are related to the good or service in question. The hedonic method is one of the indirect approaches. One main advantage of the hedonic method is that inference on valuation derives from observed behaviour in real markets. As a result, the reliability of related inference on people's valuation is enhanced compared to that derived from hypothetical methods (Arrow et al., 1993). Hence when the required data is available indirect methods are usually preferred.

In this chapter, we use the hedonic technique to infer how much people are willing to pay for access to safe and improved domestic water, which is an attribute of a house whose presence or absence may affect the willingness to pay (WTP) for the house as a whole. Hence, the structure of housing rents and prices will reflect these differentials. By using data on rent/prices of different properties we can in principle identify the contribution which water related attributes make to the value of the traded good, the house. This identifies an implicit or shadow price for these attributes, which in turn can be used to calculate total willingness to pay for their provision. The method commonly used to implement this approach is the hedonic technique pioneered by Griliches (1971) and formalized by Rosen (1974).

The objective of the analysis that follows is to examine if and by how much households in urban and rural Indonesia value the existence of various types of domestic water sources, which are situated in, or accessible from, their houses. This is attempted by indirectly testing whether the existence of these water sources is associated with the value of their houses. The analysis is performed separately for urban and rural households in order to investigate possible differences in their preferences. If respective preferences and derived WTP values for improved water sources are similar between these two samples, and if these values constitute more than 3–5% of sample-specific mean incomes, respectively, then results will provide support for the potential of the DDA. If the reverse is true, then two scenarios are possible. Low respective values of willingness to pay may be due to either the low quality of provision or to severe income constraints. Such results indicate the need for supply-side management and/or subsidization of water provision.

4. EMPIRICAL ANALYSIS

4.1 Case-study Background

Indonesia is endowed with approximately 6% of the world's total freshwater resources. Although this seems to suggest an abundance of water in the country, seasonal and spatial variability in the distribution of water resources gives rise to periodic regional water shortages, especially in some areas in the islands of Java, Bali and Nusa Tenggara. Although the percentage of the population without access to improved water sources was reduced from 31% in 1990 to 24% in 2000, this translates into more than 50 million people vulnerable to deadly health risks owing to the lack of safe water sources. The problem is more acute in urban regions, where the number of people without access to safe water sources has increased from 5.45 million in 1990 to 7.76 million in 2000.

Since 1980, government policies geared towards increasing access to safe water have mainly focused on improving physical access, by bringing in appropriate cost-effective – and in particular, capital cost-reducing – technologies for water supply. During the 1980s (also referred to as the International Decade of Water Supply and Sanitation (IDWSS)), it was thought that hand pumps and community taps were the appropriate technologies for low-income people, while in-house tap water connection was not considered an affordable option. Low access to pipe water in urban areas is also partly a result of the poor performance of publicly owned private water companies (PDAM), which are poorly regulated, financially mismanaged, priced with inefficient tariff structures and understaffed in terms of the quality of their human resources (World Bank, 1997). Moreover, public water infrastructure faces problems of unsustainability, with most systems breaking down long before their planned design lives, in spite of training in operations and maintenance by the Indonesian government and NGOs (Evans et al., 2001). Lessons learned from the IDWSS point to a lack of demand management (and the existing focus on supply-side management) as the source of the persistent problem of unsustainable use of water related infrastructure in Indonesia. Hence, the need for demand-driven management policies seems urgent.

4.2 The Dataset

The Indonesia Family Life Survey (IFLS)[2] is a continuing longitudinal socio-economic survey, the first wave of which was conducted in 1993 (IFLS1). The second wave (IFLS2) was conducted in 1997, although an additional supplement for capturing the ongoing economic crisis was conducted in 1998 (IFLS2+). The third wave, which has not yet been completed, was conducted in 2000. The sampling scheme used was stratified on provinces, and then randomly sampled within provinces. Thirteen of the nation's 26 provinces were selected with the aim of capturing a representative sample of the cultural and socio-economic diversity of Indonesia. Within each of the 13 provinces, 321 enumeration areas (EAs) – each area capturing a single village – were randomly selected, over-sampling urban EAs and EAs in smaller provinces to facilitate urban–rural and Javanese–non-Javanese comparisons. Finally, within each selected EA, households were randomly selected (Frankenberg and Thomas, 2000).

In the IFLS2 dataset, 339 households (representing 6.34% of the whole sample) rent their houses (and report their monthly rent), and 5,008 households are either self-owned or occupied (and report their imputed monthly rent). We focus our empirical analysis on households that report imputed monthly rent, in an attempt to avoid possible inconsistencies between data on actual and imputed rent. The water-related characteristics of the house are the focus variables in this hedonic analysis. In particular, we are interested in the valuation of piped, pump and well water, together with water sources located outside the house (when these are used for domestic purposes such as drinking and cooking – 'main use' – and for other uses such as bath and laundry – 'other use'). Based on this information, dummy variables for the three types of domestic water sources, that is, piped, pump and well water were constructed, together with two variables indicating distance to outside water sources, measured in metres.

Variables representing the structural characteristics of the house include the size of the house, number of rooms, house level/storey, material for wall, floor and roof, existence of toilet, quality of the ventilation, and garbage collection system. One of the important neighbourhood characteristics is the accessibility of the house to employment. This is captured by the variable indicating distance from village head office to the centre of the district, measured in kilometres. Other neighbourhood characteristics are captured by a proxy variable indicating the median per capita expenditure on food and non-food items in the neighbourhood/community. A dummy variable for each of the 13 provinces is created to capture the location-specific characteristics of a house. For the urban sample, the reference for this dummy variable is Jakarta, the province of the capital, whereas for the rural sample the reference is West Java province (the next most highly developed region after Jakarta). The reason for not using the same reference is because there is no rural area in the capital. Descriptive statistics of the variables in the dataset are presented in Table 6.1.

4.3 Estimation Model and Empirical Results

Unfortunately, the theoretical underpinnings of hedonic analysis do not suggest a specific functional form. Therefore, choosing the best functional form is merely an empirical question. To this end we employ a flexible functional form using the box-cox transformation method. The hedonic equation to be estimated is

$$y^{(\lambda)} = \alpha + \sum_i \beta_i x_{1i}^{(\lambda)} + \sum_j \gamma_j x_{2j} + \varepsilon \tag{6.1}$$

where

$$y^{(\lambda)} = \frac{y^{\lambda} - 1}{\lambda};\ x_{1i}^{(\lambda)} = \frac{x_{1i}^{\lambda} - 1}{\lambda}$$

Table 6.1 Descriptive statistics of variables in the hedonic equation

	Urban sample		Rural sample	
	mean	s.d.	mean	s.d.
Monthly rent (Rp)	474,529	(5,693,637)	94,347	(709,590)
Structural characteristics				
Size of the house (m squared)	83.162	(103.987)	71.636	(106.324)
Number of rooms	5.642	(2.212)	4.697	(1.703)
Multi-level house (1, 0)	0.185	(0.388)	0.055	(0.229)
Floor material is ceramics/tiles (1, 0)	0.486	(0.500)	0.196	(0.397)
Wall material is cements/ bricks (1, 0)	0.761	(0.427)	0.463	(0.499)
Roof material is concrete (1, 0)	0.008	(0.087)	0.001	(0.027)
Presence of toilet (1, 0)	0.746	(0.435)	0.494	(0.500)
Garbage is collected (1, 0)	0.459	(0.498)	0.009	(0.093)
Ventilation is adequate (1, 0)	0.782	(0.413)	0.735	(0.441)
Water characteristics				
Presence of piped water (1, 0)	0.204	(0.403)	0.041	(0.198)
Presence of pump water (1, 0)	0.247	(0.431)	0.061	(0.239)
Presence of well water (1, 0)	0.121	(0.326)	0.070	(0.255)
Distance to water/main use (m)	16.494	(149.995)	97.844	(371.731)
Distance to water/other use (m)	4.789	(34.811)	27.334	(123.200)
Neighbourhood characteristics				
Distance to district centre (km)	8.279	(10.536)	31.642	(32.926)
Median per capita expenditure (Rp 000)	80.773	(40.081)	42.618	(14.577)
Dummy provinces				
North Sumatera (1, 0)	0.087	(0.281)	0.037	(0.188)
West Sumatera (1, 0)	0.030	(0.170)	0.049	(0.217)
South Sumatera (1, 0)	0.034	(0.181)	0.046	(0.210)
Lampung (1, 0)	0.017	(0.129)	0.070	(0.255)
Jakarta (1, 0)	0.183	(0.387)	–	–
West Java (1, 0)	0.169	(0.375)	0.145	(0.352)
Central Java (1, 0)	0.123	(0.329)	0.173	(0.378)
Yogyakarta (1, 0)	0.071	(0.256)	0.037	(0.188)
East Java (1, 0)	0.133	(0.340)	0.154	(0.361)
Bali (1, 0)	0.038	(0.191)	0.064	(0.245)
West Nusa Tenggara (1, 0)	0.038	(0.191)	0.111	(0.314)
South Kalimantan (1, 0)	0.033	(0.178)	0.057	(0.232)
South Sulawesi (1, 0)	0.045	(0.207)	0.057	(0.231)
Number of observations	2113		2739	

with α, β, and γ representing vectors of coefficients to be estimated, y the monthly rent of the house, x_{1i} vector of variables to be transformed (that is, size of the house, number of rooms, and median expenditure of the neighbourhood), x_{2j} the vector of other non-transformed variables (dummy variables and variables that are not strictly positive and thus could not be transformed), and λ is the parameter of the transformation (the functional form is linear when $\lambda = 1$ and log-linear when $\lambda = 0$).

We use maximum likelihood (ML) to estimate equation (6.1) together with the λ coefficients for each of the two data samples. Estimated results suggest rejection of linearity and log-linearity of the hedonic function for both the urban and rural samples, with a value of λ equal to −0.164 and −0.092, respectively. The results of the OLS estimation of the non-linear hedonic equation (after variables transformation has been imposed) are shown in Table 6.2. ML estimation results of the non-linear hedonic function are reported in Appendix 6.1.

Table 6.2 Results of the hedonic equation estimation

Variables	Urban		Rural	
	Coef.	s.e.	Coef.	s.e.
Structural characteristics				
Size of the house (m squared)^	0.06204	0.012***	0.14567	0.023***
Number of rooms^	0.09169	0.014***	0.12221	0.030***
Multi-level house (1, 0)	0.02468	0.009***	0.00370	0.034
Floor material is ceramics/ tiles (1, 0)	0.03466	0.008***	0.02243	0.023
Wall material is cements/ bricks (1, 0)	0.04826	0.009***	0.06988	0.020***
Roof material is concrete (1, 0)	0.07990	0.038**	−0.23104	0.287
Presence of toilet (1, 0)	0.03670	0.009***	0.05141	0.017***
Garbage is collected (1, 0)	0.04932	0.009***	0.18936	0.084**
Ventilation is adequate (1, 0)	0.01503	0.009*	0.05427	0.019***
Water characteristics				
Presence of piped water (1, 0)	0.03321	0.010***	0.05462	0.042
Presence of pump water (1, 0)	0.02197	0.009**	0.04403	0.035
Presence of well water (1, 0)	−0.00289	0.011	0.05334	0.031*
Distance to water/main use (m)	0.00000	0.000	0.00002	0.000
Distance to water/other use (m)	0.00004	0.000	0.00006	0.000
Neighbourhood characteristics				
Distance to district centre (km)	−0.00081	0.000**	0.00061	0.000**
Median per capita expenditure (Rp 000)^	0.18868	0.021***	0.15965	0.035***

Table 6.2 (continued)

Variables	Urban		Rural	
	Coef.	s.e.	Coef.	s.e.
Dummy provinces				
North Sumatera (1, 0)	−0.15295	0.016***	−0.32628	0.046***
West Sumatera (1, 0)	−0.08419	0.022***	−0.16052	0.042***
South Sumatera (1, 0)	−0.13383	0.020***	−0.14975	0.044***
Lampung (1, 0)	−0.07120	0.027***	−0.20551	0.039***
West Java (1, 0)	−0.07233	0.012***		
Central Java (1, 0)	−0.16417	0.014***	−0.25402	0.030***
Yogyakarta (1, 0)	−0.05549	0.016***	0.02103	0.047
East Java (1, 0)	−0.14701	0.014***	−0.20792	0.030***
Bali (1, 0)	−0.07564	0.020***	−0.02619	0.040
West Nusa Tenggara (1, 0)	−0.10088	0.021***	−0.14004	0.034***
South Kalimantan (1, 0)	−0.09104	0.022***	−0.28496	0.041***
South Sulawesi (1, 0)	−0.06832	0.021***	−0.13832	0.044***
Constant	4.13952	0.068***	5.42375	0.133***
Lambda	−0.164149	0.010***	−0.091864	0.007***
Adj-R^2	0.4918		0.1819	
Mean VIF	1.53		1.45	
White statistics	276.0753		164.7198	
Number of observations	2113		2739	

Notes: ^ box-cox transformed variable; *** significant at 1% level; ** significant at 5% level; * significant at 10% level.

All structural characteristics significantly influence the rental price of urban houses. In rural areas, however, the rental value of the house is not significantly associated with whether the house is multi-level nor with the house's roof material. Other qualities of housing structure such as the house's size, number of rooms, floor and wall material, presence of toilet, garbage collection and adequate ventilation, do, however, have a significant effect on respective rental prices.

As expected, the proxy used to indicate the quality of the neighbourhood's environment (that is, the average median per capita expenditure in the neighbourhood) strongly affects the rental value of houses in both rural and urban areas. Distance to district centre captures, among other things, the degree of a house's proximity to the location of its tenants' employment. Most people living in rural areas work outside city centres because of their strong dependence on agriculture. However, people in rural areas seem to value proximity to the city centre, possibly because it allows them to trade their agricultural products in cities, at lower transportation costs. Most people living in urban areas work close to or in city centres. The unexpected negative sign of the coefficient of this variable (although not significant) could indicate a preference for living outside cities, where the provision and quality of environmental amenities is higher. In addition, the provision of improved transportation to and from district centres decreases the costs associated with choosing to live in out-of-city areas.

Geographical variation by provinces also has a strong effect on the rental value of a house. In the urban hedonic equation, all provincial dummies are significant at less than the 1% level of significance. The rental value of houses is highest in the capital of the country, which explains the negative sign in the coefficients of provincial dummy variables. Provincial dummy variables also capture location-specific variation in the cost of living and other regional differentials, for which data do not exist.

Households in urban areas do value domestic water sources as reflected in the significant coefficient indicating the presence of pumped and piped water in the house. As implicitly revealed by the estimated hedonic price function, the presence of well water – which is usually of lower quality (due to contamination) and situated in less convenient locations than piped water – does not significantly affect the price of occupying a house. For rural households, however, only well water is significant (at marginal, 10%, level of significance) in explaining variation in rental prices and the house characteristics that represent the availability of an improved domestic water source, that is, piped and pump water, are not significant.

These empirical results allow us to make inferences about the preferences of urban and rural households for the different types of domestic water sources. Households in urban areas value the existence of piped and pump water, but not well water. Households in rural areas value only well water. Piped water is generally considered the most reliable water source and has the best water quality among the three sources. It is mostly provided by the publicly owned water company (PDAM), which delivers clean, treated, water supply to households. Well water is not usually treated before use, although significantly contaminated in some regions (from chemicals and/or sea-water intrusion). As far as convenience of use is concerned, well water is considered the least convenient.

Moreover, the results have interesting policy implications as they suggest that willingness to pay for improved water sources is not as universal as some proponents of DDA argue. Households in rural areas with much lower income (the income of urban households is on average twice as high as that of rural households; see Table 6.1) are not willing to pay for improved domestic water sources. This result may highlight two possible scenarios: (a) the bad quality of service provided by the PDAM with regard to piped water or

(b) the existence of severe income constraints in rural areas. Scenario (a) indicates the failure of the Supply Driven Approach (SDA) when it functions through institutions that lack incentive structures. Scenario (b) indicates the low potential of the Demand Driven Approach (DDA) to solve water allocation problems, as heavy subsidization is still called for.

Moreover, households' valuation of proximity to outside water sources is not significant in explaining rental prices in either of the two samples. This could be explained by the fact that outside water sources are communal or public goods and as a result people free ride on their use. This is the usual free-rider problem in the provision of public goods, an issue which does not arise in the case of domestic water sources as these fall into the category of publicly provided private goods. The insignificance of distance to outside water sources confirms the findings of an earlier hedonic study in the Philippines by North and Griffin (1993).

Finally, we calculate the value of the willingness to pay for having piped and pump water for the urban sample in rupiahs (see Appendix 6.2 for relevant details). Our calculations suggest that in the urban area, monthly WTP for piped water is Rp 13,785[3] (3.6% of median expenditure) and for pump water is Rp 8,830 (2.3% of median expenditure). This suggests that, on average, people's willingness to pay for having improved domestic water sources, even in urban areas, falls below 5% of income. Interestingly, North and Griffin's (1993) study in the Philippines, also using the hedonic approach, finds that WTP for in-house piped water amounts to 2.4% of income, which is comparable to our estimates.

5. CONCLUSION AND POLICY IMPLICATIONS

Water is an economic good, but also a necessity for life, hence a fundamental right of all people. If the premise of the DDA is implemented, while that right is overlooked, it will result in a large number of poor people being prevented from accessing a good/service which is essential for their survival. It is, however, also true that the efficient provision of water should pay due attention to the premises of the DAA, as these enable optimal allocation of resources over people and time. However, once resources have been allocated, equity considerations should be considered. The challenge faced by the policy-reorientation in providing water supply in developing countries is to redistribute the increased social welfare achieved through a more optimal allocation of resources in such a way that equity considerations are addressed.

In Indonesia, the prevailing instrument that is suggested to support the implementation of the DDA is privatization of water provision, together with a substantial reduction in subsidy to investment in the water sector. Recently, the issue of privatization in the water sector has been one of the main topics of public dispute. The government is proposing a new water resource bill that will create more opportunities for the private sector to participate in water provision. However, the promotion of privatization of water provision in developing countries already faces strong resistance. Thus, if privatization could enhance the efficiency of water provision (this is still disputed in the relevant literature[4]), it has to be planned and implemented after careful study of its distributional impact on all income groups of the respective populations. Moreover, subsidy reductions should be considered in terms both of their efficiency but also of their impact on equity.

APPENDIX 6.1. RESULT OF THE HEDONIC EQUATION ESTIMATION (MAXIMUM LIKELIHOOD)

	Urban sample		Rural sample	
	Coef.	chi^2(df)	Coef.	chi^2(df)
Structural characteristics				
*Size of the house (m squared)^*	0.06204	29.04***	0.14567	38.87***
Number of rooms^	0.09169	44.12***	0.12221	16.74***
Multi-level house (1, 0)	0.02468	6.95***	0.00370	0.01
Floor material is ceramics/ tiles (1, 0)	0.03466	17.88***	0.02243	0.97
Wall material is cements/ bricks (1, 0)	0.04826	26.88***	0.06988	12.67***
Roof material is concrete (1, 0)	0.07990	4.42**	−0.23104	0.66
Presence of toilet (1, 0)	0.03670	17.39***	0.05141	9.22***
Garbage is collected (1, 0)	0.04932	33.57***	0.18936	5.14**
Ventilation is adequate (1, 0)	0.01503	2.98*	0.05427	8.20***
Water characteristics				
Presence of piped water (1, 0)	0.03321	11.38***	0.05462	1.68
Presence of pump water (1, 0)	0.02197	5.97**	0.04403	1.61
Presence of well water (1, 0)	−0.00289	0.07	0.05334	2.99*
Distance to water/main use (m)	0.00000	0.01	0.00002	0.68
Distance to water/other use (m)	0.00004	0.17	0.00006	0.97
Neighbourhood characteristics				
Distance to district centre (km)	−0.00081	5.82**	0.00061	5.64**
Median per capita expenditure (Rp 000)^	0.18868	80.64***	0.15965	20.56***

Appendix 6.1 (continued)

	Urban sample		Rural sample	
	Coef.	chi²(df)	Coef.	chi²(df)
Dummy provinces				
North Sumatera (1, 0)	−0.15295	94.90***	−0.32628	49.87***
West Sumatera (1, 0)	−0.08419	14.99***	−0.16052	14.52***
South Sumatera (1, 0)	−0.13383	43.07***	−0.14975	11.46***
Lampung (1, 0)	−0.07120	6.97***	−0.20551	28.29***
West Java (1, 0)	−0.07233	36.05***		
Central Java (1, 0)	−0.16417	133.62***	−0.25402	72.06***
Yogyakarta (1, 0)	−0.05549	12.44***	0.02103	0.20
East Java (1, 0)	−0.14701	102.81***	−0.20792	48.79***
Bali (1, 0)	−0.07564	14.49***	−0.02619	0.42
West Nusa Tenggara (1, 0)	−0.10088	23.92***	−0.14004	17.20***
South Kalimantan (1, 0)	−0.09104	17.04***	−0.28496	48.69***
South Sulawesi (1, 0)	−0.06832	10.69***	−0.13832	9.88***
Constant	4.13952		5.42375	
Log likelihood	−26063.9		−31546.2	
LR chi²(28)	1458.47		577.02	
Observation	2113		2739	

Notes: ^ box-cox transformed variable; *** significant at 1% level, ** significant at 5% level; * significant at 10% level.

APPENDIX 6.2: WILLINGNESS TO PAY CALCULATION

We rewrite the hedonic equation in box-cox form,

$$\frac{y^{\lambda}-1}{\lambda} = \alpha + \sum_i \beta_i \left(\frac{x_{1i}^{\lambda}-1}{\lambda} \right) + \sum_j \gamma_j x_{2j} + \theta w \tag{6.A1}$$

where the water characteristic in question is excluded from x_{2j} and written as w, and θ is its relevant coefficient. w is a dummy variable that has the value of 1 if the water source in question is available in the house, and 0 otherwise. Solving equation 6.A1 for y gives,

$$y(x_{1i}, x_{2i}, w) = \left[1 + \lambda\alpha + \sum_i \beta_i (x_{1i}^{\lambda} - 1) + \lambda \sum_j \gamma_j x_{2j} + \lambda\theta w \right]^{1/\lambda} \tag{6.A2}$$

We define willingness to pay for water source w as the difference between the rent (predicted by equation 6.A2) of a house with water source w available ($w = 1$) and the rent if the water source is unavailable ($w = 0$). Thus to calculate the willingness to pay for the water source in question we use:

$$\text{wtp} = y(\bar{x}_{1i}, \bar{x}_{2i}, 1) - y(\bar{x}_{1i}, \bar{x}_{2i}, 0) \tag{6.A3}$$

where the bar over the x variables indicate their mean value in the relevant sample.

NOTES

This chapter was written while Ariel Anshory Yusuf was visiting the Department of Economics/CSERGE, University College London. Both authors wish to thank Jerome Adda for helpful comments and discussions. The usual disclaimer applies.

1. Although the application of the hedonic technique in developing countries has been somewhat controversial due to the non-existence of fully developed and competitive housing markets, relevant valuation results are comparable to those derived from the application of other valuation techniques. For example, results from the application of the CVM in developing countries, a technique whose validity does not rest on the competitiveness of any underlying market, are on average comparable with those derived from hedonic analyses. See, for example, Jiwanji (2000), who provides a critical comparison of 15 CVM studies that derive willingness to pay (WTP) for water related characteristics.
2. IFLS was conducted by the Rand Institute, USA. For further information please see http://www.rand.org/labor/FLS/IFLS.
3. The exchange rate in 1997 (the year when the IFLS was conducted) was Rp 2,900/US$.
4. See Bauer (1997) and Trawick (2003).

REFERENCES

Arrow, K., Solow, R., Portney, P.R., Leamer, E.E., Radner, R. and Schuman, H. (1993), 'Report of the NOAA Panel on Contingent Valuation', *Federal Register*, **58** (10), 4601–14.

Bauer, C.J. (1997), 'Bringing Water Markets Down to Earth: The Political Economy of Water Rights in Chile, 1976–1995', *World Development*, **25**, 639–56.

Department for International Development (1999), *DFID Guidance Manual on Water Supply and Sanitation Programmes*, London: DFID.

Evans, B., Jaganathan, V., and Kingdom, W. (2001), *Serving Poor Consumers of Water Supply in Indonesia: Options for the Future*, Report to the World Bank, Washington DC: World Bank.

Frankenberg, E., and Thomas, D. (2000), *The Indonesia Family Life Survey (IFLS): Study Design and Results from Waves 1 and 2*, March 2000, Santa Monica, CA: RAND, DRU-2238/1-NIA/NICHD.

Griliches, Z. (1971), *Price Indices and Quality Change*, Cambridge, MA: Harvard University Press.

International Irrigation Management Institute (1997), 'Water as an Economic Good: A Solution or a Problem?', Research Report no. 14, Colombo, Sri Lanka.
Jiwanji, M. (2000), 'The Demand for Water in Developing Countries', MSc dissertation, University College London.
Merret, S. (2002), 'Behavioral Studies of the Domestic Demand for Water Services in Africa', *Water Policy*, **4**, 69–81.
North, J.H., and Griffin, C.C. (1993), 'Water Source as a Housing Characteristic: Hedonic Property Valuation and Willingness-to-Pay for Water', *Water Resources Research*, **29** (7), 1923–29.
Pearce, D., Whittington, D., Georgiou, S., and Moran, D. (1995), *Economic Values and the Environment in the Developing World*, A Report to the United Nations Environment Programme, UNEP.
Rosen, Sherwin (1974), 'Hedonic Prices and Implicit Markets: Product Differentiation in Pure Competition', *Journal of Political Economy*, **82** (1), 34–55.
Seppälä, O.T. (2002), 'Effective Water and Sanitation Policy Reform Implementation: Need for Systemic Approach and Stakeholder Participation', *Water Policy*, **4**, 367–88.
Trawick, Paul (2003), 'Against the Privatization of Water: An Indigenous Model for Improving Existing Laws and Successfully Governing the Commons', *World Development*, **31**, 977–96.
United Nations (2003), 'The Right to Water', Backgrounder paper to the International Year of Fresh Water 2003, United Nations.
World Bank (1997), *Indonesia Water Supply Sector Policy Framework (WSPF)*, Report to the Indonesian National Planning Agency (BAPPENAS).
World Resource Institute (WRI) (1998), *World Resource 1996–1997*, New York: Oxford University Press.

7. Conflicts in wildlife conservation: aggregating total economic values

Timothy Swanson and Andreas Kontoleon

1. INTRODUCTION

For at least 50 years economists have been arguing that identifying, assessing and then appropriating the maximum possible values for biodiversity is imperative for designing and implementing any biodiversity conserving wildlife strategy or policy (e.g. Krutilla, 1967). It would be safe to say that the economist's position has been sold and is by now almost universally acknowledged (e.g. OECD, 2002). A central concept in this reasoning is that of *Total Economic Value* (TEV) (Pearce and Turner, 1990). The concept was developed to encompass the plurality of values that individuals may hold for environmental resources. In the case of wildlife, these cover consumptive use values (e.g. wildlife products), non-consumptive use values (e.g. recreation) and non-use values. Use values (either consumptive or non-consumptive) are associated with flows derived from wildlife stocks (e.g. food, ornaments, medicines, recreational experiences and so on) that directly enter the individual's utility function. Non-use values are best seen as monetary expressions of the utility gained from knowing that certain wildlife related flows accrue to different constituencies. These beneficiaries may include other people in the present or the future as well as the species themselves. The concept of TEV has been treated as an accounting identity in which the various types of values all add up. In other words, it has been assumed that all categories of value are compatible with one another. Yet, this aggregative property of the TEV concept may not always be plausible but instead it may contain inherent trade-offs or conflicts. The source of conflict among values can be traced to the fact that different constituencies are driven by often conflicting motivations for wildlife conservation. For example, the expression of wildlife non-use values by one constituency (say through donations) may be in conflict with certain consumptive uses of the species enjoyed by another (such as hunting). In other words, often the utilization of wildlife from one constituent affects the production or utility functions of another, leading in essence to forms of production and consumption externalities between these parties. That is, conflicting values may be seen as expressions of production and/or consumption externalities.

Acknowledging and understanding the nature of such conflicts or externalities has important policy significance for two reasons. First, we argue that examining these conflicts is instrumental in understanding many of the disagreements witnessed within international wildlife conservation fora. For years different groups and constituencies have been at loggerheads over the direction that these institutions should take. The Convention on International Trade on Endangered Species of Wild Fauna and Flora (CITES) and biodiversity conventions are only the most apparent manifestations of such tormented institutions. The disagreements mostly centre upon the type and the extent of utilization practices that a particular species ought be subjected to. For example, under the auspices of CITES, African states have engaged in a battle over the future of the elephant. On the one hand, the countries of the south wish to relax CITES trade restrictions on elephant products (such as ivory, hides, meat and trophies). They argue that values appropriated from trade would provide much needed income to local rural communities as well instate the incentives for the continued conservation of the species. On the other hand, the countries of the north and west of the continent, which rely heavily on ecotourism receipts, oppose lifting current trade restrictions. Their main fear is that the resumption of trade would restore black market prices for ivory and encourage poachers to destroy their elephant herds, one of the key attractions in their tourism industry (Brown, 2000).[1] This dispute is exemplary of the case where different types of consumptive use values that are flowing towards different constituencies are in conflict. Conceptually, it is akin to a production externality. A different form of conflict surrounds wildlife species such as the minke whale or the African black rhinoceros. Here the main opposing constituencies are those in favour of numerous forms of (sustainable) utilization of the species (e.g. sport hunting, dehorning, sale of stockpiles and so on) and those groups who are only willing to support non-intrusive conservation practices (e.g. establishment of protected parks, ecotourism and so on). In essence, the consumptive uses sought out by one group are producing a type of public ‘bad’ and hence such forms of dispute resemble a typical consumption externality.

Secondly, understanding the nature of these conflicts is important for promoting one of the main conservation goals of developing countries: the appropriation of the maximum possible conservation value. Many of the problems faced by endangered species (poaching, habitat conversions) are driven fundamentally by the tight resource constraints faced by the peoples of developing countries and their governments. It is well documented that if affected state governments do not perceive the benefits that may flow from the conservation of a particular species, then they will be unlikely to allocate large amounts of available funds to anti-poaching patrols and additional protected areas. Even if they do, these allocations will usually come to nothing if the local peoples do not perceive the benefits to be derived from sharing their lands and resources with the wildlife (Swanson and Barbier, 1992). Hence, the maximization of the value of the endangered species, from the perspective of the local peoples and governments, is very likely a fundamentally important first step towards the conservation of the species. Does this mean that local policy makers should pursue all types of wildlife management policies in order to maximize the appropriated conservation value? We argue that this need not always be the case and that certain forms of wildlife utilization are problematic policies to be pursued from the perspective of value maximization. For example, it may be justified to deny consumptive uses of a species (hunting, commercial trade and so on) provided that the values derived from these uses are less than those stemming from non-consumptive uses (tourism, conservation contributions and so on), *and given that the two forms of values are in conflict with one another.* That is, the aggregate contributions to conservation may be maximized by concentrating on a single category of values (e.g. non-use) if the two do not 'add up' on account of fundamental objections of the greater one towards the other.

This chapter examines the extent and nature of these conflicts in aggregating wildlife values within the context of a contingent valuation (CV) study on the Namibian black rhinoceros. This particular endangered species has been the subject of extraordinary control measures in many of its range states. Further, the trade in all rhino products has been banned since the species was listed in CITES's Appendix 1 about 20 years ago. Yet, despite these measures, the African black rhino populations continue to be under threat. In the midst of these dire circumstances, the disagreements over the direction of rhino conservation policies continue to be as strong as ever. The main disputes are between those parties who are in favour of species conservation, supported by a broad range of policies, and those who are willing to support only non-intrusive means of conservation. Conceptually, these disputes resemble consumption externalities between different conservation parties in which the value or benefit received by one party derived from a specific wildlife flow subtracts from the utility of the other.

This study examines the extent and nature of these conflicts. In particular, we attempt to discern whether specific individuals and groups interested in the conservation of the rhinoceros (e.g. supporters of the CITES convention) will withdraw their support when other groups and individuals are contributing to conservation in a very different fashion. For example, will a group interested in contributing to the conservation of the rhinoceros for animal welfare motives withdraw their contribution in the face of conservation based on consumptive uses such as trophy rhino? Or, is it possible to aggregate across both constituencies in order to maximize the amount of value available for conservation? In other words, to what extent do conflicting perspectives on conservation imply conflicting (or accumulating) values? The case study explores whether such conflicting values exist over the conservation of the black rhino and attempts to discern the optimal policy mix that would minimize such potential conflicts, thus maximizing the total appropriable values.

Section 2 discusses the conceptual nature of conflicting perspectives in wildlife conservation. Section 3 discusses how this framework applies to the case of the black rhinoceros. Section 4 describes the details of the contingent valuation study. Section 5, 6 and 7 discuss the main findings of the study. Section 8 presents the results from a regression analysis that examined the motivational underpinnings of the elicited willingness to pay (WTP) values. Section 9 concludes the discussion.

2. CONFLICTS AND TRADE-OFFS ON TOTAL ECONOMIC VALUE

The concept of total economic value has been viewed as an aggregative concept that combines values from both stocks of living rhinos (e.g. the value obtained from retaining the option to view rhinos in the future) and the flows of goods and services deriving from currently existing rhinos (e.g. the value of rhino horn sales). The former are usually referred to as non-use values while the latter are (consumptive and non-consumptive) use values. We argue in this chapter that the main conflicts or trade-offs between values concern categories of use and non-use values. This section discusses the nature of these values in an attempt to explain why and how these values can in principle conflict.

Use values are those derived from the actual or potential consumption of flows (goods and services) derived from a particular species. Defining and empirically assessing these values is relatively uncomplicated since it simply requires the use of standard microeconomic demand analysis. Whilst conceptualizing and measuring forms of use values is considered to be straightforward, the same is not true for non-use values, where numerous conceptual and empirical issues are still troubling academics and policy makers (see Swanson et al., 2002a for a detailed review). A central problem with the concept of non-use values is that it has been interpreted as the values held for the stock of a resource. This spawns various troubles since the idea that people have pre-existing preferences regarding living things, of which they have little or no personal knowledge or experience and which they have no intention to use in any way, is to many problematic. Because of these conceptual difficulties we believe that non-use values are probably best thought of as attempts by individuals to channel flows of value to others about whom they care, rather than as a general willingness to provide stocks of the resource in the abstract. We believe that individuals are willing to pay to support policies that they believe will channel flows of value to other individuals and groups about which they care – even relatively remote groups, such as other people in this generation, future descendants or members of the endangered species itself. Willingness to pay values derived from donation data or CV studies will then be an expression of altruism value (when conservation flows are channelled to other people in the current generation), bequest values (when conservation flows are channelled to other people in future generations) and animal welfare values (when conservation flows are channelled to the species itself). Such expressed stock-related values depend crucially on the expectations of the respondent about who will receive the benefits of the flows from those stocks.

We argue that this motivational assumption regarding expressions of positive stock related values is much more fruitful than other interpretations of the concept since it avoids some of the key criticisms levelled against its use in environmental decision making. First of all, this motivational assumption can be expressed formally through well-grounded economic theory. This addresses the misconception held by many critics that the concept of non-use values has no coherent behavioural basis. More specifically, the motivational assumption evoked in this chapter can be readily modelled through a model of choice that incorporates the flows received by one party in the utility function of another 'non-user'. The non-user of a resource is thus seen as maximizing utility by optimally allocating stock related flows across time and constituencies. This form of interdependence between non-use and 'beneficiary' has been loosely termed 'altruism' and has been formally modelled in various different ways (see e.g. Johansson, 1992, and McConnell, 1997, for reviews).

Secondly, the type of altruism that most closely explains non-use values is that of paternalistic altruism. Under this form of altruism, the source of non-use value is the knowledge that particular flows accrue to specific constituencies while the impact of these flows on the welfare of these 'beneficiaries' is irrelevant to the 'benefactor'. This framework, thus, has the benefit of not requiring the conceptually difficult task of positing a welfare function for other people or species.[2] This kind of altruism resembles a consumption externality where one person's consumption of a particular flow enters another person's utility function. For the altruist or the 'non-user' of the resource, there is no trade-off between service flow to the beneficiary and (overall) utility to the beneficiary. The altruist who positively values a particular flow accruing to a certain beneficiary is better off even if the beneficiary consumes resourse services (flows) but suffers a loss in real income or a reduction in overall utility (McConnell, 1997).

Thirdly, the interpretation of non-use values discussed in this chapter is operationally more useful since it allows for the testing of empirical hypotheses. For the purposes of this chapter, the conception of non-use value described here allows for the examination of the conflicts that may be inherent in the TEV concept. This is so since it allows for these conflicts to be assessed in terms of a negative consumption externality: the disutility experienced by one group (non-users) from the consumption of particular flows by other groups.

3. THE MANY VALUES OF THE BLACK RHINO

It is clear that any species of wildlife, such as the rhinoceros, exhibits values under both the use and non-use value categories. Sport hunters and tourists spend vast sums of money each year in order to engage in the direct use of the wildlife of African countries; for example, Kenya earned approximately US$349 million in 1988 from primarily wildlife-based tourism activities, while the financial contribution of trophy hunting to Namibia in 1991 was approximately N$25 million (Cumming et al., 1990; Barnes, 1995). Equally clearly, the observed non-use values of the black rhinoceros are also quite substantial. Appeals for conservation funds for these species by organizations such as the World Wide Fund for Nature (WWF) provide funding for vast conservation programmes across these same countries. These programmes are usually being funded by means of donations from persons living on the other side of the globe from the wildlife, with little or no prospect of ever actually seeing one of the animals in its native country. In 1990, donations to wildlife conservation organizations in the US alone amounted to at least US$273 million, with $42 million flowing to the WWF (WCMC, 1992). In addition to the evidence from observed market data, use and non-use values for wildlife conservation have been exhibited in numerous stated preference studies (see Table 7.1).

Therefore, it is apparent that this form of accounting (under a wide range of values) makes sense for many wildlife species. People around the world are willing to pay for the conservation of wildlife on account of a wide range of individual motivations. Some do so for the particular function that the wildlife species is able to perform for themselves, for example, providing enjoyment in the course of recreation or providing products (leather, medicines) for their personal use in everyday life. Others do so for a wider

Table 7.1 WTP for endangered species

Species and habitats	WTP in US$ p.a., p.p.	Additional information
Namibian black rhinos	15–20	Swanson et al. (2002)
Bald eagle	19.28–28.25	Stevens et al. (1991), donation
Bald eagle	10.62–75.31	Boyle et al. (1987)
Striped shiner	1–5	Boyle et al. (1987)
Northern spotted owl	34.8	Rubin et al. (1991), p.h.
Whooping crane	31	Loomis et al. (1993), p.h.
Wild turkey	7.11–11.86	Stevens et al. (1991), donation
Coyote	3.40–5.35	Stevens et al. (1991), donation
Bottlenose dolphin	7.0	Pearce (1996), US$90
Sea otter	25	Loomis et al. (1993), p.h.
Monk seal	62–103	Samples et al. (1990), 1
Blue whale	40	Loomis et al. (1993), p.h.
Humpback whale	125–142	Samples et al. (1990), 1
Sea turtles	13	Loomis et al. (1993), p.h.

Notes:
(i) Values not adjusted for inflation
(ii) p.h.: per household; 1: once-only payment; p.p.: per person: p.a.: per annum
(iii) See Swanson et al. (2002b) for reference details.

and more complex range of reasons corresponding to the non-use values. These are best viewed as values stemming from the belief that enhanced stocks correlate with an enhanced flow of goods and services to some other beneficiary (other individuals or groups, future generations, the animals themselves).[3]

The central question we are addressing in this chapter is the extent to which the concept of TEV is not a simple accounting identity but is imbued with inherent trade-offs and conflicts between values. The source of these conflicts can be traced to conflicting motivations for conservation across constituencies. For example, expressed values for conservation that are motivated primarily by animal welfare concerns may be in conflict with certain forms of wildlife utilization that compromise the well-being of the species. It was argued in the previous section that the nature of these conflicts would resemble a consumption externality. We now proceed to examine these conflicts in a contingent valuation case study on the black rhinoceros. The study explored the extent and nature of the possible conflicts described in the previous sections. Further, the findings from this study provide insights into the choice of optimal set of wildlife conservation policies that minimizes these conflicts and maximizes total appropriable value for conservation.

4. A CONTINGENT VALUATION STUDY FOR THE PRESERVATION OF THE BLACK RHINO

The rhino survey was undertaken in the UK in a collaborative exercise between the Namibian Ministry of Parks and the Centre for Social and Economic Research for the Global Environment. The final study was conducted in 12 PTA (parent teacher association) meetings at elementary schools in Cambridgeshire during July 1996.[4] On the whole, 381 people were interviewed in group meetings involving between 18 and 72 people and lasting between 1 and 1.5 hours.[5]

Respondents were initially presented with information about the reasons for the decline in the black rhino population as having to do primarily with the poaching for rhino horn rather than habitat conversion. The consumptive uses for rhino horn were presented in a pragmatic way: as mainly an ingredient for producing traditional medicine with fever reducing properties which is widely used in Asia (and not as an aphrodisiac as is widely believed in Western societies). This first part of the group presentation ended with a reference to the institutional framework, focusing on the existing ban on international trade on rhino products. Respondents were then informed about the current anti-poaching measures existing in Namibia, highlighting the fact that they are insufficient due to lack of financial support. A proposed conservation programme for rhinos was then introduced: the Black Rhino Conservation Programme (BRCP), aiming to protect the existing Namibian black rhino population of 670 animals and to promote its increase to a population of 2000, within the next 25 years. This would be achieved through the creation of heavily guarded rhino sanctuaries.

The survey provides a unique opportunity to study the breadth and depth of the motivations driving the existence of non-use values for exotic wildlife. None of the individuals surveyed were residents of the country with which the study was concerned, none had visited this particular place, none had consumed or bought any products from rhino horn nor had any immediate intentions to do so. The surveyed group was instead being asked to assess how much they would be willing to contribute to the conservation of *another country's* wildlife for the benefit of *other* people of this or future generations and for the benefit of the rhino itself. The setting of the survey within the context of various management options then allowed for the examination of possible conflicts between the motives generating the stated values for conserving black rhino stocks.

Respondents were made aware of the fact that a current *shortfall* exists for the financing of the BRCP that would prevent its adoption. Two possible ways of covering this shortfall were described. First, by establishing an environmental tax surcharge (called the *International Direct Contribution* – IDC) levied on all UK taxpayers and secondly, by establishing a set of management programmes developing various uses of the Namibian black rhino in order to generate amounts of money, in part, to sustain their conservation efforts.

There was then a presentation on the proposed black rhino *management options*, along with the percentage of revenues that would be generated by each management option.[6] These options are denoted as A to F in Figure 7.1.

Option A involved 'increasing entry fees' to ecotourists entering the existing rhino nature reserves, and was described as being able to generate 6% of the funds required for conservation. Option B, 'sale of live rhinos', involved the sale of six rhinos per year to zoos across the world. This management option could raise 10% of the funds required for the BRCP. Option C, 'sale of stockpiled horns', involved selling the existing stockpiled horns in a controlled market setting. The rhino horn would be sold for the purposes of being used as an ingredient in the production of medicinal products that are in high demand in various Asian countries. This option could contribute 17% of the entire BRCP budget. Option D, 'dehorning operations', consisted of carefully executed procedures where trained personnel would tranquillize an adult rhino and then saw off its horn. The horn would then be sold in the same manner as the stockpiled horns. It was explained that rhino horn would re-grow in about 10 years' time. The revenues from harvesting the horns from about 80 rhinos per year would contribute towards the BRCP budget by 14%. Option E, 'darting safaris', consisted of organizing sport-hunting safaris where tourist-hunters would shoot rhinos with tranquillizer guns. Ten such expeditions per year could contribute 4% of the BRCP budget. The last management option (Option F), 'trophy hunting', involved tourist-hunters shooting and killing an adult black rhino. The hunts would be closely supervised by the park authorities so as to ensure that only one rhino per hunting expedition was killed. It was made clear that allowing for such low scale, carefully managed hunting would not endanger the survival of the rhino population. It is estimated that three hunting expeditions per year could cover 9% of the BRCP budget. Attention was called to the fact that some of these options would only be available if legal trade of rhino products was to be allowed. These options are the sale of stockpiled horns, dehorning, darting and hunting (those marked with an asterisk in Figure 7.1).

Since we used an open-ended elicitation format it would have been inappropriate to provide an exact figure for the revenue that could be raised by each management option. Instead, we only provided the *percentage* of the BRCP budget that might be raised by each management option. It has been shown that providing information on the actual distribution of cost

Option A – Increase in Entry Fees

- Photographic safaris, viewing of animals in the wild.
- *Reduce IDC by 6%*

Option B – Sales of Live Rhinos

- A small number of animals (e.g. 6 out of 670) may be sold each year on a long-term basis.
- *Reduce IDC by 10%*

Option C – Sales of Stockpiled Horns*

- Existing stockpiled horns may be marketed in a controlled trade setting.
- *Reduce IDC by 17%*

Option D – Dehorning Operations*

- Safe procedure: shooting adult rhinos with tranquillizer guns and then sawing off their horns. Rhino horn re-grows: a horn is replaced in about 10 years.
- Harvested horns could be sold in a controlled trade set-up (e.g. 83 out of 670 rhinos).
- *Reduce IDC by 14%*

Option E – Darting Safaris

- Tourist-hunters shoot rhinos with tranquillizer guns.
- Annual demand: around 10 hunts.
- *Reduce IDC by 4%*

Option F – Trophy Hunting

- Tourist-hunters shoot and kill adult black rhinos.
- In small numbers (e.g. 3 out of 670 rhinos) and in a controlled way, it would not endanger the survival of rhino populations.
- *Reduce IDC by 9%*

Note: * Option available only if legal trade of rhino products is allowed.

Figure 7.1 Management options for black rhinos

induces respondents to offer WTP amounts that reflect their 'fair share' towards the cost of the project rather than their total consumer surplus (Carson et al., 1999). By providing figures on the percentage of revenues that might be raised by each management option we avoid this problem. Also this strategy was more in line with the aims of the study which were to investigate whether different conservation policies would be associated with conflicting values and not as such to examine if stated non-use values would be sufficient to cover the entire cost of the BRCP. It is this qualitative information that is most relevant in addressing the questions regarding the interaction/conflicts between values.

Before the respondents were presented with WTP questions on the BRCP they were asked to vote on the adoption of the different set of options outlined in the presentation. They were reminded that the more options approved, the less rhino conservation would have to rely on foreign aid. This question aimed at uncovering people's attitudes towards different levels of intervention concerning the species.

Immediately after voting on these management options, respondents were faced with the valuation questions. The elicitation format was open-ended and the payment vehicle was a one-time-only tax surcharge. Three WTP questions were posed to each respondent in a step-wise order. Each respondent gave a WTP to all three questions, irrespective of the answer given to previous WTP questions. That is, the WTP questions were *not nested*. The questions sought to elicit respondents' WTP for the BRCP *given* that the programme would be financed via combinations of management options and direct taxation. Three such alternative combinations of financing schemes were presented.

The first WTP question asked for an individual WTP for the full BRCP, when all the management options previously described were being used to help finance it (WTP_{FP}). This entailed that 60% of the project would be covered by the revenues from the uses and the remaining 40% from taxation (i.e. *via* the IDC). In the second WTP question, hunting was deleted as an option to finance the BRCP (WTP_{H}). This entailed that UK taxpayers would have to provide an extra 9% of the BRCP budget via direct taxation to make up for the loss in revenue from not allowing the hunting option. The remaining 51% of the budget would be financed by the other management options. In essence, respondents were asked for their new WTP amount to avoid trophy hunting as a management option. The third elicitation question asked for WTP when all the options that implied legal trade were deleted (sales of stockpiled horns, dehorning operations, darting safaris and trophy hunting) (WTP_{LT}). This implied that only 16% of the budget could be covered by revenues generated by uses while the remaining 84% would have to be covered by UK taxpayers. This is basically the status quo option where the only possible way to endogenously generate funds for wildlife conservation is by increasing entry fees in national parks and selling animals to zoos and other parks. The question was designed to assess the benefits that may accrue from re-opening the legal trade of rhino horn products.

By using the information from these estimated welfare measures, we were able to assess which types of use values conflict with non-use values. Our main hypothesis concerned the potential conflict between welfare and conservation interests. These conflicts could be identified in various ways. If welfare concerns predominated over a general interest in conservation, the full BRCP would be the set of management options that would receive the lowest WTP, because it entailed the most intrusive set of management programmes (all six) while generating the most conservation funding. In addition, given the general public's dislike for sport hunting, it was anticipated that the elimination of rhino hunting would generate a significantly higher WTP than the full BRCP. Moreover, if welfare effects are strong, the elimination of further intrusive regimes (dehorning operations and darting safaris), and the denial of the commercial trade as well as sport hunting, may increase the WTP over that registered for the full BRCP minus sport hunting. Hence, it is interesting to investigate how the subtraction of further intrusive programmes affects the non-use value.

More formally, the specific hypotheses that were tested in the context of the current experiment were:

1. Use and non-use values for conservation associated with *hunting* are in conflict. The null and alternative hypotheses would be:

$$\mathrm{H}_0\text{: } WTP_H = WTP_{FP}$$
$$\mathrm{H}_1\text{: } WTP_H \neq WTP_{FP}$$

If H_0 is rejected in favour of H_1 then individuals would be willing to pay a statistically significant additional amount for conservation in order to eliminate hunting as a management option. In this case non-use and use values for conservation associated with hunting would be in conflict.

2. Use and non-use values for conservation associated with *all* trade options are in conflict. The null and alternative hypotheses would be:

$$\mathrm{H}_0\text{: } WTP_{LT} = WTP_{FP}$$
$$\mathrm{H}_1\text{: } WTP_{LT} \neq WTP_{FP}$$

If H_0 is rejected in favour of H_1 then individuals would be willing to pay a statistically significant additional amount for conservation in order to eliminate all forms of rhino utilization that involve trade in rhino products. In this case non-use and use values for conservation associated with all available trade options would be in conflict.

3. Use and non-use values for conservation associated with trade options *apart from hunting* are in conflict. The null hypothesis would be:

$$H_0: [WTP_{LT} - WTP_{FP}] = [WTP_H - WTP_{FP}]$$
$$H_1: [WTP_{LT} - WTP_{FP}] \neq [WTP_H - WTP_{FP}]$$

If H_0 is rejected in favour of H_1 then individuals would be willing to pay a statistically significant additional amount for conservation in order to eliminate all forms of rhino utilization *beyond* hunting. In this case non-use and use values for conservation associated with all available trade options except hunting would be in conflict.

5. ATTITUDES TOWARDS WILDLIFE MANAGEMENT POLICIES

Table 7.2 presents the attitudes of respondents towards various forms of wildlife management. As can be seen, the great majority of the sample is strongly opposed to trophy hunting (91%) and darting safaris (61%). Table 7.3 also reveals a strong correlation between the two policies (ρ = 0.41): those who oppose hunting tend also to vote against darting. This finding is not unexpected and, being more than a general interest in animal welfare, confirms the UK public's distaste for blood sports and for enjoyment in harvesting wildlife.

Table 7.2 *Attitudes towards rhino management options*

	In favour %	Against %
Increase entry fees	93.44	6.56
Sale of rhinos to zoos	55.64	44.36
Sale of stockpiled horns	82.68	17.32
Dehorning operations	77.17	22.83
Darting safaris	38.85	61.15
Sport hunting	9.19	90.81
Trade of wildlife products	74.80	25.20

Note: N = 381.

Table 7.3 Correlation coefficients between attitudes on management options

	Entry fees	Rhino sales	Stockpiles	Dehorning	Darting	Hunting	Trade
Entry fees	1						
Rhino sales	0.127 (0.0131)	1					
Stockpiles	−0.0181 (0.7251)	0.1503 (0.0033)	1				
Dehorning	−0.0916 (0.0741)	0.1223 (0.0169)	**0.4841** (0.0000)	1			
Darting	−0.0216 (0.6743)	0.2149 (0.0000)	**0.3773** 0.0000	**0.4585** (0.0000)	1		
Hunting	−0.0121 (0.8141)	0.1989 (0.0001)	(0.1902) 0.0002	0.1864 (0.0003)	**0.4124** (0.0000)	1	
Trade	−0.0236 (0.6459)	0.1158 (0.0238)	**0.4851** (0.0000)	**0.3995** (0.0000)	**0.2489** (0.0000)	0.0330 (0.5205)	1

Notes: Significant correlation coefficients in bold; Level of significance in parentheses.

In contrast, non-intrusive policies like increasing entry fees in safari parks and selling stockpiled horns seem to generate widespread support. The endorsement of the latter option is indicative of some support for a controlled legal trade in rhino products – the survey also explicitly elicited respondents' views on this issue with only 25% voting against legal trade (see Table 7.2).

Perhaps the most interesting part of the analysis relates to respondents' attitudes towards the sale of live rhinos and dehorning operations. Of the six proposed management options, these two are arguably the most clear indicators of concern for animal welfare. Increasing entry fees and selling stockpiled horns are non-intrusive regimes that do not reflect welfare concerns, while darting and trophy hunting may generate a disutility either from a concern for the welfare of the rhinos themselves or from the hunters' enjoyment derived from molesting the animals. Hence, a more 'refined' indicator of animal welfare concerns can be obtained from people's attitudes towards dehorning and live sales options. Selling rhinos will remove the animals from their natural original habitat and may have disruptive effects on animal life while shooting rhinos with tranquillizer guns and sawing off their horns is an obviously distressing operation.

The survey shows that only 56% of the sample supported the sale of live rhinos while a much larger 77% voted for dehorning operations. Given that the latter is presumably more disturbing for the animals, this result is somewhat surprising – the fact that dehorning operations, apart from potentially generating money from the sale of rhino horns, make the animals less attractive to poachers may have influenced the results. In any case, altruistic values (i.e. the value non-users placed on the flows from rhino conservation consumed by other people) seem to dominate, on average, over animal welfare concerns. This finding is endorsed by the low and insignificant correlation coefficient between hunting and dehorning and other legal trade options, suggesting that different factors may be behind respondents' attitudes towards these different options.

6. WTP FOR THE FULL BLACK RHINO CONSERVATION PROGRAMME

On average, respondents were willing to pay between £5 and £12.67 (depending on whether the median or the mean is used to summarize the data) for the full management Black Rhino Conservation Programme, as a one-time-only contribution (see Table 7.4). We have thus identified a positive and non-trivial WTP for the conservation of the Namibian black rhinoceros; however, that value was derived by reference to a conservation programme that includes various types of management options, some of which are perceived as being detrimental to the animal's welfare (e.g. trophy hunting with a 91% disapproval rating). As Table 7.4 shows, the public clearly does hold preferences over the sorts of intrusions it would prefer to apply in conservation. Hence, individuals may have withdrawn some of their support for conserving the rhino in lieu of certain uses under the first policy regime. This suggests that the WTP attributed by UK citizens to the specified full management BRCP might not result in the greatest aggregate return (when combining BRCP and the WTP). That is, this aggregate amount might still be maximized if some of the 'less preferred'

Table 7.4 Summary statistics of WTP for all three scenarios

	WTP for the full BRCP	WTP for the BRCP with no hunting	WTP for the BRCP with no legal trade options
Mean	12.67	15.18	13.68
St. error	*(0.96)*	*(1.08)*	*(1.12)*
Median	5	10	5

Note: Units are pounds sterling. Sample size = 381.

options were omitted from the BRCP. The next section will explore this possibility further.

7. CONFLICTS BETWEEN USE AND NON-USE VALUES

We now turn to investigate whether various use and non-use values for the black rhino are in conflict. This was achieved by assessing the impact of varying management regimes on the values offered in support of the full BRCP and then by testing the hypotheses laid out in Section 4.

The WTP for a management regime that is devoid of sport hunting has a mean value of £15.18 (see Table 7.4), which indicates that, on average, respondents are willing to pay an extra £2.51 to avoid trophy hunting of black rhinos (see Table 7.5). This difference is statistically significant according to both the Student's *t*-test of paired comparisons and the paired-rank Wilcoxon non-parametric test (see Table 7.6). The preferred measure of average WTP also indicates this difference in stark fashion: the median WTP doubles from £5 to £10 with the elimination of the use of the rhino for sport hunting. We can thus reject the first hypothesis and conclude that non-use values are in conflict with the presence of this particular use.

Next, the potential conflict between non-use values and the use of the products that the black rhinoceros can generate was evaluated. Specifically, the survey groups were queried on the sensitivity of their WTP to the commercial usage of the horn of the black rhinoceros; that is, the regimes that implied the existence of a legal trade for rhino horn sales of stockpiled horns, dehorning operations, darting safaris and trophy hunting. Returning to Table 7.4, the mean WTP for the BRCP without these options – the *status quo* scenario – is £13.68, an increase of about £1 over the full BRCP. However, this slightly higher amount is not substantial

Table 7.5 Value of several components of the BRCP: summary statistics

	Value of legal trade options minus hunting	Value of hunting	Value of all legal trade options
Mean	1.50	−2.51	−1.01
St. error	*(0.60)*	*(0.28)*	*(0.66)*
Median	0	0	0

Note: Units are pounds sterling. Sample size = 381.

Table 7.6 Hypothesis testing

	Null hypothesis	t-statistic decision	Wilcoxon test
Avoiding trophy hunting	$WTP_H = WTP_{FP}$	*Reject*	*Reject*
Avoiding all legal trade options	$WTP_{LT} = WTP_{FP}$	*Cannot reject*	*Cannot reject*
Legal trade options minus hunting	$[WTP_{LT} - WTP_{FP}] = [WTP_H - WTP_{FP}]$	*Reject*	*Reject*

Notes: All tests are two-sided and all decisions on H_0 are at the 95% level.
WTP_H for WTP for programme without hunting.
WTP_{FP} for WTP for full programme with all management policies.
WTP_{LT} for WTP for programme without any management policies that require legal trade.

enough to be statistically different from the WTP for the full programme with all management options included, as both the t-test of paired comparisons and the paired-rank Wilcoxon test show (Table 7.6). That is, on the basis of this sample size, it is not possible to reject the second hypothesis that the WTP within the UK is identical for both management programmes (i.e. those with and without trade in rhino horn). This leads to the conclusion that respondents are not against having this set of options included in the programme; that is, there is no perceived conflict between the non-use value that the respondents are expressing and the use values derived from rhino horn trade. These two forms of value appear to be aggregative.

Further insights into the nature of respondents' preferences are possible from examining the third hypothesis. It was just shown that respondents were willing to pay £1.01 in order to avoid the complete set of options that imply a commercial use of the black rhino and related horn products ($WTP_{LT} = WTP_{FP}$). Further, it was shown that respondents were willing to pay £2.51 in order to avoid hunting ($WTP_H = WTP_{FP}$). The difference between these two values (i.e. $[WTP_{LT} = WTP_{FP}] - [WTP_H = WTP_{FP}]$) provides a measure of how much individuals were willing to pay to avoid all uses of the species apart from hunting. This difference is statistically different from zero (see Table 7.6) and is found to be equal to −£1.50 (Table 7.5). The negative sign attached to this value implies that individuals are willing to pay this sum in order to allow for certain types of rhino utilization except hunting. It appears that respondents are not giving a negative welfare-based valuation to some management options, such as dehorning and darting, while they are to others that are similar in intrusiveness, such as trophy hunting. Therefore, it may be concluded that there is a clear conflict between

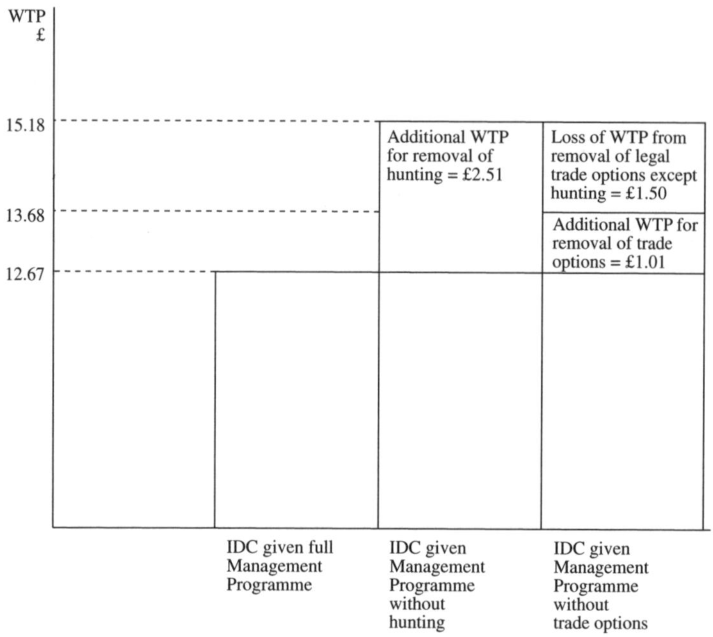

Figure 7.2 Decomposition of black rhino values

use and non-use values in the case of trophy hunting, but not in the case of the other uses (darting, dehorning, commercial uses and live sales).

(Figure 7.2 illustrates and summarizes the arguments presented in this section. The mean non-use value for the existence of black rhinos lies somewhere within the range of £12.67 to £15.18 per UK household (or between £5 and £10 if the median is used), depending upon the lifestyle afforded to the animal in that jurisdiction. There is a mean positive WTP in support of both the removal of sport hunting from the BRCP (about £2.51) and of the inclusion of the rhino horn trade (about £1.50).

8. MOTIVATIONS BEHIND CONFLICTING VALUES

In this section we use regression analysis to try to explore the motivations behind the conflicts presented above. More specifically we will be examining the impact of various attitudinal and socio-economic variables on the WTP distributions obtained from the study. Two types of WTP responses were elicited which required a different econometric modelling approach. The first type of WTP response was in the form of total WTP responses directly obtained for each of the three conservation scenarios. Since these three WTP distributions were collected in a step-wise fashion *from the same* individual, it may well be the case that they were not independent (Hoehn, 1991). This possible interdependence would be captured by a significant contemporaneous correlation between the error terms of the three WTP functions. The correlation of the stochastic elements of the three main WTP equations as well as the form of the associated variance-covariance matrix introduces additional information over and above that available when the individual equations are considered separately. Neglecting this information (by treating each WTP function as separate) may lead to inefficient parameter estimates (Srivastava and Giles, 1987).

To account for this contemporaneous correlation between the error terms associated with the three dependent variables we employ an asymptotically efficient feasible GLS estimation model (or seemingly unrelated regression (SUR) model). The GLS model applies to the stacked model:

$$\mathbf{WTP}_m = \mathbf{X}_m \, \hat{\mathbf{a}}_m + \mathring{\mathbf{a}}_m \tag{7.1}$$

where the subscript refers to $m = 1 \ldots 3$ equations, $\mathbf{WTP}_m$, $\hat{\mathbf{a}}_m$ and $\mathring{\mathbf{a}}_m$ are vectors, $\mathbf{X}_m$ is a data matrix.

It is assumed that $\mathring{\mathbf{a}}_m \sim N(\mathbf{0}, \grave{\mathbf{u}})$ and the variance-covariance matrix of $\boldsymbol{\varepsilon}_m$ has the general form:

$$\mathbf{\Omega} = \begin{bmatrix} \sigma_{11} & \sigma_{21} & \sigma_{21} \\ \sigma_{21} & \sigma_{22} & \sigma_{32} \\ \sigma_{31} & \sigma_{23} & \sigma_{33} \end{bmatrix} \tag{7.2}$$

The disturbances are assumed to be uncorrelated *within* each equation but are contemporaneously correlated *across* WTP responses.[7] A GLS framework has frequently been used for the estimation of systems of demand equations where there is no simultaneity problem (i.e. demand equations do not interact) but the cross-equation error terms are related. That is, the demand equations are linked not structurally (as in a system of simultaneous equations) but statistically through the 'jointness of the error terms' and through the non-diagonality of the associated variance-covariance matrix. This framework was extended to model CV data where we have multiple WTP responses from the same individual. The estimation procedure followed was a two stage Feasible GLS approach described in Greene (1997) and Srivastava and Giles (1987) and is similar to the seemingly unrelated regression model (SUR) when the $\grave{\mathbf{u}}_{mm}$ is unknown.

The second type of WTP data obtained from the study were the *marginal* WTP values for the avoidance of additional intrusive management policies. These were the (implicit) WTP values for avoiding trophy hunting and the WTP to avoid all intrusive polices expect hunting. Whereas the modelling of the distribution for the total WTP values had to address the issue of cross-equation correlation, the choice of the appropriate econometric specification for marginal WTP had to tackle the potential problems generated by the large percentage of zero responses found in these two distributions.[8] The distribution of WTP to avoid hunting contained 50% zero responses while that for having trade options (except hunting) contained 48% zero responses. Using simple linear regression in this case will lead to biased and inconsistent results (Greene, 1997). We thus used a limited dependent variable modelling approach which is suitable for the analysis of open-ended WTP data that contain non-trivial percentages of zero responses (see Kontoleon, 2003 for a review).

The specific limited dependent variable model employed for these data was the inverse hyperbolic sign double hurdle dependent model. Details of this model can be found in Kontoleon (2003). The model suggests that these marginal WTP distributions are generated by a two-tier decision making process. The first decision or hurdle that the individual has to overcome is whether they are indifferent between alternative conservation regimes that entail different management options. Given that the individual is *not* indifferent but has a preference in favour of a particular option, a second decision is made as to the size of the bid that the individual would be willing to pay in support of this option.

This double hurdle data generating process can be described by the following observability rule:

$$\begin{array}{lll} WTP_n = WTP_n^* & \text{if } WTP_n^* = \boldsymbol{\beta}'\mathbf{X}_n + \varepsilon_n > 0 \textit{ and } I_n^* = \mathbf{\acute{a}}'\mathbf{Z}_n + v_n > 0 & \\ WTP_n = 0 & \text{otherwise} & (7.3) \end{array}$$

The variable, I^*, represents a latent variable that determines whether one is indifferent between the *means* of conservation and WTP_n^* is the latent/notional WTP that determines the form of the observed WTP distribution (note that no restrictions are placed on the range of WTP^*, i.e. $WTP_n^* \in (-\infty, +\infty)$). The vectors **X** and **Z** include the variables that determine the latent continuous variables and $\mathbf{\hat{a}}'$ and $\mathbf{\acute{a}}'$ are their associated parameter vectors. The terms ε and v denote the disturbances of each decision. A feature of such a model is that the determinants of each decision are allowed to differ while the common variables (in **X** and **Z**) may have opposite effects. Also, in its most general form, the above model does not impose any restriction on the relationship between the two decisions. That is, it allows for the possibility of the error terms ε and v being correlated by following a pre-defined joint probability distribution.

Using (7.3) and assuming that ε and v follow a bivariate normal distribution,[9] we can construct a likelihood function with the form:

$$\begin{aligned} L_{DHD} = & \prod_{0} [1 - P(v_n > -\mathbf{\acute{a}}'\mathbf{Z}_n) \cdot P(\varepsilon_n > -\mathbf{\hat{a}}'\mathbf{X}_n / v_n > -\mathbf{\acute{a}}'\mathbf{Z}_n)] \\ & \times \prod_{1} P(v_n > -\boldsymbol{\alpha}'\mathbf{Z}_n) \times \prod_{1} P(\varepsilon_n > -\boldsymbol{\beta}'\mathbf{X}_n / v_n > -\boldsymbol{\alpha}'\mathbf{Z}_n) \\ & f(y_n / \varepsilon_n > -\mathbf{\hat{a}}'\mathbf{X}_n, v_n > -\mathbf{\acute{a}}'\mathbf{Z}_n) \end{aligned} \quad (7.4)$$

The first segment of equation 7.4 captures the probability of being indifferent between the means of conservation, while the remaining two components determine the payment decision *given* that an individual is not indifferent. This particular hurdle model that allows for the possibility that the error terms of the two decisions are correlated is akin to the 'double hurdle dependent' model (see Blundell and Meghir, 1987; Jones and Yen, 1994; Garcia and Labeaga, 1996).

Two additional elements were added to the modelling process. The first catered for the violations of the assumption of bivariate normality of the error terms. This was achieved by applying an inverse hyperbolic sine (IHS) transformation of the dependent variable (see Kontoleon, 2003 for details). Secondly, the variance of the likelihood function was parameterized in order to account for heteroscedasticity.[10]

The best-fit results from the analysis of both the GLS and the hurdle model are presented in Tables 7.9 through 7.11.[11, 12] The description of the explanatory variables that were used is provided in Table 7.7. These include both socio-economic and attitudinal variables. The latter included proxy variables for the latent motives underpinning people's stated WTP values. For example, the variables 'extinction' and 'genetic value' were used as proxies for latent concerns over preserving a species as a source of (consumptive and non-consumptive) use-related flows. Also, the dummy variable 'children' (which equals 1 when children are present in the household) was used as a proxy for bequest motivations for conservation. Finally, the variable 'animal welfare' aimed at capturing any animal welfare concerns that may motivate WTP for conservation.[13] The impact of these explanatory variables on the elicited WTP values is discussed in the following two sub-sections.

8.1 Regression Results from GLS Model on Total WTP Values

Turning to the coefficients estimates from the GLS model, we first note that higher order polynomials were used for age and income, signifying some non-linearities between these covariates and the dependent variable.

Table 7.7 Explanatory variables for regression analysis

Variable	Description
Sex	Sex = 1 for male
Age	Age in years
Age^2	Age squared
Income	Annual disposable income
Income^2	Annual disposable income squared
Children	Children = 1 if children present in the household
Education	Years of education
Genetic Value	Concern for the conservation of the genetic value of species
Extinction	Concern for the extinction of species
Animal welfare	Concern for the well-being of wildlife
Opinion index	Opinion about questionnaire
Trade	Attitudes towards trade in wildlife products
Hunting	Attitudes towards wildlife hunting
Dehorning	Attitudes towards dehorning
Horn sale	Attitudes towards sale of stockpiles

Table 7.8 Regression results from GLS model

	Coefficient	St. error	*t*-value
Sex	−0.998	0.524	−1.907
Age	−0.244	0.120	−2.032
Age^2	0.003	0.002	1.781
Income	0.000	0.001	0.117
Income^2	0.000	0.000	−0.402
Children	0.489	0.228	2.146
Education	0.190	0.110	1.729
Genetic value	0.712	0.321	2.217
Opinion index	1.127	0.233	4.835
Trade	1.117	0.520	2.148
Constant	1.268	2.758	0.460
Adjusted R^2		0.1866	
F-statistic		4.635067	
P-value		0.0000	
WTP_H			
Sex	−1.169	0.450	−2.598
Age	−0.155	0.080	−1.938
Age^2	0.002	0.001	1.415

Table 7.8 (continued)

	Coefficient	St. error	*t*-value
Income	0.001	0.001	1.375
Income^2	0.000	0.000	−2.280
Children	0.465	0.196	2.374
Education	0.093	0.124	0.744
Opinion index	0.936	0.200	4.671
Trade	0.881	0.447	1.971
Constant	0.316	2.363	0.134
Adjusted R^2		0.1945	
F-statistic		4.942606	
P-value		0.0000	
WTP_{LT}			
Sex	−2.195	0.529	−4.150
Age	−0.243	0.130	−1.869
Age^2	0.003	0.001	2.827
Income	0.001	0.001	1.489
Income^2	0.000	0.000	−1.810
Children	0.189	0.230	0.820
Education	0.055	0.146	0.378
Animal welfare	1.046	0.578	1.810
Opinion index	0.892	0.238	3.757
Trade	−0.468	0.526	−0.889
Constant	2.588	2.804	0.923
Adjusted R^2		0.1740	
F-statistic		4.869285	
P-value		0.0000	

Table 7.9 Correlation matrix of residuals

	WTP_{FP}	WTP_H	WTP_{LT}
WTP_{FP}	1		
WTP_H	0.8167	1	
WTP_{LT}	0.6626	0.6224	1

Notes: Breusch-Pagan test of independence: $chi^2(3) = 568.975$, $Pr = 0.0000$. Independence can be rejected.

Table 7.10 IHS regression results: WTP to have trade options except hunting

	Coefficient	Std. error	*t*-statistic
Indifference decision			
Education	0.531	0.346	1.536
Income	0.001	0.001	1.754
Extinction	0.973	0.504	1.931
Animal welfare	−0.028	1.114	−0.025
Constant	−2.976	1.610	−1.849
Payment Decision			
Sex	1.122	0.703	1.595
Income	0.000	0.000	0.265
Horn sale	0.685	0.216	3.180
Hunting	−0.736	0.239	−3.075
Family	0.495	0.269	1.838
Extinction	0.442	0.214	2.065
Animal welfare	−1.161	1.092	−1.063
Constant	−4.967	2.009	−2.472
Variance			
Sex	0.258819	0.142035	1.822
Constant	1.432697	0.138175	10.369
ρ	0.2650148	0.0609802	4.346
N		318	
Log likelihood		−678.51671	
Wald chi²(4)		5.39	
Prob > chi²		0.00249	

The presence of such quadratic effects are consistent with many other findings from regression analysis of WTP data (e.g. Johansson, 1999). To account for multicollinearity between the polynomials we expressed the age and income variables in deviation form (Bradley and Srivastava, 1979). The coefficients on age are significant in all three equations, whereas those for income are significant only for the WTP_H and WTP_{LT} distributions. Women are associated with a lower WTP in all three management scenarios while people with a higher education level would be WTP more for the full programme (WTP_{FP}). The presence of children in each household has a significant and positive influence on WTP for the WTP_{FP} and WTP_H scenarios but not for WTP_{LT}. This last finding suggests

Table 7.11 IHS regression results: WTP to avoid hunting

	Co-efficient	Std. error	*t*-statistic
Indifference decision			
Dehorning	0.129	0.052	2.468
Hunting	−0.415	0.099	−4.214
Education	0.113	0.066	1.720
Extinction	−0.142	0.285	−0.497
Animal welfare	0.802	0.382	2.098
Constant	−0.694	0.711	−0.976
Payment Decision			
Sex	−0.609	0.354	−1.720
Income	0.000	0.000	1.712
Hunting	−0.138	0.379	−0.364
Dehorning	−0.094	0.122	−0.769
Opinion index	0.355	0.230	1.544
Children	0.375	0.196	1.914
Extinction	1.433	0.976	1.468
Animal welfare	1.619	0.787	2.059
Constant	−2.852	2.069	−1.379
Variance			
Education	0.305968	0.122539	2.497
Constant	0.833041	0.23207	3.59
ρ	0.341509	0.100383	3.402
N		378	
Log likelihood		−715.28771	
Wald chi²(5) =		23.29	
Prob > chi²		0.0003	

the presence of possible strong bequest (relative to animal welfare) motives: individuals value the prospect of certain rhino flows being channelled to their children in the future (e.g. ecotourism, rhino horn products and so on).

Turning to the attitudinal variables, we see that WTP for rhino conservation using all available management options (WTP_{FP}) is positively associated with a higher appraisal for the genetic importance of wildlife (the coefficient on the gene-value index is significant and positive) while WTP for conservation that would not allow for utilization of the species (WTP_{LT}) is positively affected by one's animal welfare sentiments ('animal welfare').

People's opinion about the conservation programmes has a significant positive effect in all three decisions, signifying the importance of reliability in designing CV experiments. Finally, individuals' attitudes towards re-opening legal trade positively influence WTP for the two scenarios that include trade options (WTP_{FP} and WTP_H) but has no effect on the scenario where trade options are excluded (WTP_{LT}). The results suggest that altruistic concerns are associated with higher WTP for the scenarios involving human utilization of the species, while animal welfare concerns are the driving force behind higher WTP values for the scenario involving limited uses for humans but enhanced welfare for rhinos.

We, thus, see that overall, the demographic variables are consistent with economic theory and are in line with past CV studies. Moreover, the attitudinal and taste variables provide a logical explanation of the direction and magnitude of the WTP responses that is consistent with the discussion on the motivational assumptions underpinning non-use values.

8.2 Regression Results from the Hurdle Model on Marginal WTP Values

Both demographic and attitudinal/motivational questions were used in the specification of the indifference and payment decisions of the hurdle models. Our discussion will focus on the motivational variables since these are of primary concern in this section. In particular, it is of interest to examine why non-users would still be willing to support conservation that entailed certain uses of the species (such as sale of rhino horns) rather than others (such as sport hunting). Following the reasoning developed in Section 2, it can be assumed that support for rhino utilization other than hunting would be compatible with a desire to provide these flows to other people. This would be the result of a form of 'altruistic effect'. Conversely, one's disapproval of sport hunting would be motivated by a relatively stronger 'animal welfare effect'.

Looking first at the decision on whether one is indifferent with regard to the introduction of commercial uses of rhinos (Table 7.10), we see that both effects have the anticipated sign: positive for the altruistic effect (captured by the 'extinction' variable) and negative for the animal welfare effect (captured by the 'animal welfare' variable). We also observe that the altruism effect dominates the animal welfare effect (i.e. the coefficient on 'extinction' is larger than that on 'animal welfare' while the latter is also insignificant).[14]

This finding also carries over to the payment decision (WTP_{LT}). The results clearly suggest that concern for the flows that wildlife generates through trade policies for the benefit of *other* people (altruism effect) outweighs concerns about decreased animal well-being from wildlife utilization (animal welfare effect).

Turning to the indifference decision concerning the use of trophy hunting, we see that the animal welfare effect dominates the altruistic effect. That is, the likelihood of being unwilling to support a conservation regime that allows hunting increases as ones animal welfare concerns increase.

Looking at the payment decision we also see that a higher WTP to avoid hunting is associated with higher animal welfare motives. We can thus conclude that both the decision to support a ban on rhino hunting and the decision on how much one would be willing to pay to attain/sustain such a ban can be largely explained by a strong negative animal welfare effect from the introduction of hunting.

Although this negative animal welfare effect from hunting is clearly supported by the data, closer examination of the results suggests that there may be an *additional* conflict between those who enjoy particular forms of wildlife uses (particularly, sport hunters) and those who receive disutility from their enjoyment. Looking at the regression results of Table 7.11 we see that people's attitudes towards the act of hunting (as captured by the variable 'hunting') have a very strong *negative* effect on the likelihood of supporting the ban on hunting. On the other hand, we see that the coefficient on attitudes towards dehorning, a policy with similar intrusiveness to hunting, has a *positive* and significant effect on the likelihood of supporting the ban on hunting. It thus appears that the disutility experienced by the non-user from other people's enjoyment of hunting (and not simply the loss of animal welfare) may provide an additional explanation for the conflict between non-use values and hunting.

This effect may be interpreted as kind of *vicarious disutility:* the act of hunting enters the non-user's utility function as a 'bad'. Following the discussion of Section 2, we can accommodate this interpretation of the regression results within the framework of the paternalistic altruism model. Past models on altruism implicitly assume that non-use would only receive *positive* utility from another agent's use of a resource and that this utility should be *additive* in cost benefit calculations. The present study suggests that non-users may receive *disutility* from *certain* flows (in our case hunting) enjoyed by certain users (hunters) and that this value would conflict (and not aggregate) with other non-use values. It has been argued that this conflict is conceptually similar to a negative consumption externality.

The current study has shown that non-users do not receive disutility from flows associated with other management options (e.g. sale of stockpiles for medicinal purposes) which are consumed by *other* groups of users (Asian consumers of rhino horn medicine). On the contrary non-users expressed an *enhanced* welfare when such uses were allowed (WTP for trade option except hunting was positive), while the probability of supporting such options was positively related to respondents' altruistic sentiments. These findings translate to non-users having a positive WTP to ban certain kinds of wildlife uses (hunting) while supporting others (e.g. dehorning, selling of stockpiles).

9. DISCUSSION

Different people and constituencies see the object of wildlife conservation very differently: some would like to maintain large stocks of wildlife in order to trade it commercially or to hunt it, others would like to leave some wilderness to their grandchildren, and others still would like to know that there are some beasts on earth living a natural and undisturbed life. Is it possible for all of these different people to come together in the effort to conserve wildlife and their habitats, or are there fundamental conflicts between these different motivations that will always prevent them from co-operating? This is the issue that we have attempted to address in the context of the conservation of the Namibian black rhinoceros. It was in this context that the capacity for the aggregation of use values (derived from various managed uses there) together with non-use values of the citizens of the UK (derived from the maintenance of a specified lifestyle for a stock of live rhinos) was examined.

This experiment found that non-use values for the black rhino conservation programme that included a broad range of utilization policies are substantial. If the conservative median estimate for the 'full BRCP' at £5 is at all accurate, then this would indicate a non-use value *within the UK* of about £110 million.[15] Even if this estimate is an order of magnitude too great, this would still indicate that very substantial non-use values inhere in northern countries that should be channelled to conservation purposes. What is more, the study suggests that non-use values can be doubled by banning certain kinds of uses of this natural resource.

The indicated non-use values in the UK alone are potentially capable of supplying the full amount of funding required for the conservation of the black rhinoceros in Namibia, and it should clearly be able to supplement fully the funding derived from the various uses occurring within Namibia. However, if non-use value is intended to supplement rather than displace domestic management programmes, then to what extent is this possible? How well do non-use and use values add up?

The study demonstrated that conservation policies that include torture of the species, such as hunting, are associated with negative WTP values (people were found to be WTP to avoid such a policy). These negative non-use values associated with the use of hunting were found to be explained by a negative animal welfare effect induced by animal suffering but also from a negative altruistic effect associated with the act of hunting itself (a vicarious disutility effect).

These findings support the argument of this chapter that non-use values conflict (and do not aggregate) with specific use values and that these conflicts can be viewed as forms of consumption externalities. That is, they emerge when the utilization of wildlife from one constituent affects the utility functions of another.

It is also clear that there are other motivations for non-use values. Some of these motivations include the desire to maintain live stocks of rhinos for the benefit of future generations and future uses, and they are clearly not incompatible with any uses that aid the conservation of rhino stocks. Regression analysis revealed that this finding could be explained by a clear 'altruism effect': individuals were willing to support policies that entailed wildlife utilization provided that this aids conservation but also provides flows of goods and services to various other groups of people.

There are lessons to be learned from this case study that are much broader than this single context. It is clear that developing countries cannot cope with the expenses of conserving and maintaining the stock of their wildlife. Two important alternative financing mechanisms available to them are direct contributions from international funds and revenues raised from various wildlife utilization policies. The former are mainly supported by non-users while the latter allow for users of the resource to contribute towards its conservation. Developing countries and conservation agencies should instate the optimal amount and type of markets for both users and non-users so as to maximize conservation revenues. In doing so it is imperative to understand how these markets interact. Can the introduction of one market jeopardize the efficiency of another? Should sustainable utilization of the species or the preservation of animal welfare be the overriding objective?

The black rhino study examined the extent to which conflicting perspectives on conservation imply conflicting (or accumulating) values and attempted to discern the optimal policy mix that would minimize such potential conflicts. Our study indicates that in order to maximize the non-use values from rhino existence, the most successful formula seems to be the banning of options that involve an element of enjoyment in harvesting the rhinos (hunting and darting) while allowing other commercial uses of the animal like the sale of stockpiled horns and dehorning operations. Interestingly, it does not appear that there is any additional withdrawal of support associated with intrusive management options other than those associated with sporting activity. Therefore, there are conflicts between the various values of wildlife, but these are not perhaps as substantial as the paralysis in international policy making may suggest. From our research we believe that most people in the UK do support the commercial use of wildlife and wildlife products in support of conservation, but they reject the concept of encouraging the taking of pleasure in the process. An optimal conservation policy would make use of those uses of wildlife which are compatible with non-use value, and would especially make substantially greater efforts at harnessing the non-use values that exist in the northern countries.

NOTES

The authors would like to acknowledge financial assistance from the European Commission's Framework V Programme (BIOECON–VK2-CT-2000-00086) and from the Convention on International Trade in Endangered Species (CITES). We would also like to thank David Pearce, Joe Swierzbinski and Susana Mourato for useful comments on previous drafts of this chapter.

1. CITES lists fully protected species in which all international trade is banned in Appendix I. Those in which a limited, highly regulated trade is allowed are in Appendix II. The southern African states want their elephants listed in Appendix II; Kenya wants them to be in Appendix I.
2. This feature of the model also avoids issues of double counting pure altruistic preferences (Johanson, 1992).
3. If the benefactor was able to separate out and provide for these flows directly to these groups, then the stock related value would not exist. Positive statements of stock related values, in this framework, act as surrogates for flows that are unable to be thought out and arranged otherwise. Expressed preferences over enhanced stocks then act as very crude instruments for the channelling of flows of goods and services in the desired direction.
4. Given the complexity of the proposed task, the survey development stage lasted several months in 1995–96. Survey design and development included consultation of experts (valuation, biologists and rhino policy experts), a focus group session and three pre-tests which included debriefing sessions with randomly selected participants.
5. In many CV experiments, group surveys have been found to exhibit the advantages of in-person interviews while also allowing for greater consistency in the presentation of material (e.g. Morey et al., 1999). In fact, since no interaction was allowed between respondents, the entire procedure is almost identical to in-person interviews. In addition, group interviews may reduce the interviewer bias and decrease non-response rates to 'sensitive questions' (e.g. income level) since group settings offer more privacy to respondents (Weinberg, 1983).
6. The Namibian government provided detailed information on the various management options available for the conservation of the black rhinoceros, and the funding that each would generate. We would like to acknowledge the co-operation of the Namibian Ministry of Parks in providing the data that supported this research exercise. Nigel Patchings was the member of the Ministry who supplied the necessary effort. Malan Lindeque was the director of research who developed the collaborative link.
7. By allowing for the possibility of contemporaneous correlation between the error terms across equations, the variance-covariance matrix will not necessarily be diagonal.
8. Multivariate least squares regression suggested that there was no correlation between the WTP to avoid hunting and WTP to have trade options. Thus, the main modelling challenge here was to address the presence of large percentages of zeros.
9. With the form:

$$(\varepsilon, \text{v}) \sim \text{BVN}(0,\Omega), \text{ where } \Omega = \begin{bmatrix} \text{ó}_{\text{á}} & \text{ó}_{\text{á}} \cdot \text{ñ} \\ \sigma_{\varepsilon} \cdot \rho & 1 \end{bmatrix}$$

10. Since we had poor *a priori* knowledge as to which variable should be used to parameterize the variances of the WTP decisions, we followed an iterative process examining various specifications. The variables that satisfied the IM test were 'education' for the WTP_H model and 'sex' for the WTP_{LT} model. We see that both these coefficients were highly significant.
11. Before we turn to discussion of parameter estimates, two observations must be made on the results of the FGLS model. First, note in the table the high correlation coefficient between the WTP decisions ranging between 0.6 and 0.83 (see Table 7.10) A Breusch-Pagan ML test suggests that these coefficients differ highly significantly from zero. Thus, the error variance-covariance matrix, $\grave{\mathbf{u}}_{mm}$, is *not* diagonal. Also note that not all WTP equations had the same specification. That is, X_m is not the same across all m. The specification of each model was reached using repeated incremental F-tests (bottom-top approach). If all the three equations were specified by the same covariates and/or the variance-covariance matrix, $\grave{\mathbf{u}}_{mm}$, was diagonal, the use of a GLS model would be superfluous. Yet, these two findings suggest that the use of the joint GLS model (as opposed to using three separate models for each WTP equation) was justified.
12. The information matrix (IM) test (Chesher, 1984) was used to jointly test for homoscedasticity and normality in the two regression models in their standard (un-transformed versions). The construction of the test statistic followed the approach taken in Reynolds and Shonkwiler (1991) and Gao et al. (1995). After employing the IHS transformation and parameterizing, the IM test could not reject the null of joint normality and homoscedasticity in both models. Also note that the correlation coefficient, ρ, between the error terms of the indifference and payment decision was found to be statistically different from zero. These results suggest that the appropriate IHS double hurdle dependent model provided the appropriate specification.
13. Hence, the variables, 'children', 'extinction' and 'genetic value' would capture the concern to provide flows from rhino conservation to other people or 'altruism effect', while the 'animal welfare' variable is intended to capture concerns for the species itself ('animal welfare effect').
14. These are not the true marginal effects on the *probability* of indifference but are the marginal effects on the latent variable I^*. Since here we are interested in the sign and magnitude of the difference between coefficients, reporting the latter would suffice.
15. There are 22 million households in the UK.

REFERENCES

Barnes, I (1995), Department of Environmental Affairs, Namibia, mimeo.

Blundell, R., and Meghir, C. (1987), 'Bivariate Alternatives to the Tobit Model', *Journal of Econometrics*, **34**, 179–200.

Bradley, R.A., and Srivastava, S.S. (1979), 'Correlation and Polynomial Regression', *American Statistical Association*, **33**, 11–14.

Brown, P. (2000), 'Traders say Profit can be Motive for Preservation', *Guardian*, 17 April.

Carson, R., Groves, T., and Machina, M.J. (1999), 'Incentive and Informational Properties of Preference Questions', Plenary Address at the annual conference of the European Association of Resource and Environmental Economists, Oslo, Norway, June.

Chesher, A. (1984), 'Testing for Neglected Heterogeneity', *Econometrica*, **52**, 865–72.

Cumming, D.H.M., Tout, R.F.D., and Stuart, S.N. (1990), *African Elephants and Rhinos: Statutes and Conservation Actions Plan*, Report, IUCN/SCC, Switzerland: African Elephant and Rhino Specialist Group.

Gao, X.M., Wailes, E.J., and Cramer, G.L. (1995), 'Double-Hurdle Model with Bivariate Normal Errors: An Application to U.S. Rice Demand', *Journal of Agricultural and Applied Economics*, December, **27** (2), 363–76.

Garcia, J., and Labeaga, Jose M. (1996), 'Alternative Approach to Modelling Zero Expenditure: An Application to Spanish Demand for Tobacco', *Oxford Bulletin of Economics and Statistics*, **53** (3), 489–506.

Greene, W. (1997), *Econometric Analysis*, 3rd edition, New York: Macmillan.

Hoehn, J.P. (1991), 'Valuing the Multi-Dimensional Impacts of Environmental Policy. Theory and Methods', *American Journal of Agricultural Economics*, **73**, 289–99.

Johansson, M.V. (1999), 'Determinants of Charitable Giving. Evidence from Hypothetical Data on Willingness to Pay', Working Paper, Department of Economics, Umea University.

Johansson, P.O. (1992), 'Altruism in Cost-Benefit Analysis', *Environmental and Resource Economics*, **2**, 605–13.

Jones, A.M., and Yen, S.T. (1994), 'A Box-Cox Double Hurdle Model', *IFS Working Paper Series*, No. W94/6.

Kontoleon, A. (2003), 'Essays on Non-market Valuation of Environmental Resources: Policy and Technical Explorations', Ph.d. Dissertation, Department of Economics, University College London.

Krutilla, J. (1967), 'Conservation Reconsidered', *American Economic Review*, **57** (4), 777–86.

McConnell, K.E. (1997), 'Does Altruism Undermine Existence Value?', *Journal of Environmental Economics and Management*, January, **32** (1), 22–37.

Morey, E., Rossmann, K.G., Chestnut L., and Ragland, S. (1999), 'Modelling and Estimating E(WTP) for Reducing Acid Deposition Injuries to Cultural Resources: Using Choice Experiments in a Group Setting to Estimate Passive-Use Values', forthcoming in S. Navrud and R.C. Ready (eds), *Valuing Cultural Heritage*, Cheltenham, UK, Northampton, MA, USA: Edward Elgar Publishing.

OECD (2002), *Handbook of Biodiversity Valuation: A Guide for Policy Makers*, Paris: OECD.

Pearce, D.W., and Turner, R.K. (1990), *Economics of Natural Resources and the Environment*, Baltimore: Johns Hopkins University Press.

Reynolds, A., and Shonkwiler, J.S. (1991), 'Testing and Correcting for Distributional Misspecifications in the Tobit Model', *Empirical Economics*, **16,** 313–23.

Srivastava, V.K., and Giles, D.E.A. (1987), *Seemingly Unrelated Regression Equation Models: Estimation and Inference*, New York: Marcel Dekker Inc.

Swanson, T., and Barbier, E. (1992), *Economics for the Wilds*, London: Earthscan.

Swanson, T., Kontoleon, A., and Macrory, R. (2002a), 'Individual Preference Based Values and Environmental Decision Making: Should Valuation have its Day in Court?', *Journal of Research in Law and Economics*, **20**, 179–216.

Swanson, T., Kontoleon, A., Mourato, S., and Swierzbinski, J. (2002b), 'Conflicts in Conservation: The Many Values of The Black Rhinoceros', in D.W. Pearce, C.G. Pearce and Charles Palmer (eds), *Valuing Environmental Benefits. Volume I: Case Studies from the Developing World*, Cheltenham, UK, Northampton, MA, USA: Edward Elgar.

WCMC (1992), *Global Biodiversity: Status of the Earth's Living Resources*, UK: Chapman & Hall.

Weinberg, E. (1983), 'Data Collection: Planning and Management', in P.H. Rossi (ed.), *Handbook of Survey Research*, New York: Academic Press.

8. Contingent ranking of river water quality improvements

Stavros Georgiou, Ian Bateman, Matthew Cole and David Hadley

1. BACKGROUND

The River Tame rises as three tributaries in the urbanized areas of Wolverhampton, Walsall and Oldbury before flowing through the city of Birmingham. It then turns north and eventually flows into the River Trent which, in turn, drains into the North Sea.

The river was once a small, high quality stream, but, during the last century, as industrial activity and population began to increase in the West Midlands region, the water quality of the river began to suffer. The last salmon were seen in the river in 1876 and by 1945 the river was dead, devoid of all life (Environment Agency, 1998). Since then there has been some improvement in water quality due to improvements in sewerage systems. However, the water quality of the river as it flows through the Metropolitan West Midlands region is still classified by the Environment Agency as very poor. This means that only very pollution tolerant life is supported in small numbers, for example, snails, worms, leaches and a few small fish (sticklebacks) as well as limited numbers of aquatic plants. Additionally, the water in the river is hazardous to human health because of high bacterial levels and it is definitely not suitable for water-based recreational activities.

There are a number of different sources of pollution that cause this poor state of water quality. Effluent from sewage works remains a problem although these facilities are currently being improved (Environment Agency, 1998). Other important sources are urban run-off[1] and contaminated land.

Urban run-off is a particular problem in urban areas where little rainwater is absorbed into the ground and where it can quickly flow down into the river system. Once in the river, this run-off discolours the water giving it a cloudy, grey appearance because of the high levels of solids suspended in it. These solids can then settle on the riverbed, smothering plants and animal life. It can also be toxic and can reduce oxygen levels in the water, causing further decreases in the water quality.

For example, in July 1995 there was a period of heavy rainfall over Birmingham after a long dry period and high temperatures. The impact of urban run-off on the Tame was very serious as oxygen levels in the river fell rapidly, resulting in the loss of 90% of fish stocks downstream of Birmingham and even killing fish in the River Trent (Environment Agency, 1998).

Contaminated land also has an effect on the water quality of the Tame. Because of the long industrial legacy of the West Midlands conurbation, there are several sites of old mine workings, industrial sites and tips, in-filled canals and disused railway lines. Some of these sites drain directly into the river and impair the water quality by seepage of nickel, copper and zinc, as well as other pollutants. Some of these metals and other chemicals can be toxic to plant and animal life, as well as humans, when present in high enough concentrations.

Options required to alleviate problems that are currently adversely affecting water quality in the Tame will involve expense. This will fall on a number of different bodies (local authorities, the Environment Agency, water companies and landowners), but it is likely that local authorities will fund a large part of the bill. For example, where possible, paying the bill for cleaning up contaminated land will be the responsibility of the landowner. But, in the West Midlands there are areas of land that were contaminated up to 100 years ago and so it would be impossible to trace responsibility for that contamination back to one individual or company. In this case the local authority will be responsible.

Given the large costs involved in clean-up of the river, the question arises as to whether such spending constitutes value for money or if some alternative use of the money would be more beneficial. There will be a trade-off between environmental improvements and the public's willingness to pay for environmental improvements. This means we have to decide upon acceptable pollution control (and thus environmental improvement) levels.

Economic theory posits that the objective of society is to maximize human welfare. Since welfare to the economist is a state of human perception, great emphasis is placed on how individuals perceive their welfare and hence on the concept of preference. Economic theory asserts that there exists a utility function that represents preferences. The aim of the individual is thus to attain the highest level of utility. This is the axiom of utility maximization. Looking at pollution control/acceptable environmental policy from an economic perspective therefore requires that rational policy decisions regarding resource allocation be based on an informed assessment of the utility (or benefits) of controlling pollution/environmental improvement.

In estimating such benefits, economic analysis of individual behaviour focuses upon the trade-offs used to infer values of environmental improvements. Hence the value of environmental improvement is measured by how much of another good a person will give up to get the reduction. Economic assigned values then are expressed in terms of individual willingness to pay (WTP) and willingness to accept compensation (WTA).

We develop estimates of the economic value of the benefits from improving the water quality of the River Tame, in particular focusing on improvements to biodiversity and recreational opportunities.

The following section details the particular benefits that may arise from the various improvements considered to the quality of water in the River Tame. We then discuss the particulars of the benefit estimation technique employed in the case study, along with issues of questionnaire survey design and structure. There then follows a results section that includes discussion and interpretation. The final section outlines the conclusions.

2. BENEFITS OF WATER QUALITY IMPROVEMENTS IN THE RIVER TAME

As water quality is improved, the types and numbers of fish and other life the river could support would increase. With a small improvement in quality, roach and gudgeon would begin to be seen in the river and with further improvements the numbers of these fish would grow. A greater diversity of plants – such as reeds and rushes – would grow in the river water and along its edge, and these would encourage waterfowl (moorhens, coots, ducks, geese and swans) to use the river. At this stage it would still not be advisable to paddle or swim in the river, but the river would be suitable for canoeing, for example.

As quality improved further, fish species such as perch, dace, chub, eel and pike would migrate up the river and it would now become a good coarse fishery. The number and types of insects living in and around the river would increase, for example, mayflies, dragonflies, and these would attract greater numbers of birds and other wildlife. Now the water, whilst not drinkable, would be relatively safe for humans and paddling and swimming in the river might be possible.

Finally, the water quality in the river could be restored to what it was before the industrial revolution. This would mean that trout – and even salmon – could live in the river along with freshwater shrimp. In some of the open spaces along the upper reaches of the river, such as in Sandwell Valley Country Park, it might be possible for otters to survive. At this level of quality, the water would be clear and although it still would not be a good idea to drink it, it would definitely be safe for paddling and swimming.

3. BENEFIT ESTIMATION OF WATER QUALITY IMPROVEMENTS

In order to assess the benefits of water quality improvements in the River Tame, we have developed a questionnaire survey in which respondents face a contingent ranking exercise in which they are asked to rank three potential water quality schemes along with the current status quo.

Contingent ranking (Smith and Desvousges, 1986) is a survey-based technique designed to isolate the value of individual product characteristics (attributes) which are typically supplied in combination with one another. In a CR elicitation respondents are asked to rank or rate a series of 'product profiles' that describe products having specific attribute levels. The expressed trade-offs between respondents' assessments and product attributes then can be used to estimate the marginal utility of each attribute. Since price is usually one of the attributes, it is possible to rescale the ranking (utility) index in money terms and so derive estimates of willingness to pay for particular attribute bundles.

Such ranking activities are especially useful for valuing environmental programmes, which often have several features, such as cleaner water, and so on. It is thus useful to divide the programme into its different components to assess people's willingness to pay for each programme attribute. Using this technique we have the advantage of allowing for the valuation of both the programme as a whole and the various attributes of the programme. The technique allows respondents to systematically evaluate trade-offs among multiple environmental attributes or among environmental and non-environmental attributes. In addition, the trade-off process encourages respondent introspection and consistency checks can be made on response patterns. However, CR elicitation can be cognitively challenging since some trade-offs are difficult to evaluate or may involve some unfamiliar attributes.

Using various environmental and non-environmental attributes we evaluate a number of scenarios/programmes. Each scenario/programme consists of the various attributes combined together such that variation in the choice of attribute levels gives rise to the different scenarios/programmes.

A random utility model, a widely applied model of consumer behaviour that involves discrete choices, is used to model the observed rankings. In a random utility model, the individual is assumed to select alternatives that provide the highest utility level. The present study follows the methodology of Beggs et al. (1981). This methodology takes advantage of the greater set of information provided by a full set of ranked choices. Such a full set arises in the present contingent ranking case since we have more than one alternative in the choice set, and this generates more than one response for each respondent. Each response is differentiated by the rank of a given alternative and by the levels of the attributes of that alternative.

Information on the choice ranked first by the respondent indicates that his/her utility for that choice is greater than the utility for any alternative choice they have. We can then define a probability model for any alternative, that gives the probability that utility for the alternative is greater than the other alternatives. The full set of rankings will give us information on respondents' relative utilities for each of the alternatives. A probability model can then be defined based on the ordered data, giving the probability of a complete ordering.

So, if equation (8.1) describes a random utility function, then individual *i*'s probability of selecting alternative *j*, given *i*'s characteristics Z_i, is defined by the probability that *i*'s utility of *j* will exceed the utility of all other alternatives.

$$\Pr[U_{i1} > U_{i2} > \ldots > U_{ij}] \tag{8.1}$$

$$U_{ij} = V_{ij}(X_{ij}, Z_i) + \varepsilon_{ij} \tag{8.2}$$

Where

i = individuals
j = choice alternatives
U_{ij} = total utility individual *i* receives from choice alternative *j*
V_{ij} = observed or deterministic part of the utility function
X_{ij} = choice alternative specific attributes
Z_i = individual specific attributes
ε_{ij} = stochastic portion of utility

The stochastic component is assumed to follow some distribution function. If this distribution function is assumed to be logistic, then we can derive the following model which shows the probability of a complete ordering of choices 1 to *J*:

$$\Pr[U_{i1} > U_{i2} > \ldots > U_{i,J}] = \prod_{j=1}^{J}\left\{\exp(V_{ij}) / \left[\sum_{k=j}^{J}\exp(V_{ik})\right]\right\} \tag{8.3}$$

A likelihood function can then be derived defining the joint probabilities of the rank orderings as a function of the parameters of the indirect utility function (assuming the indirect utility function *V* is linear in parameters).

Maximum likelihood estimation can then be used to find the coefficients of the indirect utility function that maximize the probability that a given respondent ranks the choices in the order in which they are actually selected. This enables one to estimate the marginal rates of substitution between scheme attributes.[2] As such it is possible to get valuations of the individual scheme attributes as well as for the scheme as a whole.

4. SURVEY DESIGN, STRUCTURE AND DATA

The questionnaire first contained a section on administrative information, relating to when and where the survey was completed, as well as a brief introductory statement of the purpose of the survey and permission to proceed.

The next section related to the respondent's residential details, visitation and use of the River Tame. These can be important determinants of the responses to the valuation questions. The attitudes of respondents towards environmental problems and towards current problems that exist in the UK more generally are then elicited using a Likert type scale. The respondents were asked to rate the importance of the various problems on a scale ranging from 1 = not important to 5 = very important. Respondents were also asked to state how interested they were in environmental issues, again on a Likert scale from 1 = not interested at all to 5 = very interested.

Knowledge and perception questions relating to the River Tame were then asked. Respondents were first asked to rate the quality of the river water on a scale ranging from −3 = very poor to +3 = very good. Then after being given some information about the current state of the river and causes of this state they were asked if they already knew this information. The information was as follows:

> The river was once a small, high quality trout stream, but, over the last century the water quality has decreased and is currently classified by the Environment Agency as very poor. Fish stocks are now virtually non-existent, plants find it difficult to grow in the river and hence insect, bird and animal life around the riverbanks is limited. Additionally, the water in the river is unsuitable for boating, paddling or swimming.
>
> The main causes of the current poor state of the water quality in the river are effluent from sewage works, urban run-off and seepage of pollutants from contaminated land. By urban run-off we mean the rainwater that runs off roads, industrial and housing estates.

The next section contained the valuation scenarios outlining the water quality improvements possible. Three separate possible improvement scenarios were specified as follows:

Small improvement – here a few species of fish, such as roach, would begin to be seen in the river, and more plants such as reeds and rushes would grow in the water and along the river edge. These would encourage waterfowl to use the river. The river would also become suitable for boating. However, one still would not be able to paddle or swim in the river.

Medium improvement – water quality is now improved such that some game fish species, such as perch, would migrate up the river and it would now become good enough for fishing as well as boating. The number and types of insects, such as mayflies and dragonflies, which live in and around the river, would increase, and these would attract greater numbers of birds and other wildlife. However, one still would not be able to paddle or swim in the river.

Large improvement – the water quality in the river is restored to what it was before the industrial revolution. This would mean that trout – and even salmon – could live in the river. In some of the open spaces along the upper reaches of the river, such as in Sandwell Valley Country Park, it might be possible for otters to survive. At this level of quality the water would be good enough to paddle and swim in, as well as for fishing and boating.

The respondents were then asked to indicate how important it was to them that the water in the River Tame should be clean on a Likert type scale ranging from 1 = not important at all to 5 = very important.

Some information was then given on what was necessary for the improvements to occur, including the fact that for the improvements to occur, expense would be required, mainly in terms of higher council tax levels paid by residents. Respondents were reminded that they already currently paid towards some water improvements as part of the taxes and water rates, and that any amount they stated would then be unavailable for other purchases.

The contingent ranking exercise question then followed in which respondents were asked to rate four combinations of water quality levels and amounts that they might be willing to pay in order to obtain those levels. The three improved levels of water quality were considered as well as the current status quo. This is because, in order to avoid imposing linearity on respondents' preferences, a minimum of three levels of each attribute are required. These levels should be chosen so as to maximize the amount of information contained in the survey responses, in particular with reference to the implicit prices embodied in the choice between alternative scenarios.

The WTP amounts considered were increases in council tax levels per household per year (also given as the equivalent monthly payment). The actual WTP amounts proposed were decided upon by pilot testing the questionnaire using different sets of combinations of amounts matched to water quality levels, and looking at how the distribution of rankings varied across the different sets of combinations. Ideally one should choose the WTP amounts such that they span the range of true willingness to pay amounts in the population, and such that the alternatives are not ranked solely on the basis of either the WTP amount or water quality level (otherwise trade-off estimates could not be determined). The final WTP amounts and associated water quality characteristics used are shown in Table 8.1 (note zero increase in WTP amount for current status quo). Respondents had to rate the combinations from 1 to 4, where 1 is the most preferred and 4 the least preferred.

The final section of the questionnaire contained questions on the socio-economic characteristics of the respondents. These included questions on sex, age, education, household numbers, marital status, employment status, the council tax charge band the respondent's property was classified under, and income. Some questions were also included for interviewers in order to

Table 8.1 WTP amounts and water quality characteristics for improvements

Water quality level	Characteristics of water quality level			£ extra council tax	
	Fishing	Plants & wildlife	Boating & swimming	Per year	Per month
Large improvement in quality (Level L)	Trout and salmon return Good game fishing possible	Increase in plants and wildlife Possible for otters to survive	Water good enough for boating and swimming	£30	£2.50
Medium improvement in quality (Level M)	Some game fish species return (e.g. perch) Good enough for fishing	Increase in number and types of insects Greater numbers of birds and wildlife	Suitable for boating, but not swimming	£15	£1.25
Small improvement in quality (Level S)	A few fish species return (e.g. roach)	More plants would grow, waterfowl can use river	Suitable for boating, but not swimming	£5	£0.42
Current situation (Level C)	Fish stocks virtually non-existent	Plant growth, insects, birds and animal life limited	Unsuitable for boating and swimming	£0	£0

assess respondents' understanding and the consideration given to the valuation questions.

5. RESULTS

Survey data collection was carried out by in-person interview of local residents in the Birmingham area. Respondents were interviewed in their place of residence and interviews were undertaken over the period August and September 1999. Each interview lasted about 10–15 minutes and total sample size was 675.

The socioeconomic composition of the sample is shown in Table 8.2. It should be pointed out that the refusals on the income question are uncharacteristically rather high. This may be due to respondents being sensitive about disclosing this information, especially since interviews were conducted at their place of residence.

We now consider information relating to people's visitation, use and perceptions of the River Tame area. Table 8.3 shows the frequency of visits to the river area during a typical year, as well as the mean distance from residence to the river area for each of the visitation frequencies. As can be seen, a majority of the sample has never visited the river area. Interestingly, it

Table 8.2 General characteristics

Characteristic	
Income £ (mean)	19023
£ (median)	21000
(% don't know/refused)	50.07
Age (mean)	48.4
Sex (% of men)	45.9
No. of household residents (mean no. of people in household)	2.97
Employment (% currently employed, full or part time)	51.19
Owner occupation (% own property)	88.86
Education level attained (% of sample who completed)	
• primary	99.85
• secondary (to 16 yrs)	97.78
• upper secondary (to 18 yrs)	45.93
• professional qualification	28.44
• university degree	17.93
Council tax £ (mean)	850.69
(% don't know)	24.15

Table 8.3 Frequency of visits

Frequency of visits	% of sample (number of respondents)	Mean distance from residence to river (miles)
Daily	4.30 (29)	1.05
At least once a week	6.81 (46)	1.24
At least once a month	6.81 (46)	1.81
At least once a year	5.93 (40)	2.35
About once a year	6.37 (43)	1.58
Less than once a year	16.00 (108)	2.04
Have never visited	53.78 (363)	3.04

Table 8.4 Reasons for visiting the River Tame area

Reason for visiting the river	% of those who have visited the river area who stated reason	% of sample who stated reason (number of respondents)
To relax and enjoy the scenery/sightseeing	26.92	12.44 (84)
To walk a dog	10.90	5.04 (34)
For a walk/jogging	31.41	14.52 (98)
For a picnic	2.88	1.33 (9)
To go bird-watching/wildlife observation	1.92	0.89 (6)
To take part in outdoor sports	3.53	1.63 (11)
Cycling/fishing/horse-riding/ pass by river	30.13	13.93 (84)

Note: more than one reason may be stated by any individual.

appears roughly that as visitation rate falls the mean distance from residence to the river increases. There was in fact a statistically significant relationship ($\alpha = 1\%$) between the frequency of visits and the distance from the respondent's residence and river area.

Table 8.4 shows the main reasons why people visit the river along with the percentage of those who have visited the river area, as well as of the total sample, who stated this reason as to why they visited the river. As can be expected for such a river area, the main reason for visiting is to go for a walk/jogging.

Table 8.5 shows respondents' subjective rating of water quality for the Tame. Ratings are also shown for the sub-sample of respondents who have

Table 8.5 Water quality rating

Water quality rating	Full sample	Respondents who have visited at least once	Respondents who have never visited
Mean	−0.72	−0.62	−0.95
Median	−1.00	−1.00	−1.00
% who gave 'don't know' response	50.52	24.36	73

Notes: Scale: −3 = very poor quality to +3 = very good quality.

made at least one visit to the river, as well as those who have made no visits, to see if perceptions differ between the two groups. As shown, respondents who have never visited the river have a lower mean rating of river water quality[3] (statistically significant at $\alpha = 10\%$), as well as much greater uncertainty in terms of ability to give a rating in the first place (statistically significant at $\alpha = 1\%$) than those who have visited the river.

After answering the water quality rating question, respondents were given some factual qualitative information regarding the river water quality and sources of pollution, after which they were asked if they already knew this information. Table 8.6 shows the responses to the question for the entire sample as well as for the visitors/non-visitors sub-samples as before. Awareness was higher among those respondents who had visited the river at least once previously than for those who had not visited (statistically significant at $\alpha = 1\%$).

After this awareness question, respondents were then asked some questions regarding their opinions about problems (general and environmental) which currently exist in the UK. The problems are listed in Tables 8.7 and 8.8 along with their mean and median rating of importance (rated by each respondent on a scale of 1 = not important to 5 = very important). Note that the order in which problems are presented in the table is the same order in which they appeared to respondents in the questionnaire.

Table 8.6 Awareness of water quality information

Aware of water quality information	Full sample	Respondents who have visited at least once	Respondents who have never visited
Yes (%)	28.44	35.58	22.31
No (%)	49.04	38.78	57.85
Some of it (%)	22.52	25.64	19.83

Table 8.7 Importance of some general problems currently existing in the UK

Problem	Mean rating	Median rating
Unemployment	4.23	5
Crime	4.69	5
Damage to the environment	4.30	5
Education	4.25	5
The Health Service	4.36	5
Public transport	3.69	4

Table 8.8 Importance of some environmental problems currently existing in the UK

Problem	Mean rating	Median rating
Air pollution	4.33	5
Poor drinking water quality	3.63	4
Pesticide residues in food	4.03	4
Water pollution at beaches	4.29	5
Loss of animal and plant species	4.24	5
Pollution of rivers and lakes	4.40	5
Damage to the countryside	4.28	5
Growth of genetically modified crops	3.80	4

'Crime' and the 'Health Service' are rated as the most important general problems overall, followed by 'Damage to the environment'. The higher rating for 'Crime' was in fact higher than for all the other problems by a statistically significant amount ($\alpha = 1\%$).

With regard to environmental problems currently existing in the UK, the highest rating was given to pollution of rivers and lakes, again the rating being higher than all the other environmental problems by a statistically significant amount ($\alpha = 1\%$). However, this question was ordered such that it came after the questions relating to use of the River Tame and, as such, respondents may have been made more sensitive to the problem of pollution of rivers relative to the other problems.

Respondents' interest in environmental issues was also established on a scale of 1 = not interested at all to 5 = very interested. Mean and median scores for the overall sample as well as for the visitors/non-visitors subsamples are shown below in Table 8.9. Environmental issues were rated as having more interest among those respondents who had visited the river at

Table 8.9 Interest in environmental issues

Interest in environmental issues	Full sample	Respondents who have visited at least once	Respondents who have never visited
Mean	3.92	4.00	3.86
Median	4	4	4

Table 8.10 Importance of clean-up

Importance of clean-up	Full sample	Respondents who have visited at least once	Respondents who have never visited
Mean	4.29	4.44	4.17
Median	5	5	4

least once previously than for those who had not visited at all (statistically significant at $\alpha = 10\%$).

The Valuation Questions

Respondents were first informed of the current situation in the River Tame and the various levels of improvement that could be implemented along with their implications for recreation and biodiversity. Prior to the ranking exercise they were asked to indicate how important it was to them that the water in the River Tame should be clean, using a scale of 1 = not important at all to 5 = very important. Table 8.10 shows the mean and median scores for the overall sample as well as for the visitors/non-visitors sub-samples. Importance of clean-up was rated higher among those respondents who had visited the river at least once previously than among those who had not visited (statistically significant at $\alpha = 1\%$).

Ranking Exercise

The contingent ranking question asked respondents to rank from 1 (most preferred) to 4 (least preferred) combinations of water quality levels and amounts they might be willing to pay per year to obtain those levels.

Table 8.11 shows the frequency distribution for all the rankings that are possible. As can be seen, the group of individuals who seem to rank on one criterion (either water quality or payment) dominates the sample rankings. Slightly less than half the sample was spread amongst the intermediate rankings although the distribution of frequencies for these rankings shows that there is some degree of preference for the medium and small improvements. We feel that the domination of the extreme rankings over the intermediate was not sufficiently high to indicate an ambiguous trade-off between payment and water quality.

Table 8.11 Frequency distribution for the rankings of water quality and payment

Ranking[a]	Frequency	Percent
LMSC	208	31.37
LMCS	2	0.30
LSMC	1	0.15
LSCM	0	0
LCMS	7	1.06
LCSM	1	0.15
MLSC	36	5.43
MLCS	2	0.30
MSLC	61	9.20
MSCL	51	7.69
MCLS	0	0
MCSL	0	0
SLMC	0	0
SLCM	0	0
SMLC	71	10.71
SMCL	11	1.66
SCLM	0	0
SCML	32	4.83
CLMS	4	0.60
CLSM	0	0
CMLS	1	0.15
CMSL	0	0
CSLM	0	0
CSML	175	26.40
Total	663	100

Notes: [a]The rankings are from highest to lowest level, with the alternatives defined as follows:
C = status quo
S = small improvement
M = medium improvement
L = large improvement.

Empirical Estimation of the Utility Function

The rankings of water quality and WTP were analysed using a rank ordered logit model in order to derive the indirect utility function, specified as a linear function of alternative scenario attributes. This, as we shall see below, enables one to estimate the marginal rates of substitution between scheme attributes (characteristics). As such, it is also possible to obtain valuations of individual scheme attributes as well as for the scheme as a whole.

The rank ordered logit model (McKelvey and Zaviona, 1975) is estimated for all observations. The estimation was made easier by the fact that there were no tied rankings.[4] The rank-ordered maximum likelihood estimation procedure, from Stata 6.0 (Stata Corporation, 2000), finds the coefficients that maximize the likelihood that a randomly selected individual ranks the alternatives in the order in which they were chosen. Negative coefficient estimates imply that an increase in the respective attribute will reduce utility (the probability of higher ranking for alternatives with higher levels of the respective attribute is decreased).

The attributes of the scenarios that are considered in the modelling procedure include those for water quality and cost of scenario. The cost attribute is simply the annual payment of extra council tax shown in Table 8.1. As discussed in the section on survey design (Table 8.1), the water quality attributes (characteristics) included fishing, plants and wildlife, and boating and swimming. It was not possible to include these individual characteristics as separate elements in the rank ordered logit model, since some form of numeric scale is required for each. However, it is possible to represent the overall nature of the characteristics by way of a proxy for them in the form of a water quality level scale. One such scale that has been previously used (Smith and Desvousges, 1986) is the Resources for the Future (RFF) Water Quality Index (Vaughan, 1981). This is a 10-point index of technical water quality measures and informed judgement linking recreational activities and water quality. Alternatively, one might use technical water quality measures such as levels of dissolved oxygen, biological oxygen demand, and total ammonium. Table 8.12 shows the water quality level improvements used in the survey, along with their associated RFF water quality index values and other technical measure values.

Whilst the RFF index does not specifically incorporate the plant and wildlife characteristics in defining the water quality, these are considered to be consistent with the index value pertaining to each of the recreational activity levels (boating, fishing and swimming – see Table 8.1). Such an interpretation of the RFF index is subject to a certain degree of qualification. Others may interpret it somewhat differently and this may have some effect on the results. Nevertheless we feel that our interpretation is on balance defensible. Similarly, the extent to which the values of the other

Table 8.12 Water quality improvements and RFF water quality index

Water quality level	RFF water quality index	Dissolved oxygen[a] (% saturation)	Biological oxygen demand (BOD)[a] (mg/litre)	Total ammonia[a] (mg N/litre)
Large improvement – L	7.0	80	2.5	0.25
Medium improvement – M	5.0	65	5	0.95
Small improvement – S	2.5	50	8	2.5
Current situation – C	0.8	20	15	9

Notes: [a]The correspondence of these technical measures to the RFF index scores and water quality improvement levels considered is derived from the UK Environment Agency's River Ecosystem Classification scheme, which has been used to describe rivers according to their suitability for fish in terms of these technical measures. Given that both the RFF index and the water quality improvement levels considered in this study are also characterized by their suitability for fish, it has thus been possible to match up the various technical measures to the water quality improvement levels and the RFF index values.

indices correspond to the water quality improvement levels considered here can be questioned (see Table 8.12 for more on the justification for their use). Whilst the modelling estimation undertaken here is for the RFF index (which we feel is also more defensible in terms of its relationship with the water improvement levels considered), we nevertheless report the final WTP values for these other indices for illustrative purposes.

Table 8.13 shows the results of the modelling procedure. The dependent variable is the ranked position of the policy and the independent variables are the policy attributes (we assume for simplicity at this stage that the rankings are unaffected by socioeconomic factors).

The coefficient on Payment is negative as expected, indicating that as the payment required for a scheme increases, utility decreases and so schemes requiring higher payment are more likely to receive lower ranked positions. Conversely, the coefficient on Water Quality is positive (as expected) indicating that utility increases as the water quality index increases. Schemes with higher water quality are more likely to receive higher ranked positions. The coefficients are both highly significant.

Estimation of WTP Estimates from Ranking Exercise

In order to calculate WTP estimates from the ranking exercise we follow the approach of Lareau and Rae (1985). The trade-off between attribute levels and disposable income is found by first assuming an indirect utility function

Table 8.13 Contingent ranking ordered logit results

Dependent variable: ranked position of water quality improvement

Variable	Coefficient	Std. error	*Z*	P>|*z*|	95% Conf. interval
Payment (£)	−0.2415	0.0164	−14.680	0.000	−0.2737: −0.2092
Water quality (RFF score)	1.2256	0.0797	15.364	0.000	1.0693: 1.3820

Notes:
Number of obs = 2649
LR $chi^2(2)$ = 248.77
Prob > chi^2 = 0.0000
Log likelihood = −3547.9068
Pseudo R^2 = 0.0339

in which the deterministic portion is specified as a linear function of the attribute levels, as shown by the following form:

$$V = \alpha c + \beta q$$

where c is the vector of payment associated with the scheme in question, q is the vector of the level of the other attributes associated with the scheme (in this case river water quality), and α and β are the respective coefficient parameters which represent the relative importance of each attribute in determining a respondent's ranking (or the marginal (dis)utility associated with a one-unit change in the attribute). In accordance with welfare theory, a respondent's maximum WTP for an increase in river water quality generated by a unit increase in q is such that his/her overall level of utility is constant. The change in payment relative to the change in river water quality necessary to keep welfare constant is $\Delta c/\Delta q$, which is given by the ratio β/α. This is the marginal rate of substitution between the water quality and payment attributes (ratio of marginal utilities). Calculating this for the specification shown in Table 8.13 gives an estimated WTP trade-off of £5.08 per household per annum (for a unit increase in RFF Water Quality Index).

As mentioned earlier, the WTP trade-offs were also estimated for the alternative water quality technical measures considered in Table 8.12. The results of the various unit trade-offs are shown in Table 8.14.

More complicated specifications of the indirect utility function involving income, demographic and socioeconomic variables can also be developed, though this is beyond the scope of the present study.[5]

Table 8.14 WTP per unit change in water quality indices

Unit change in water quality index	WTP per household per annum (£)
Unit increase in RFF index	5.08
1% saturation increase in dissolved oxygen	0.61
1 mg/litre decrease in biological oxygen demand	3.06
1 mg N/litre decrease in total ammonia	5.05

It should be noted that the econometric model used is based on the *Ranked Data* type of model used by Lareau and Rae (1985), and this is the dominant model used in the literature. Whilst this model is generally more efficient, in that it makes use of all the information on rankings contained in the dataset, it is, however, more restrictive in terms of the assumptions it imposes upon ranking behaviour (that all rankings are assumed to follow a logistic distribution and to be independent of each other. The alternative to this is to assume that only the selection of the first choice option is assumed to be governed by a logistic distribution). Further work is necessary to see whether the restrictive assumptions of the *Ranked Data* model give any cause for concern.

Another unattractive implication of the standard *Ranked Data* model is the use of a linear functional form (which thus does not allow the marginal utility of particular attributes to vary in accordance with their levels). A logarithmic transformation of the attribute levels was undertaken in order to account for this potential problem. Whilst direct comparison of the coefficient estimates is not possible given the logarithmic transformation of the data, the transformed model displayed uniformly smaller *t*-ratios as well as a lower value of the maximized log-likelihood function, indicating worse statistical performance. As such, there is no statistical case for preferring the logarithmic functional form to the linear one.

7. CONCLUSIONS

This study has been the first of its kind in the UK (to the knowledge of the authors) to estimate the benefits of river water quality improvements in terms of the objective water quality indices using a contingent ranking methodology.

Our case study considers improvements to an inner city river, the River Tame in Birmingham. In particular, we look at recreational and biodiversity improvements. The benefits of river water quality improvements were found for unit changes in various water quality indices. For example, the benefits were found to be around £5 per household per annum for a unit increase in the RFF water quality index scale. Whilst the RFF scale can be related to specific water quality conditions, relating mainly to recreational use of water bodies, we believe that these conditions should also pertain to the improvements in biodiversity levels described in the valuation scenarios.

Mention should be made of the relative ease with which respondents appeared to undertake the ranking exercise (less than 2% unable to give a ranking response), in contrast to the difficulties often found in contingent valuation studies (especially with open-ended CV elicitation formats).

These results come at a timely moment for consideration by the authorities responsible for water management in the UK. Recent interest in the use of stated preference methods has been expressed by bodies such as the Environment Agency, who are in the process of developing guidelines for the assessment of river water quality improvements. This study hopes to provide a useful input into the debate over the use of monetary valuation techniques in this context and should serve to show some of the relative merits and limitations associated with the techniques discussed.

NOTES

This research was funded by a grant from the University of Birmingham's Interdisciplinary Research Fund.

1. By urban run-off we mean the rainwater that runs off roads, individual factory yards and roofs, industrial and housing estates and any other hard surfaces which might collect atmospheric pollution and spillages of oils and other substances during dry periods.
2. Since the coefficients can be interpreted as the marginal utility associated with a one-unit change in any of the attributes, and the marginal rate of substitution simply equals the ratio of marginal utilities of the attributes of interest.
3. This is not surprising, since it can be argued that if you think that quality is low then you don't visit.
4. In such a situation it is necessary to undertake some form of 'censoring' in order to incorporate the ties. This, however, results in giving extra weight to tied ranks, so to overcome this it is necessary to use a weighted sample approach (Cox et al., 1999).
5. These variables can be incorporated in two ways. First, the variables of interest can be interacted with the payment or water quality attribute, though this can add to the burden of estimation and make interpretation of resulting coefficients complicated. Alternatively, one can divide the data up according to the particular socioeconomic variable of interest and estimate the model separately for each subset. The effect of the variable can then be deduced by comparing the magnitude and sign of the coefficients for each subset.

REFERENCES

Beggs, S., Cardell, S., and Hausman, J. (1981), 'Assessing the Potential Demand for Electric Cars', *Journal of Econometrics*, **16**, 1–19.

Cox, M., Barbier, E.B., and White, P.C.L. (1999), 'Using Contingent Rating Data in a WTP Study of Rabies Prevention Policies in the UK', mimeo, University of York, York.

Environment Agency (1998), *West Midlands-Tame Local Environment Agency Plan Consultation Report*, Lichfield: Environment Agency.

Lareau, T.J., and Rae, D.A. (1985), 'Valuing Willingness to Pay for Diesel Odor Reduction: An Application of the Contingent Ranking Technique', *Southern Economic Journal*, **55** (3), 728–42.

McKelvey, R., and Zaviona, W. (1975), 'A Statistical Model for the Analysis of Ordinal Level Dependent Variables', *Journal of Mathematical Sociology*, **4**, 103–20.

Smith, V.K., and Desvousges, W.H. (1986), *Measuring Water Quality Benefits*, Kluwer: Boston.

Vaughan, W.J. (1981), 'The Water Quality Ladder', appendix II, in R.C. Mitchell and R.T. Carson, *An Experiment in Determining Willingness to Pay for National Water Quality Improvements*, Draft Report, Washington DC: Resources for the Future.

9. Environmental resource information and the validity of non-use values: the case of remote mountain lakes

Ben Groom, Andreas Kontoleon and Timothy Swanson

1. INTRODUCTION

The suitability and validity of using non-use values (NUVs) in environmental decision making has been the subject of continuing debate ever since Krutilla's 1967 seminal paper which introduced the concept (though not the term) of NUVs into the mainstream of environmental economic theory and policy. Though the validity of NUVs has been debated on conceptual and philosophical grounds (see Kontoleon et al., 2001 for a survey), the bulk of the discussion has been preoccupied with issues of measurement. Since the commonly accepted method for measuring NUV is the contingent valuation method,[1] the debate over measurement of NUVs understandably reverts to one over the validity of the estimates derived from such a method (Mitchell and Carson, 1989; Bateman and Willis, 1999).[2] One of the main issues concerning the validity of NUV estimates from contingent valuation (CV) studies concerns the effect and role of environmental resource information that is provided to respondents participating in the contingent market.

Both the NOAA panel (Arrow et al., 1993) and CV practitioners have acknowledged the potential biases, framing effects as well as the possible confusion, manipulation and inducement of CV survey responses that can result from providing inappropriate types and quantities of information. Moreover, it has been accepted that the problems of information provision are more likely to be augmented for environmental goods for which individuals have mainly non-use values, low levels of information and familiarity or low levels of relevance (Arrow et al., 1993; Blomquist and Whitehead, 1998; Ajzen et al., 1996; Cameron and Englin, 1997). Supplying the optimal type and quantity of information is thus crucial for the validity of contingent valuation estimates and for the use of NUVs for environmental policy and damage assessment purposes.

In this chapter, we follow NOAA panel guidelines and undertake two tests of the validity of CV responses that are related to the effects and role of the provision of environmental resource information. The tests are explored in a case study that estimates the non-use values for a highly unfamiliar environmental resource, namely remote mountain lakes (RMLs). These ecosystems constitute a perfect example of a complex environmental good with which respondents are unfamiliar and for which non-use values are most likely the predominant element of total economic value. In the first validity test, the effects of varying levels of information on stated WTP are examined. This is a theoretical validity test in that it examines whether information provided to CV participants affects their WTP in a manner consistent with economic theory (Mitchell and Carson, 1989). Such theoretical validity tests have been undertaken with varying results by numerous researchers.[3] These studies provide different levels of information within or across groups of CV respondents and examine whether and in what way their WTP is affected. Conformity to economic theory is taken to provide an indication that CV responses are not random but instead follow some consistent pattern and are thus theoretically valid. Most of these studies have dealt with environmental goods for which people have mainly use values and/or a high degree of familiarity. In contrast, the experiment presented in this chapter explores the information effects on individual preferences and WTP of a highly unfamiliar and obscure environmental resource for which individuals have only very indirect use or non-use value, namely RMLs. The theoretical validity test is accomplished by designing a CV experiment that obtains WTP for the conservation of RMLs from different sub-groups of respondents who have been provided with different levels of information. A simple welfare theoretic model of the effects of information on individual preferences is presented. The theoretical model allows for the formation of empirically testable hypotheses that examine the effects of information on WTP.

Though the results from such tests may enhance our understanding of the effects of information on WTP, they provide little insight as to the question of the optimal level of information that must be provided. The issue of optimality is more adequately addressed by reference to some external benchmark or baseline against which to judge the outcome of the CV study (Mitchell and Carson, 1989). The NOAA panel has suggested that this can be achieved through the use of a type of external or convergent validity that 'compare[s] . . . contingent valuation's outcomes with those provided by a panel of experts' (p. 4607) as an alternative validity test for contingent valuation experiments. Some form of 'convergence' or conformity of CV responses to those obtained from an expert panel assessment would provide some external validation of the reliability of the former while the NOAA guidelines state that such a comparison 'will help to check whether respondents are reasonably well informed' (p. 4607). We thus follow Boyle et al. (1995) and interpret the NOAA guidelines as prescribing a form of external validity test for the reasonableness or optimality of the information provided. Few studies have endeavoured to follow the NOAA panel recommendations and compare expert opinions with individual preferences (Kenyon, 1998; Boyle, 1996), and still fewer have focused on the effect of information on the conformity of individual preferences with expert opinion (Kenyon, 1998). None has addressed these issues in the context of non-use values, the very class of economic values for which problems of validity and information issues are most pervasive.

This external validity test is undertaken through a comparison of the CV results with those obtained from a Delphi survey. This comparison allows us to assess the credibility and validity of using CV as an input into policy decisions as opposed to relying on expert based appraisal methods. We consider a situation that is commonly encountered by policy makers: the selection for conservation purposes of a small number of sites from a larger population. Such a policy decision requires considerations of trade-offs between the attributes of sites as well as some form of rating and ranking of these sites. Budgetary restrictions dictate such a prioritization of ecological sites. In this study, we obtained the ranking of four types of RMLs from a panel of experts participating in a Delphi survey. We then compared these results with those from a CV experiment in which we obtained the implicit ranking of the same types of RMLs (through the stated WTP bids) from three different groups, each receiving a different level of information. The objective of such an ordinal comparison was to investigate whether the provision of increasing levels of information would make CV respondents provide responses consistent with those obtained from experts and to draw some conclusions on the optimal level of information that should be provided in CV studies.

Note that this is not an external or convergent validity test of the *accuracy* of CV results. This would require a comparison of CV values with values obtained from revealed preference data sets. The latter are considered as 'true' values that serve as a benchmark with which we can compare the accuracy of 'stated' or 'hypothetical' values. In this sense, the validity test performed in this study, which involves an ordinal comparison between rankings of experts and lay-people, is not a strict convergent validity test in that we do not assume that expert opinion provides some 'true' value. Yet, expert panel assessments can be used as an external baseline for assessing the effects and optimality of the information provided to respondents and in this sense can serve as the basis for an external validity test on the reliability of CV studies.

The validity tests highlighted above provide guidance towards understanding the validity of stated preference techniques, but also allow us to draw some more general implications for using CV and individual preference based values in environmental policy. An attempt is made to address these issues in order to guide environmental policy in general and for the particular case in hand, the remote mountain lakes.

2. RESOURCE INFORMATION AND ENVIRONMENTAL DECISION MAKING

2.1 The Role and Effect of Information in Eliciting Non-use values

The credibility and validity of stated preference techniques have been questioned when respondents are asked to value complex environmental goods about which they have little prior information, and for which preferences may not be well formed or consistent (Munro and Hanley, 2000). In such cases respondents bring prior information and beliefs to the contingent market, and these beliefs may or may not be an accurate representation of the world, or ensure consistent preferences over choices. As a result, respondents are faced with uncertainty as to their preferences, which may manifest itself in any number of distortions from the 'true' response. Moreover, if the contingent valuation is a constructive process, as some authors claim, the economic value (in other words, the stated WTP) is constructed during the interview. Again, this is more likely when respondents have little knowledge or experience of the environmental good to be evaluated (Ajzen et al., 1996).[4] In sum, when the good in question is not used by people, for the most part and when it harbours qualities which are more scientifically/research oriented, respondent familiarity becomes more of an issue, and the level of information becomes important (Munro and Hanley, 2000).

To the extent that validity and credibility problems arise through lack of information, there is an incentive to provide individuals with additional information concerning the environmental good being valued in order to ensure responses are built upon correct assumptions and to reduce uncertainty (Munro and Hanley, 2000). From a methodological perspective, information concerning environmental goods is thought to reduce the embedding effect (Arrow et al., 1993), reduce the use of 'incorrect' heuristic valuation related to core characteristics of the good (Hutchinson et al., 1995; Fischoff et al., 1980; Ajzen et al., 1996; or Blamey, 1998), and fix the meaning, and the perception, of the good for the respondent (Hutchinson et al., 1995). Similarly, some authors have suggested that there is a need to supply additional information to individuals as a result of the public good nature of environmental assets, about which individuals are generally unaware (Sagoff, 1998).

Information can affect at least three aspects of CV studies, including: (i) the subjective probabilities that individuals hold about potential states of the world, (ii) the credibility of the scenario, (iii) the strategic bias (Munro and Hanley, 2000). The resultant effect of information upon the distribution of WTP responses will depend upon the beliefs that people bring to the survey and whether the information provided is 'positive' or 'negative' (Munro and Hanley, 2000).[5] There is much evidence to suggest that the distribution of WTP responses varies considerably depending upon the amount and complexity of the information provided to individuals (e.g. Blomquist and Whitehead, 1998; Bergstrom et al., 1990, MacMillan et al., 2000). In particular Ajzen et al. (1996) report that additional information has a very strong impact on the stated willingness to pay and this effect is magnified when the good is of high personal relevance. Further information effects have been analysed empirically with respect to a number of different elements of the contingent market: for example, information about the resource to be evaluated (Samples et al., 1986; Bergstrom et al., 1990), about budget constraints and other people's contingent values (Loomis et al., 1994; Bergstrom et al., 1989) and about related environmental goods like the existence and the properties of complement and substitute goods (Whitehead and Blomquist, 1991). Information may also effect an increase in participation in the contingent market (a reduction of zero responses), again affecting moments of the bid distribution (Munro and Hanley, 2000). Similarly, the provision of information about the relative efficiency (perceived marginal efficiency) of alternative money expenditures towards achieving preservation objectives may affect reported willingness to pay (Samples et al., 1986).

Additional exogenous information for respondents is recommended in order to focus responses on some 'true' value, the suggestion being that, whatever the effect of information on the distribution of WTP, it is a desirable effect. However, another problem related to providing information in contingent valuation studies is that respondents may not receive information that is suited to their individual needs. As the level of information required to make a decision will vary from individual to individual, standardized information sets, no matter how well designed, will unavoidably run the risk of leaving respondents either (a) unconvinced by the simplistic nature of the questionnaire: information underload, or (b) simply confused by the amount of information they have to process: information overload (MacMillan et al., 2000). Moreover, if contingent markets become too complex, people may make hasty choices which do not reflect their true preferences, like 'yeah-saying', 'don't know' responses or 'protesting' and terminating the interview quickly, as well as resorting to heuristics (Clark et al., 2000, or MacMillan et al., 2000).

2.2 Processing of Information by Respondents

Another issue is related to how people process information; so far it has been assumed that any piece of information provided by the CV practitioners is processed in the 'appropriate' way by all the respondents. In the real world, the standard level of information incorporated in a questionnaire is processed differently by different respondents according to a great number of factors, the most important being the personal relevance of the good and previous knowledge of the topic.

As pointed out by Cameron and Englin (1997), an interaction exists between exogenously provided and endogenously determined/prior information. While it is very easy to control the effect of the former on the willingness to pay, it is more difficult to check either the extent or the effect of the latter. Endogenously determined information is usually modelled as a function of past recreational habits, observed behaviour, degree of education and kind of employment, but most of the time it must be simply written off as unobserved behaviour. In most of the studies, it is implicitly assumed that the endogenously determined experience (prior knowledge) does not influence the results of the questionnaire. Abstraction from this kind of knowledge may be justified in the case of very obscure commodities, but usually respondents already have some information about the good to be evaluated and this will influence how they process the information incorporated in the questionnaire. Unfortunately, a formal model of the interaction between endogenous and exogenous information is still missing in the literature.

Similarly, it has been generally assumed that information provided in contingent valuation studies is ingested by the respondents in the same way in which it is communicated by the investigators. In other words, it is assumed that respondents process information very carefully. Ajzen et al. (1996) point out that this is not always true. According to the authors, one of the most important factors in determining the way in which respondents process information is the personal relevance of the good. In the absence of personal relevance, respondents are thought to adopt a peripheral processing mode so that the final judgement is deeply influenced by factors which are unrelated to the content of the message. Such factors include relatively superficial issues, implicit moods and motivations or cognitive heuristics. Therefore, it is important not only to provide information about the good but also to be sure that respondents are processing information effectively.

2.3 The Optimal Provision of Information in CV Studies

It is clear from the survey of the previous two sections that the amount of information is an important factor in ensuring the credibility of CV estimates, because it directly affects the stated WTP. Similarly, it is important to establish that information is being processed 'correctly'. Thus, as the possibility of information overload reveals, it is not simply *more* information that will produce credible results; it is the correct level (amount and type). The question therefore remains; what is the optimal level of information that should be provided to CVM respondents?

Several perspectives exist as to the level of information that respondents should be provided with. At the one extreme, there are those who suggest that the practitioner must accept the respondents' ignorance and provide only the amount of information which is necessary to create a realistic market situation. At the other extreme, it is thought that the practitioner must provide complete information about the resource being evaluated, its complements, its substitutes, the perceived efficiency of the management plan to be implemented and whatever other pieces of information are considered relevant to the particular issue.

The NOAA panel recommendation for stated preference valuation techniques falls somewhere in between. It suggests analysts should 'decide . . . the standard of knowledgeability of the respondents that [they] want to impose on a contingent valuation study. It is clear that it should be at least as high as that which the average voter brings to a real referendum' (p. 4607). However, the recommendations also state that 'if contingent valuation surveys are to elicit useful information about willingness to pay, respondents must understand exactly what it is they are being asked to value' (Arrow et al., 1993, p. 14, our emphasis). A similar view argues against the extremes and for a middle way. Hoevenagel and van der Linden (1993) argue that the level of information should be less than that which causes 'information overload' but sufficient to overcome 'information thresholds'. In this framework, the assumption is that there is a non-linear relationship between the amount of information and its effects on WTP, such that an informational threshold exists at the point at which it is decided to participate in the contingent market, and at the point at which confusion sets in.[6] In short, the question of the optimal level of information can be addressed on a case by case basis and by reference to the impact on the distribution of WTP responses (Munro and Hanley, 2000).

2.4 Information Provision through Alternatives to CV

As described above, the NOAA panel recommendation emphasizes the need to ensure that respondents are at least as informed as an average voter in a real referendum, and that respondents understand exactly what it is they are being asked to value. Yet, as the discussion above suggests, conveying the appropriate level of information in a stated preference study is very difficult, especially for unfamiliar and complex environmental resources. Indeed, this seems to be an almost insoluble difficulty due to the very nature of CV studies. First, CV practitioners with a limited budget face time constraints on each interview, within which the environmental good is explained, the proposed scenario described and respondents process this information in order to make their (stated) choice. The brief time allocated to each interview is clearly insufficient when dealing with complex and unfamiliar environmental resources. Second, as seen above, respondents may not receive information that is suited to their individual needs (cognitive ability, prior knowledge and so on). CV practitioners can endeavour to provide information that can be understood by the 'average' individual, yet the level of information required to make a decision will vary from individual to individual, leading to information over- or underload in standardized information sets (MacMillan et al., 2000).

Numerous studies have shown that participants in CV studies have a very poor understanding of the environmental resource in question (e.g. Chilton and Hutchinson, 1999) and resort to constructing various heuristics or to relying on survey cues (e.g. wording) while making their choices (e.g. Ajzen et al., 1996; Blamey, 1998). Also, the complexity of CV settings may cause people to make hasty choices which do not reflect their true preferences.[7]

The acknowledgement that individual preferences do have a role in environmental decision making, coupled with the recognition that stated preferences techniques are dented by difficulties in conveying the appropriate information, have led some to propose *other* methods of incorporating individual participation in environmental decision making. Most notably, the citizen jury or the similar planning cell technique have been suggested as viable alternatives (Brown et al., 1995; Crosby, 1995; Dienel and Renn, 1995). Here we focus on their potential role in overcoming the 'informational' difficulties encountered in stated preference techniques. Compared to respondents in CV studies, those in citizen juries (CJs) are much better informed about the issue because they are deliberating for several days, interviewing an array of experts, and discussing the issue among their peers to reach a consensus about the particular environmental issue (or 'charge') presented to them. Yet, CJs do not provide *economic* values associated with any particular project nor do they pronounce upon whether a particular allocation decision constitutes an efficient use of resources. These weaknesses have recently prompted economists to develop new methods that attempt to combine stated preference techniques (necessary to provide information on efficiency questions) with jury-type methods (that allow citizens to be better informed and thus provide more meaningful choices). Examples of this work are MacMillan, et al. (2000) who develop the 'Market Stall' method and Kenyon and Hanley (2001) who explore the 'valuation workshop' approach.

3. MODELLING RESOURCE INFORMATION AND WILLINGNESS TO PAY

Blomquist and Whitehead (1998) develop a model for analysing the effect of information within the framework of consumer theory. It is within this framework that we address the effects of information upon the WTP for RMLs. The model provides general insights into the effects of exogenous information upon individual WTP. Blomquist and Whitehead define WTP as the difference between two individual expenditure functions whose arguments are the two states or quality levels of the good, q, and a given level of utility, u. The perceived quality of an environmental good is a function of the 'objective' quality of the resource, θ, and the exogenous information provided in the CVM questionnaire, I. Thus the individual's perceived quality of RML i, under information level k, can be modelled as:

$$q[\theta,I] = \beta\theta + \delta I \quad (9.1)$$

β and δ are learning parameters, β for prior information and δ for information provided exogenously in the contingent market. In entering into the contingent market, individuals may have less than perfect information about the quality of the resource they must value. This may manifest itself in either under- or overestimation of the perceived quality of the resource. The provision of information to the respondents is intended to correct these perceptions towards the true quality levels represented by the objective quality θ.

It is postulated that should the perceived resource quality be higher than the objective resource quality, the effect of additional information on perceived quality will be negative, bringing perceived quality into line with objective quality. This would be represented by $\delta < 0$. Conversely, where perceived quality is less than objective quality, the effect of exogenous information about the quality of the resource will be positive, again bringing perceived quality into line with objective quality.[8] This can be represented by $\delta > 0$. The WTP for quality changes in environmental resources, using the definition of perceived quality can be defined as:

$$WTP = e(q^1[\theta,I],u) - e(q^0[\theta,I],u) \quad (9.2)$$

where q^1 is the perceived quality after the change while q^0 is the original perceived quality. Substituting in the indirect expected utility function, $u = v(q^0[\theta,I],m)$, (9.2) becomes:

$$WTP = e(q^1,v(q^0[\theta,I],m)) - m \tag{9.3}$$

Given (9.3), the marginal effect of I on WTP is given by the partial derivative of (9.3) with respect to I. By the chain rule this gives:

$$\frac{\partial WTP}{\partial I} = \frac{\partial e}{\partial v}\frac{\partial v}{\partial q^0[\theta,I]}\frac{\partial q^0[\theta,I]}{\partial I} \tag{9.4}$$

Assuming the marginal utility of income and the marginal utility of perceived quality are both positive, the first two terms on the right-hand side (RHS) of (9.4), which represent the marginal effect of perceived quality on WTP, are non-negative. That is, '[w]illingness to pay will increase (decrease) with an increase (decrease) in perceived resource quality since increasing quality increases the utility loss associated with degraded quality'. However, as described above, the effect of exogenously provided information, I, upon WTP may be either positive or negative depending on the relationship between objective and perceived quality, that is, whether δ is less than or greater than zero. Rewriting (9.4) with reference to (9.1) provides:

$$\frac{\partial WTP}{\partial I} = \frac{\partial WTP}{\partial q^0[\theta,I]}\frac{\partial q^0[\theta,I]}{\partial I} = \frac{\partial WTP}{\partial q^0[\theta,I]}\delta \gtrless 0 \tag{9.5}$$

Following the assertions above, it is clear from this representation that if perceived quality is less than objective quality, that is, people currently underestimate the quality of the resource in question, information about resource quality will increase perceived resource quality, $\delta > 0$, and therefore increase stated WTP towards that associated with the objective quality. On the other hand, if perceived resource quality is greater than the objective quality, that is, people are currently overestimating the quality of the resource, information will reduce perceived resource quality, $\delta < 0$, and reduce the stated WTP, again towards that associated with the objective quality of the resource. Interpreting the objective quality as representative of the 'true' state/quality of the world, the information effect is always desirable in that the stated WTP (conditional on additional information) will be closer to the WTP associated with the objective quality of the resource.[9]

4. ENVIRONMENTAL RESOURCE INFORMATION AND THE VALIDITY OF WTP: AN APPLICATION TO RMLs

The preceding model was employed to formulate hypotheses that were used to explore the validity tests described in the introduction. The tests were examined within a CV study on the management of remote mountain lakes. RMLs were chosen as the subject matter of the CV study owing to the public's unfamiliarity with these ecosystems and their high non-use value component.

RMLs are defined as those aquatic ecosystems that are above the regional timberline. In Europe, such lakes are dispersed in mostly remote regions far from any human settlements. Owing to the harsh climatic conditions, RMLs host very few plant and insect species. There are no animal species present, although some lakes have fish populations (largely brown trout). Human interaction with these ecosystems is minimal. In fact, most lay-people have very little (if any) knowledge about these lakes. In contrast, European scientists (primarily ecologists, limnologists, biologists, chemists and meteorologists) have extensively studied these ecosystems over the past couple of decades. This research has provided data that feed into air-born pollution and climate change modelling. Their research mainly focuses on studying water chemistry as well as the condition of algae and fish populations in these lakes.[10] Scientific research has shown that acidification has taken its toll even in these remote ecosystems, affecting primarily the composition of algae species.

The benefits to humans of the RMLs are of the non-use type (from the knowledge that these ecosystems are preserved when no personal direct present or future use is contemplated) and of a very indirect kind (providing habitat to some algae, plant and insect species as well as providing scientific information on climate change and atmospheric pollution). Moreover, the impacts of atmospheric pollution on these lakes are equally obscure to most non-experts. According to natural scientists, the sensitivity of RMLs makes them particularly vulnerable to environmental change and also enables them to act as excellent indicators of both pollution and climate change. The corollary of this is that RMLs are the most difficult environments for which to attain environmental standards. Research into the ecological benefits (or non-attainment costs) of adherence to ecological standards has never previously been undertaken for the RMLs, and as such the implementation of environmental agreements such as the UNECE Second Sulphur Protocol has not been guided or optimized by such measures.[11] A number of studies are currently under way to redress this omission using stated preference techniques.[12] However, as argued above, questions exist as to the validity of economic valuation techniques when applied to environmental assets such as RMLs, which are in general unfamiliar and complex environmental goods whose economic value to members of the public lies largely in potentially nebulous existence values.

The first validity test examined whether individual preferences would converge to that of lake experts if appropriate information was provided. This was achieved by comparing the implied ranking of types of RMLs with the ranking provided by experts. Individual preferences were ascertained within the CV study while expert opinion was obtained using the Delphi method. To investigate such external validation of CV responses we had to establish the implicit ranking, or absence thereof, of the four types of lakes to be valued by each individual. Hence, we were able to investigate the implicit ranking of four programmes through the pair-wise testing of the following null hypothesis:

$$\text{Null Hypothesis 1:} \qquad H_0^1 : WTP_{ik} = WTP_{jk}$$

for the kth information level, and for RMLs $i > j$, for all combinations of RMLs. This comparison of WTP reduces to a comparison of perceived quality changes across lakes. These changes are composed of the effect of perceived changes upon the objective quality (from θ_i^0 to θ_i^1), and the level of exogenous information.[13] In terms of the model, and using (9.6), null hypothesis 2 can also be represented as:

$$WTP_{ik} - WTP_{jk} = e(q_{ik}^1, v(q_{ik}^0[\theta_i^0, I_{ik}], m)) - e(q_{jk}^1, v(q_{jk}^0[\theta_j^0, I_{jk}], m)) = 0 \tag{9.6}$$

This hypothesis was explored for each information level, k, so as to examine if and how the ranking of sites varied across information groups and whether any particular level of information would make individual responses converge to those obtained from experts.

The second validity test sought to examine the effect of information on the intensity of individual preferences for such a remote and unknown environmental good.[14] Based on information from a Delphi study (see next section) as well as direct consultations with experts, three levels of information about RMLs were devised. The RMLs were grouped into four types of lakes, each group containing lakes with similar characteristics and levels of services. A CV study was then designed such that three sub-groups of individuals were asked to provide their WTP for conserving each of the four types of RMLs. Hence, individuals in each of the three information groups ($k = 1, 2, 3$) were asked to value four different types of lakes ($i = 1, 2, 3, 4$). We thus received three WTP bids for a particular group of lakes i: one from each individual that had access to one of the k levels of information. In terms of the model described above, the null hypothesis testing the effect of information on WTP is given by:

$$\text{Null Hypothesis 2:} \qquad H_0^2 : \overline{WTP_{ik}} = \overline{WTP_{il}}$$

for information levels $k \neq l$, and for RML i, where, noting that the perceived quality of lake i at information level k can be written as:

$$q_{ik}[\theta_i, I_{ik}] = \beta_i \theta_i + \delta_{ik} I_{ik} \tag{9.7}$$

the effect of additional information on WTP for lake i at current information level k can be written as:

$$\frac{\partial WTP_{ik}}{\partial I} = \frac{\partial WTP_{ik}}{\partial q_{ik}^0[\theta_i, I_{ik}]} \delta_{ik} \tag{9.8}$$

Given the assumptions concerning equation (9.4), in effect we are testing the sign of the learning parameter for exogenous information δ_{ik}, and making no *a priori* assumptions concerning the sign of β_i in equation (9.6).[15] δ_{ik} is not assumed constant across lakes within the k information levels, since although the information levels provide the same 'type' of information for each of the i lakes, naturally the actual components of the information differ for each lake. Similarly, δ_{ik} is not assumed to be constant across information levels.[16]

5. THE DELPHI STUDY

In this section we report on the design, implementation and results from the Delphi study. The Delphi methodology is a systematic method of collecting opinions from a group of experts through a series of questionnaires in which feedback on the group's opinion distribution is provided between question rounds (Helmer, 1972). In this way a significant portion of the effort needed for experts to communicate is shifted from the respondents group to the monitoring team. The Delphi method is particularly useful when (a) the decision in question does not lend itself to precise analytical techniques but may benefit from subjective judgements on a collective basis, and (b) individuals who are needed to contribute to the examination of the problem represent diverse backgrounds with respect to experience and expertise (Linstone and Turoff, 1976). It is in this sense that the Delphi method may be a useful decision mechanism for environmental policy concerned primarily with non-use values of environmental resources, may provide a useful alternative to CVM, or may be used as a test of the validity of CVM preference orderings. The recommendations of the NOAA panel can perhaps be understood in this sense.

Unlike other methodologies used in environmental economics (for example, CV) the Delphi method is particularly unstructured. It is the duty of the monitoring team to adapt and apply the basic rules of the methodology to the subjects being examined. The main principles of the Delphi are: (i) the experts interact only through the feedback mechanisms provided by the monitoring team: this is to avoid the group dynamics which characterize face-to-face meetings such as domineering personalities or unwillingness to contradict individuals in a higher position, and (ii) answers are anonymous to provide the experts with the greatest degree of individuality and freedom from restriction on their expression (Turoff, 1976).

In the current study, we used three rounds in the Delphi study, the internal aims of which were manifold. The study was implemented during the period July to August 2001. First, we sought to reach a consensus between experts of different disciplines on the most important ecological criteria to evaluate the ecological importance of generic RMLs (rounds 1 and 2). This information was used to construct the information scenarios for the CVM study described in Section 6.1. Secondly, we required our experts to rank four specific RMLs on the basis of their 'ecological interest' with respect to the chosen criteria (round 3).

Round 1 of the Delphi study started within information about a hypothetical management plan[17] being designed for the conserving RMLs. The management plan consisted of a programme of applying lime (a natural mineral) to the lakes as a means of combating the effects of acidification. It was explained that because of budgetary restrictions not all RMLs could be included in the programme. We asked the experts for their opinions on the various criteria that could be used to choose the most suitable regions of lakes to be included in this management plan.[18] In order to help the experts assess the criteria and in order to provide a framework for their judgement we introduced a 5-point Likert 'importance scale' such that '1' denoted 'highly important' and '5' 'highly unimportant'.

Round 2 of the Delphi questionnaire provided the experts with each criterion's average mark and the variance of the mark and asked them to evaluate the criteria again. The results from rounds 1 and 2 of the Delphi questionnaire are summarized in Table 9.2. It is worth pointing out that the ranking of the criteria obtained in round 2 is substantially different from that obtained in round 1. Moreover, it seems that knowing the opinion of fellow members of the panel allowed scientists to reduce uncertainty about their judgement as represented by the general drop in the value of the variance. In sum, round 2 of the Delphi shows a deeper consensus compared to that of round 1.

Table 9.1 Composition of the expert panel

Ecologists	4
Limnologists	6
Biologists	6
Economists	1
Meteorologists	1
Chemists	2
Physicists	1
Pollution modellers	3
Total	24

In *Round 3*, following Kenyon and Edward-Jones (1998), the expert panel were asked to rank the four RMLs according to their 'ecological interest', as defined by the scientific criteria shown in Table 9.1. Prior to this, measurable scientific information about the criteria deemed important from the findings of rounds 1 and 2 were collected for the four RMLs to be ranked in round 3. The RMLs considered in this section of the questionnaire were chosen on the basis that they were distinct from one another. As the difficulty of the ranking process is thought to be inversely proportional to the similarities among areas, we required the maximum possible diversity among the lakes in order to make the ranking exercise as straightforward as possible.[19]

A number of criticisms are levelled at the Delphi method. The lack of clear guidelines for the development of the questionnaire, for example, the ecological criteria for ranking environmental sites, and selection of members for expert panels are high among them. With regard to the former criticism, we follow Kuo and Yu (1999) by ensuring that the ecological criteria introduced in our questionnaire were well known in previous research on natural reserves and national parks and in the ecological literature.[20] We predicted that this would limit both the need to provide definitions and any potential misunderstanding between the monitoring team and the expert panel.

With regard to the latter criticism, the experts in our study were drawn from the EMERGE project, which is the largest and oldest network of European scientists explicitly studying RML. The composition of the Delphi panel is shown in Table 9.1. This ensured that members of the Delphi panel had a very high level of understanding of RMLs. Moreover, choosing EMERGE scientists as expert panellists for this study has ensured that the level of involvement and of interest in our study has been particularly high. As pointed out by May and Green (1990) involvement and interest in the study are the most influential variables on the response rate.

Table 9.2 describes the results of the feedback process of rounds 1 and 2 of the Delphi study. In general, these results suggest that the expert panel are

Table 9.2 Rounds 1–2: Ranking of ecological criteria in defining the ecological importance of RMLs

Ecological criteria	Rank in round 2	Mean in round 2	Variance in round 2	Rank in round 1	Mean in round 1	Variance in round 1
Pollution already present in the lake	1	1.33	0.24	3	1.6	0.48
Sensitivity	2	1.43	0.37	2	1.47	0.48
Naturalness	3	1.52	0.47	1	1.43	0.38
Species, habitat and community diversity	4	1.9	0.6	4	1.79	0.78
Species rarity	5	1.95	0.79	5	1.79	1.21
Isolation of the RML	6	2.75	1.14	11	2.42	1.7
Recorded data	7	2.79	0.39	7	2.36	0.82
Geographical location across Europe	8	2.79	0.87	6	2.18	0.89
Potential for research	9	3.00	0.83	9	2.41	1.03
Presence of nearby natural park	10	3.06	0.78	10	2.42	0.78
Geological nature of the catchment	11	3.17	0.88	8	2.38	1.61
Accessibility of the RML	12	3.21	0.87	12	2.54	1.21
Topography of the catchment	13	3.34	1.03	14	2.82	1.51
Morphology of the RML	14	3.38	0.72	13	2.66	1.39
Landscape attractiveness	15	3.42	0.79	15	2.83	1.36
Amenity value or beauty of the sight	16	3.61	1.31	16	3.08	1.35
Proximity to other RMLs	17	4.02	0.79	17	3.08	1.35

Table 9.3 Round 3: ranking of the lakes by the expert panel

Lake	Ranking	1	2	3	4	Total
Osvre Neådalsvatten (Norway)	1	13	5	3	3	24
Loch Nagar (Scotland)	2	4	9	9	2	24
Lago Paione Inferiore (Italy)	3	2	7	6	9	24
Dlugi Staw Gasienicowy (Poland)	4	2	4	8	10	24

concerned more with conserving the lakes and ascertaining their scientific value than with their potential amenity value (criteria 12, 15, 16 and 17).[21] These attributes were consistently ranked in the bottom five.

Curiously, a low level of importance was given to some criteria considered extremely important in the literature on RMLs: for example, morphology of the lake (criterion 14), and geological nature of catchment (criterion 11). Clearly, this could be a consequence of the composition of a panel of which ecologists and biologists made up only half. Indeed, the number of members with a specialization in chemistry and physics, those scientists who might better have appreciated the criteria mentioned above, were respectively one and three. The final ranking of RMLs based on the attributes arising from round 3 is shown in Table 9.3.

The Delphi experiment shows how, in cases where environmental assets are remote and obscure, decisions concerning conservation and other environmental policies can be made by reference to panels of experts closely associated with the good in question. The recursive nature of the method employed meant that a degree of consensus could be reached between panel members concerning the important attributes of RMLs. Subsequently, panel members were able to provide ordinal preferences concerning the four RMLs under consideration, thereby acting as a guide to policy makers. The Delphi method can be seen as one of various decision making tools that can provide relevant information to policy makers owing to its ability to prioritize the focus of policy by reference to expert opinion (Kontoleon et al., 2002).

6. ASCERTAINING WTP FOR REMOTE MOUNTAIN LAKES

The CVM survey was undertaken to elicit the non-use values held by UK individuals for RMLs in the UK. Three separate focus groups (of about 30 members) were used over a period of three days during August to September 2001. All interviews were undertaken in London. The moderator used visual aids to describe the information levels and the scenarios to be valued while respondents were guided through the questionnaire in a highly structured and controlled manner. No interaction between respondents was allowed, although private consultations (for further clarification) between individual respondents and the moderator were permitted. Each experimental session had a duration of 1.5 hours, considerably above the average time spent on most personal face-to face CV studies. An augmented survey time was rendered necessary so that respondents could assimilate the information provided.

6.1 Information Levels

In order to test the effect of information on the stated WTP three versions of the questionnaire were designed, each with a different information level. The information levels were progressively increased in the three versions such that the first version contained only information level 1, the second contained information levels 1 and 2, and the third contained all three levels of information. The information scenarios were constructed using the results from our consultations with European lake scientists as well as from the results of the Delphi study.

The *first* information level[22] started by defining what constitutes a remote mountain lake. We then informed respondents that there exist four main types of such lakes. These types corresponded to the four representative lakes ranked in the Delphi study. The following attributes were described for each type of lake: (i) presence of a conservation area surrounding the lake, (ii) use of lake by tourists, (iii) walking distance from the closest road, (iv) level of acidity, and (v) a listing of algae, macro-invertebrates, aquatic plants, fish and birds present in each type of lake. Lastly, we explained the effects of acid rain on each of the four types of RML.

In the *second* information level[22] we added further ecological information on RMLs: (i) the degree of biodiversity present in RMLs, (ii) the role of nutrients in supporting the fauna and flora of lakes, and (iii) the biological effect of increasing acidity. We explicitly made clear that the services and functions arising from these kinds of lakes may include recreational use services as well as other services related to preservation of ecosystems, habitats and species diversity. In addition, for each group of living organisms, we provided a qualitative evaluation of the status of the fauna and flora described in the first level of information, and distinguished between acid and non acid-sensitive species.

In the *third* information level, we added a description of the scientific services and functions arising from RMLs. We then explained that these functions are related to the fact that some species living in RMLs may act as bioindicators[23] of both pollution and climate change. We also provided a qualitative assessment (derived from the Delphi study) of each lake's importance both for scientific research and as indicator of past and present levels of pollution and climate temperature.

6.2 The Contingent Market

After providing information about RMLs, the *same* scenario for the contingent market was presented. Initially, we referred to the threats RML ecosystems are facing. For reasons of simplicity, we focused on the threat of increased acidity levels from air pollution resulting from the generation of electricity. The scenario then stated that scientists had grouped all the 400 UK remote mountain lakes into four types or groups of lakes. It was stated that each group contained roughly the same number of lakes with similar characteristics. The characteristics and level of services of each group of lakes was then described. Respondents were then told how the actual level of acidity is expected to reach the same levels in each of the four groups of lakes in ten years time. Individuals were then presented with a programme of liming that aimed at maintaining the level of acidity at its current level. Respondents were then told that the government is considering a programme of applying lime to RMLs in order to combat the effects of acidification. Furthermore, respondents were informed that due to governmental budgetary constraints only one of the four conservation programmes would be implemented. That is, the conservation programmes were emphasized as being mutually exclusive. Four WTP questions were then presented to each individual – one for each type of lake – in which they were asked to state the maximum amount of money they would be willing to pay for a the programme of liming described above.[24] The payment vehicle used was a fixed supplement[25] to every UK household's electricity bills for the next ten years.[26]

7. RESULTS

The mean and standard error of WTP for each RML are shown in Table 9.4 while Figure 9.1 provides a visual comparison of both the ranking of the lakes in terms of mean WTP, and of the effect of information on the mean WTP for the four RMLs.[27] An initial inspection of these results suggests that increased levels of information on the scientific service flows from RMLs have a positive effect on stated WTP. Yet, more formal hypothesis testing is required to fully understand this informational effect as well as to explore the statistical significance of the implicit ranking of the various types of RMLs.

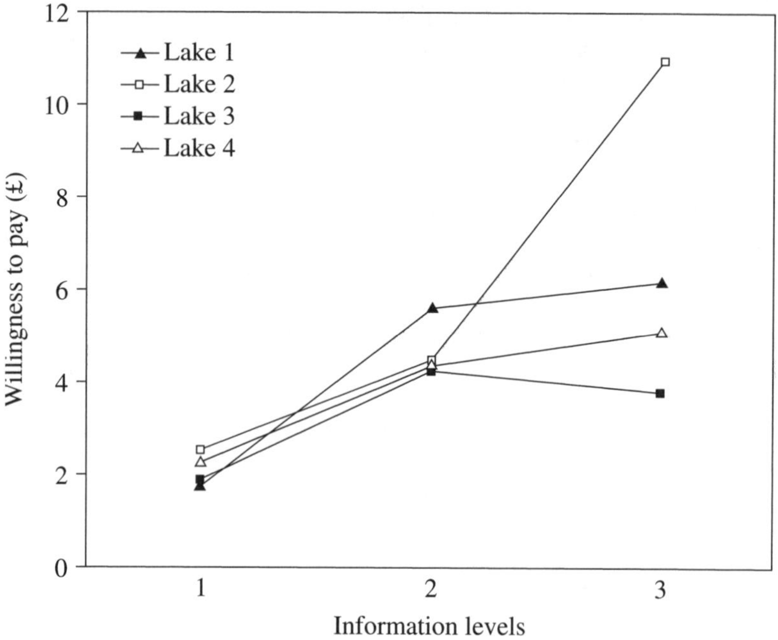

Figure 9.1 *The evolution of WTP bids for the remote mountain lakes over information levels*

We have two different families of hypotheses to test. Null hypothesis 1 amounts to a test of whether or not a statistically significant implicit ranking can be established for the lakes for a given level of information: that is, a comparison of the mean WTP of each RML across information sets. Null hypothesis 2 represents a test of the effect of information on WTP bids.

7.1 Testing for Implicit Ranking of Lakes and Comparison with Expert Ordering

Since the WTP responses provided by the each individual cannot be assumed to be independent we employed a paired-sample test for the comparison of bids under the following alternative hypothesis:

$$\text{Alternative Hypothesis 1} \qquad H_1^1 : \overline{WTP}_{ik} > \overline{WTP}_{jk} : i > j$$

The standard paired-sample t-test employs parametric assumptions concerning the distribution of the WTP bids, i.e. it assumes they are normally

Table 9.4 Mean WTP for the RMLs across information scenarios (£)

Remote mountain lake		First information level	Second information level	Third information level
		Mean (standard error)	Mean (standard error)	Mean (standard error)
Lake 1	Loch Nagar (Scotland)	1.79 (2.17)	5.67 (9.30)	6.25 (6.83)
Lake 2	Osvre Neådalsvatten (Norway)	2.54 (3.25)	4.50 (9.48)	11.03 (12.13)
Lake 3	Dlugi Staw Gasienicowy (Poland)	1.90 (2.25)	4.29 (4.73)	3.85 (6.52)
Lake 4	Lago Paione Inferiore (Italy)	2.28 (3.10)	4.40 (7.17)	5.17 (6.92)
	Sample size	27	27	26

distributed. Yet, the Anderson-Darling test revealed that the normality assumption does not hold for the observed WTP responses and thus the use of a non-parametric test should be employed.[28] The Wilcoxon paired signed rank test is often a more efficient and powerful test for paired samples. The null hypothesis for this test is that the population underlying the samples is identical. The results of the non-parametric tests are shown in Table 9.5.

The results in Table 9.5 allow us to examine the implicit rankings of the lakes under the different information scenarios.[29] Under the first information scenario, strict preference orderings over all the lakes are not revealed. If we assume a strict preference requires a disparity of mean bids at a 10% significance level, lakes 2 and 4 are both strictly preferred to lake 1. Similarly, lake 4 is strictly preferred to lake 3. It should also be noted that there appears to be a 'weak' preference for lake 2 over lake 3, at something approaching a 10% significance level.

In the treatment group receiving the second information scenario, the preference ordering is even less clear and even contrary to those revealed under the first information scenario. At the 10% significance level, it is only possible to establish strict preferences for lake 1 over lakes 2 and 4. Clearly the preferences are reversed for lakes 2 and 4 over lake 1 when compared to the first information scenario. In the treatment group receiving the third

Table 9.5 Wilcoxon paired signed rank test for paired samples within information groups[a]

Null hypotheses (1)[b]	First information level		Second information level		Third information level	
	W-stat	P-value under Ha	W-stat	P-value under Ha	W-stat	P-value under Ha
$WTP_{1k} = WTP_{2k}$	30.5	0.083†	35.0	0.992**	129.5	0.028*
$WTP_{1k} = WTP_{3k}$	29.5	0.419	80.5	0.586	57.5	0.962*
$WTP_{1k} = WTP_{4k}$	55.0	0.025*	19.5	0.996**	31.0	0.992**
$WTP_{2k} = WTP_{3k}$	24.0	0.880	135.0	0.131	58.0	0.993**
$WTP_{2k} = WTP_{4k}$	88.5	0.285	92.0	0.388	44.5	0.988*
$WTP_{3k} = WTP_{4k}$	95.0	0.0813†	80.0	0.727	143.5	0.433

Notes: ** Refers to significance at the 1% level, * at the 5% level and † at the 10% level.

[a] The p value comes from a test which is corrected for the number of ties in the ranked differences. This entails an assumption that the ranked differences, rather than the observations themselves, are distributed normally.

[b] The null hypothesis for the non-parametric test is no longer a test of the equality of mean WTP, but, as stated, a test of the distribution of the bids across lakes (Wonnacott and Wonnacott, 1995).

information scenario, a clear preference ordering is revealed. Lake 2 is strictly preferred to lakes 1, 3 and 4, whilst lake 1 is strictly preferred to lakes 3 and 4. Respondents were indifferent between lakes 3 and 4, perhaps having a weak preference for lake 4. But for the apparent indifference between lakes 3 and 4, this represents a strict preference ordering over all lakes.

In sum, respondents seem to be initially unfamiliar with RMLs and unable to develop strict preferences over different types of lakes until they are provided with sufficient information concerning their characteristics. It appears that the second level of information concerning their characteristics. It appears that the second level of information concerning details about the ecological attributes of the lakes served only to weaken the preference ordering, allowing only lake 1 to be revealed as strictly preferred to the others. Lastly, the third level of information concerning the scientific value of the lakes seems to have exceeded some cognitive threshold for respondents, allowing them to make distinct choices over the lakes. One reason for this may be that this information enabled respondents to 'contextualize', or digest the previous ecological information. In addition, the scientific information may increase the 'relevance' of the goods, in the

Table 9.6 Preference ordering of RMLs according to stated WTP

Lake	First information level rank	Second information level rank	Third information level rank
Lake 1: Loch Nagar	2	1**	2
Lake 2: Osvre Neådalsvatten	1*	2	1
Lake 3: Dlugi Staw Gasienicowy	2	2	4^
Lake 4: Lago Paione Inferiore	1*	2	3

Notes: * These lakes are both strictly preferred to the others. ** There is a weak preference for these lakes over at least one other. ^ Weakly not preferred.

sense of Ajzen et al. (1996). The implicit ranking that arises from the Wilcoxon paired signed rank test undertaken above is shown in Table 9.6.

In the contingent valuation experiment we obtained an implicit ranking from the elicited WTP values form each group of respondents (operating under different information levels) while in the Delphi study the experts (operating under high levels of information) provided a direct ranking of the four representative RMLs in accordance with ecological criteria. The results from the pair-wise test in Tables 9.5 suggest that we only obtained a clear ranking at the third information level. More importantly, as shown in Table 9.6, this ranking coincides with that obtained from the expert panel.

7.2 Testing the Effect of Information on the Mean Willingness to Pay for RMLs

To test the impact of varying levels of information on mean WTP for RMLs we employed a mean test for independent samples. Yet, the Anderson-Darling test revealed that the normality assumptions required by this test was rejected[30] and thus we used the Mann-Whitney test with the following alternative hypothesis:

Alternative Hypothesis 2 $$H_1^2: \overline{WTP_{ik}} > \overline{WTP_{il}} : k > l$$

for information levels ($k = 1, 2, 3$), and for lake i. That is, under this alternative hypothesis the provision of exogenous information has a positive effect on mean willingness to pay for lake i. This alternative hypothesis was used on the assumption that on the whole individuals would be unfamiliar with RMLs, and that the incremental information provided essentially concerned 'positive' attributes of the individual lakes (in the sense of Munro and Hanley, 2000). In terms of the model described in Section 3, this is a test of the sign of δ_{ik}, the learning parameter associated with exogenous information. This suggests that, we can conclude that, overall, individuals' perceived quality concerning RMLs was less than the so-called objective quality, and that the provision of information in the contingent market moved people towards the higher objective quality, and hence, given the assumptions contained in equation (9.3), increased WTP. The results of the Mann-Whitney test are shown in Table 9.7.

The Mann Whitney test indicates that only in five cases out of 12 is the null hypothesis rejected, i.e. information is seen to have significantly positive effect on WTP bids. If we assume that each of the independent samples are representative of the population, we can derive useful implications over the magnitude of the information effect from Table 9.6. For example, we notice that the preference ordering for lakes 1 and 4 is reversed between information scenarios 1 and 3, suggesting that the information was relatively more 'positive' for lake 1, than for lake 4. This is borne out by the level of significance of the positive information effect on lake 1. Indeed it can be seen that the preference ordering is driven by the significant information effect on lakes 1 and 2.[31]

When differences between information levels 1 and 2 are compared, we reject the null hypothesis only in the cases of lakes 1 and 3. To some extent this explains the change in the preference ordering over information scenarios 1 and 2 between lakes 1 and 2, and lakes 1 and 4 shown in Table 9.6. The information provided in scenario 2 is particularly 'positive' for lake 1. Similar changes in preferences are noted for lake 3 as a result of information level 2, suggesting that the information was relatively 'positive' for lake 3 also. Lastly, in the third information scenario, the null hypothesis is rejected only in the case of lake 2, for which information concerning the scientific indicator value is most 'positive'.

8. DISCUSSION AND CONCLUDING REMARKS

The chapter examined the effects of resource information on the validity of WTP for non-use values as obtained from contingent valuation studies. Following NOAA panel guidelines, two tests of validity of WTP were explored: a theoretical validity test that examined whether varying degrees of information affected WTP in a manner consistent with a basic welfare-theoretic model and an external validity test which examined the optimal level of information that should be offered to respondents by reference to

Table 9.7 Mann-Whitney test of median WTP differences of lakes across information scenarios

Null hypothesis (2)	First lake		Second lake		Third lake		Fourth lake	
	U-stat	P-value	U-stat	P-value	U-stat	P-value	U-stat	P-value
$WTP_{i1} = WTP_{i2}$	497.5	0.010**	375.0	0.573	262.5	0.038*	301.5	0.188
$WTP_{i1} = WTP_{i3}$	512.5	0.002**	206.5	0.005**	314.0	0.254	306.5	0.213
$WTP_{i2} = WTP_{i3}$	310.5	0.235	219.5	0.009**	408.5	0.848	340.0	0.515

Notes: P-values represent the normal approximation corrected for ties in all cases. ** Refers to significance at the 1% level, * the 5% level.

a benchmark level of information provided by an external panel of experts. We explored these tests with the aid of a controlled CV experiment and a Delphi study on the management of remote mountain lakes. This environmental resource was chosen on the basis of its high unfamiliarity and the predominantly non-use nature of the good.

The results of the Delphi study suggest that experts can provide useful information as to the important attributes of RMLs that can be utilized in the formation of the 'information package' provided to CV participants. Moreover, the expert panel was able to provide an ordinal classification of four representative RMLs. The input from the Delphi study was subsequently used to design a controlled CV experiment that provided three different levels of information to three sub-groups of respondents. All information was provided in a highly controlled and structured manner by experienced moderators and with the aid of visual and presentational material. The first group received information about the recreational possibilities of these remote ecosystems and a brief listing and description of their fauna and flora. The second group received the first level of information but was also provided with a much more detailed description of the ecology, water chemistry and biodiversity of the lakes. The third level of information included the information from the first and second levels but also added a description of the scientific services and ecosystem functions arising from RMLs. The study focused on UK lakes which were grouped into four types of lake that corresponded to the representative lakes that preoccupied the Delphi study. The four lake groups differed with respect to their attributes and the level of services they provided. A scenario was presented in which all lakes would be further acidified in the next ten years, causing a reduction in the level of services that each type/group of lake provides. A conservation programme involving liming was described that would prevent such damage from occurring. Respondents in each information group were asked to provide their WTP for each of the four types of lakes.

With respect to the effect of information, we see that its impact is twofold. First, the results clearly suggest that, for resources with low familiarity (i.e. $\beta < 1$), increasing the quality of information is associated with an increase in mean WTP, suggesting a positive value of the learning coefficient for exogenous information δ. This result is consistent with those found in Blomquist and Whitehead (1998) and Bergstrom et al. (1990). The WTP for each type of lake increased as we moved from the base-line to the higher information levels. Second, the study showed that differences between the stated WTP within groups for different types of lakes were not statistically significant at the first and second levels of information. In contrast, the individuals presented with the third level of information were able to focus on the scientific value of the RMLs, acknowledge the *relative* importance and difference between types of lakes and provide a subsequent ranking. In combination, the results suggest that the effects of information were found to be consistent with a basic welfare-theoretic model of individual choice which supports the theoretical validity of our results.

Moreover, the results suggest that the information in the first two groups was not sufficient for respondents to provide a full ranking of the four types of lakes, while respondents receiving the third level of information were able to provide a full ranking of the four sites, and providing such information resulted in a convergence between individual and expert opinion. We can conclude that the third level of information provides sufficient information for individuals to distinguish between ecological sites and to make decisions which are consistent with those of experts. Further, the results suggest that information from a panel of experts can be used as an external benchmark to provide validity and reliability to CV estimates in the manner suggested by the NOAA panel.

In closing, a few caveats are worth considering. First, some doubts may arise as to the meaning of the comparison of WTP bids from respondents who have received different levels of information. These primarily have to do with whether additional information changes the nature of the good itself. This remains an unresolved issue amongst CV practitioners. The crux of the debate concerns how we define q in equation (9.2). The assumption made in this study follows that in Bergstrom, et al. (1990) and Blomquist and Whitehead (1995), where characteristics of the environmental resource itself are objective while the type and level of services they provide/support are subjective. This reasoning can be better understood within Lancaster's household production framework in which (objective) environmental resource characteristics combined with a divisible market resource make up the final (subjective) services or flows (both use and non-use) that people receive. In this sense, providing additional information of the type offered in this study alters the subjective services and not the environmental good itself. In terms of the model of Section 3, by providing additional information I, the analyst affects the perceived resource quality, q, that approximates the objective resource quality θ.

Second, studies such as the one considered here involving issues of information and NUVs raise interesting issues concerning the aggregation of these values. The NOAA recommendations suggest that one of the responsibilities of the survey designer is to ensure that the information brought to the survey by the respondent reflects the level of information that the average voter brings to a referendum. The study has shown that it is possible to provide respondents with a sufficient quantity of information about a previously unfamiliar public good, for which non-use values are the predominant class of resource value, such that their preference ordering over these goods will coincide with that of a panel of experts. However, although this process appears to validate the CVM in the sense of the NOAA recommendations, it brings to light the question as to whether or not the level of information that effects the coincidence of the preference ordering still reflects that of the average individual, the preferences of whom should essentially be driving decisions made on the basis of CBA/CVM analyses such as these. These points have been raised by numerous authors. For example, Dunford et al. (1997) and Johnson et al. (2001) have argued that people with no or poor knowledge about the resource and/or its injury do not, in fact, have true non-use values. That is, the lack of such demand for information tells us something about the true preferences of these individuals. NUVs are defined as being a matter of conception, which in turn, their argument goes, involves some prior knowledge. Information acquisition activities involving opportunity costs are thus indicators of one's interest in (or of the intensity of one's preferences for) a particular natural resource. Respondents in CV studies that have not (endogenously) acquired such information nevertheless receive (exogenous) information from the study itself. The authors in essence are claiming that expressed non-use values from individuals with no prior or no intended demand to acquire information are somehow 'induced', constructed, 'hypothetical' or even 'fictional' preferences and that the subsequent estimated losses would not have occurred if the respondent had not been sampled. Hence, attempts to measure *aggregate* losses in NUVs over informationally unrepresentative sub-samples of larger populations may be inconsistent with the *revealed* knowledge and concerns of that population (Johnson et al., 2001, p. 61). In our case, the CV participants provided induced responses that cannot be generalized to the rest of the population that has very poor, if any, prior information about RMLs. Hence, using such estimates to aggregate non-use values for RMLs from individuals who, it may be argued, have been driven into behaving like experts may not be representative of societal preferences, and thus may lead to prescribing socially sub-optimal resource allocations. There are various counter-arguments to such a critique which are beyond the scope of this chapter (see Swanson and Kontoleon, 2002, for a discussion). Here, it suffices to say that the resolution of issues of the validity of providing information to CV respondents may depend on what the analysis intends to do with the results. It may be reasonable to argue that supplying information to respondents makes good sense in 'traditional' non-use value studies designed to help policy makers evaluate the potential benefits of *policy alternatives*. These are *ex ante* studies of proposed changes and thus neither the entire number of constituents of a society nor the sample used in a stated preference study can have knowledge of the proposed changes. Yet, supplying information to respondents when the CV is to be used for *damage assessment* is much more questionable and the arguments raised by Dunford et al. (1997) and Johnson et al. (2001) are not easily addressed. Hence, it does not appear to be necessarily valid to provide additional information (such as that from experts) when assessing *ex post* compensation for actual welfare losses from a sample of respondents representing the general population (Dunford et al., 1997), while it may be considered reasonable to provide such information for *ex ante* studies intended for policy evaluation.

Third, all of the additional information provided in this study was 'positive' or 'beneficial'; that is, information about positive attributes of the lakes was provided in successive information levels. The theoretical validity of the effect of information on WTP estimates should be further explored by providing 'negative' information.

Finally, Boyle et al. (1996) have recognized that 'a lack of comparability between CV estimates and expert opinions does not refute the validity of CV. Experts are a self-selected group and there may be very good reasons why their opinions might differ from those of a sample of individuals responding to a CV survey'. Yet, a comparison between CV and expert panel could trigger investigation as to the reason for this difference. There are many reasons why individual and expert opinions may differ. For example, one reason for such a divergence can be attributed simply to different preference structures between the two groups. In addition, Kuitunen and Törmälä (1994) and Kuo and Yu (1999) have empirically demonstrated that experts and uninformed lay-people focus on different attributes when evaluating the same environmental good. It is therefore likely that a different order of ranking of ecological sites and/or environmental goods would be produced by the two sets of respondents. In the current study, however, we have seen that individual preferences and expert opinion coincided for the third information level, that is, when the information concerning overall scientific interest was provided. Clearly, the observed convergence is suggestive of a coincidence of the attributes considered important to individuals and experts. Table 9.2 suggests that the expert panel are particularly concerned to conserve these lakes to ascertain their scientific value, almost exactly the information that was provided at level 3 of the CVM. This is likely to be driving the coincidence of the preference ordering. This result complements that found in Kenyon and Edward-Jones (1998), in which additional information about the ecological characteristics and services of ecosystems allowed individual preferences to coincide with expert opinion. Hence, using such auxiliary information from expert studies enhances both our understanding of how CV participants respond to survey questions as well as the credibility of the overall contingent valuation method. Clearly, further research as to the importance of providing information about the ecological and systemic functions of environmental resources is warranted.

NOTES

The authors would like to acknowledge the financial support of the EMERGE project funded under the EU Fifth Framework Programme. We also appreciate highly the useful input from Stale Navrud, Ian Bateman and Philip Cooper.

1. See Larson (1992) for an alternative view on how revealed preference data could potentially be used to estimate NUVs.
2. NUVs can also be measured by other forms of stated preference technique such as choice experiments. Yet, their application for the measurement of NUVs has only recently been explored. In any event, the issues raised in this chapter are of equal relevance to all forms of stated preference valuation techniques.
3. Most notably by Ajzen et al. (1996), Bergstrom et al. (1985), Blomquist and Whitehead (1998), Bergstrom et al. (1990), Samples et al. (1986), and Boyle et al. (1989).
4. An example of the learning process which is at work during the contingent valuation studies is provided by Samples et al. (1986) where the same questionnaire is administered twice to the same two groups of people. While the first group of people is provided with more information during the second round of the questionnaire, the second group received the same questionnaire with an unchanged amount of information. Surprisingly, the average WTP of both groups changes.
5. 'Positive' information is that which increases the subjective probabilities for good attributes: Milgrom's 'good news' idea (Milgrom, 1981).
6. It is worth pointing out that the existence of these kinds of thresholds has been widely accepted in studies about the effect of advertising for market goods and it constitutes one of the principles guiding marketing strategies.
7. E.g. 'yeah-saying', 'don't know' or 'protesting', mentioned above (Clark et al., 2000, in MacMillan et al., 2000).
8. Clearly in the Blomquist and Whitehead additive formulation, objective and exogenous information are seen as substitutes for one another.
9. Bergstrom et al. (1990) draw similar conclusions. Addressing the effect of additional information concerning the services provided by environmental assets, they conclude that while the direction of this information effect is uncertain, the information effect itself is argued to be desirable, as it increases the completeness and accuracy of the evaluation of environmental goods.
10. ALPE, MOLA, EMERGE are three major research projects funded by the European Commission over the past ten years.
11. Some research has been undertaken into the costs associated with acidification for different ecosystems however; see ApSimon et al. (1997).
12. See other work being undertaken for the EMERGE project by Bateman et al.
13. It is assumed that the quality changes described in the contingent market enter through the objective quality parameter θ_i.
14. Information can have several effects on the distribution of the WTP bids, the effect on the mean being just one. Other tests might include a test of the change in the variance of bids with one alternative hypothesis being a narrowing or focusing of bids, i.e. a diminished variance. Another test might be on the number of zero bids. Both of these tests have been considered but do not provide much insight in this case.
15. The form of the hypothesis should be noted here. The parameter δ_{ik} refers to the effect of information changes when at information level k. Our experiment consists of three information levels, thus three tests will be undertaken. The first will be a comparison of WTP at information level 2 with level 1, a test of δ_{i1}, then at level 3 and level 1, a test of δ'_{i1}, and then at level 3 and level 2, a test of δ_{i2}.

16. θ_i and β_i remain constant for each lake over information levels as they reflect the prior knowledge or perception of the lake.
17. The main features of this management plan are:
    - The pollution affecting remote mountain lakes (RMLs) cannot be tracked to its source with any accuracy.
    - It is almost certain that the pollution coming from a specific region affects more than one region of RMLs (for example, the pollution from the Ruhr district in Germany may affect the RMLs in both South Norway and on the Tatra Mountains).
18. The exact question asked was 'In case you were asked to suggest the region of lakes to be selected for this management plan, how important in formulating your consultation would the following criteria be?'
19. We were concerned about the possibility that the experts might not accept the scientific plausibility of the ranking exercise. According to some of the literature (see for example Tans, 1974), a very large amount of information is required to rank different areas. Asking scientists to comment on our study anonymously was one of the few methods we had to verify their judgement on the scientific value of the ranking exercise. The responses we received made us confident that our approach was acceptable.
20. We chose this branch of natural science literature because of the similar rationale between choosing where to set a natural reserve and the question asked in our Delphi questionnaire.
21. Clearly this list of criteria is not exhaustive. Indeed, several criteria related to single components of pollution were dropped from the study. The expert panel was asked whether they preferred to evaluate pollution as a single item or consider its main components individually. As only six out 21 experts chose the latter, we decided not to include individual criteria in the second round.
22. This level of information coincided with the format of the CV questionnaire used by an accompanying study looking into the non-use values for RMLs.
23. 'All organisms have evolved to exist in different environmental conditions, some tolerating a very wide range of conditions while others tolerating a very narrow range. The latter are called bioindicators as their distribution and numerosity of the community is quickly affected when the environmental conditions of the habitat where they live change: these environmental conditions include physical and chemical factors, soil conditions and other organisms' (Carvalho and Anderson, 2001).
24. Following the work by Bateman et al. (2001) we attempted to minimize ordering effects and warm glow bias by providing advanced warning to respondents of the size of the choice set instead of describing the four possible scenarios in a step wise manner.
25. We defined 'fixed' as same per household and same amount for each of the 40 quarters.
26. In order to make the plan accountable, we specified that the fixed supplement would be listed as a separate item on people's bills. The Electricity Companies would pass this money on to the Department of the Environment who would only use it for liming the lakes. Any excess funds collected would be rebated to customers.
27. We defined £50 as the maximum acceptable bid. All bids with a higher value were considered outliers and reduced to the next highest bid level.
28. The Anderson-Darling statistic for WTP for each lake was never less than 1.7, compared to the critical value of 0.752, at 5% significance. The null hypothesis that the bids are normally distributed is thus rejected.
29. Where the p-value is close to one and the *t*-statistic is shown to be significant at some level, this represents rejection of the null hypothesis when faced with an alternative hypothesis with a strict inequality in the other direction to that posited above, i.e. Alternative Hypothesis 1': $\overline{WTP_{ik}} - \overline{WTP_{il}} < 0 : k > l$. It is necessary to take this approach in order to establish a strict ranking.
30. The Anderson-Darling statistic for WTP for each lake was never less than 1.7, compared to the critical value of 0.752, at 5% significance. The null hypothesis that the bids are normally distributed is thus rejected.
31. There is clearly no control for group differences.

REFERENCES

Ajzen, I., Brown, T.C., and Rosenthal, L.H. (1996), 'Information Bias in Contingent Valuation: Effect of Personal Relevance, Quality of Information and Motivational Orientation', *Journal of Environmental Economics and Management*, **30**, 43–57.

Arrow, K., Solow, R., Leamer, E., Portney, P., Radner, R. and Schuman, H. (1993), 'Report of the NOAA Panel on Contingent Valuation', *Federal Register*, **58**, 4601–14.

Bateman, I.J., Cole, M., Cooper, P., Georgiou, S., Hadley, D., and POE, G.L. (2001), 'Visible Choice Sets ad Scope Sensitivity: An Experimental and Field Test of Study Desig Effects upon Contingent Values', Paper submitted to *The Eleventh Annual Conference of the Europea Association of Environmental and Resource Economists (EAERE)*. University of Southampton, United Kingdom, 28 June–30 June 2001.

Bateman, Ian and Willis, K.G. (eds). (1999), *Valuing Environmetal Preferences: Theory and Practice of the Congtingent Valuation Method in the US, EU, and Developing Countries*, New York: Oxford University Press.

Bergstrom, J.C., Stoll, J.R., and Randall, A. (1989), 'Information Effects in Contingent Markets', *American Journal of Agricultural Economics*, **71** (3), 685–91.

Bergstrom, J.C., Stoll, J.R., and Randall, A. (1990), 'The Impact of Information on Environmental Commodity Valuation Decisions', *American Journal of Agricultural Economics*, **72**, 614–21.

Blamey, R.K. (1998), 'Decisiveness, Attitude Expression and Symbolic Responses in Contingent Valuation Surveys', *Journal of Economic Behaviour and Organisation*, **34**, 577–601.

Blomquist, G.C., and Whitehead, J.C. (1998), 'Resource Quality Information and Validity of Willingness to Pay in Contingent Valuation', *Resource and Energy Economics*, **20**, 179–96.

Boyle, K.J. (1989), 'Commodity Specification and the Framing of Contingent Valuation Questions', *Land Economics*, **65**, 57–63.

Boyle, K.J., Welsh, M.P., Bishop, R.C., and Baumgartner, R.M. (1995), 'Validating Contingent Valuation with surveys of Experts', *Agricultural and Resource Economics Review*, October, 247–54.

Brown, Thomas C., Peterson, George L. and Tonn, Bruce E. (1995), 'The Values Jury to Aid Natural Resource Decisions. (Speculations).' *Land Economics*, **71** (2): 250–60.

Cameron, T.A., and Englin, J. (1997), 'Respondent Experience and Contingent Valuation of Environmental Goods', *Journal of Environmental Economics and Management*, **33**, 296–313.

Chilton, S.M., and Hutchinson, W.G. (1999), 'Exploring Divergence between Respondent and Researcher Definitions of the Good in Contingent Valuation', *Journal of Agricultural Economics*, **50** (1), 1–16.

Clark, J., Burgess, J., and Harrison, C.M. (2000), 'I Struggled with this Money Business: Respondents' Perspectives on Contingent Valuation', *Ecological Economics*, **33**, 45–62.

Cooper, C.F., and Zedler, P.H. (1980), 'Ecological assessment for regional Development', *Journal of Environmental Management*, **10** (3), 285–96.

Dunford, Richard W., Johnson, F.R., Sandefur, R.A., and West, E.S. (1997), 'Whose Losses Count In Natural Resources Damages?', *Contemporary Economic Policy*, **15** (4), 77–87.

Edward-Jones, G., Edward-Jones, E.S., and Mitchell, K. (1995), 'A Comparison of Contingent Valuation Methodology and Ecological Assessment as Techniques for Incorporating Ecological Goods into Land-use Decisions', *Journal of Environmental planning and Management*, **38** (2), 215–30.

Fischoff, B., Slovic, P., and Lichenstein, S. (1980), 'Knowing What You Want: Measuring Labile Values', in *Cognitive Process in Consumer and Decision Behaviour* (ed Wallstein T. S.), Lawrence Erlbaum Associates, Hillsdale, New Jersey.

Helmer, O. (1972), 'On the Future State of the Union', Report 12–27, Institute for the Future, Menlo Park, California.

Hoevenagel, R., and van der Linden, J.W. (1993), 'Effects of Different Descriptions of the Ecological Good on Willingness to Pay Values', *Ecological Economics*, **7**, 223–38.

Hutchinson, G.W., Chilton, S.M., and Davis, J. (1995), 'Measuring Non-use values of Environmental Goods using the Contingent Valuation Method: Problems of Information and Cognition and the Application of Cognitive Questionnaire Design Methods', *Journal of Agricultural Economics*, **46** (1), 97–112.

Johnson, F. Reed *et al* (2001), 'Role of Knowledge in Assessing Non-use Values for Natuarl Resource Damages', *Growth and Change*, **32** (1), 43–68.

Kenyon, W., and Edward-Jones, G. (1998), 'What Level of Information Enables the Public to Act Like Experts when Evaluating Ecological Goods?', *Journal of Environmental Planning and Management*, **4184**, 463–75.

Kenyon, W., and Hanley, N. (2001), 'Economic and Participatory Approaches to Environmental Evaluation', mimeo.

Kontoleon, A., Swanson, T.M., and Macrory (2001), 'Individual Preferences, Expert Opinion and Environmental Decision Making: An overview of the issues', Paper presented at the Symposium on Law and Economics of Environmental Policy, UCL, 6–7 September 2001.

Kuitunen, M., and Törmälä T. (1994), 'Willingness of Students to Favour the Protection of Endangered Species in a Trade-off Conflict in Finland', *Journal of Environmental Management*, **42**, 111–18.

Kuo, N.-W., and Yu Y.-H (1999), 'An Evaluation System for National Park Selection in Taiwan', *Journal of Environmental Planning and Management*, **42** (5), 735–45.

Linstone, H.A., and Turoff M. (1976), *The Delphi Method, Techniques and Applications*, Addison-Wesley Publishing company, London.

Loomis, J., Gonzales-Caban, A. and Gregory, R. (1994), 'Do Reminders of Substitute and Budget Constraints Influence Contingent Valuation Estimates?', *Land Economics*, 70, 499–506.

MacMillan, D.C., Hanley, N., Philip, L., and Begona, A. (2001), 'Valuing the Non-market benefits of Wild Goose Conservation: a Comparison of Individual Interview and Group-based Approaches', Mimeo, University of Glasgow.

May, G.H., and Green, D.H. (1990), 'Planning for the Future: the Application of the Delphi Techniques to the Unitary Development Plan Process', CUDEM Working Paper Series: 7, Metropolitan Leeds University, Leeds.

Milgrom, Paul (1981), 'Good News and Bad News: Representation Theorems and Applications', *Bell Journal of Economics*, **12** 380–91.

Mitchell, R.C. and Carson, R.T. (1989), *Using Surveys to Value Public Goods: The Contingent Caluation Method*, Johns Hopkins University Press.

Munro, A. and Hanley, N.D. (2000), 'Information, Uncertainty, and Contingent Valuation', in (eds) I. Bateman and K. Willis, Oxford University Press.

Sagoff M. (1998), 'Aggregation and Deliberation in Valuing Environmental Public Goods: A Look Beyond Contingent Pricing, *Ecological Economics*, **2** (2–3), 213–30.

Samples, K.C., Dixon, J.A., and Gowen, M.M. (1986), 'Information Disclosure and Endangered Species Valuation', *Land Economics*, **62** (3), 306–12.

Swanson, T. and Kontoleon T. (2004), 'What Future for Environmental Liability? The Use of Liability Systems for Environmental Regulation in the Courtrooms of the United States and the European Union', in Norman Vig and Michael Faure (eds)., *Green Giants? Environmental Policy of the United States and the European Union*, Boston: MIT Press, 2004.

Tans, W. (1974), 'Prority Ranking of Biotic Natural Areas', *Michigan Botanist*, **13**, 31–9.

Whitehead, J.C., and Blomquist, G.C. (1991), 'Measuring Contingent Values for Wetlands: Effect of Information about Related Environmental Goods', *Water Resources Research*, **27**, 2523–31.

Wonnacot, T.H. and Wonnacot, R.J. (1995), 'Introductory Statistics', John Wiley and sons, Canada.

PART III

Estimation under uncertainty

10. The role of risk properties and farm risk aversion on crop diversity conservation

Salvatore Di Falco and Charles Perrings

1. INTRODUCTION

The loss of biodiversity is causing major concern worldwide. Conservationists are, nowadays, less concerned with the extinction of a specific species but more with the overall loss of biological diversity. This is because the loss of genetic diversity implies a loss of the potential informational contributions embodied in species stock (Barrett, 1993). Biodiversity contributes also to the stability of ecosystems and a certain amount of biological diversity is vital to assure the capability of a system to work. In fact, 'there is a threshold of Biodiversity below which most ecosystems cannot function under any given environmental condition' (Perrings et al., 1995). Diversity is a fundamental component of the ability of the environment to support and sustain economic activities such as consumption and production. Environmental productivity plays a crucial role in short-term and long-term overall productivity. Following Pearce and Moran (1994), biodiversity can be described in terms of genes, species and ecosystems. This description corresponds to three fundamental and hierarchically related levels of biological organization:

- genetic diversity;
- species diversity;
- ecosystem diversity.

Genetic diversity is the sum of genetic information that is contained in the genes of individual plants, animals and micro-organisms. Species diversity is considered to correspond to a population within which gene flow occurs under natural conditions. Ecosystem diversity relates to the diversity and variety of habitats, biotic communities and ecological processes in the biosphere, and can be described at different levels. At all these levels, there is some reason to look at the source of value of biodiversity. Heal (2000) noted that 'the full diversity of organisms in an ecosystem is required for that system to function and to provide services to human societies, and the removal or addition of even a single type of organism can have far reaching consequences'. This is particularly true of so-called keystone species. Removing these species causes dramatic changes in the system and it is impossible to foresee the consequences of these alterations. Their conservation for the stability of the system becomes very important. In this chapter, we focus on a particular ecosystem: the agroecosystem.

An agroecosystem is 'an ecological and socio economic system, comprising domesticated plants and or animals and the people who husband them, intended for the purpose of producing food, fibre or other agricultural products' (Conway, 1993). The number of crops selected by farmers affect the level of agrobiodiversity and it is recognized that the reduction of crop genetic resources has crucial effects on food production, health and life-support systems (for instance, 80% of agricultural production is related to a small group of crops). Farmers' acreage allocations to different varieties are among the most important forces driving diversity conservation. Keeping agrobiodiversity is instrumental in fostering the existence of variation in crop characteristics owing to the creation of different production niches and unique sets of selection pressures. The agroecosystem is subject to stresses caused by inadequate rainfall and soil moisture, randomness of temperature, and potential evaporation. All have the potential to shape wheat development and variation. Sumner et al. (1981) reported that a reduction of crop genetic diversity promotes the build-up of crop pest and pathogen populations. This is because the greater the diversity between or within species and functional groups, the greater is the tolerance or resistance to pests. Greater agrobiodiversity is also important with respect to pest resistance. Pests have more ability to spread through crops with the same genetic base (Altieri and Liebman, 1986; Brush, 1995). Furthermore, crop diversity plays an important role in soil-nutrient interactions. In fact, interactions between the fungal communities associated with the roots of the plants and the diversity of the fungi in the soil affects the effectiveness of nutrient uptake. Building the soil through increased biomass production and protecting the soil from erosion (because it is covered for the most of the cropping cycle) has important long-term spillover in terms of resilience and sustainability. Recently, Smale et al. (1997) in a study on the Punjab of Pakistan found that genealogical distance and number of varieties in wheat are associated with higher mean and lower variances of yields. However, in irrigated areas, a high concentration of areas with fewer species has an important effect on the expected yields. Widawsky et al. (1998), in a study on rice varieties in the Chinese agricultural system, showed that increasing varieties and adopting host plant resistance for pest management increase would lead to a higher productivity than a low diverse pesticide intense farming system. Widawsky and Rozelle (1998) adopted a Just and Pope (1978) specification to test the correlation between yield variability and varietal abundance. They find that as the number of planted varieties increase, the coefficient of variation decreases.

The relationship between diversity and the variance of yields bears an important piece of information: the risk property of agrobiodiversity. In fact, if keeping agrobiodiversity implies a reduction in the variance of yields, one would expect that risk averse farmers will select more species than risk neutral farmers. This chapter's focus is on this link, and it presents a theoretical and empirical investigation of the role of crop diversity on the mean and variance of farmers' income.

1.1 Risk and Agrobiodiversity

Uncertainty and risk are quintessential features of agricultural activities. Agricultural production interacts with the ecosystem in a circular manner. Farmers' production choices affect the environment, for instance runoff of nutrients, pesticides, tillage practices and varietal choices. From these, damage to ecosystems may follow. On the other hand, soil quality and use affect productivity, in the short and in the long run. Because of the complexities of physical and economic systems, the unfolding of most processes that we consider exhibits attributes that cannot be forecast with precision. Rainfall, temperatures, biological processes, for example, are fundamental factors basically out of our control. The immediate implication of this *uncertainty* for economic agents is that many possible outcomes are usually associated with any one chosen action. Thus decision making under uncertainty is characterized by risk (Moschini and Hennessy, 2001) and it is a common approach to incorporate production or price risk into models of farmers' behaviour.

The benchmark model of decision making under uncertainty is the Expected Utility framework (Von Neumann and Morgenstern, 1944) which explicitly recognizes the mutually exclusive nature of the random consequences faced by farmers. When farmers are risk neutral, only the most profitable and risky crop is chosen. But as the farmer becomes more and more risk averse, optimal crop combinations shift from a small and profitable number of risky crops to a more diversified, less risky and less profitable combination.

Sandmo (1971), relying on the Expected Utility framework, provided a model of optimal output for a risk averse firm facing price uncertainty.

He showed that the optimal output would be less than for the deterministic setting, because the production reduction is the way the firm reduces its risk exposure. Feder and Zilberman (1985) extended the analysis to the output uncertainty case, getting similar conclusions. However, the Sandmo model does not allow for land allocation decisions and considers just the first moment of the distribution of the random variable. Therefore, it cannot be used for farmers' land allocation choices regarding different cultivars or crops.

Allocating land to different varieties of crop is one way to deal with uncertainty, when farmers are risk averse and production is stochastic. Using the certainty equivalence approach, one can show that a portfolio of assets decreases risk. Kenneth Arrow in 1971 suggested a specification which models a risk averse investor's choice between two alternative strategies, one non-risky with a certain rate of return and the other risky with a stochastic rate of return. The optimal solution is a diversification of the initial endowment (wealth) between these two assets.

It is the mean-variance approach which specifies risk in terms of the average return and its variability.

Feder (1982) and Just and Zilberman (1985) addressed the question of land allocation to modern crop varieties in developing countries. Both used the Expected Utility framework and found out that diversification is an optimal strategy for risk averse farmers. Just and Zilberman (1985) provided a more general model considering randomness in both strategies available to farmers. Risk is influenced by the mean, variance, and covariance of yields under various alternatives. It implies that only the first two moments enter into the decision making process (see Antle, 1983, for the inclusion of additional moments). Finkelstein and Chalfant (1991) considered the case in which diversity is consumption led. When households are also consumers (in large percentage) of their yield, the diversity in demand arises from consumption demand for basic grains and the demand for cash income in the production of other crops. Farmers decide how much of their land is to be devoted to each of a number of crop varieties, and hence determine the level of crop diversity. That is, they choose the interspecific and the intraspecific diversity of both cultivated and ancillary species. In so doing, farmers consider the impact of diversity on the variance of yields.

The next section will introduce a theoretical model in which farmers' crop choices determine agrobiodiversity in an uncertain environment.

2. THE THEORETICAL FRAMEWORK

In the standard agricultural economics literature, crop diversity choices (Newbery and Stiglitz, 1981; Heisey et al., 1997) have been explained as a standard risk hedging strategy. Risk averse farmers respond to uncertainty in agricultural production and prices by increasing their varietal diversity range. Along the same lines, in this section we consider a model of farmers' crop diversity choices where uncertainty is at play on the production side. The farmer determines the level of crop diversity by choosing the land allocated to different species. In the empirical section a diversity index (e.g. Simpson, Shannon index) will be used to represent the spatial diversity decision. Let the land allocation be represented by the vector x. It is assumed that spatial diversity is a representation of crop genetic diversity. Furthermore, to simplify the analysis, it is assumed that once the land allocation among the species is decided, other management decisions follow. That is, there is a fertilizers, pesticide and cultivation regime corresponding to each crop type. This simplifies the analysis, and is not too strong an assumption. The farmer is assumed to be risk averse. Given a Just and Pope (1978) production function, their crop choice affects both the mean and variance of output. That is, the production function is the following

$$y = (f(x) + h(x)\varepsilon)$$

where x represents the level of spatial diversity of the managed agroecosystem, ε is a random component and y is output. Following Leathers and Quiggin (1991), it is assumed that $\varepsilon = \varepsilon^* + \tau(\varepsilon^* - E(\varepsilon^*))$, where ε^* is a random variable with the same mean as ε and τ is a positive constant. Then, $E(\varepsilon^*) = E(\varepsilon) = \mu_\varepsilon, Var(\varepsilon) = \tau^2 Var(\varepsilon^*)$ and $\sigma_\varepsilon = \tau\sigma^*_e$. This way of representing the random component allows a mean-preserving change in ε to be indicated by μ_ε and a mean-preserving multiplicative spread of ε to be indicated by a change in τ, hence, $\partial\sigma_\varepsilon/\partial\tau > 0$. The farmer's problem is to choose the land allocation regime to maximize the expected utility of income, hence:

$$\max EU(\pi(x))$$

where U is a continuously differentiable utility function defined on income π. At any level of spatial diversity, x_i corresponds to a random variable π_i:

$$\pi_i = p(f(x_i) + h(x_i)\varepsilon) - wx_i$$

Hence, the farmer's problem is 'one of choosing an element of the set of random variables containing π_i'. If the elements vary only by location and scale parameters then conditions to apply the Meyer (1988) analysis hold.

Specifically let F_i and F_j be cumulative density functions of the random variables π_i and π_j, then

$$F_i(k) = F_j(\beta k + \alpha)$$

where β and α are non-stochastic terms. Leathers and Quiggin (1991) showed that this holds because

$$\begin{aligned} F_i(k) &= \Pr(\pi_i < k) = \Pr(\varepsilon < [k + wx_i - p(f(x_i)]/ph(x_i) \\ &= \Pr(\varepsilon < [k + wx_j - p(f(x_j)]/ph(x_j) + \alpha/ph(x_j) \\ &= \Pr[p(f(x_j)] + ph(x_j)\varepsilon - wx < \beta k + \alpha) = \Pr(\pi_j < \beta k + \alpha) \\ &= F_j(\beta k + \alpha) \end{aligned}$$

where $\beta = ph(x_j) + ph(x_i)$ and $\alpha = ph(x_j)[wx_i - pf(x_i)]/ph(x_i) - [wx_j - pfx_j]$. Thus, the farmer's problem may be restated as:

$$\mathrm{Max}_x V(\mu, \sigma)$$

where $\mu = p(f(x) + h(x)\mu_\varepsilon) - wx$ and $\sigma = ph(x)\tau\sigma^*_\varepsilon$. The first order conditions associated with the maximization of the problem are

$$V_\mu(\partial\mu/\partial x) + V_\sigma(\partial\sigma/\partial x) = 0$$

or

$$(\partial\mu/\partial x) - S(\partial\sigma/\partial x) = 0$$

or

$$\Psi = pf' + ph'\mu_\varepsilon - w - S(\mu, \sigma)ph'\tau\sigma^*_\varepsilon = 0$$

where $S(\mu, \sigma)$ is the slope of an indifference curve recording preferences over μ and σ and is equal to $S = -V_\sigma(\mu, \sigma)/V_\varepsilon(\mu, \sigma)$. Under risk aversion this is positive. Since the sign of the first order condition $pf' + ph'\mu_\varepsilon - w = S(\mu, \sigma)ph'\sigma^*_\varepsilon$ is determined by h', the risk averse farmer will choose a more diverse cropping regime if greater spatial diversity of crops is a risk reducing strategy. The h' represents the risk property of diversity. Hence, if farmers are risk averse and if diversity is a risk reducing strategy, we would expect the agroecosystem to be characterized by greater crop diversity.

2.1 The Model

In this subsection we exploit the Leathers and Quiggin result to develop a dynamic model of crop diversity choices. Let us assume that farmers decide the level of biodiversity in the agroecosystem by allocation of land among crops (intraspecies diversity). In practice, though, farming decisions have implications for the stock of diversity available in the future. Let $\mathbf{g}_t$ be a vector describing the farmers' land allocation at time t, and let D_t be an index of crop genetic diversity derived from $\mathbf{g}_t$. For simplicity, as before, it is assumed that each land allocation decision embeds decisions with respect to all the other inputs (e.g. fertilizers, pesticides). Therefore, once the land allocation strategy is decided, the corresponding fertilizer and pesticide regime follows. We thus have a very simple production function:

$$Q_t = Q(\mathbf{g}_t, D_t) \tag{10.1}$$

Production, Q_t, is a function of land allocation decisions $\mathbf{g}_t$ and the associated crop genetic diversity D_t. The function is assumed to be continuous, twice differentiable and concave in its arguments. Crop genetic diversity depends on the relative area under each crop variety. The ith element of the vector $\mathbf{g}_t$ describes the share of land allocated to the ith crop, implying that $0 < g_{it} \leq 1$. If $g_{it} = 1$, $D_t = 1$ and the farmer's land is devoted to a single crop or species. If a multicropping strategy is chosen, $g_{it} < 1$ for all i and $D_t < 1$. The technological properties of the production function are the following, neglecting time indices:

$$Q_{\mathbf{g}_i} > 0; \, Q_{\mathbf{g}\mathbf{g}_i} \leq 0$$

Costs depend on the land allocation choice: $C = c(\mathbf{g})$, and it is assumed that

$$C_{\mathbf{g}_i} > 0$$

Farmers face risks that affect either the output of agricultural activities (the risk affects the quantity or quality of crops produced) or agricultural markets (the risk affects the prices of agricultural inputs or outputs).[1] Farmers hedge risks, primarily through their land allocation decisions. It follows that different degrees of risk and risk aversion will both affect the level of crop genetic diversity observed in the agroecosystem. To capture risk, the model includes a multiplicative random term. The problem for the farmer may be stated as follows:

$$\mathrm{Max}_{\mathbf{g}_t} E(\pi) = \int_{t=0}^{\infty} E\{\pi(Q_t, p_t, \theta_t)\} e^{-rt} dt \qquad (10.2)$$

where the revenue function, $\pi(Q_t, p_t, \theta_t)$, now depends upon the quantity produced, price and a stochastic component. The latter is assumed to be identically, independently and normally distributed, and to affect the output of Q only. The function is assumed to be continuous, twice differentiable and concave. To see how output risk affects land use decisions we need an appropriate specification of the production function. Once again we use that due to Just and Pope (1978, 1979), who suggest a stochastic function of the form:

$$Q(D_t, \mathbf{g}_t, \theta_t) = f(\mathbf{g}_t, D_t) + h(\mathbf{g}_t, D_t)\theta_t \qquad (10.3)$$

$f(\mathbf{g}_t, D_t)$ is a deterministic function of land allocation in period t, $\mathbf{g}_t$, and the diversity of crops in the agroecosystem in that period, D_t and $h(\mathbf{g}_t, D_t)\theta_t$ is a stochastic additive component that depends upon the same arguments as the deterministic function together with θ_t – a stochastic disturbance. The farmer's problem in the face of output uncertainty is to:

$$\mathrm{Max}_{\mathbf{g}_t} \int_{t=0}^{\infty} E\{[p_t(f(\mathbf{g}_t, D_t) + h(\mathbf{g}_t, D_t)\theta_t) - C(\mathbf{g}_t)]\} e^{-rt} dt \qquad (10.4)$$

subject to

$$\dot{D} = D_t - D(\mathbf{g}_t), \text{ and } D(0) = D_0 > 0.$$

Let H denote the current value Hamiltonian which is assumed to be concave,

$$H = E\{[p_t(f(\mathbf{g}_t, D_t) + h(\mathbf{g}_t, D_t)\theta_t) - C(\mathbf{g}_t)]\} + \lambda[D_t - D(\mathbf{g}_t)]$$

where λ is the current value shadow price for diversity. The first order conditions are:

$$H_g = E(\pi_g) + \lambda D_{\mathbf{g}}(\mathbf{g}) = 0$$
$$H_D = E(\pi_D) + \lambda D_D(\mathbf{g}) = r\lambda - \dot{\lambda}$$
$$\dot{D} = D_t - D(\mathbf{g}_t)$$

Setting price equal to unity, the first order necessary conditions imply that:

$$f_{\mathbf{g}}(\mathbf{g}_t^*, D_t^*) + [h_{\mathbf{g}}(\mathbf{g}_t^*, D_t^*) - \frac{D_{\mathbf{g}}(\mathbf{g}_t^*)}{r} h_D(\mathbf{g}_t^*, D_t^*)] \frac{\mathrm{Cov}\{\pi_t\}}{E\{\pi_t\}} - C_{\mathbf{g}}(\mathbf{g}_t^*) = \frac{D_{\mathbf{g}}(\mathbf{g}_t^*)}{r} f_D(\mathbf{g}_t^*, D_{tt}^*) \qquad (10.5)$$

The term $\mathrm{Cov}\{\pi_g\}/E\{\pi_g\}$reflects the structure of profit risks. The term $h_{\mathbf{g}}(\mathbf{g}_t, D_t) - [D_{\mathbf{g}}(\mathbf{g}_t)/r]h_D(\mathbf{g}_t, D_t)$ represents the risk factor. It reflects both the marginal productivity of a change in the land allocation decision $h_{\mathbf{g}}(\mathbf{g}_t, D_t)$ and the impact of a change in land allocation on the diversity of crops $h_D(\mathbf{g}_t, D_t)$.

Assuming D to be equal to a Simpson's index for biodiversity, $(\Sigma_{i=1}[g^i/G])^2$ and assuming that g^i is the share of farmland allocated to the ith crop then we have that $D_g = 2g^i$. Substituting the latter in (10.5), yields:

$$g^i = \frac{1}{2}\left[\frac{C_g(g) - h_g \dfrac{\mathrm{Cov}\{\pi_g\}}{E\{\pi_g\}} - f_g}{f_D + h_D \dfrac{\mathrm{Cov}\{\pi_g\}}{E\{\pi_g\}}}\right] \qquad (10.6)$$

We can use this to evaluate the effect of biodiversity on the mean and variance of yields on the area planted g^i, that is,

$$\frac{\partial g^i}{\partial f_D} = -\left[\frac{2\left(C_g(g) - h_g \dfrac{\mathrm{Cov}\{\pi_g\}}{E\{\pi_g\}} - f_g\right)}{\left[f_D + h_D \dfrac{\mathrm{Cov}\{\pi_g\}}{E\{\pi_g\}}\right]^2}\right] \qquad (10.7)$$

and

$$\frac{\partial g^i}{\partial h_D} = -\left[\frac{2\dfrac{\mathrm{Cov}\{\pi_g\}}{E\{\pi_g\}}\left(C_g - h_g \dfrac{\mathrm{Cov}\{\pi_g\}}{E\{\pi_g\}} - f_g\right)}{\left[f_D + h_D \dfrac{\mathrm{Cov}\{\pi_g\}}{E\{\pi_g\}}\right]^2}\right] \qquad (10.8)$$

These are all for the ith q in the addition (10.5) and for the optimal g^i (i.e. g^*).

Aside from the structure of profits risk, the effect of biodiversity on farm incomes depends on the sign of the numerator given by $(C_g(g) - h_g[\mathrm{Cov}\{\pi_g\}/E\{\pi_g\}] - f_g)$. If it is positive $\partial g^{*i}/\partial f_D < 0$ and $\partial g^{*i}/\partial h_D > 0$. If it is negative $\partial g^{*i}/\partial f_D > 0$ and $\partial g^{*i}/\partial h_D < 0$. The area optimally allocated to a given crop will increase if the marginal effect on mean yields is negative and vice versa. It will also increase if the impact of greater diversity on the variance of yields is positive and vice versa. Next the impact of crop diversity on both mean and variance of income[2] will be empirically tested.

3. ESTIMATING RISK PROPERTIES

In order to estimate the risk properties of biodiversity the Just and Pope specification is chosen. In fact, Just and Pope (1978, 1979) provided a methodology to analyse separately the impact of an input on the mean and the variance of production. We assume the following production function specification:

$$y = A\left(\prod_{i=1}^{n} X_i^{\alpha i}\right)e^{\varepsilon} \tag{10.9}$$

where y is output, X is a vector of inputs and ε it is a stochastic disturbance term with $E(\varepsilon) = 0$, $V(\varepsilon) > 0$. We have that the marginal effect of input use on production variability:

$$V(y) = A^2\left(\prod_{i=1}^{n} X_i^{2\alpha i}\right)V(e^{\varepsilon})$$

$$\frac{\partial V(y)}{\partial X_i} = \frac{2\alpha i A^2}{X_i}\left(\prod_{i=1}^{n} X_i^{2\alpha i}\right)V(e^{\varepsilon}) \tag{10.10}$$

is positive if $\alpha > 0$. In other words, the marginal effect of an increase on inputs always leads to an increase in production variability. Given that

$$\frac{\partial y}{\partial X_i} = \frac{\alpha_i y}{X_i}$$

$$V\left(\frac{\partial y}{\partial X_i}\right) = \frac{\alpha_i^2}{X_i^2}V(y)$$

$$\frac{V\left(\dfrac{\partial y}{\partial X_i}\right)}{\partial X_i} = -1(1-\alpha)\frac{2\alpha_i^2 A^2}{X_i^3}\left(\prod_{i=1}^{n} X_i^{2\alpha i}\right)V(\varepsilon) < 0$$

the effect of increasing input use is to reduce the variability of marginal products (at least for concave production functions). These are both rather restrictive conditions. In fact, a reduction in input use may well imply an increase in yield variability (e.g. pesticides). The variability of marginal productivity may also increase with increasing input use. Therefore 'if any input has a positive effect on output, then a positive effect on variability of output is imposed' (Just and Pope, 1979). Recognizing the shortcomings of this production function, Just and Pope (1978) suggested a method of estimating a two-moment stochastic production function by three-stage non-linear least squares:[3]

$$y = f(X) + h^{1/2}(X)\varepsilon$$

where y is the output and X is a vector of input choices. The function $f(X)$ determines the conditional mean and the function $h(X)$ determines the variance of y, $E[\varepsilon] = 0$, $\mathrm{Var}[\varepsilon] = 1$.

Production is modelled as the sum of two functions: $E(y) = f(X)$ and $V(y) = h(X)$. This makes the effect on mean and variance independent. Therefore

$$\frac{\partial V(y)}{\partial X} = h_i(X)$$

$$-\frac{\partial y}{\partial X_i} = f_i(X) + \frac{1}{2}h^{-1/2}(X)h_i(X)\varepsilon \tag{10.11}$$

and

$$\partial\left(\frac{\partial y}{\partial X_i}\right) = h_i^2(X)/4h(X)$$

$$\frac{\partial V(y/\partial X_i)}{\partial X_i} = \frac{h_i(X)[h(X)h_i(X) - h_1^2(X)]^2}{2h^2(X)} \tag{10.12}$$

The algebraic signs of (10.11) and (10.12), are not a priori determined. It is possible to have risk increasing or risk reducing inputs, and inputs are not assumed to have the same effect on both average output and its variability. The Just and Pope specification has had immediate and widespread application in the agricultural economics literature because of its simplicity and flexibility. For estimation purposes, the functions f and h in the equation:

$$y = f(X) + h^{1/2}(X)\varepsilon$$

Table 10.1 The Just and Pope estimation procedure

1	An NLS regression of y_{it} on $f(X_{it}, \alpha) = e^{[(\ln X_{it})\alpha]}$ obtaining $\hat{\alpha}$
2	An OLS regression of $\lvert \ln \varepsilon_t^* \rvert = \ln\lvert y_{it} - f(X_{it}, \hat{\alpha})\rvert$ on $\ln X_{it}$ to obtain $\hat{\beta}$
3	An NLS regression of $y_{it}^* = y_{it} h^{-1/2}(X_{it}, \hat{\beta}) = y_t e^{[-\frac{1}{2}(\ln X_{it})'\hat{\beta}]}$ on $f^*(X_{it}, \alpha) = e^{[(\ln X_{it})'\alpha]} - \frac{1}{2}(\ln X_{it})'\hat{\beta}$ obtaining $\hat{\alpha}$

may follow a popular Cobb Douglas form and in the case of log linearity we have:

$$y_t = f(X_t, \alpha) + \varepsilon^* \tag{10.13}$$

where

$$\varepsilon_t^* = h^{1/2}(X_t, \beta)\varepsilon$$

and $E(\varepsilon^*) = 0$, $E(\varepsilon_t^* \varepsilon_\tau^*) = 0$ for $t \neq \tau$. Following the Malinvaud procedure (1970), (10.13) can be considered as a heteroscedastic non-linear regression and may be used to get a consistent estimate of α. In order to determine the effect of input use on risk, it is estimated in three stages represented in Table 10.1.

The standard estimation procedure has been modified using the GLS estimator in order to estimate the model coefficients. The feasible generalized least squares is adopted because it improves the efficiency of the estimation when there is multiplicative heteroscedasticity. Hence,

$$y_t = f(X_t, \beta) + \varepsilon_t$$

where $E[\varepsilon_t] = 0$, $E[e^2] = \sigma^2 = \exp\{z_t' \alpha\}$, $E[e_t e_s] = 0$ where $t = 1, \ldots T$ and $t \neq s$ and z is a vector containing $t - th$ observations ($Sx1$) on non-stochastic variables and α is a vector of the same dimension containing unknown parameters. The GLS estimator for β is

$$\hat{\beta} = \left[\sum_{t=1}^{n} \exp(-z_t'\alpha)\mathbf{x}_t\mathbf{x}_t'\right] \sum_{t=1}^{n} \exp(-z_t'\alpha)\mathbf{x}_t y_t \tag{10.14}$$

and for α

$$\log \hat{e}_t^2 = z_t'\alpha + v_t \tag{10.15}$$

where $v_t = \log(\hat{e}_t^2/\sigma^2)$.

Table 10.2 The mean and the variance of income and crop diversity, south of Italy 1970–92

	Mean function	Variance function
Diversity	0.9* (0.02)	− 2.45* (0.7)
Sigma		0.29* (0.04)
$R^2 = 0.2$		
Wald statistic = 384*	Breush Pagan test = 230*	

Notes:
Significance level * = 1%; ** = 5%; *** = 10%.
Please note standard errors are in parentheses.

The Just and Pope approach has been widely scrutinized and alternatives have been suggested for estimating production technologies and the effect of inputs on yield moments. Love and Buccola (1991) proposed a method of jointly estimating production technologies and the risk preferences of farmers. This method provides an improvement in efficiency and in the consistency of parameters while input use is endogenous. However, as observed by Smale et al. (1997), this model is more applicable for estimating technology and risk parameters for conventional inputs than 'for estimating the effect on crop production of unobserved genetic resource characteristics of varieties'. Finally, the framework, while having important limitations, has as its main advantage that it can provide a straightforward way of testing the so-called 'risk property' of the arguments of the function. In fact, it allows the partial derivative with respect to the argument to be positive or negative independently with respect to the mean function and the variance function. This latter determines whether the argument is risk increasing or risk reducing. The risk effect of interspecies crop diversity strategy may be tested using the data at hand plus locational and time shifters to remove time and regional specific effects in both mean and variance. The results are reported in Table 10.2. Note that the Breush and Pagan test rejects the null hypothesis of homoscedasticity so the application of the model is appropriate.

The model[4] shows that expected farm profits are positively related to crop genetic diversity and that the variance of farm profits is negatively related to crop genetic diversity.

The use of a Just and Pope production function provides a straightforward way of testing the effect of crop genetic diversity on income risks. Note, however, that the impact of diversity on expected profits means that we are unable to infer a great deal about the effect of risk aversion on farmers' choices, since farmers have an incentive to opt for a high diversity strategy irrespective of the impact on the variance of production.

4. CONCLUSIONS

This chapter assessed the potential role of risk properties in crop diversity conservation. It has been found that the impact of biodiversity on the variance of farm profits, along with farmers' risk aversion, has a pivotal role in determining agrobiodiversity. In fact, adopting a simple model in the spirit of Leathers and Quiggin (1991), we have shown that if diversity is negatively related to production variance, the agroecosystem will have more diversity. The adoption of a Just and Pope specification provides a straightforward way of modelling farmers' crop diversity choices when uncertainty exists, and to estimate the effect of agrobiodiversity on the mean and the variance of farm income. An applied example, based on data from the south of Italy, is presented. This geographical area has been classified as a *Vavilov megadiversity area* for cereals. It has been found that diversity is negatively related to the variance of production. Hence, at least in the long run, maintaining crop diversity is a risk reducing activity.

NOTES

1. This work is concerned only with output uncertainty. This is because the price level for cereals has been set by the European Union during the time span considered.
2. With price constant.
3. See Harvey (1976).
4. Cf. Di Falco and Perrings (2003).

REFERENCES

Altieri, M., and Liebman, M. (1986), 'Insect, Weed, and Plant Disease Management in Multiple Cropping Systems', in C. Francis (ed.), *Multiple Cropping Systems*, New York: Macmillan.
Antle, J.M. (1983), 'Testing the Stochastic Structure of Production: A Flexible Moment Based Approach', *Journal of Business and Economic Statistics*, **1** (3).
Antle, J.M. (1987), 'Econometric Estimation Procedures of Producer's Risk Attitudes', *American Journal of Agricultural Economics*, 509–22.
Arrow, Kenneth J. (1971), 'A Utilitarian Approach to the Concept of Equality in Public Expenditure', *The Quarterly Journal of Economics*, **85** (3), 409–15.
Barrett, S. (1993), 'Optimal Economic Growth and the Conservation of Biological Diversity', in E. Barbier (ed.), *Economics and Ecology*, London: Chapman.

Brush, S.B. (1995), 'In Situ Conservation of Landraces in Centers of Crop Diversity', *Crop Science*, **35**.
Brush, S.B., Taylor, J.E., and Bellon, M.R. (1992), 'Technology Adoption and Biological Diversity in Andean Potato Agriculture', *Journal of Development Economics*, **39** (2).
Conway, G.R. (1993), 'Sustainable Agriculture: The Trade-offs with Productivity, Stability and Equitability', in E.B. Barbier (ed.), *Economics and Ecology: New Frontiers and Sustainable Development*, London: Chapman and Hall.
Di Falco, S., and Perrings, C. (2003), 'Crop Genetic Diversity, Productivity and Stability of Agroecosystems. A Theoretical and Empirical Investigation', *Scottish Journal of Political Economy*, **50** (2).
Dillon, J.L., and Scandizzo, P.L. (1978), 'Risk Attitudes of Subsistence Farmers in Northeast Brazil: A Sampling Approach', *American Journal of Agricultural Economics*, **60**.
Feder, G., (1982), 'Adoption of Interrelated Agricultural Innovations: Complementarity and the Impacts of Risk, Scale, and Credit', *American Journal of Agricultural Economics*, **64**.
Feder, G., and Zilberman, D. (1985), 'Adoption of Agricultural Innovations in Developing Countries: A Survey', *Economic Development and Cultural Change*, **33**.
Finkelstein, I., and Chalfant, J.A. (1991), 'Marketed Surplus under Risk: Do Farmers Agree with Sandmo?', *American Journal of Agricultural Economics*, **73**.
Folke, C., Holling, C.S., and Perrings, C. (1996), 'Biological Diversity, Ecosystems and the Human Scale', *Ecological Applications*, **6** (4). Reprinted in K.Turner, K.J. Button, and P. Nijkamp (eds), *Ecosystems and Nature*, Aldershot, UK and Brookfield, US: Edward Elgar, pp. 26–32.
Grepperud, S. (2000), 'Optimal Soil Depletion with Output and Price Uncertainty', *Environment and Development Economics*, **5**.
Harvey, A. (1976), 'Estimating Regression Models with Multiplicative Heteroscedasticity', *Econometrica*, **44**.
Heal, G. (2000), *Nature and the Marketplace: Capturing the Value of Ecosystem Services*, New York: Island Press.
Heisey, P.W., Smale, M., Byerlee, D., and Souza, E. (1997), 'Wheat Rusts and the Costs of Genetic Diversity in the Punjab of Pakistan', *American Journal of Agricultural Economics*, **79**.
Heywood, V. (ed.) (1995), *Global Biodiversity Assessment*, Cambridge: Cambridge University Press.
Hiebert, D. (1974), 'Risk, Learning and the Adoption of Fertilizers: Responsive Seed Varieties', *American Journal of Agricultural Economics*, **56**.
Just, R.E., and Pope, R.D. (1978), 'Stochastic Representation of Production Functions and Econometric Implications', *Journal of Econometrics*, **7**.
Just, R.E., and Pope, R.D. (1979), 'Production Function Estimation and Related Risk Considerations', *American Journal of Agricultural Economics*, May.
Just, R.E., and Zilberman, D. (1983), 'Stochastic Structure, Farm Size and Technology Adoption in Developing Agriculture', *Oxford Economic Papers*, **35** (2).
Leathers, H.D., and Quiggin, J.C. (1991), 'Interactions between Agricultural and Resource Policy: The Importance of Attitude toward Risk', *American Journal of Agricultural Economics*, August.
Love, H.A., and Buccola, S.T. (1991), 'Joint Risk Preferences – Technology Estimation with a Primal System', *American Journal of Agricultural Economics*, **73**.

Magurran, A.E. (1988), *Ecological Diversity and its Measurement*, London: Croom Helm.
Meyer, J. (1988), 'Two Moment Decision Models and Expected Utility Maximization', *American Economic Review*, **77**.
Moschini, G., and Hennessy, D.A. (2001), 'Uncertainty, Risk Aversion, and Risk Managment for Agricultural Production Functions', in B.L. Gardner and G.C. Rausser (eds), *Handbook of Agricultural Economics*, UK: North-Holland.
Newbery, D.M.G., and Stiglitz, J.E. (1981), *The Theory of Commodity Price Stabilization*, Oxford: Clarendon Press.
Pearce, D., and Moran, D. (1994), *The Economic Value of Biodiversity*, London: Earthscan.
Perrings, C., Mäler, K.-G., Folke, C., Holling, C.S., and Jansson, B.-O. (eds) (1995), *Biological Diversity: Economic and Ecological Issues*, Cambridge: Cambridge University Press.
Sandmo, A. (1971), 'On the Theory of the Competitive Firm under Uncertainty', *American Economic Review*, **61**.
Smale, M. (ed.) (1998), *Farmers, Gene Banks, and Crop Breeding: Economic Analyses of Diversity in Wheat*, Boston: Kluwer Academic Publishers and CIMMYT.
Smale, M., Just, R.E., and Leathers, H.D. (1994), 'Land Allocation in HYV Adoption Models: An Investigation of Alternative Explanations', *American Journal of Agricultural Economics*, **76** (3).
Smale, M., Hartell, J., Heisey, P.W., and Senauer, B. (1997), 'The Contribution of Genetic Resources and Diversity to Wheat Production in the Punjab of Pakistan', *American Journal of Agricultural Economics*, **80**.
Sumner, D.R., Doupnik, B., and Boosalis, M.G. (1981), 'Effects of Tillage and Multicropping on Plant Diseases', *Annual Review of Phytopathology*, **19**.
Tilman, D., and Downing, J.A. (1994), 'Biodiversity and Stability in Grasslands', *Nature*, **367**.
Tilman, G.D., Wedin, D., and Knops, J. (1996), 'Productivity and Sustainability Influenced by Biodiversity in Grassland Ecosystems, *Nature*, **379**.
Trenbath, R. (1999), 'Multispecies Cropping System in India', *Agroforesty Systems*, **45**.
Von Neumann, J., and Morgenstern, O. (1944), *Theory of Games and Economic Behaviour*, Princeton: Princeton University Press.
Widawsky, D., and Rozelle, S. (1998), 'Varietal Diversity and Yield Variability in Chinese Rice Production', in M. Smale (ed.), *Farmers, Gene Banks, and Crop Breeding*, Boston: Kluwer.
Widawsky, D., Rozelle, S., Jin, S., and Huang, J. (1998), 'Pesticide Productivity, Host-plant Resistance and Productivity in China', *Agricultural Economics*, **19**.

11. Stochastic production in a regulated fishery: the importance of risk considerations

Phoebe Koundouri and Marita Laukkanen

1. INTRODUCTION

Variability of output, often referred to as production risk, is inherent in marine fisheries susceptible to changing environmental conditions. Risk plays an important role in input use decisions. Input quantities not only determine the volume of output produced but some of these inputs also affect the extent of production risk. In this chapter we address the implications of production risk for controlling fishing effort in a regulated fishery within a framework where fishers maximize expected utility of profit. We focus on controlling effort through season closures that limit the number of days the fishery is open to harvest each year.

Risk attitudes of economic agents are an important factor in input allocation decisions and hence in output produced (see, for example, Stiglitz, 1974; Just and Pope, 1978; Antle, 1987). Risk considerations are necessary in the analysis of the fishery sector as there exist a number of possible cases where policy formulation should consider not only the marginal contribution of input use to the mean of output, but also the marginal reduction in the variance or higher moments of output. To this end, we investigate fishers' behaviour towards production risk, their input choices and the respective effects on output, and discuss the policy implications of production risk for regulating a fishery through controlling season length. In particular we consider fishers' capacity choice and fishing effort, approximated by the number of days at sea.

Despite the uncertainty inherent in the fishing industry, the theoretical articles that address the choice of fishing effort and capital inputs in fisheries largely assume away uncertainty. Gordon (1954), Scott (1955) and others have shown that open access to fisheries results in effort levels that result in overharvesting and dissipation of economic rents. Clark, Clarke and Munro (1979) were the first to explicitly account for optimal investment in fleet capital. McKelvey (1985, 1986) studied the capital investment decisions of an individual fisher operating in an open access fishery, and showed that open access results in excessive capital investment as compared to the optimal management scenario. Homans and Wilen (1997) studied the regulated open access case, where TACs are in place in order to conserve the fish stock but no effective attempts are made to control the fleet size. They showed that economic overfishing will emerge in the regulated open access fishery as well.

The overfishing and overcapitalization demonstrated by the above research is caused by misguided incentives arising from the absence of well-defined property rights. The problem could thus be expected to persist in models explicitly including uncertainty in the analysis of the regulator's and individual fishers' optimal effort and capital choice. However, the extent of the discrepancy between the individually and socially optimal choices may depend on the uncertainty characterizing the industry as well as on fishers' risk preferences. In order to steer fisheries towards efficient input use, policies aiming at controlling fishing effort or fishing capacity should take into account the uncertainty inherent in fisheries, fishers' risk preferences and the effect of controls on both expected profit and on higher moments of profits.

Individual transferable quotas have been shown to be an optimal instrument for regulating fisheries in that they effectively define property rights and thereby correct the incentives of individual fishers (Clark 1980; Anderson 1992). In spite of this, suboptimal instruments such as season closures, input restrictions and limited entry restrictions are used in many fisheries. In addition to being an economically suboptimal instrument, season closures add risk in the fishery in that openings may occur during extreme weather conditions, such as storms. As season closures are nevertheless widely used as a regulatory instrument, we focus on their effect on fishers' input choice when fishers' production risk behaviour is explicitly accounted for.

Early studies involving the estimation of production functions in order to establish a relationship between inputs and outputs in fisheries include, among others, Hannesson (1983), Squires (1987), Pascoe and Robinson (1998) and Campbell and Lindner (1990). More recently, interest in technical efficiency has driven a shift towards the estimation of production frontiers.[1] These were estimated using Data Envelopment Analysis (DAE), which allows the study of technical and allocative inefficiency. Relevant studies include Pascoe, Coglan and Mardle (2001), Tingley, Pascoe and Mardle (2003) and Vestergaard, Squires and Kirkley (2003). However, as DAE is non-parametric, it is sensitive to random error, and also does not provide estimates of the impact of individual inputs on the level of outputs, or the relationship between the outputs themselves. To overcome these shortcomings, a number of papers estimate stochastic production frontiers for fisheries; see, for example, Kirkley, Squires and Strand (1995, 1998), Grafton, Squires and Fox (2000) and Pascoe and Coglan (2002). Stochastic production frontiers account for the possible influence of data noise, arising from measurement error or model misspecification, upon the shape and positioning of the frontier. Estimating these frontiers involves the specification of a frontier function with an error term with two components: a symmetric error to account for noise and an asymmetric error to account for inefficiency. All of these studies neglect uncertainty and risk.[2]

In the general production function literature the impact of the choice of inputs on production risk has been studied more extensively. The traditional theoretical studies implicitly assume that inputs increase risk. Examples of such studies are Stiglitz (1974), Batra (1974) and Bardhan (1977). These studies utilized multiplicative stochastic specifications, which are restrictive in the sense that inputs that marginally reduce risk are not allowed. Just and Pope (1978) identified this limitation and proposed a more general stochastic specification of the production function. Their model includes two general functions: one which specifies the effects of inputs on the mean of output, and another one which determines the effects on its variance, thus allowing inputs to be either risk-increasing or risk-decreasing.

While Just and Pope's model is a generalization of the traditional model in that it does not restrict the effects of inputs on the variance to be related to the mean, Antle (1983, 1987) has shown that it does restrict the effects of inputs across the second and higher moments in exactly the way traditional econometric models do across all moments. Thus Antle's departure point was to establish a set of less restrictive general conditions under which standard econometric techniques could be used to identify and estimate risk attitude parameters as part of a structural econometric model. More specifically, Antle's moment-based approach begins with a general parameterization of the moments of the probability distribution of output, which allows the identification of risk parameters for more flexible representations of output distributions. Moreover, Antle's approach places the emphasis on the distribution of risk attitudes in the population, which constitutes a departure from existing literature which focuses on measurement of the risk attitudes of the individual producer (see, for example, Hazell, 1982; Pope, 1982; and Binswanger, 1982).

Love and Buccola (1991, 1999) also proposed an extension of Just and Pope's model including producers' attitude towards risk in the model. They assumed an implicit form of the utility function and considered producers' risk preferences in a joint analysis of input allocation and output supply decisions. Just and Pope's work has also been extended in a series of studies on salmon farming. Kumbhakar (2002a) examines joint estimation of production and risk preference functions in the presence of production risk and output price uncertainty, using a quadratic specification for the production and utility functions.[3] In another recent study by Kumbhakar (2002b), risk preference functions are derived without assuming an explicit form of the utility function and any distribution of the error term representing production risk. Two sources of risk, namely production uncertainty and technical efficiency, are considered. Kumbhakar and Tveterås (2003) use a system approach to simultaneously estimate production risk, risk preferences and firm heterogeneity. Kumbhakar and Tsionas (2002) use a nonparametric approach to estimate the production function, the risk function and risk preference function associated with production risk, thereby avoiding the need to specify a functional form for either the production or risk functions.[4]

All of the above studies use the Just and Pope specification in the sense that they do not allow for the identification of the effect of inputs on the higher moments of output. In this study we instead apply Antle's (1983, 1987) moment-based approach, which enables estimation of the stochastic production function and fishers' risk attitudes without any ad hoc specification of the form of the risk preferences. We study stochastic production, input choice and fishers' risk attitudes in the North Sea Fishery. The extensive requirements in terms of functional form specification of the various distributions (stochastic production function, risk function, utility function under risk) involved in the analytical solution of the model lead us to attempt an empirical approximation to this model. Antle's flexible moment-based approach readily lends itself to estimating the empirical approximation.

The chapter is organized as follows. In Section 2 we present the underlying model of fishers' behaviour under risk and discuss implications of risk aversion for policies that regulate inputs. The empirical model is described in Section 3. The model is applied to an unbalanced panel from the North Sea Fishery. The relevant data-set is described in Section 4 and estimation results in terms of derived input-specific risk attitude characteristics (absolute Arrow-Pratt and down-side risk aversion coefficients and risk premia) are presented in Section 5. Section 6 concludes the chapter by discussing the impact of regulating inputs in a stochastic fishery in terms of input use and moments of profit, and the policy implications of such regulations.

2. THEORETICAL MODEL: FISHERS' BEHAVIOUR UNDER RISK

In this section we analyse the impact of season closures on the production decisions of a fisher operating in a risky environment. The model of the fishery we employ is necessarily a seasonal one. We follow Homans and Wilen (1997) and assume that vessel capital is non-malleable only on an intra-seasonal basis.[5] Our focus here is on inputs whose choice and mixture may be modified by the fisher on a seasonal basis in order to hedge against production risk. Fishers are assumed to be price-takers, so that a modification in their input allocation decision will affect neither output nor input prices.

Assume a management authority regulates the fishery and limits season length in the fishery. An economically optimal management strategy would entail choosing both the capital utilization and the resource investment policy simultaneously in order to maximize the expected utility of harvest over time. As long as property rights to the resource stock are not well defined, individual fishers have an incentive to expend effort in excess of the socially optimal levels. Season closures are used to limit effort in fisheries even though they have been shown to be inefficient in economic literature (see, for example, Clark, 1980; Homans and Wilen, 1997). In reality season length is often limited by biological stock conservation objectives rather than economic considerations. Neglecting risk consequences may have unforeseen consequences both in terms of meeting the conservation goals of regulations and the economic performance of the industry.

An important aspect of our framework is that from the fishers' point of view the season length restriction is exogenous, so that once it is chosen, fishers decide on their production plans considering the season length as given. Both problems (choice of season length and decision on the level of production) are thus completely separated. This is because the management authority's criterion is based upon the whole resource stock and the entire fishing fleet, whereas each fisher only considers his individual expected utility and this is too small to influence the agency's decision.

A key ingredient in assessing accurately the performance of such resource management policy is naturally studying the fishers' input choices and their effect on harvest under such a policy. This requires, first, an adequate representation of the technology, but also of fishers' preferences towards risk.

It is well known that ignoring possible distortions in production decisions due to risk aversion can lead to misleading results (Just and Pope, 1978). When production risk originating for example from climatic or ecological conditions is likely to be significant, producers may hedge against risk by modifying their input choices. Stochastic factors such as extreme weather conditions and variation in the size and distribution of the fish stock make the production process in marine capture fisheries risky. There is, however, considerable scope for controlling the level of output risk through input quantities. For example, the effect of labour quality such as crew skill and experience may be important, since production outcomes depend on measures taken by the crew as a response to changing weather conditions and other environmental variation. Further, large vessels are less susceptible to bad weather.

The Production Model

In this section, the basic representative agent production model under risk is developed. As noted above, we assume an exogenously given season length whose determination is not detailed here.

Let p denote output price for a single composite output, $f(\cdot)$ is the production function, X is the K vector of inputs, and r is the corresponding vector of unit input prices. We approximate fishing effort by days at sea. The season length restriction is directed towards this single input. We denote days at sea by X_D with associated unit price r_D. We then have $X' = (X_1, X_2, \ldots, X_{k-1}, X_D)$ and $r' = (r_1, r_2, \ldots, r_{k-1}, r_D)$. The restriction imposed on X_D is written

$$X_D \leq \bar{X}_D \tag{11.1}$$

where $\bar{X}_D$ is a restriction in absolute terms. We assume that there exists a single source of risk affecting production yield, denoted ε, whose distribution $G(\cdot)$ is not affected by fishers' actions (weather conditions and the like). In addition, we assume prices p and r to be non-random, so that the only source of risk is production risk through the random variable ε. Let us suppose further that $f(\cdot)$ is continuous and twice differentiable. The representative agent's problem is to maximize expected profit if she is risk-neutral, or to maximize the expected utility of profit if she is risk-averse, subject to condition (11.1). In the latter case, the agent's problem is

$$\text{Max}_x E\,[U(\pi)] = \text{Max}_x \int [U(pf(\varepsilon, X) - r'X)]\, dG(\varepsilon) + \lambda(\bar{X}_D - X_D), \tag{11.2}$$

where $U(\cdot)$ is the Von Neumann-Morgenstern utility function and λ is the Lagrange multiplier associated with (11.1). The optimal solution for action X would then depend upon (p, r) and on the shape of functions $U(\cdot)$, $f(\cdot)$ and $G(\cdot)$. The first-order condition associated with this problem for the fishing effort represented by days at sea X_D is:

$$E\,[r_D \times U'] = E\left[p\frac{\partial f(\varepsilon, X)}{\partial X_D} \times U'\right] - \lambda$$

$$\Leftrightarrow \frac{r_D + \lambda/E(U')}{p} = E\left(\frac{\partial f(\varepsilon, X)}{\partial X_D}\right) + \frac{\text{cov}(U', \partial f(\varepsilon, X)/\partial X_D)}{E(U')}, \quad (11.3)$$

because p and r_D are not random, and where $U' = \partial U(\pi)/\partial\pi$. It is apparent that the shape of the utility function (whose curvature is increasing with the degree of absolute risk aversion) will determine the magnitude of the departure from the risk-neutrality case. For a risk-neutral fisher, the price ratio under the season closure policy, $(1/p)[r_D + \lambda/E(U')]$ equals the expected marginal productivity of X_D. When the fisher is risk averse, the second term in the right-hand side of (11.3) is different from zero, and measures deviations from the risk-neutrality case. More precisely, this term is proportional and has the opposite sign to the marginal risk premium with respect to X_D. If the latter is risk-increasing, the marginal risk premium increases with X_D and the desired level of that input decreases, all other things being equal.

3. EMPIRICAL MODEL: ASSESSING RISK ATTITUDES

In principle, solving equation (11.3) for X_D yields the equilibrium fishing effort in terms of p, r, $\bar{X}_c$ and λ. However, the problem is empirically difficult. In addition to the choice of production function specification, the distribution of ε needs to be known and the agent's preferences need to be specified through the utility function. We thus choose a flexible approach that has the advantage of requiring only information on profit, price and input quantities. The key feature of this approach is to note that the solution to the fisher's problem can be written as a function of input levels alone. More precisely, maximizing the expected utility of profit with respect to any input, subject to the season length restriction, is equivalent to maximizing a function of moments of the distribution of ε, those moments themselves having X as an argument. There is no loss of generality here, because such a function of the moments, denoted $F(\cdot)$, is completely unspecified. The fisher's programme becomes:

$$\text{Max}_X E[U(\pi)] = F[\mu_1(X), \mu_2(X), \ldots, \mu_m(X)] \text{ subject to } X_D \leq \bar{X}_D, \quad (11.4)$$

where μ_j, $j = 1, 2, \ldots, m$ is the mth moment of profit.

Based on the expression above, Antle (1983, 1987) proposes a moment-based approach to estimating the risk-attitude parameters of a population of producers. Focusing on the population instead of focusing on each individual agent has two main advantages. It avoids any problem of aggregation of individuals and allows the identification of the risk-attitude parameters from a cross-sectional data-set. However, this approach relies on some assumptions. First, the agent solves a single-period maximization programme in which inputs are predetermined variables. Second, all agents harvest with similar technology. Below, this stochastic technology is represented by the corresponding distribution of profit, which amounts to assuming that the same profit distribution applies to each fisher and that all fishers form the same expectations. We now describe more precisely Antle's method. From the first-order condition, in matrix form:

$$\frac{\partial \mu_1(X)}{\partial X} = (-1/2!)\frac{\partial \mu_2(X)}{\partial X} \times \frac{\partial F(X)/\partial \mu_2(X)}{\partial F(X)/\partial \mu_1(X)} - (1/3!)\frac{\partial \mu_3(X)}{\partial X} \times \frac{\partial F(X)/\partial \mu_3(X)}{\partial F(X)/\partial \mu_1(X)} - \cdots - (-1/m!)\frac{\partial \mu_m(X)}{\partial X} \times \frac{\partial F(X)/\partial \mu_m(X)}{\partial F(X)/\partial \mu_1(X)}. \quad (11.5)$$

As before we index the inputs used in harvesting by $k = 1, \ldots, K$ and we denote by α_{jk} the expression $(\partial F(X)/\partial \mu_j(X))/(\partial F(X)/\partial \mu_1(X))$. α_{jk}, ($j = 2, \ldots, m$), represents the jth average population risk-attitude parameter related to input k. For each input k, we will thus have $(m-1)$ unknown parameters. Each of the K equations described below will be estimated separately.

$$\frac{\partial \mu_1(X)}{\partial X_k} = -\alpha_{2k} \times (1/2!)\frac{\partial \mu_2(X)}{\partial X_k} - \alpha_{3k} \times (1/3!)\frac{\partial \mu_3(X)}{\partial X_k} - \cdots - \alpha_{mk} \times (1/m!)\frac{\partial \mu_m(X)}{\partial X_k} \quad (11.6)$$

The marginal contribution of input k to the expected profit is given by $\partial \mu_1(X)/\partial X_k$, which is written as a linear combination of the marginal contributions of input k to the other moments (variance: $\partial \mu_2(X)/\partial X_k$, skewness: $\partial \mu_3(X)/\partial X_k, \ldots$). α_{mk} measures the 'weight' attributed by the fisher to the mth moment of his profit distribution. The analysis is made input by input because each input contributes in a different manner to the moments of the profit distribution. In general, we expect that all inputs increase the expected profit but, for the second and higher-order moments, we can find risk-increasing as well as risk-decreasing inputs.

The following model will be estimated for each input k:[6]

$$\frac{\partial \mu_1(X)}{\partial X_k} = \theta_{1k} + \theta_{2k}\frac{\partial \mu_2(X)}{\partial X_k} + \theta_{3k}\frac{\partial \mu_3(X)}{\partial X_k} + \cdots + \theta_{mk}\frac{\partial \mu_m(X)}{\partial X_k} + u_k \quad (11.7)$$

where $\theta_{2k} = -\alpha_{2k} \times (1/2!)$, $\theta_{3k} = -\alpha_{3k} \times (1/3!)$, . . . , $\theta_{mk} = -\alpha_{mk} \times (1/m!)$ and u_k is the usual econometric error term. A nice feature of this model is that the parameters θ_{2k} and θ_{3k} are directly interpretable as Arrow-Pratt and down-side risk aversion coefficients respectively. The Arrow-Pratt (*AP*) absolute risk aversion coefficient is defined by:

$$AP_k = -\frac{E(U''(\pi))}{E(U'(\pi))} \cong -\frac{\partial F(X)/\partial \mu_2(X)}{\partial F(X)/\partial \mu_1(X)} = 2\theta_{2k}. \tag{11.8}$$

A positive *AP* coefficient means that the fisher is risk-averse. Down-side (*DS*) risk aversion is measured by:

$$DS_k = \frac{E(U'''(\pi))}{E(U'(\pi))} \cong \frac{\partial F(X)/\partial \mu_3(X)}{\partial F(X)/\partial \mu_1(X)} = -6\theta_{3k}. \tag{11.9}$$

A positive *DS* coefficient means that the fisher is averse to down-side risk.[7] *AP* and *DS* coefficients can then be used to compute the risk premium *RP*. Assuming that the fisher is concerned about the first three moments of the distribution only, we have $RP = \mu_2(AP_k/2) - \mu_3(DS_k/6)$ for each k, where μ_2 and μ_3 are respectively a measure of the second- and third-order moments of the distribution. $RP_k > 0$ would mean that the fisher is characterized by a positive willingness to pay to be insured against the risk associated with the use of input k. Coefficients α_{2k} and α_{3k}, directly related to AP_k and DS_k, can also be interpreted as a measure of the marginal contribution of each moment to the risk premium.

4. DESCRIPTION OF THE DATA-SET: THE NORTH SEA FISHERY

The North Sea is the major fishing area in European Community waters. Commercial activity in the region is mostly undertaken by fishers from the UK, Denmark, the Netherlands, France, Germany, Belgium and Norway. Transboundary stocks are shared between the EU and Norway. The total value of the allowable catch in 1999 was estimated to be about 1.5 billion euros. This is an underestimate of the true value of landings as the guide prices are generally lower than market prices. However, it provides an indication of the order of magnitude of the value of the fishery.

This study focuses on two main fleet segments that make up the majority of the UK North Sea fleet; one composed of mobile and the other composed of static vessels. Most of the stocks exploited by the fleet are heavily overfished. In addition, the fishery has been targeted for decommissioning as it is considered to have considerable excess capacity. Fleet size has been almost halved between 1994 and 2000 as a result of the reduced North Sea quotas, pushing some boats into the English Channel and/or Celtic Sea, and decommissioning.

Despite being subject to quota controls, the quotas were not binding over the period examined. Since the introduction of the FQAs in 1999, the only binding quotas for North Sea species were for saithe and sole in 2000. For most species, quota uptake ranged between 70% and 90% (DEFRA). An analysis of the available beam trawl logbook and quota allocation data for 2000 found that over 75% of the vessels did not fill their quota allocation, with the remainder exceeding the allocation (presumably through quota leasing). Given the apparent abundance of quota and the apparent effectiveness of the quota leasing market, it was assumed for the purposes of this study that the quotas were not effectively constraining output.

Logbook production data and boat characteristics information from the central fleet registry for the trawlers operating in the North Sea were used in the analysis. The data is an unbalanced panel, including the following years: 1996, 1997, 2000, 2001 for both the static and mobile segments of the fleet. Mobile gears include beam, dredge, otter and pelagic gears, while static gears include pots, nets and lines. Tables 11.1 and 11.2 present the relevant descriptive statistics.

Catches of the key species used in the construction of the profit variable incorporated into the model varied over the period examined, largely as a result of changes in stock conditions. Accounting for variations in stock abundance in fisheries production functions is generally undertaken either through the direct inclusion of the stock, or through the use of dummy variables. A particular problem exists for the use of stock indexes in multi-output production functions, in that each stock measure relates directly to only one of the outputs, although it may indirectly affect the output of the others by affecting fishing patterns. A composite stock variable cannot effectively capture the

Table 11.1 Descriptive statistics of variables: mobile vessels

Variable	Mean	Standard deviation
Profit	152 731.99	145 814.40
Capital value	215 372.18	222 597.88
Days at sea	206.295	58.60
Length of the vessel	16.07	7.64
Engine power (kW)	177.67	170.58
Age of the vessel	19.71	12.59

Note: Number of observations: 167.

Table 11.2 Descriptive statistics of variables: static vessels

Variable	Mean	Standard deviation
Profit	54 765.83	90 617.43
Capital value	52 119.46	103 764.36
Days at sea	178.25	65.72
Length of the vessel	9.38	4.07
Engine power (kW)	84.09	88.81
Age of the vessel	16	11.29

Note: Number of observations: 269.

stock changes of the different species, since these do not follow a consistent pattern. To overcome these problems, the catches in each time period were normalized using the stock indexes, that is, the catch in each time period was divided by the stock index in that time period. This allows the effects of changes in stock size on catch to be incorporated into the analysis, but imposes the implicit assumption of unitary output elasticity with respect to stock size. This assumption is most likely valid given the nature of the resources, in that they are widely dispersed, fairly uniform in density across their areas of distribution and exploited across their whole areas of distribution.

While several physical characteristics of vessels were available in the dataset, for example, length, age and engine power (kW), only vessel capital value and days at sea, the latter being the restricted input, were used in the production function estimation. Vessel age and engine power were used as instruments in the last stage of the estimation procedure two-stage least squares (2SLS). Vessel length was found to be highly correlated with engine power (r = 0.94) and as a result was excluded from the model.

Since one of the requirements of Antle's approach is for the agents in the panel to have the same production technology, we apply the approach separately to the two samples of our panel: the one with the mobile gears and the one with the static gears.

5. ECONOMETRIC ESTIMATION AND RESULTS

Measurement of Risk-attitude Parameters

Following Antle (1987), we propose to estimate the sample-average risk-attitude parameters. As before, we distinguish between two groups of producers, fishers with mobile and static vessels, and two inputs, capital value and days at sea. We wish not to impose a priori the equality of risk-attitude parameters between the two different inputs. For each of the two groups, our estimation methodology is as follows. First, we estimate the conditional expectation of profit using a quadratic functional form: total observed profit is regressed on all levels, squared, and cross-products of inputs. The residuals of the latter regression are then used to compute conditional higher moments (variance and skewness), which are then regressed on all levels, squared, and cross-products of inputs.

Analytical expressions for derivatives of these moments with respect to each input are then computed. We finally fit a 2SLS equation of the estimated derivative of the expected profit on derivatives for higher moments for each input. Age of vessel and engine power were used as instruments in the 2SLS estimation. The parameters associated with the second and third moments will respectively be denoted by θ_{2k} and θ_{3k} for each input k. Estimated parameters were then used to recover Arrow-Pratt (AP) and down-side (DS) risk aversion measures using the following relationships: $AP_k \cong 2\hat{\theta}_{2k}$ and $DS_k \cong -6\hat{\theta}_{3k}; k = 1, \ldots, K$. These estimates were finally used to compute the average risk premium ρ_k as a proportion of expected net returns for each input k, which is approximately equal to $\rho_k/\mu_1 = [\mu_2 AP_k/2\mu_1] - [\mu_3 DS_k/6\mu_1]$ where μ_2 and μ_3 are respectively a measure of the second- and third-order moments of the distribution.

Estimation results for the sub-group of mobile vessels are found in Table 11.3. The Wald test rejects the null hypothesis of equal parameters between the effects of the choice of the two inputs. For both inputs, the parameters θ_2 associated with the second moment (variance of profit) are positive and significant whereas the parameter linked to the third moment is negative and significant. Signs of these coefficients are 'as expected', showing risk aversion of mobile vessel producers (through both the Arrow-Pratt and down-side risk measures). The average relative risk premium is similar across inputs, ranging from 17% (for capital) to 20% (for days at sea) of expected profit.

Results for the static vessels sub-group are reported in Table 11.4. The Wald test rejects the null of parameter equality with regards to effects of these two inputs on expected profit. The parameter linked to the variance is positive and significant in both models. Thus, we get positive Arrow-Pratt risk-aversion measures for both capital and days at sea inputs. Moreover the down-side risk measure is positive and significant for both inputs. The relative risk premia are lower in the static vessels group (7% and 9%, for capital and days at sea, respectively) compared to the group of mobile vessels.

We note that the constant term is not significant in either of the two models. We know that by definition we should not observe a significant constant term in the model linking the derivatives of moments of expected

Table 11.3 Estimation of the risk-aversion measures: mobile vessels

	Capital value		Days at sea	
	Est.	Std. err.	Est.	Std. err.
Constant	−0.0245	0.0715	0.1169	0.0729
θ_{2k}	1.2726	0.4159	2.1143	0.2139
θ_{3k}	−0.5222	0.6936	−0.6346	0.8011
AP	2.55	0.83	4.23	0.43
DS	3.13	4.16	3.81	4.81
RP	17%		17%	

Note: Wald test of parameters equality: 1771.0 (p-value: 0.0000).

Table 11.4 Estimation of the risk-aversion measures: static vessels

	Capital value		Days at sea	
	Est.	Std. err.	Est.	Std. err.
constant	0.1433	0.0400	0.1432	0.0222
θ_{2k}	0.8595	0.1672	7.8820	0.7078
θ_{3k}	−1.4992	0.4680	−20.7043	2.0907
AP	1.72	0.33	15.76	1.42
DS	9.00	2.81	124.23	12.54
RP	7%		9%	

Note: Wald test of parameters equality: 1570.3 (p-value: 0.0000).

profit with respect to each input (see equation 11.7). A significant constant term indicates model misspecification, or that the input under consideration is inefficiently used and more precisely, a positive (negative) sign means that the input under consideration is overused (underused) in the sense that the expected marginal return is less (greater) than the factor price. Our result indicates correct model specification and no production inefficiency.

6. POLICY IMPLICATIONS

This chapter has dealt with estimation of the production technology and input choice decisions when producers face exogenous production risk. We estimated the production technology and risk preferences using Antle's flexible moment-based approach on data from the North Sea Fishery.

Our results show that, first, fishers are risk averse. Second, failure to include risk aversion behaviour in the characterization of the production function might bias parameter estimates and give wrong results on technological parameters. Third, risk aversion behaviour is translated in terms of a risk premium, which is viewed as the implicit cost of private risk bearing. Risk premium as a percentage of mean profit is found to be different between mobile and static gears, with mobile gears exhibiting higher premia by 10% and 8% of profit, for capital and days at sea inputs, respectively. Fishers using static gears (pots, lines and nets) involving smaller fixed costs often have other sources of income and are thus less susceptible to variations in the harvest yield.

As shown in Section 2 of the chapter, if fishers are risk averse, the value of the marginal product of variable inputs exceeds their market price. This result might be used to argue (erroneously) that vessels are not efficient in allocating their variable inputs and that regulation regarding input choices is needed to enhance the economic performance of the fishery. Furthermore, neglecting risk considerations when assessing impacts of regulation policies on input choices and expected harvest could provide misleading guidance to the policy makers concerned about sustainable harvest levels. This constitutes a significant warning to all policy makers who contemplate regulation of stochastic production processes in general, and fisheries in particular.

NOTES

The authors want to thank Sean Pascoe and Trond Björndal for making the data availabe. We are also in debt to Celine Nauges for comments and suggestions regarding the empirical part of the chapter.

1. There are also theoretical reasons why the estimation of production frontiers has advantages over the estimation of production functions (see Kumbhakar, 2002b).
2. A common feature of these studies is the reliance on a single measure of output. However, unlike many other industries, fisheries are characterized by joint production. Multi-output distance functions in fisheries have been studied by Alvarez and Orea (2001), Fousekis (2002) and Bjørndal, Koundouri and Pascoe (2003), who examine the implications of output substitution in multi-species fisheries for quota setting.
3. Kumbhakar considers an exogenous production shock rather than input dependent production risk in the sense of Just and Pope.
4. However, non-parametric estimations involve the selection of the kernel and bandwidth, which are not specification free.
5. This assumption is a reasonable one for a fishery where vessels participating in harvest could readily be diverted to other fisheries.
6. We should check that θ_{1k} is not significantly different from zero in each model.
7. Down-side risk is concerned with asymmetric (skewed) statistical distributions of profit.

REFERENCES

Alvarez, A., and Orea, L. (2001), 'Different Approaches to Model Multi-species Fisheries Using a Primal Approach', *Efficiency Series Paper 3/2001*, Department of Economics, University of Oviedo.

Anderson, L.G. (1992), 'Consideration of the Potential Use of Individual Transferable Quotas in US Fisheries, Vol. 1: Overview Document', Report prepared for the National Oceanic and Atmospheric Administration (NOAA), 1992.

Antle, J. (1983), 'Testing the Stochastic Structure of Production: A Flexible Moment-Based Approach', *Journal of Business and Economic Statistics.* **1**, 192–201.

Antle, J. (1987), 'Econometric Estimation of Producers' Risk Attitudes', *American Journal of Agricultural Economics*, 509–22.

Bardhan, P. (1977), 'Variations in Forms of Tenancy in a Peasant Economy', *Journal of Development Economy*, **4**, 105–18.

Batra, R. (1974), 'Resource Allocation in a General Equilibrium Model of Production under Uncertainty', *Journal of Economic Theory*, **8**, 50–63.

Bjørndal, T., Koundouri, P., and Pascoe, S. (2003), 'Output Substitution in Multi-species Trawl Fisheries: Implications for Quota Setting', FEEM (Fondazione Enrico Mattei) Working Papers Series, Nota di Lavoro N. 30 2004, Downloadable from http://www.feemit/Feem/Pub/Publications/Wpapers/default. htm.

Binswanger, H. (1982), 'Empirical Estimation and Use of Risk Preference: Discussion', *American Journal of Agricultural Economics*, **64**, 391–3.

Campbell, H.F., and Lindner, R.K. (1990), 'The Production of Fishing Effort and the Economic Performance of Licence Limitation Programmes', *Land Economics*, **66**, 55–66.

Clark, C.W. (1980), 'Towards a Predictive Model for the Economic Regulation of Commercial Fisheries', *Canadian Journal of Fisheries and Aquatic Sciences*, **37**, 1111–29.

Clark, C.W., Clarke, F.H., and Munro, G.R. (1979), 'The Optimal Exploitation of Renewable Resource Stocks: Problems of Irreversible Investment', *Econometrica*, **47**, 25–47.

Fousekis, P. (2002) 'Distance vs. Ray Functions: An Application to the Inshore Fishery of Greece', *Marine Resource Economics*, **17**, 251–68.

Gordon, H.S. (1954), 'The Economic Theory of a Common Property Resource: The Fishery', *Journal of Political Economy*, **62**, 124–42.

Grafton, R.Q., Squires, D., and Fox, K.J. (2000), 'Private Property and Economic Efficiency: A Study of a Common-Pool Resource', *Journal of Law and Economics*, **43** (2), 679–713.

Hannesson, R. (1983), 'Bioeconomic Production Function in Fisheries: Theoretical and Empirical Analysis', *Canadian Journal of Fisheries and Aquatic Science*, **13** (3), 367–75.

Hazell, P. (1982), 'Application of Risk Preference Estimates in Firm-Household and Agricultural Sector Models', *American Journal of Agricultural Economics*, **64**, 384–90.

Homans, R., and Wilen, J. (1997), 'A Model of Regulated Open Access Resource Use', *Journal of Environmental Economics and Management*, **32**, 1–21.

Just, R., and Pope, R. (1978), 'Stochastic Representation of Production Functions and Econometric Implications', *Journal of Econometrics*, **7**, 67–86.

Just, R., and Pope, R. (1979), 'Production Function Estimation and Related Risk Considerations', *American Journal of Agricultural Economics*, 276–84.

Kirkley, J., Squires, D., and Strand, I. (1995), 'Assessing Technical Efficiency in Commercial Fisheries: The Mid-Atlantic Sea Scallop Fishery', *American Journal of Agricultural Economics*, **77** (4), 686–97.
Kirkley, J., Squires, D., and Strand, I. (1998), 'Characterizing Managerial Skill and Technical Efficiency in a Fishery', *Journal of Productivity Analysis*, **9**, 145–60.
Kumbhakar, S.C. (2002a), 'Specification and Estimation of Production Risk, Risk Preferences and Technical Efficiency', *American Journal of Agricultural Economics*, **84**, 8–22.
Kumbhakar, S.C. (2002b). 'Risk Preference and Productivity Measurement under Output Price Uncertainty', *Empirical Economics*, **27**, 461–72.
Kumbhakar, S.C. and Tsionas E.G. (2002), 'Estimation of Production Risk and Risk Preference Function: A Nonparametric Approach', mimeo.
Kumbhakar, S.C. and Tveterås, R. (2003), 'Risk Preferences, Production Risk and Firm Heterogeneity', *Scandinavian Journal of Economics*, **10** (2), 275–93.
Love, H.A., and Buccola, S.T. (1991), 'Joint Risk Preference-Technology Estimation with a Primal System', *American Journal of Agricultural Economics*, **73**, 765–74.
Love, H.A., and Buccola, S.T. (1999), 'Joint Risk Preference-Technology Estimation with a Primal System: Reply', *American Journal of Agricultural Economics*, **81**, 245–47.
McKelvey, R. (1985), 'Decentralized Regulation of a Common Property Renewable Resource Industry with Irreversible Investment', *Journal of Environmental Economics and Management*, **12**, 287–307.
McKelvey, R. (1986), 'Fur Seal and Blue Whale: The Bioeconomics of Extinction', in M. Cohen (ed.), *Applications of Control Theory in Ecology, Lecture Notes in Biomathematics*, Heidelberg: Springer-Verlag, pp. 57–82.
Pascoe, S. and Coglan, L. (2002), 'Contribution of Unmeasurable Factors to the Efficiency of Fishing Vessels: An Analysis of Technical Efficiency of Fishing Vessels in the English Channel', *American Journal of Agricultural Economics*, **84** (3), 45–57.
Pascoe, S., Coglan, L., and Mardle, S. 'Physical versus Harvest Based Measures of Capacity: The Case of the UK Vessel Capacity Unit System', *ICES Journal of Marine Science*, **58,** 1243–52.
Pascoe, S., and Robinson, C. (1998), 'Input Controls, Input Substitution and Profit Maximisation in the English Channel Beam Trawl Fishery', *Journal of Agricultural Economics*, **49** (1), 16–33.
Pope, R. (1982), 'Empirical Estimation and Use of Risk Preference: An Appraisal of Estimation Methods that Use Actual Economic Decisions', *American Journal of Agricultural Economics*, **64**, 376–83.
Scott, B. (1955), 'The Fishery: The Objectives of Sole Ownership', *Journal of Political Economy*, **63**, 116–24.
Squires, D. (1987), 'Fishing Effort: Its Testing, Specification, and Internal Structure in Fisheries Economics and Management', *Journal of Environmental Economics and Management*, September, **14,** 268–82.
Stiglitz, J. (1974), 'Incentives and Risk Sharing in Sharecropping', *Review of Economic Studies*, **41**, 219–55.
Tingley, D., Pascoe S., and Mardle, S. (2003), 'Estimating Capacity Utilisation in Multi-purpose, Multi-metier Fisheries', *Fishing Resources*, **63**, 121–34.
Vestergaard, N., Squires, D. and Kirkley J. (2003), 'Measuring Capacity and Capacity Utilization in Fisheries: The Case of the Danish Gill-net Fleet', *Fishing Resources*, **60**, 357–68.

12. Is irrigation water demand really convex?

Christophe Bontemps, Stéphane Couture and Pascal Favard

1. INTRODUCTION

In many countries of the world, water scarcity has significant environmental, health and other domestic consequences. Competition between users is increasing and the current water allocation mechanisms need to reflect this new reality (Tsur and Dinar, 1997). Water underpricing has played a major role in the development of irrigation and has favoured wasteful use of water and inefficient farming choices. 'Getting prices right' is seen as particularly important to solve inefficient water use (Johansson et al., 2002) and the related problems such as scarcity, conflicts between users, equity, waste, which are mainly due, or at least attributed, to water use for irrigation. The theory of efficient water pricing is well-defined (Tsur et al., 2002; Johansson et al., 2002), and its application would help farmers to use water more efficiently. One of its crucial elements is the derived demand for irrigation water.

Tsur et al., suggest two main approaches to estimate this derived demand: an econometric and a mathematical programming approach. Only a few works focus on econometric estimation of irrigation water demand. In France, to our knowledge, only one econometric estimation of irrigation water demand has yet been published (Michalland, 1995). The main reason is probably that appropriate data required for econometric estimation are difficult to collect. Another reason is that, when the data exist, few fluctuations in the prices are observed and sometimes water price is null for many users. Therefore it is difficult to estimate an irrigation water demand function using an econometric approach. Nevertheless, some researchers have done such estimates. The methods used by all the authors are based on the dual approach to production theory using dual input demand specifications (Moore and Negri, 1992; Moore et al., 1994a; Belhaj Hassine and Thomas, 2001). Estimates of irrigation water demand are relying on actual farmer behaviours and are usually based on cross-sectional data. Farmers are represented as multicrop production firms that make decisions about crop choices, and crop-level allocations of land in the long run, and applied water quantities in the short run. The main result of these econometric studies on irrigation water demand is the unresponsiveness of water demand to change in prices. This result is probably due to the lack of appropriate data on crop-level water use, and, for that reason, due to an imprecise description of short-run decisions.

At the same time, there exists a more intensive economic literature on irrigation water demand based on programming models (Shunway, 1973; Howitt et al., 1980; Montginoul, 1997; Hooker and Alexander, 1998; Varela-Ortega et al., 1998; Tsur et al., 2002; De Fraiture and Perry, 2002). The derived demand for irrigation water is based on the mathematical formalization of the farmer's behaviour. An estimation of the production technology is done, generally based on a pre-specified crop yield response function to irrigation water, prior to the estimation. The programming method is then based on the following scheme: For a given price, one calculates the quantity of water maximizing the farmer's profit, by computer simulations. Variations in water prices induce different levels of maximized water quantities that directly represent the derived demand for irrigation water. Most of these studies conclude that irrigation water demand is completely inelastic below a threshold price, and elastic above. These findings are strongly linked to the specification of the water-yield function, while it is proved that such functions are too simple to give a precise representation of the biological process of plant growth.

Two main points should be noticed from this brief review of the literature on irrigation water demand. First, water is a complex input that enters the production process in a specific manner. This specificity requires an appropriate representation of the production process. Second, irrigation water demand estimates seems to strongly depend on the method considered. The main result emerging from the literature is that seasonal irrigation water demand:

- when estimated with econometric models (Ogg and Gollehon, 1989; Moore and Negri, 1992; Moore et al., 1994b; Belhaj Hassine and Thomas, 2001) seems to be inelastic;
- when estimated with the programming approach (Shunway, 1973; Howitt et al., 1980; Montginoul, 1997; Hooker and Alexander, 1998; Varela-Ortega et al., 1998; Tsur et al., 2002; De Fraiture and Perry, 2002) seems to be inelastic below a threshold price, and elastic beyond that point.

No general or precise form of the irrigation demand function appears, even if some estimations can be found in this literature. Surprisingly, while the concern over the economic regulation of irrigation water demand is increasing, no general modelling approach of this demand under uncertainty has been developed. This issue, which necessitates taking into account the stochastic environment, information structure, and farmers' preferences in the formalization, has not been directly addressed in the literature on water demand estimation using programming methods. Therefore, the idea of a smooth, regular and convex curve is still in everybody's mind, even if it may not be the case.

Our goal is to propose a framework for estimating irrigation water demand under uncertainty, to estimate and characterize irrigation water demand function and show how it should be specified. To achieve that purpose, we estimate irrigation water demand under uncertainty without any *a priori* assumption about its shape. This estimation is reached by extending the method for estimating irrigation water demand under deterministic weather conditions, presented by Bontemps and Couture (2002), to a stochastic environment, in the following way: we take into account uncertainty (stochastic weather conditions), risk aversion (farmers' preferences), and information (open-loop or feedback information structure). These modifications allow us to have more realistic conditions to estimate the irrigation water demand precisely. This approach is used to characterize and quantify irrigation demand functions under stochastic weather conditions. The distribution of these demand functions reveals patterns of great importance and helps answer the following questions: *What is the general shape of the irrigation demand function under uncertainty? Is it really convex? What is its distribution? How sensitive is it to the strategy used (or to the information set)? How should it be modelled?* and finally, *What are the implication of misspecifying it?*

The chapter is structured in the following manner. In the next section, we briefly present the theoretical framework for calculating demand functions, that is, the dynamic model of the farmer's decisions, and briefly describe the procedure for resolution and estimation. In the following section, we present an application in the south-west of France. The main results and estimations are reported, as well as graphical schematic representation of the demand functions. We also give some comments and recommendations on *ad-hoc* parametric specification of demand functions. The policy regulation implications of these results are developed and analysed. Finally, there is a brief concluding section.

2. MODEL DESCRIPTION AND PROCEDURE

A detailed description of the model is available in Bontemps and Couture (2002) and Bontemps et al. (2003). This discussion is limited to a brief account of the relevant components. The general framework of the model is presented in Annex A.

2.1 Principles and Extensions

We use the programming model framework to derive an inverse water demand. As presented by Tsur et al., 2002, the inverse water demand is obtained by calculating the optimal crop production programme under various water supply constraints and valuing the associated shadow price of water at each level of water constraint. This suggests using a mathematical model to describe the farmer's behaviour in response to changing resource constraints. This constrained optimization problem is solved in some papers using either linear programming (Shunway, 1973), quadratic programming (Howitt et al., 1980; Hooker and Alexander, 1998; De Fraiture and Perry, 2002) or Positive Mathematical Programming methods (Tsur et al., 2002).

All the previous programmes are special cases of the profit maximizing farmer programme that constitutes a non-linear programming problem.[1] Little has yet been done to take into account that input decisions could depend on uncertainty due to the weather (Bontemps and Couture, 2003). Standard results apply for decisions under certainty, be they about output and input prices or yield. Many empirical and theoretical considerations however reveal that uncertainty may explicitly affect the farmer's decisions. In this chapter we take into consideration past research and propose three main improvements:

- *Stochastic environment* The complete knowledge assumption was relaxed to reflect the stochastic weather environment. We take into account the impact of uncertainty on farmers' decisions and therefore on demand. We incorporate yield uncertainty due to climate and investigate the influence of temporal uncertainty[2] on optimal economic decisions. At each stage of the multi-stage decision process, some weather information becomes available. The farmer's decision process can incorporate this information, and can improve the decision accordingly.
- *Information structure* Similarly to the deterministic case, the problem of optimal allocation of irrigation water under stochastic conditions can be modelled as an optimal control problem. The classes of stochastic control policies are defined depending on the information on past and anticipated future observations. According to the amount of information used, two classes of stochastic control policies have been distinguished: open-loop and feedback. The only

difference between them resides in the anticipation of future knowledge. Of these two policies, the optimal stochastic control belongs to the feedback class. The complexity involved in modelling the stochastic feedback policy has led us to use the stochastic open-loop feedback control as an alternative for this study. The optimization problem is quite complex and is solved numerically (see also Bontemps and Couture, 2003).

- *Farmers' preferences* All the previous studies are based on the strong assumption that the farmer is risk neutral and that he maximizes his profit, while it is recognized in the literature that farmers are risk averse (Chavas and Holt, 1996). Neglecting the risk-averse behaviour in agricultural models can lead to significant overstatement of the output level and to biased estimation of the irrigation water value as well as to incorrect prediction of choices. We specify a constant relative risk aversion utility function as an objective function which appears appropriate to describe the farmer's behaviour.

2.2 Model Resolution

Bontemps et al. (2003) give a detailed description of the general procedure for estimating irrigation water demand; this section is limited to a brief presentation of the procedure. The procedure contains two main parts; in the first we propose a numerical resolution of the decision problem while we estimate the objective and demand functions in the second. First, the numerical procedure of resolution integrates the agronomic model, EPIC-Phase, the economic model, and an algorithm of search for the solution, and is based on a method of global optimization. We find the maximized irrigation schedule, and the corresponding maximized objective function. We repeat this procedure for different quantities of water, and obtain couples (*quantity of water, maximized objective function*) for various climatic years. Second, this database is used to estimate the maximized objective function and its derivative, the farmer's water value. We use a nonparametric method to estimate these functions. A major advantage of nonparametric estimation is that it is designed to estimate an unknown function without assuming its form.

3. APPLICATION AND DISCUSSION

In this section, as in the perfectly known environment (Bontemps and Couture, 2002), we estimate the irrigation water demand for a crop, a French farmer, located in the south-west of the country, and three climatic years. We use this application to draw some general results on irrigation water demand and derive some policy implications.

3.1 Irrigation Water Demand Estimates

The stochastic variability is presented in these results through three years: a 'medium' one corresponding to real data of the year 1991, a 'dry' year (1989) and a 'humid' one (1993). We may use these last two years, 1989 and 1993, as high and low bounds of the distributions under study. Figure 12.1 reveals that the shapes of the demand functions are quite similar. Obviously, given a water quantity, the willingness to pay is increasing with the dryness of the weather. In the same way, within a climatic year, the more information you have, the higher the utility, the higher the water demand.

The shapes of the demand functions are similar whatever the information set, and can be schematically represented in Figure 12.3.

Each demand function presents three areas: In the first one $[0, \underline{Q}]$, the curve is highly decreasing, it becomes almost flat in the second $[\underline{Q}, \bar{Q}]$, and decreases again in the third. In the latter area, the absolute value of the elasticity is, however, smaller than in the first. To explain these different areas, remember that water is considered as an essential input but also as a means

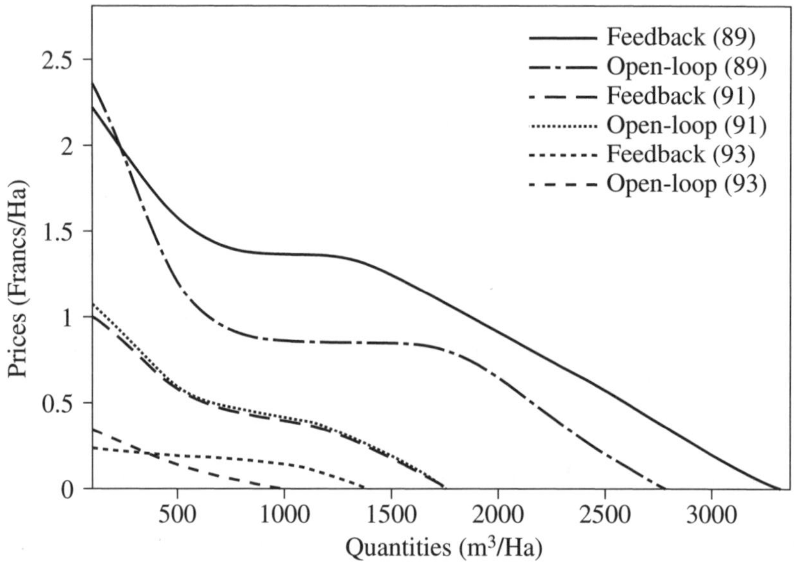

Figure 12.1 Demand functions for 'dry', 'medium' and 'humid' year

to insure against risk, and that two main factors, the water (irrigation plus rainfall) and the temperature, can be limiting production factors. The convex shape of the demand function in the first area is classical, it is decreasing and the absolute value of elasticity is high. This is not surprising since the water is an essential good. Note that the length of this area is just the same whatever the climate, that is, $\underline{Q}$ is almost the same for the three years. In the region under study, even in a humid year, the temperature for emergence and flowering is always sufficient. So in this first area, even if generally temperature and water are complementary goods, the only factor that can stress the plant is the water. In this first area, the water is the limiting factor. Obviously, in a humid year this amount is reached with a smaller irrigation water quantity, because of rainfall, and $\underline{Q}_{89}$ is a little bigger than $\underline{Q}_{93}$. The decreasing slope of the demand curve will depend on the climatic condition. The drier the weather, the stronger the water limiting factor, and therefore, the greater the willingness to pay. Now let us explain the more surprising part of the demand curve, the second area. The flat shape is due to agronomic characteristics of the crop growth process which implies a particular rate of return. This statement is sufficient to justify here the use of an agronomic model. Indeed, in this area, variations in marginal profit are almost null, and therefore, risk aversion is not an explanatory component of the farmer's decisions.[3] Therefore, the flat shape is also present in the perfectly known environment estimates but at different levels in price and quantity.

Another feature of the curves is that the length of this flat area is decreasing with the humidity of the season. So, for a dry year and therefore a warm year, the length of this area is significantly greater than for a humid, chilly year and we observe in the figure that $\bar{Q}_{89} \geq \bar{Q}_{91} \geq \bar{Q}_{93}$. Contrary to the other areas, the temperature is the limiting factor here. At the end of the second phase the biomass level is at a maximum. The third area corresponds to the maturity of the plant. Intuition suggests that there exists a finite quantity of water such that the willingness to pay is nil, whatever the climate. So the curve must reach the horizontal axis. In this third phase, demand is decreasing again, but is not convex. The concave shape of the demand function in this area appears, however, less intuitive than the convexity of the first. The main reason is that there is no other smooth possibility of reaching zero from a flat curve. In this third area, in our region, the temperature is not the limiting factor. This fact explains why, whatever the climate, the length of this area is almost the same. So, there exists a water quantity such that the plants keeps their grain yield.[4] Obviously, if the year is humid, rainfall contributes to this amount more than in a dry year. Another reason is the importance of the insurance component of water in this area. Though marginal profits are low in this area, variations in marginal profit induce high variations in objective function, and, therefore, the farmer wants to insure against risk.

3.2 Parametric versus Nonparametric Estimates

The nonparametric estimation of irrigation water demand provides a precise estimation of the shape of the demand function without assuming any parametric specification. However, it may be interesting to have a parametric, and more practical, form for this function. Since all irrigation demand studies use some *ad-hoc* parametric specifications for the profit or production functions (Moore et al., 1994a; Belhaj Hassine and Thomas 2001), we have estimated parametrically, by nonlinear regression, the mean demand functions[5] using the data generated by the nonparametric procedure. We have tested several *ad-hoc* specifications of the demand function. Table 12.1 gives the estimation results of the specifications we have tested and their associated R^2.

The parametric curves chosen here give a good estimation of the nonparametric curves, at least on the basis of the R^2. But these parametric functions are, by construction, convex (see Figure 12.2). This means that the three areas we have discussed earlier, and which are of great importance, are no longer present in the demand functions. To summarize: the fit is good but the shape is not. Therefore the use of 'convex' parametric representations of the demand function for policy analysis may be misleading even if their global adjustment to the data is good.[6]

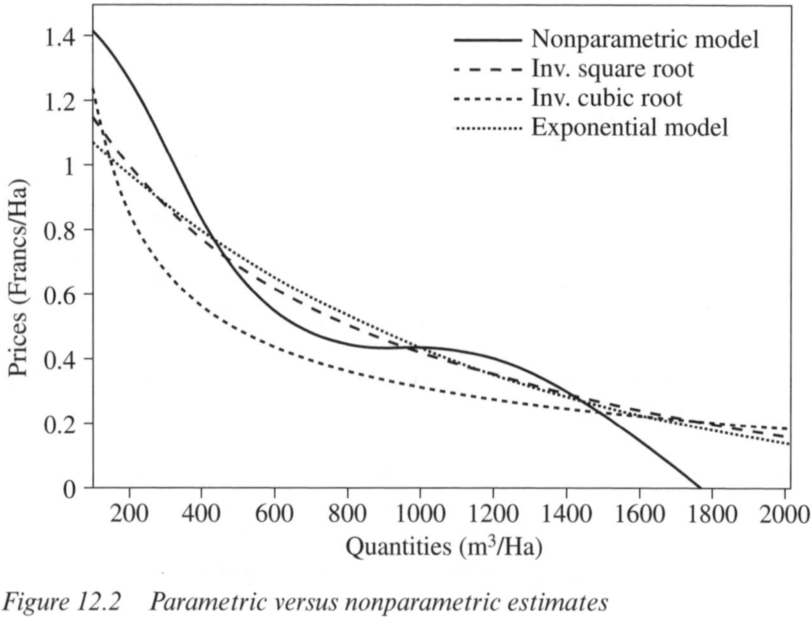

Figure 12.2 Parametric versus nonparametric estimates

Table 12.1 Results of nonlinear regressions

Specifications	Parameters	Demands	
		Feedback	Open
(1) $P = \alpha_1 + \beta_1 \cdot exp(-\gamma_1 \cdot Q)$	$\hat{\alpha}_1$	−0.043948	−0.058292
(*exponential model*)	$\hat{\beta}_1$	1.220422	1.216876
	$\hat{\gamma}_1$	0.000941	0.001006
	R^2	0.993415	0.9951764
(2) $P = \alpha_3 + \beta_3/\sqrt{Q}$	$\hat{\alpha}_3$	−0.113706	−0.147926
(*inverse square root model*)	$\hat{\beta}_3$	13.498286	13.459313
	R^2	0.896510	0.898665
(3) $P = \alpha_4 + \beta_4/\sqrt{Q} + \gamma_4/\sqrt[3]{Q}$	$\hat{\alpha}_4$	−1.388966	−1.4001683
(*inverse cubic root model*)	$\hat{\beta}_4$	−42.634237	−41.660033
	$\hat{\gamma}_4$	31.563734	30.994017
	R^2	0.99467271	0.994237

Our analysis is obviously partial, being for only one crop (corn) and for a specific region. Moreover, in order to get our results we have solved a structural programme. In this sense, it may appear to the reader that it could be hard to reproduce the estimation for all crops and all regions. A solution could be to use a reduced form and specify, as usually assumed in the literature, a parametric demand function. But, definitively, the specification chosen should be flexible enough to allow some non-convexity that is at least two inflexion points. For example, the simplest parametric specification could be a polynomial of degree three for the demand function, or of degree four for the production function.

3.3 Policy Analysis

We restrict our policy analysis here to the optimal feedback irrigation water demand. Before applying a price policy, the regulator has to know whether the current price lies in the second or in the third part of the demand curve (see Figure 12.3). In a region where farmers do use irrigation, the current irrigation price is not in the first part of the demand curve. Unless the regulator's objective is to eradicate irrigation in a specific region, he will never set a price reaching the first part. If the regulator doesn't know the real demand function, and assumes, as in the literature, that the curve is convex, he will not take too many political risks, since a marginal increase in price will imply, on a convex curve, a marginal effect on farmer's profit.[7] But we showed that the real irrigation demand curve is not convex. If, after a marginal price increase, the new price still lies in the third area, the profit variation will also

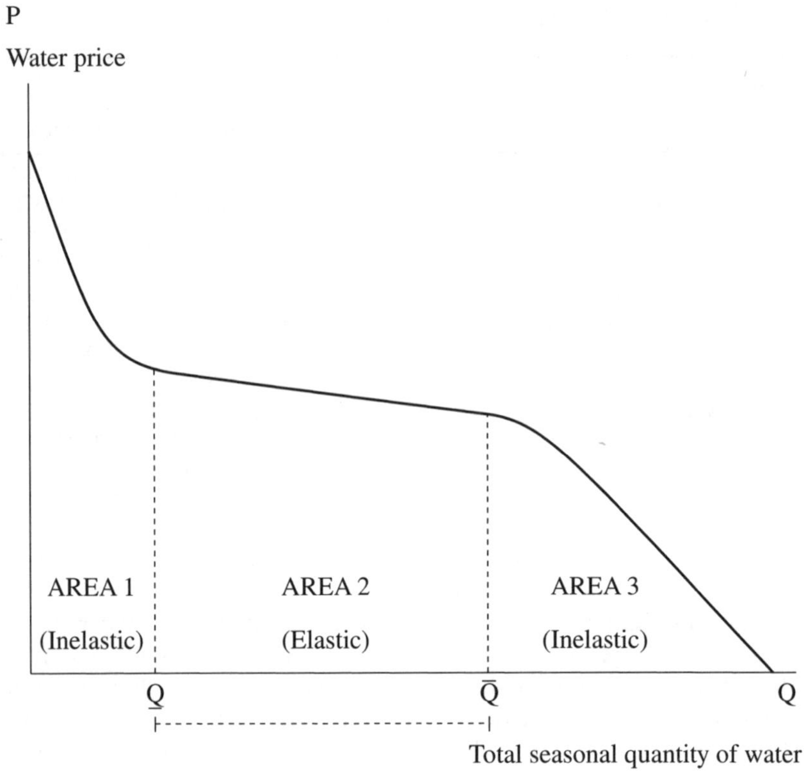

Note: The length of the flat section depends on weather conditions.

Figure 12.3 Schematic representation of the seasonal irrigation water demand curves

be marginal. In this case the policy is 'politically correct'. However, if unfortunately after the marginal price variation the price switches to the second area, the farmers may not be really happy, since we showed that the induced profit variation is not marginal any more. This pattern is obvious considering the flat shape of the demand curve in this area. Let us consider the 'medium' year and illustrate numerically the facts explained above. On the demand curve, we see that a marginal 1% increase in price from 0.49 francs/m^3 up to 0.495 francs/m^3, leads to a non-marginal water reduction of 45%. The loss in terms of farmers' revenue is also non-marginal (6.7% of the initial surplus). So, since politically it is always difficult to decrease the farmer's surplus non-marginally, the regulator may be reluctant to implement a water pricing policy. However, if we compare the surplus loss (6.7%)

to the water savings (45%), the economist may be more enthusiastic. If a country decides to increase the irrigation water price in order to decrease irrigation water quantity, it is because the water saving valuation and/or other users' water valuation is greater than the farmer's water valuation. Given that, it does not seem unrealistic, considering the important water savings (45%), to subsidize the farmers using lump sum transfers.

4. CONCLUSION

One may wonder if the results presented here are important, and if they justify the methodology used. To summarize, here are some arguments that should convince the reader of the utility of our work. First of all, we showed that the irrigation water demand was known only approximately, even if there are many papers estimating it in the literature. Second, no paper, to our knowledge, integrates a crop growth model in the irrigation water demand estimation under uncertainty. The non-convex shape of the demand function we obtained justifies by itself the integration of the agronomic model EPIC-Phase. Third, we have used a dynamic decision model to represent the farmer's behaviour under uncertainty, and relaxed assumptions in the estimation procedure. Finally, the policy implications drawn from the non-convex shape of the demand curve show that this feature is not a subtle theoretical matter and may have practical implications, at least on the irrigation water demand specification.

Our purpose here, and our final word, is to convince applied economists to take into account the probable presence of inflexion points in the irrigation water demand curve. If they disregard this, their policy recommendations could be misleading.

ANNEX A: THE GENERAL FRAMEWORK OF THE MODEL

We distinguish the three sets of climatic information Ω, I_t, and ω_t. Ω is the stochastic climate of the whole season. I_t is the farmer's climatic information set over the period t; ω_t is the vector of real weather factors such as wind, rain, temperatures, and radiation, realized during the period t. In our model we assume that only rainfall and temperature are in I_t, and thus influence the Bayesian revision process.

Consider a farmer facing a sequential decision problem of irrigation under uncertainty. At date $t = 1$, the farmer knows the total quantity of water available for the season, Q, the initial water stock in soil, $\bar{V}$, the state of crop biomass, $\bar{M}$, and the past weather. The farmer has to take decisions on irrigation at each date $t = 1, \ldots, T - 1$, and must choose the quantity of irrigation water denoted q_t. Therefore, we have a dynamic model of sequential choice under limited water supply with uncertainty, integrating three state variables (M_t, V_t, Q_t) *for* $t = 1, \ldots, T - 1$. The dynamics of the latter variable are the following:

$$M_{t+1} - M_t = f_t(M_t, V_t, \omega_t) \qquad (12A.1)$$

$$V_{t+1} - V_t = g_t(M_t, V_t, q_t, \omega_t) \qquad (12A.2)$$

$$Q_{t+1} - Q_t = -q_t \qquad (12A.3)$$

The change in the level of the biomass at any date (equation 12A.1) is a function (f_t) of the current date state variable, water stock in soil, and climatic conditions during the period. The change in water stock in soil (equation 12A.2) depends moreover on the decision taken, q_t at the current date. The total quantity of water has a simple decreasing dynamic (equation 12A.3).

The irrigation water supply is constrained as follows:

$$\sum_{t=1}^{T-1} q_t \leq Q \qquad (12A.4)$$

The application level, q_t – if this quantity is selected positive – is subject to technological and institutional constraints:

$$\underline{q} \leq q_t \leq \bar{q} \ \ for \ q_t > 0 \qquad (12A.5)$$

with $\underline{q}$ and $\bar{q}$ exogenous.[8]

The final date ($t = T$) corresponds to harvesting when actual crop yield becomes known. Let Y denote the crop yield function, that quantity depends only on the final biomass at date T and is denoted $Y(M_T)$.

The farmer's profit per hectare can be written as:

$$\Pi = r.Y(M_T) - C_{FT} - \sum_{t=1}^{T-1}(c.q_t + \delta_t.C_F) \tag{12A.6}$$

where r denotes the output price; C_{FT} denotes fixed production costs; c is the variable cost for each m^3 of water applied; δ_t is a dummy variable taking the value 1 if the farmer irrigates and 0 if not. C_F represents the fixed irrigation capital costs. We assume in the following that there is no uncertainty on output price.

The farmer is represented by a strictly monotonic, increasing and concave Von Neumann-Morgenstern utility function, denoted U. We chose the most common CRRA utility function:

$$U(\Pi) = \left(\frac{1}{1-\beta}\right)\cdot\Pi^{(1-\beta)} \tag{12A.7}$$

with β ($\beta \neq 1$), the relative risk aversion coefficient. We have assumed a risk aversion coefficient of 0.001, in accordance with the literature[9] (Jayet, 1992).

In the feedback framework, the farmer incorporates all the information he gets during the decision process. At date 1, the farmer takes the decision q_1 according to his weather expectations (I_1). At date 2 he integrates the decision made at date 1 and the climate realized during period 1 (ω_1), he may revise his weather expectations using a Bayesian rule:

Let Ω_j denote a particular climate. We assume that the corresponding probabilities $P[\Omega_j]$ as well as the conditional probabilities $P[I_t|\Omega_j]$ are known.[10] Then from the Bayes formula we find, for each decision date, t, the *a posteriori* probability:

$$P[\Omega_j|I_t] = \frac{P[I_t|\Omega_j]\cdot P[\Omega_j]}{\sum_j P[I_t|\Omega_j]\cdot P[\Omega_j]} \tag{12A.8}$$

This procedure can be repeated up to date $T-1$.

Through these computations the decision taken at date t clearly depends on the weather conditions observed during the period $[t-1, t]$ and on the past decisions $q_1, \ldots, q_{t-1}$. Formally, the farmer's sequential problem is:

$$\text{Max}_{q_1} E_{\Omega}\left[\text{Max}_{q_2} E_{\Omega|I_1}\left[\ldots \text{Max}_{q_{T-1}} E_{\Omega|I_{T-2}}\left[E_{\Omega|I_{T-1}} U\left[[rY(M_T)] - C_{FT} - \sum_{t=1}^{T-1}(c.q_t + \delta_t.C_F)\right]\right]\ldots\right]\right] \tag{12A.9}$$

$$s/c \quad \begin{cases} M_{t+1} - M_t = f_t(M_t, V_t, \omega_t) \\ V_{t+1} - V_t = g_t(M_t, V_t, q_t, \omega_t) \\ Q_{t+1} - Q_t = -q_t \end{cases} \tag{12A.10}$$

and subject to the technical constraint

$$and\ s/c \quad \begin{cases} \delta_t = \begin{cases} 0 & si \quad q_t = 0 \\ 1 & si \quad q_t > 0 \end{cases} \\ \underline{q} \le q_t \le \overline{q} \quad iff \quad q_t > 0 \\ M_t \ge 0, \quad V_t \ge 0, \quad Q_t \ge 0 \\ M_1 = \overline{M}, \quad V_1 = \overline{V}, \quad Q_1 = Q \end{cases} \tag{12A.11}$$

Where

E_{Ω} denotes the expectation over the climatic area for the whole season or *a priori* distribution.

$E_{\Omega|It-1}$ represents the conditional expectation on Ω revised from the Bayes formula or a *posteriori* distribution.

NOTES

We would like to thank Philippe Bontemps, Robert Chambers and Céline Nauges for helpful comments on an earlier draft. We are also grateful to the participants at the EAERE and AAEA 2001 Congress for critical remarks.

1. It is proved that the crop production function, that is, the relation between water applied to the crop and crop yield, does not admit a linear, or a Leontief, or a quadratic form, but has a more complex form depending on physical, weather and soil factors (Cabelguenne et al., 1999).
2. Temporal uncertainty corresponds to the situation where decisions are made over time as new information becomes available, modifying the anticipations of the farmer concerning the current uncertainty.
3. In this area, risk aversion does not matter because the CRRA utility function specification ensures that marginal utility is constant as marginal profit is constant.
4. As, whatever the climate, the shape of the demand function is the same, we may think that the quantity axis is also a temporal axis, regardless of the scale. The first area corresponds to emergence and flowering, the second to grain filling, and the third to maturity. These facts allowed us to use the above temporal explanations.
5. The mean demand functions are obtained from the distribution bounds of irrigation water demand under uncertainty that we have previously found. These curves are certainly the ones a regulator would look at closely before setting either a price or a quota in situations where water is scarce.
6. To have a better comparison and test between parametric and nonparametric curves one may use specific tests (see Härdle and Mammen, 1993). This is beyond the scope of the simple illustration presented here.
7. Of course, here we consider Q, the total seasonal water supply, corresponding to the second and third areas.

8. Farmers can face some limitations on the quantity q_t of water applied to each irrigation since investments are fixed in the short term.
9. The choice of this parameter is beyond the scope of this chapter.
10. We used a 14 year database to compute these probabilities for the numeric application.

REFERENCES

Belhaj Hassine, N., and Thomas, A. (2001), 'Aversion au Risque et Décisions de Production: L'Agriculture Irriguée en Tunisie', *Economie Rurale*, **266**, 91–108.

Bontemps, C., and Couture, S. (2002), 'Irrigation Water Demand for the Decision Maker', *Environment and Development Economics*, **7**, 643–57.

Bontemps, C., Couture, S., and Favard, P. (2003), 'Estimation de la Demande en Eau d'Irrigation sous Incertitude', *Economie Rurale*, **276**, 17–24.

Cabelguenne, M., Debaeke, P., and Bouniols, A. (1999), 'EPIC-Phase, a Version of the EPIC Model Simulating the Effects of Water and Nitrogen Stress on Biomass and Yield, Taking into Account of Developmental Stages: Validation on Maize, Sunflower, Sorghum, Soybean and Winter Wheat', *Agricultural Systems*, **60**, 175–96.

Chavas, J.P., and Holt, M.T. (1996), 'Economic Behavior under Uncertainty: A Joint Analysis of Risk Preferences and Technology', *Review of Economics and Statistics*, **78**, 329–35.

De Fraiture, C., and Perry, C. (2002), 'Why is Irrigation Water Demand Inelastic at Low Price Ranges?', Conference on Irrigation Water Policies: Micro and Macro Considerations, Agadir, Morocco.

Härdle, W., and Mammen, A. (1993), 'Comparing Nonparametric versus Parametric Regression Fits', *Annals of Statistics*, **21** (4), 1926–47.

Hooker, M.A., and Alexander, W.E. (1998), 'Estimating the Demand for Irrigation Water in the Central Valley of California', *Journal of the Association Water Resources Association*, **34**, 497–505.

Howitt, R.E., Watson, W.D., and Adams, R.M. (1980), 'A Reevaluation of Price Elasticities for Irrigation Water', *Water Resources Research*, **16**, 623–8.

Johansson, R.C., Tsur, Y., Roe, T.L., Doukkali, R., and Dinar, A. (2002), 'Pricing Irrigation Water: A Review of Theory and Practice', *Water Policy*, **4**, 173–99.

Michalland, B. (1995), 'Approche Économique de la Gestion de la Ressource en Eau pour l'Usage de l'Irrigation', Ph.D dissertation, University of Bordeaux.

Montginoul, M. (1997), 'Une Approche Économique de la Gestion de l'Eau d'Irrigation: Des Instruments, de l'Information et des Acteurs', Ph.D dissertation, University of Montpellier I.

Moore, M.R., and Negri, D.H. (1992), 'A Multicrop Production Model of Irrigated Agriculture, Applied to Water Allocation Policy of the Bureau of Reclamation', *Journal of Agricultural and Resources Economics*, **17**, 30–43.

Moore, M.R., Gollehon, N.R., and Carrey, M.B. (1994a), 'Alternative Models of Input Allocation in Multicrop Systems: Irrigation Water in the Central Plains, United States', *Agricultural Economics*, **11**, 143–58.

Moore, M.R., Gollehon, N.R., and Carrey, M.B. (1994b), 'Multicrop Production Decisions in Western Irrigated Agriculture: The Role of Water Price', *American Journal of Agricultural Economics*, **76**, 859–74.

Ogg, C.W., and Gollehon, N.R. (1989), 'Western Irrigation Response to Pumping

Costs: A Water Demand Analysis using Climatic Regions', *Water Resource Research*, **25**, 767–73.

Shunway, C.R. (1973), 'Derived Demand for Irrigation Water: The California Aqueduct', *Southwestern Journal of Agricultural Economics*, **5**, 195–200.

Tsur, Y., and Dinar, A. (1997), 'On the Relative Efficiency of Alternative Methods for Pricing Irrigation Water and their Implementation', *World Bank Economic Review*, **11**, 243–62.

Tsur, Y., Dinar, A., Doukkali, R.M., and Roe, T.L. (2002), 'Efficiency and Equity Implications of Irrigation Water Pricing', Conference on Irrigation Water Policies: Micro and Macro Considerations, Agadir, Morocco.

Varela-Ortega, C., Sumpsi, J.M., Garrido, A., Blanco, M., and Iglesias, E. (1998), 'Water Pricing Policies, Public Decision Making and Farmers' Response: Implications for Water Policy', *Agricultural Economics*, **19**, 193–202.

PART IV

Recent advances in econometrics methods applied to natural resource management

13. Contrasting conventional with multi-level modelling approaches to meta-analysis: expectation consistency in UK woodland recreation values

Ian J. Bateman and Andrew P. Jones

1. INTRODUCTION

The past two decades have witnessed an increasing reliance upon benefit-cost analysis (BCA) as a tool for project appraisal and to inform decision making. In the UK, a typical example of this trend is provided by the 1995 Environment Act which brought into being the Environment Agency (EA) and imposed 'general duties' upon the Agency to take account of the costs and benefits arising from its policies (HM Government, 1995). For many agencies, particularly those which have explicitly environmental or public good responsibilities, the assessment of benefits necessitated by adopting BCA approaches has led to a growing interest in tools for the monetary valuation of preferences for environmental goods and services. Consequently, expressed preference methods such as contingent valuation (CV) and conjoint analysis (CA) together with revealed preference techniques such as hedonic pricing (HP) and individual and zonal travel cost (TC) have enjoyed an unprecedented increase in application. However, use of such methods raises theoretical, empirical and practical issues. At a theoretical level, certain of these various techniques yield different measures of value. Furthermore, the validity of certain modes of application and analysis has been questioned. They are associated with recognized biases, exhibited as empirical regularities within the published literature. These issues place an onus upon the analyst to explain to decision makers the consequences of adopting certain study designs. However, from a decision perspective, a further and pressing practical issue concerns the fact that individual applications incur both direct and time related costs.

Consequently, the proliferation of valuation studies has coincided with increased interest in the potential for benefit transfer.

Rosenberger and Loomis (2000) define benefit transfer as 'the application of values and other information from a "study" site with data to a "policy" site with little or no data' (p. 1097). A number of approaches to undertaking transfers are available[1] including simple transfer of unadjusted point estimates, transfer of benefit demand functions and meta-analysis. As the simplest approaches cannot incorporate the characteristics of a given site within the transfer exercise, considerable attention is being given to the development of methods for transferring benefit demand functions (Loomis, 1992; Bergland et al., 1995; Loomis et al., 1995; Downing and Ozuna, 1996; Kirchhoff et al., 1997; Brouwer and Spaninks, 1999). However, results are mixed, with some studies reporting considerable success while others indicate abject failure. Given this and the empirical difficulties of such studies, a substantial literature has developed regarding the applications of meta-analysis techniques as a basis for benefit transfer.

Meta-analysis is the statistical analysis of the summary findings of prior empirical studies for the purpose of their integration (Glass, 1976; Wolf, 1986). Developed over the last 30 years, it has most commonly been applied in the fields of experimental medical treatment, psychotherapy, and education. Typically, these experiments took place in well-controlled circumstances with standard designs. Deviation from such specifications increases the problems with any cross-analysis (Glass et al., 1981).[2]

Despite problems, meta-analysis offers a transparent structure with which to understand underlying patterns of assumptions, relations and causalities, so permitting the derivation of useful generalizations (Hunter et al., 1982). It permits the extraction of general trend information from large datasets gleaned from numerous studies which would otherwise be difficult to summarize. In comparison with other benefit transfer techniques, Rosenberger and Loomis (2000) identify three advantages of adopting a meta-analysis approach: (i) it typically collates information from a greater number of studies, (ii) it is relatively straightforward to control for methodological differences between valuation source studies, (iii) benefit transfer is readily affected by setting explanatory variable values to those at the desired target site be it a previously surveyed, unsurveyed or just proposed (i.e. currently non-existent) site.

Table 13.1 extends reviews by Van den Bergh et al. (1997) and Smith and Pattanayak (forthcoming) to provide a brief summary of meta-analysis studies in this area. As can be seen, while analyses have addressed a number of issues, the bulk of applications have been within the field of recreation benefits valuation.

Table 13.1 Meta-analysis studies in environmental and resource economics

Subject area	Study authors
Recreation benefits	Bateman et al. (1999a, 2000), Markowski, et al. (2001), Rosenberger and Loomis (2000), Shrestha and Loomis (2001), Smith and Kaoru (1990a), Sturtevant et al. (1995), Van Houtven et al. (2001), Walsh et al. (1990, 1992)
Price elasticity in TC studies	Smith and Kaoru (1990b)
CV versus revealed preference	Carson et al. (1996)
Multiplier effects of tourism	Baaijens et al. (1998), Van den Bergh et al. (1997, ch. 9)
Wetland functions	Brouwer et al. (1999), Woodward and Wui (2001)
Groundwater quality	Boyle et al. (1994), Poe et al. (2001)
Price elasticity for water	Espey et al. (1997)
Urban pollution valuation	Smith (1989), Smith and Huang (1993), Smith and Huang (1995), Schwartz (1994), Van den Bergh et al. (1997, ch. 10)
Noise nuisance	Button (1995), Nelson (1980), Van den Bergh et al. (1997, ch. 4)
Congestion and transport	Button and Kerr (1996), Van den Bergh et al. (1997, ch.13 and 14), Waters (1993)
Visibility and air quality	Desvousges et al. (1998), Smith and Osborne (1996)
Endangered species	Loomis and White (1996)
Valuation of life estimates	Mrozek and Taylor (forthcoming), Van den Bergh et al. (1997, ch. 11)

The empirical applicability of meta-analysis to any given context is determined by the number, quality and comparability of studies available to the researcher (Desvousges et al., 1998). Here there is a difficult trade-off between the desire to expand analyses so as to enhance the applicability of results to different goods, provision changes, locations, contexts, etc., and the consequent increase in data demands which such expansions entail. For example, Rosenberger and Loomis (2000) consider a wide range of outdoor recreation activities (ten separate categories ranging from fishing to rock climbing to snowmobiling) across a very extensive area, the US and Canada. This analysis requires a large valuation dataset and their study utilizes 682 value estimates from 131 separate studies. By contrast the meta-analysis presented in this chapter considers just one type of activity, recreation in open-access woodlands, and just one geographical area, Great Britain, a land area just over 1% the size of that considered by Rosenberger and Loomis. Our analysis is initially restricted just to measures obtained by application of the CV method yielding a dataset of 44 value estimates from 11 studies. A second analysis supplements these data with results obtained from six TC studies, bringing the total number of value estimates to 77.[3] While this is less than the size of the Rosenberger and Loomis dataset (reflecting the smaller number of studies conducted in Great Britain), the much smaller geographical boundaries of our study, and its focus upon just one activity, mean that data are placed under considerably less stress, enhancing the reliability of resultant benefit transfer estimates. The disadvantage of this focus is that our results are not readily applicable to other activities or to areas outside Great Britain.

The study described here embraces two objectives. The minor of these concerns the extent to which meta-analysis confirms expectations, derived from theory and empirical regularities, regarding the relationship of values derived from the various permutations of study design represented in our assembled dataset. In so doing we seek to highlight to decision makers (and researchers) the influence upon value estimates of adopting different methods or analytical techniques and so directly address concerns regarding the variability of valuation estimates for apparently similar goods. As a direct extension of this investigation we address the issue of whether, after allowing for design choice, different authors are associated with significantly different valuation estimates. Evidence for such effects would constitute a substantial criticism of valuation studies, raising the charge that authors tailor findings to the desires of those commissioning research. However, the principal objective of this study is analytical as we detail alternate approaches to the construction of meta-analysis models.

The first and second meta-analyses presented here are conducted by applying conventional regression techniques to, initially, the subset of CV estimates and subsequently to the full set of CV and TC estimates. These analyses provide a basis for illustrating the limitations of such conventional regression techniques in comparison with a third analysis obtained through application of multilevel modelling (MLM) methods (Goldstein, 1995) to the full dataset of CV and TC observations. As discussed in detail subsequently, the MLM approach allows the researcher to explicitly incorporate potential nested structures within the data, permitting examination of a number of key issues and criticisms of both meta-analysis and valuation studies. Crucially, the MLM approach allows the researcher to relax strong and commonly adopted assumptions regarding the independence of estimates with respect to the numerous natural hierarchies within which they reside. For example, we might expect estimates derived for a given forest to be more similar than those obtained from different forests. Furthermore, whilst not in accord with any theoretical expectation, it might be observed that estimates produced within the same study (or, as highlighted above, by the same author) were more similar than other estimates.[4] While many previous meta-analyses have failed to acknowledge this issue by implicitly assuming independence between estimates (e.g. see some of the studies reported in Van den Bergh et al., 1997), others have adopted weighting approaches, typically by dividing the data associated with each estimate by the number of estimates within the study concerned (e.g. Markowski et al., 2001; Mrozek and Taylor, forthcoming).[5] However, both approaches are flawed; independence ignores the real possibility of similarity between nested estimates, while weighting schemes such as those described here result in all studies receiving equal weight irrespective of the fact that we have more information about those containing higher numbers of valuation estimates. Furthermore, such studies typically only address the nesting of estimates within studies and ignore other equally plausible hierarchies such as the nesting of estimates within sites or within authors.

By explicit incorporation of data hierarchies within the analysis, the MLM approach both provides insight into areas in which the independence assumption fails to hold and, through improved modelling of such nesting, ensures that standard errors on parameter estimates are correctly estimated and the significance of explanatory variables accurately assessed. Such a meta-analysis can then defensibly be used to investigate the extent to which valuation estimates conform to expectations. This then links together our analytical objectives with the validity aims of the chapter. We can use our refined MLM model to examine both expected differences, such as those associated with different methods and analytical techniques, and unexpected differences, such as the clustering of estimates within authors as described above.

The remainder of the chapter is organized as follows. In Section 2 we provide some background to the case study and detail the theoretical and empirical expectations embraced by this application. Section 3 sets out and reports a conventional meta-analysis of our data. Section 4 repeats this process for our MLM based model discussing in detail the nature of this approach and how it differs from the conventional approach. Section 5 concludes by highlighting advantages and limitations of the MLM approach, examining the implications of our findings for the validity of valuation exercises and distilling messages for policy makers within this area.

2. THE RECREATIONAL VALUE OF FORESTS

2.1 Background and Data

In terms of land use, British forestry has always been the poor cousin of agriculture. A history of deforestation meant that, by 1900, only 4% of England and Wales and 2% of Scotland and Ireland was forested, by far the lowest level in Europe (Rackham, 1976). The establishment of the FC (Forestry Commission) in 1919 has done much to reverse this trend and over 10%[6] of the land area of Great Britain is under woodland today. This constitutes the largest single source of open-access land, generates approximately 24–32 million recreational visits per annum (NAO, 1986; Benson and Willis, 1990; 1992), and produces a national aggregate consumer surplus value estimated at between £40 million (Bateman, 1996) and well over £50 million (Benson and Willis, 1992) at current prices. From an economic perspective, the recreational value of forestry is therefore one of its most important benefit streams.

The initial stage of any meta-analysis involves a survey of the relevant literature to identify potential base data studies. Table 13.2 presents summary details from some 30 studies of UK woodland recreation value yielding over 100 benefit estimates. As can be seen, these studies embrace a diversity of recreation value units including per annum, capitalized and per forest values. This variety is not readily incorporated within a meta-analysis and so our study concentrates upon the largest single group of estimates: the per person per visit values.

As outlined above, an initial analysis focused solely upon those estimates obtained from applications of the CV method. Here survey respondents were asked to state their willingness to pay (WTP) for the recreational value of the forests concerned.[7] Table 13.2 indicates that there are eight studies yielding 28 estimates of the direct 'use value' of the recreational services provided by forests. Three studies also asked respondents about their WTP for both the present and possible future use (or 'option value'; Weisbrod, 1964; Pearce and Turner, 1990) of forests, providing a further 16 estimates of this wider recreational value. In total therefore, these studies yield 44 value estimates.[8]

A second analysis was conducted by expanding the dataset to include a further 23 per person per visit value estimates obtained from TC studies. These estimates can be further subdivided. There are 16 individual TC estimates of which nine use ordinary least squares (OLS) estimators. A further seven use maximum likelihood (ML) estimators.[9] There are also 17 zonal TC (*ZTC*) estimates all of which use OLS estimators.

Taken together, these CV and TC studies yield 77 value estimates across 21 forests (methods were well represented across these forests[10]). The

Table 13.2 Studies of open-access woodland recreation value in Great Britain

Value type	Recreation value unit	Valuation method	No. of studies	Date conducted[1]	No. of value estimates	Value range (£, 1990) (m = million)
Use	Per person per visit	CV	8[a]	1987–93	28	£0.28–£1.55
Use + option	Per person per visit	CV	3[b]	1988–92	16	£0.51–£1.46
Use	Per person per visit	ZTC	3[c]	1976–88	17	£1.30–£3.91
Use	Per person per visit	ITC	3[d]	1988–93	16	£0.07–£2.74
Use	Per person per year	CV	3[e]	1989–92	7	£5.14–£29.59
Use	Per household capital[2]	CV	3[f]	1990	3	£3.27[3]–£12.89
Use	FC forests/conservancy[4]	TC	1[g]	1970	13	£0.1m–£1.1m
Use	Total UK value	TC	6[h]	1970–98	6	£6.5m–£62.5m
–	All studies	–	30	1970–98	106	–

Notes:

1 = Dates refer to the year of study survey rather than publication date.
2 = These studies use a once-and-for-all willingness to pay per household question.
3 = We have recalculated this figure by including those who refused to pay as zero bids.
4 = The FC at the time divided the area of Great Britain into a number of Forest Conservancies and large forests to which these estimates relate.

Study references:
a = Whiteman and Sinclair (1994); Hanley and Ruffell (1991); Bishop (1992); Willis and Benson (1989); Hanley (1989); Willis et al. (1988); Bateman and Langford (1997); Bateman (1996).
b = Bishop (1992); Willis and Benson (1989); Willis et al. (1988).
c = Benson and Willis (1992); Hanley (1989); Everett (1979).
d = Willis and Garrod (1991); Bateman (1996); Bateman et al. (1996).
e = Whiteman and Sinclair (1994); Bishop (1992); Bateman (1996).
f = Hanley and Munro (1991); Hanley and Ecotec (1991); Hanley and Craig (1991).
g = HM Treasury (1972).
h = HM Treasury (1972); Grayson et al. (1975); NAO (1986); Willis and Garrod (1991); Benson and Willis (1992); Bateman (1996).

following list of variables which might potentially influence value estimates were identified:

Method: A set of four binary variables indicating the method/estimation technique adopted to produce the value estimate:

CV	=	1 for contingent valuation method used; 0 otherwise
ITCols	=	1 for individual travel cost method with ordinary least squares estimators used; 0 otherwise
ITCml	=	1 for individual travel cost method with maximum likelihood estimators used; 0 otherwise
ZTC	=	1 for zonal travel cost method with ordinary least squares estimators used; 0 otherwise

Option (CV studies only): 1 = use value plus option value requested in WTP question, 0 = use value alone

Elicit (CV studies only): A set of five binary variables identifying the WTP elicitation method employed (variable names as follows: *OE* = open ended, *IB* = iterative bidding, *PC* = payment card, *PCH* = high range payment card, *DC* = dichotomous choice).

Forest: A set of 21 binary variables identifying each of the forests included in at least one of the studies (variable/forest names as follows: *Mercia, Thames Chase, Gt. Northern Forest, Aberfoyle, Derwent Walk, Whippendell Wood, New Forest, Cheshire, Loch Awe, Brecon, Buchan, Newton Stewart, Lorne, Ruthin, Castle Douglas, South Lakes, North York Moors, Durham, Thetford, Dean, Dalby*)

Author: A set of six binary variable identifying authors common to a set of studies (studies can be identified via notes to Table 13.2; variable names as follows: *Bateman, Bishop, Everett, Hanley, Whiteman, Willis*)

Year: Continuous variable; the number of years before (negative) or after (positive) the base year (1990)

Table 13.3 reports summary descriptive statistics for the value estimates disaggregated by the various *Method* and *Author* variables. All values were adjusted to a common base year (1990) set roughly in the middle of the density of collated estimates. The table highlights two important features of the dataset that are the subject of subsequent investigation. First, the data are dominated by estimates derived from studies conducted by Willis et al., reflecting their leading role in this field. Second, while the number of estimates is too small to permit calculation of confidence intervals, values do appear to vary by *Method* (e.g. the *ZTC* estimates appear to be substantially higher than those from other approaches) and possibly by *Author* (although it is clearly important to control for the effect of *Method* here). These initial observations provide focal points for the analyses described subsequently.

Table 13.3 Per person per visit woodland recreation value estimates (£, 1990) disaggregated by study author and valuation/estimation method

Method	Whiteman & Sinclair	Hanley et al.	Bishop	Willis et al.	Bateman et al.	Everett	All
CV	3	6	4	28	3	0	44
	0.78	1.30	0.89	0.71	1.08	–	0.84
	(0.66–	(0.85–	(0.46–	(0.28–	(0.47–	–	(0.28–
	0.93)	1.55)	1.46)	1.29)	1.55)	–	1.55)
	[0.14]	[0.27]	[0.46]	[0.27]	[0.55]		[0.36]
ITCols	0	0	0	6	3	0	9
	–	–	–	1.46	1.35	–	1.42
	–	–	–	(0.47–	(1.07–	–	(0.47–
	–	–	–	2.74)	1.58)	–	2.74)
ITCml	0	0	0	6	1	0	7
	–	–	–	0.57	1.20	–	0.66
	–	–	–	(0.07–	(1.20–	–	(0.07–
	–	–	–	1.13)	1.20)	–	1.20)
				[0.47]	[–]		[0.49]
ZTC	0	1	0	15	0	1	17
	–	2.14	–	2.53	–	1.30	2.43
	–	(2.14–	–	(1.58–	–	(1.30–	(1.30–
	–	2.14)	–	3.91)	–	1.30)	3.91)
		[—]		[0.66]		[–]	[0.71]
All	3	7	4	55	7	1	77
	0.78	1.41	0.89	1.27	1.21	1.30	1.24
	(0.66–	(0.85–	(0.46–	(0.07–	(0.47–	(1.30–	(0.07–
	0.93)	2.14)	1.46)	3.91)	1.58)	1.30)	3.91)
	[0.14]	[0.40]	[0.46]	[0.95]	[0.38]	[–]	[0.83]

Notes:
Cell contents are as follows:
Number of estimates
Mean value (£/person/visit)
(Range: minimum to maximum value)
[StDev of values]

2.2 Theoretical and Empirically Derived Expectations

Taken together, theory and empirical regularities reported in the valuation literature provide a rich set of expectations regarding how our valuation estimates may vary according to the differing combinations of valuation methods and analytical techniques from which they were obtained. This means that we can use our various meta-analyses to examine the extent to which value estimates conform to these expectations. If we were to assume that all our meta-analyses were equally robust we could use them to provide a commentary upon the validity of our valuation estimates. However, as highlighted previously, we have good reason to suspect that our MLM meta-analyses provide a superior alternative to conventionally estimated models. Therefore we can reverse the direction of our test by examining the differing extents to which our various meta-analyses provide results which conform to expectations. Here improved conformity with expectations may be taken as indicating superior performance of a given meta-analysis technique.

What then are the relationships which we might expect to observe within our valuation estimates? Considering the subset of CV studies first, an initial expectation is that questions seeking to elicit the sum of option plus use value should yield higher values than those addressing use values alone (Pearce and Turner, 1990).

Staying within the CV studies, theory also provides clear guidance regarding the impact of changing WTP elicitation method across the various permutations identified in our list of variables. Carson et al. (1999) extend earlier work by Hoehn and Randall (1987) to provide a comprehensive critique of the incentive compatibility of differing WTP elicitation approaches. They note that a simple open ended (OE) WTP question, such as 'What are you willing to pay?', is liable to free-riding behaviour, typically leading to understatement of WTP. Conversely, following the work of Farquharson (1969), Gibbard (1973) and Satterthwaite (1975), Carson et al. show that 'no response format with greater than a binary . . . can be incentive compatible without restrictions on preferences' (p. 11).[11] This provides a powerful argument in favour of CV studies adopting the single bound dichotomous choice (DC) format wherein respondents may only choose to accept or reject an interviewer-specified discrete WTP sum. For our purposes the DC approach also provides a useful benchmark for testing the theoretical compatibility of our various meta-analyses. For example, we can expect that estimates of WTP derived from OE elicitation techniques should be below those provided by the DC format. Similarly, the iterative bidding (IB) approach, in which respondents can bid up or down from a given starting point, opens the possibility of free-riding again resulting in values which are lower than those derived from DC designs. However, these theoretical expectations can be modified in the light of empirical regularities, repeatedly observed in the literature. So, for example, IB studies have been shown to exhibit significant starting point biases (Roberts et al., 1985; Boyle et al., 1985) and in comparative tests have provided value estimates which lie below those given by DC methods but above those derived from

OE formats (Bateman et al., 1995). The situation with payment card (PC) approaches, in which respondents choose values from a range presented to them, is equally complex. While recent years have seen a renaissance in the use of PC approaches (Rowe et al., 1996), they fail an incentive compatibility test and in the face of free-riding are again likely to yield underestimates of true WTP. Furthermore, changes in the PC range given to respondents may induce psychological effects, resulting in further biases. It is an examination of one such possible bias which yields our high range payment card (PCH) study (Bateman, 1996) which compares various payment cards including those deliberately designed to stretch well beyond the distribution of woodland WTP measures as obtained by a more typical PC range. This test found that measures derived from the PCH were significantly higher than those obtained from other, conventionally designed, PC approaches.

In summary, we have a variety of theoretically and empirically derived expectations regarding elicitation effects in CV studies. If we rely solely upon theoretical expectations then, in the presence of strategic free-riding within non-incentive compatible formats, we might expect DC derived measures to exceed those obtained from other formats. However, if we temper these theoretical expectations with observed empirical regularities then, while we would still expect OE estimates to be below those from DC studies, we would expect IB values to lie between these values. PC measures also suffer incentive incompatibility, although we expect those obtained from the PCH format to exceed those from other PC analyses.

Widening our analysis to include the TC estimates, again both theory and practice provide some guidance regarding expectations. Comparing these with CV estimates, while the latter yield direct Hicksian welfare measures of WTP, TC methods provide Marshallian consumer surplus estimates. The relationship of these measures depends upon the relative shape of the underlying compensated and uncompensated demand curves for the goods and provision changes concerned (Just et al., 1982; Boadway and Bruce, 1984). Carson et al. (1996) review 83 studies from which 616 comparisons of CV to revealed preference (RP; including TC) estimates are drawn, yielding a whole sample mean CV:RP ratio of 0.89 (95% CI = 0.81 to 0.96), i.e. CV estimates were found to be significantly lower than TC values.

As noted in the preceding section, we can identify a number of distinct types of TC analysis. Certain of the TC based estimates of woodland recreation value rely upon theoretically inappropriate OLS estimation techniques (labelled above as *ITCols* measures). Such techniques are liable to lead to over-estimates of benefits due to an inability to reflect the truncation of non-visitors within an on-site TC survey sample. In contrast other estimates (labelled as *ITCml* measures) have been derived using appropriate maximum likelihood estimators which explicitly model the truncation of non-visitors and are not upwardly biased in this respect. There are also a number of zonal TC (*ZTC*) estimates. These are also likely to yield over-estimates of values both because, in this instance, all used OLS estimators and because of a systematic upward bias in most zonal estimates of travel time and distance (and hence consumer surplus) recently identified by Bateman et al. (1999b).

Taken together, these theoretical and empirical factors lead to clear expectations regarding the relationships which should hold in our meta-analyses. In summary these are that, within CV estimates, those derived from OE methods should yield the lowest values and that IB estimates should lie above these but below those from DC formats. The relation with PC estimates is less clear other than that PCH estimates should exceed those from other PC designs. A general expectation is that TC studies should produce higher values than CV analyses and that within TC estimates those from ZTC and *ITCols* designs should be higher than *ITCml* measures.

Considering the remaining variables identified from our set of estimates, the *Forest* variables are included to identify any influences that variations in the nature of individual sites (e.g. facilities) may have upon stated WTP. We have no theoretical expectations regarding these variables. However, empirical work by Brainard et al. (1999, 2001) examining the drivers of demand for forest recreation found that site facilities had very little discernible impact upon observed demand for woodland recreation which was instead driven primarily by locational factors (a result which supports the use of TC methods). This would suggest that the *Forest* variables are likely to prove relatively weak predictors of variation between value estimate. The *Year* variable seems most likely to reflect perceived changes in the availability or desirability of open-access woodland recreation over time and therefore has no prior expectation (although its observed sign is clearly of policy interest). Finally, while we have no theoretical expectation that the *Author* variables should impact significantly upon values, if this did prove to be the case it would constitute a problem for valuation research, giving support to the criticism that some authors yield unusually high or low value estimates.

Together these expectations provide a basis for validating and comparing our various meta-analyses. As outlined above, these open, in Section 3, with conventionally modelled analyses, initially for just our CV estimates after which we expand to include the TC estimates. Section 4 then re-estimates the latter model using MLM techniques.

3. CONVENTIONALLY ESTIMATED META-ANALYSES

3.1 Conventional Meta-analysis of the CV per Person per Day Values

Our initial meta-analysis applied conventional regression methods to our set of CV derived value estimates. This restriction removed the *Method* variables defined previously. However, all other variables were considered within this analysis. Within the *Elicit* variables the *DC* dummy was omitted as an incentive compatible base case against which all other elicitation effects could be observed. Collinearity between the *Author* and *Forest* variables was too high to permit their simultaneous inclusion within a single model (e.g. all studies by Hanley et al. were conducted in Aberfoyle forest although others also undertook studies in this forest). When tested separately the *Forest* variables proved, as per expectations outlined above, to be almost always insignificant predictors of WTP. Given this, the first model reported in this chapter concentrates instead upon the *Author* variables. Here we hold the Bateman et al. studies as the base case (as these fall roughly in the middle of values reported by other researchers) and include all other *Author* dummies. Inspection of the *Year* variable indicated little variation across CV estimates relative to our wider dataset and this variable was reserved for subsequent analysis. Tests indicated that a linear model performed better than other functional forms, yielding the model given in Table 13.4.[12]

Table 13.4 Conventionally modelled meta-analysis of CV estimates of per person per visit recreation values (£, 1990) for open-access woodland in Great Britain

Variable	Coefficient	95% CI	p
Intercept	1.061	0.999–1.684	>0.001
Option	0.419	0.290–0.549	>0.001
OE	−0.443	−0.784–0.102	0.032
IB	−0.419	−0.901–0.064	0.144
PC	−0.129	−0.53–0.276	0.589
PCH	0.489	−0.052–0.971	0.090
Bishop	0.065	−0.303–0.434	0.764
Hanley	0.497	0.156–0.838	0.017
Whiteman	0.161	−0.215–0.537	0.466
Willis	-0.118	−0.443–0.208	0.538

Notes: $R^2 = 0.718$; R^2(adj.) = 0.643; n = 44.

The model detailed in Table 13.4 fits the data well and conforms well with our theoretical and empirical expectations. The *Option* variable provides a strong, positive and highly significant influence upon stated WTP; as expected respondents facing a 'use plus option value' question stated higher WTP sums than those facing 'use value alone' questions. The *Elicit* variables also conform well with prior expectations. Compared to the incentive compatible *DC* base case all methods yield negative departures (suggesting the anticipated presence of free-riding strategies) except for the *PCH* method (where the psychological pressure exerted by the high range payment card seems to have raised stated WTP above that predicted via the *DC* approach; a result which is just significant at the 10% level). The size and significance of estimated coefficients also conforms well with expectations, with the *OE* method exerting the largest downward pressure upon estimates (this being the only effect which is clearly significant at the 5% level), while the *IB* approach results in a lesser negative effect followed by the *PC* results, with both of these proving insignificant. Overall this ordering conforms in all aspects with our prior expectations, providing some considerable support for this model. However, this is not the case for our set of *Author* variables. Here the expectation is of no significant effect and while this is generally the case, this is not true of the *Hanley* variable which yields a clearly significant positive effect. This latter result is somewhat worrying as it appears to suggest that reported valuation estimates are partly dependent upon the researcher carrying out the study. We therefore move to our wider dataset, boosted by the TC estimates and re-examine this and the other issues raised above.

3.2 Conventionally Estimated Meta-analysis of the CV and TC per Person per Day Values

The analysis was subsequently expanded by the addition of the 23 estimates of per person per visit woodland recreation values obtained using TC methods. In addition to increasing the total observations to 77, this also adds the set of *Method* variables which defines the four method/estimation combinations used (*CV*, *ITCols*, *ITCml* and *ZTC*, of which the *CV* studies are held as the base case in subsequent analyses).[13] The *Elicit* variables were omitted from this analysis as they did not apply to the TC studies. However, the expanded period covered by the wider dataset permitted inclusion of the *Year* variable. Models were estimated using conventional regression technique.[14] Table 13.5 details results for a number of model specifications. In each case, tests of functional form indicate that the linear specification performs roughly as well as other standard forms and is retained for comparability and ease of interpretation.

Table 13.5 Conventional meta-analyses of CV and TC estimates of per person per visit recreation values (£, 1990) for open-access woodland in Great Britain

	Models				
	A	B	C	D	E
Intercept	1.1980	0.8368	0.6687	0.6796	0.7697
	(0.1057)	(0.0764)	(0.0862)	(0.0886)	(0.0910)
	[11.34]	[10.95]	[7.75]	[7.67]	[8.46]
	{0.000}	{0.000}	{0.000}	{0.000}	{0.000}
Option			0.2717	0.2626	0.3414
			(0.1436)	(0.1469)	(0.1434)
			[1.89]	[1.79]	[2.38]
			{0.063}	{0.078}	{0.020}
Forest:	−0.3780		−0.4029	−0.4153	−0.3962
Cheshire	(0.3839)		(0.2163)	(0.2203)	(0.2109)
	[−0.98]		[−1.86]	[−1.88]	[−1.88]
	{0.328}		{0.067}	{0.064}	{0.065}
Loch Awe	0.5653		0.4379	0.4212	0.4154
	(0.4881)		(0.2760)	(0.2812)	(0.2690)
	[1.16]		[1.59]	[1.50]	[1.54]
	{0.251}		{0.117}	{0.139}	{0.127}
Aberfoyle	0.4445		0.5491		
	(0.3104)		(0.1799)		
	[1.43]		[3.05]		
	{0.156}		{0.003}		
Method:		1.5973	1.6988	1.7253	1.8461
ZTC		(0.1447)	(0.1378)	(0.1418)	(0.1427)
		[11.04]	[12.33]	[12.17]	[12.94]
		{0.000}	{0.000}	{0.000}	{0.000}
		0.5876	0.8005	0.7910	0.7994
ITCols		(0.1854)	(0.1767)	(0.1805)	(0.1727)
		[3.17]	[4.53]	[4.38]	[4.63]
		{0.002}	{0.000}	{0.000}	{0.000}
ITCml		−0.1811			
		(0.2062)			
		[−0.88]			
		{0.383}			
Author:				0.4926	0.4390
Hanley				(0.1955)	(0.1881)
				[2.52]	[2.33]
				{0.014}	{0.023}

Table 13.5 (continued)

	Models				
	A	B	C	D	E
Year					0.0755 (0.0276) [2.74] {0.008}
R^2(adj.)	0.020	0.531	0.690	0.678	0.705
n	77	77	77	77	77

Notes:
Cell contents are: Estimated coefficient
(StDev)
[*t*-value]
{*p*-value}

where:

Dependent variable = recreational value (£) per person per visit;
Option = 1 where the value estimate relates to the sum of use plus option value and 0 where the value estimated is use value alone (note that all TC studies relate to use value alone);
Cheshire = 1 for studies conducted at Cheshire forest and 0 otherwise;
Loch Awe = 1 for studies conducted at Loch Awe forest and 0 otherwise;
Aberfoyle = 1 for studies conducted at Aberfoyle forest and 0 otherwise;
ITCols = 1 if study uses the individual travel cost method with an OLS estimator and 0 otherwise;
ITCml = 1 if study uses the individual travel cost method with an ML estimator and 0 otherwise;
ZTC = 1 if study uses the zonal travel cost method (all employ OLS estimators) and 0 otherwise;
Hanley = 1 if study conducted by Hanley et al. and 0 otherwise;
Year = Continuous variable; the number of years before (negative) or after (positive) the base year (1990);

In Table 13.5, Model A restricts investigation to the 21 *Forest* variables referring to study site effects, reporting only the three most significant of these dummies. Even these prove highly insignificant, a result which conforms to our expectations as set out previously. In Model B these variables are removed in favor of the *Method* dummies which yields a dramatic increase in explanatory power. Perhaps more importantly the sign and significance of these variables conforms well with our prior expectations. Remembering that CV studies form our base case, we find no significant effect from the *ITCml* variable (a result which persisted throughout our analysis such that we omit this variable from subsequent analyses in Table 13.5 for which the base case now becomes *CV* and *ITCml* estimates) but strongly significant and positive effects associated with the *ITCols* and *ZTC* variables. This result again confirms our prior expectations, suggesting that these latter estimates are upwardly biased.

Model C adds the *Option* and previously considered *Forest* variables producing a further substantial improvement to model fit which does not change substantially in remaining models. As expected, the *Option* variable yields a positive and significant ($\alpha = 10\%$) effect upon values. Interestingly, two of the *Forest* variables also prove significant. However, as mentioned previously, one of these, the site variable for *Aberfoyle* forest, is strongly correlated with the author variable *Hanley* (all of the Hanley et al. studies were conducted at Aberfoyle although other authors also provide estimates for this forest). Given the insignificance of all but one other of the *Forest* variables and our results of Table 13.4, it seems reasonable to investigate the possibility that it is this *Author* variable which is the root of this effect. Accordingly, Model D exchanges the *Aberfoyle* variable with that for *Hanley*, the latter also proving significant.

Taken together, the results of Model D and that reported in Table 13.4 could be seen as supporting the argument that valuation estimates may be subject to authorship effects. An alternative explanation is that the Hanley et al. estimates are elevated because of some characteristics of the Aberfoyle site for which they were estimated. Yet a further explanation might be that this result is in some way a product of the conventional modelling approach adopted in this meta-analysis. All of these possibilities are explored subsequently.

Model E adds the final variable *Year* into the analysis. This yields a small, positive and significant coefficient. The result is not particularly robust, becoming insignificant ($p = 0.181$) when the oldest estimate (that provided by Everett, 1979 is omitted, yet even then the sign and size of the coefficient remain similar ($\beta = 0.0526$). This suggests that, given a longer data period, a positive trend in valuations might become more clearly established. While emphasizing statistical uncertainties regarding this result, its general message seems plausible, suggesting an increasing relative interest in outdoor, environmentally based recreation over the last three decades and echoing the seminal work of Krutilla and Fisher (1975).

In summary, with the exception of the *Hanley* variable, the relationships detailed in Model E conform well to expectations. Values are positively related to the *Option* variable which in this best fit model is now significant at the 5% level. Similarly, the *Method* variables *ITCols* and *ZTC* both have significant and positive coefficients reflecting their expected relationship with the CV and *ITCml* values which form the base case of this analysis. Here the only *Forest* variables to prove significant ($\alpha = 10\%$) is that for *Cheshire.* The negative coefficient on this variable may reflect the high visitor congestion observed in studies of this forest (Willis and Benson, 1989).[15] As noted, the positive and significant *Year* variable also seems highly plausible. Model E also provides the best fit to our data and, given the generally desirable characteristics noted above, provides a typical example of a meta-analysis estimated using conventional statistical modelling approaches. We now consider an alternative to this approach and examine the extent to which this may provide superior insight into the nature and robustness of these postulated relationships.

4. AN MLM APPROACH TO META-ANALYSIS

The various models reported in Tables 13.4 and 13.5 all assume independence between estimates. However, in recent years a suite of 'Multilevel Modelling' (MLM) techniques have been developed within the fields of epidemiology and education research to allow the researcher to relax this assumption and develop models which explicitly incorporate natural hierarchies or 'levels' within which data is clustered (Goldstein, 1995). This is achieved by modelling the residual variance of estimates in two parts; that due to the effect of given levels upon estimates, and that remaining due to true unexplained error. In effect, this approach allows for the possibility that variation within value estimates may differ between levels thus violating the independence assumption. In order to relax this assumption and examine the advantages of an MLM approach, this technique is now applied to our meta-analysis of woodland recreation estimates.[16]

A potential limitation of the application of conventional regression techniques in meta-analysis occurs if the observations being modelled possess an inherent hierarchy. Within conventional estimation strategies, some of the variables used to predict recreation may be specific to each individual study (examples being the study design and elicitation method used). However, others, such as the author, study or forest to which a given estimate pertains, may be constant across a set of such estimates. These former categorizations can be conceptualized as higher level variables, and in this sense the data may be viewed as possessing a hierarchical structure. The data structure from the above examples can be seen as actually corresponding to a range of hierarchical levels; of value estimates (level 1) within studies (level 2), of value estimates (level 1) within forests (level 2), or alternatively of value estimates (level 1) within authors (level 2).[17] Given sufficient data, this hierarchy could be extended with further levels representing, for example, regions or even nations.

Hierarchical data structures cannot be easily accommodated within the traditional regression framework. Here, the values of author or study location related variables must be collapsed to the level of the individual value estimate and simply replicated across all observations sharing those characteristics. This procedure is problematic in that it provides no information on, for example, the probability of estimates made in the same forests, or by the same authors producing similar value estimates. This limitation may be circumvented, as employed in the examples given in Tables 13.4 and 13.5, by the use of dummy variables to indicate forest location or authorship. However, this solution can present difficulties. With the present data, there are only a limited number of authors and forest sites, and hence the number of dummy variables that need to be added to the models are manageable. However, it is readily apparent that any model estimated using dummies will quickly become extremely large and complex if the dataset contains numerous observations at each level of the hierarchy.[18] An alternative to the use of dummy variables to model hierarchical data structures is to fit a series of separate regression models. For example, separate models could be fitted for each forest or author. However, this approach defeats the objective of meta-analyses when the variables found to be significant may differ between models. Furthermore, unreliable results may be produced due to small sample sizes when there are relatively few estimates for each forest, as in the present case.

Aside from methodological considerations, a further limitation of traditional analyses stems from the fact that they may contain poorly estimated parameters and standard errors (Skinner et al., 1989). Problems with standard error estimation arise due to the presence of intra-unit correlation: the fact that recreation value estimates from studies within the same forest, or by the same author, may be expected to be more similar than those drawn from a random sample. If intra-unit correlation is small, then reasonably good estimates of standard errors may be expected (Goldstein, 1995). However, where intra-unit correlation is significant, then conventional regression strategies will tend to under-estimate standard errors, meaning that confidence intervals will be too short and significance tests will too often reject the null hypothesis.

For simplicity, a two level hierarchy of i value estimates (at level 1) within j authors (at level 2) is considered in the examples below. As with a traditional generalized linear model, the observed responses y_{ij} are the published mean per person per visit recreation value estimates in 1990 pounds sterling. Considering a situation with just one explanatory variable, *OPTION* (defined as before) being tested, a simple model may be written as:

$$y_{ij} = \beta_{0j} + \beta_1 OPTION_j + \varepsilon_{ij} \qquad (13.1)$$

Here the subscript i takes the value from 1 to the number of value estimates in the model, and the subscript j takes the value from 1 to the number of authors in the sample. Using this notation, items with two subscripts ij vary from estimate to estimate. However, an item that has a j subscript only varies across authors but is constant for all the estimates made by each author. If an item has neither subscript it is constant across all studies and authors.

As the authors included in the analysis are treated as a random sample from a population, Equation (13.1) may be re-expressed as:

$$\beta_{0j} = \beta_0 + \mu_j$$
$$\hat{y}_{ij} + \beta_0 + \beta_1 OPTION_{ij} + \mu_j \tag{13.2}$$

where β_0 is a constant and μ_j is the departure of the j-th author's intercept from the overall value. This means that it is an author level (level 2) residual that is the same for all estimates nested within an author. In other words, this term describes, after holding constant the effect of the explanatory variables within the model, the residual influence of the author in determining the outcome for each individual mean WTP estimate they published.

The notations expressed in Equation (13.2) can be combined. Introducing an explanatory variable *cons*, which takes the value 1 for all estimates (and hence forms a constant or intercept term), and associating every term with an explanatory variable, the model becomes as shown in Equation (13.3):

$$y_{ij} = \beta_0 cons + \beta_1 OPTION_{ij} + \mu_{0j}\, cons + \varepsilon_{0ij} \tag{13.3}$$

Finally the coefficients can be collected together and written as:

$$y_{ij} = \beta_{0ij}\, cons + \beta_1 OPTION_{ij}$$
$$\beta_{0ij} = \beta_0 + \mu_{0j} + \varepsilon_{0ij} \tag{13.4}$$

In Equation (13.4), both μ_j (the level 2 or author level residuals) and ε_{ij} (the level 1 or estimate level residuals) are random quantities whose means are estimated to be equal to zero. A comparison between the multilevel model expressed in Equations (13.3) and (13.4) and the original non-hierarchical structure depicted in Table 13.4 illustrates the tenet of multilevel models. Traditionally, the residual error term of a model, ε, is seen as an annoyance and the aim of the modelling process is to minimize its size. With multilevel models the error term is of pivotal importance in model estimation. Rather than a single error term being estimated, it is stratified into a range of terms, each representing the residual variance present at each level of the hierarchy. Viewed in this sense, μ_j represents author level effects, whilst ε_{ij} represents those operating at the level of the value estimate.

If, after holding constant the influence of the x_{ij} explanatory variables in the model, $\mu_j > \varepsilon_{ij}$, then this would suggest that some factors associated with the authors themselves are of greatest importance in explaining the residual variation in WTP estimates. If instead $\mu_j < \varepsilon_{ij}$ then some un-modelled factor associated with the elicitation of each estimate (which, for example, could be associated with the characteristics of each specific study, or might simply be random variation in each elicited WTP value) is more important. A common scenario is that, whilst both μ_j and ε_{ij} are large in a model containing few x_{ij} explanatory variables, both will decrease as further explanatory variables are added and the residual variance in the model is explained.

The structure presented in Equation (13.4) is known as a variance components model (Lin, 1997). For ease of interpretation the estimated parameters may be classified as either being of a *fixed* or *random* nature. The fixed parameters are those for which a just single coefficient is estimated, and hence correspond to those that would be found in a conventional analysis. In this example both *CONS* and *OPTION* are fixed. In contrast, the random parameters are those where individual estimates are made for every unit at each level of the hierarchy. Here both μ_j and ε_{ij} are random, as a value of ε_{ij} is estimated for each value estimate (at level 1 of the model) and a value of μ_j is estimated for each author (at level 2 of the model). Hence, in terms of model interpretation, it is the stratification of the error term to form these random parameters that differentiates a multilevel model from more traditional regression analysis techniques. Remembering that $OPTION_{ij}$ is a dummy variable that represents whether the elicited WTP requested use plus option value (OPTION = 1) or use value alone (OPTION = 0), the variance components model depicts the relationship between OPTION and the value estimate as being constant, but (provided $\mu_j > 0$) recreation values are modelled as being higher for some authors than others.

Whilst there are various methods available for parameter estimation in multilevel models, an approach known as Iterative Generalized Least Squares (IGLS) was adopted in our subsequent analysis. The statistical theory underpinning IGLS is described in detail by Goldstein (1995). Briefly, initial estimates of the fixed parameters are derived by traditional regression methodologies ignoring the higher-level random terms. The squared residuals from this initial fit are then regressed on a set of variables defining the structure of the random part to provide initial estimates of the variances/covariances. These estimates are then used to provide revised estimates of the fixed part, which is in turn employed to revise the estimates of the random part, and so on until convergence. Crucially, a difficult estimation problem is decomposed into a sequence of linear regressions that can be solved efficiently and effectively, providing maximum-likelihood estimates.[19]

It is important to note that the slopes and intercepts that are estimated for units within level 2 and above of the hierarchy will not be the same as those that would be obtained from a traditional generalized linear solution. They are in fact residuals which have, to a greater or lesser extent, shrunk towards the average regression line giving the predicted relationship between mean WTP and the explanatory variables across all authors. Taking our example of a two level model, at the author level, if $\sigma^2_{e0} = \text{var}(\varepsilon_{0ij})$ and $\sigma^2_{u0} = \text{var}(u_{0j})$ then each author level residual is estimated using Equation (13.5):

$$\hat{u}_j = \frac{n_j \sigma^2_{u0}}{n_j \sigma^2_{u0} + \sigma^2_{e0}} \tilde{y}_j \tag{13.5}$$

Here, n_j is the total number of estimates produced by author j, $\tilde{y}_j$ is the raw residual associated with the author (the mean estimate level residual for all estimates made by author j) and $\hat{u}_j$ is the shrunken residual. From this, it can be seen that if n_j is large and there are many value estimates made by an author, then the predicted level-2 residuals will be closer to the raw residual than when n_j is small. If n_j is small, then the residual will be shrunken towards the mean. Similarly, if σ^2_{e0} is large and there is a lot of variability in the recreation value estimates produced by an author, then the predicted residual will also be shrunken. In this sense, the MLM approach provides conservative estimates of variability at different levels of the hierarchy where units based on a small sample or a very variable outcome are considered to provide little information. This is particularly pertinent here because, as has already been considered, the statistically significant positive coefficient observed for *Hanley* in Table 13.5 was based on studies that were all conducted at a single forest (Aberfoyle).

A multilevel re-analysis of the meta-analysis data was undertaken using the MLwiN package (Rasbash et al., 2000) developed by the Multilevel Models Project at the Institute of Education, London. Three sets of model were produced: one with a hierarchy of WTP estimates nested within authors, one of estimates within study locations and finally one of estimates within published studies. The results of the model of estimates nested within authors are given in Table 13.6. Here those CV elicitation techniques which produced estimates which were insignificantly different from the incentive compatible DC approach have been merged with the latter to yield a base case set of estimates from which departures are estimated. This leaves two CV elicitation techniques; the variable *CVOE* identifying those CV estimates produced using the OE format, while *CVPCH* refers to CV studies using the PCH format.

Although technically different, the fixed parameters in the model in Table 13.6 can be interpreted in the same way as an ordinary regression. The results detailed in the fixed part of the model now conform entirely with our theoretically and empirically derived expectations. As before, the *Option* variable yields a significant and positive effect. Considering the CV elicitation variables and remembering the DC results that form our base

Table 13.6 MLM model estimates

Variable	Coefficient	95% CI	p
	FIXED EFFECTS		
Constant	0.703	0.952 – 0.954	<0.001
Option	0.391	0.083 – 0.699	0.013
CVOE	−0.593	−1.081 – −0.105	0.018
CVPCH	0.887	−0.089 – 1.863	0.075
ZTC	1.917	1.609 – 2.220	<0.001
ITCols	0.823	0.452 – 1.193	<0.001
ITCml	0.041	−0.355 – 0.436	0.841
Year	0.071	0.010 – 0.132	0.021
	RANDOM (HIERARCHICAL) EFFECTS		
	Variance	95% CI	p
Level 1 (Value estimate)			
Variance σ^2_{e0}	0.218	0.142 – 0.295	<0.001
Level 2 (Author)			
Variance σ^2_{u0}	0.021	−0.021 – 0.121	0.673

Note: −2*loglikelihood (IGLS) = 86.759 (n = 77).

case, the *CVOE* variable is associated with a clear negative effect while the coefficient on *CVPCH* is strongly positive; both results conforming to expectations. Turning to the *Method* variables, as expected, the *ZTC* and *ITCols* variables both produce strong positive effects while, as observed previously, the *ITCml* variable is statistically insignificantly different to the DC base case; given that these are the most theoretically and methodologically defensible of the TC and CV methods this seems a reassuring result. Finally, the positive and significant coefficient on the *Year* variable is reconfirmed.

In summary, therefore, the fixed part of the multilevel model reported in Table 13.6 conforms entirely with our prior expectations. However, one of the prime objectives of fitting such a model was to determine if, after controlling for the variables in the fixed part, there was still statistically significant variation in WTP estimates between authors. These random effects are shown in the lower part of Table 13.6. This part of the model is relatively simple. Although the multilevel methodology involves estimating a separate intercept value for each author (μ_j) and a separate residual for each value estimate (ε_{ij}), the variance between the two levels of the model may be neatly summarized by the two parameters σ^2_{u0} and σ^2_{e0} These are the same parameters used in the calculation of the shrinkage factor illustrated in Equation (13.5) and known as variance parameters, as they indicate the variance in the μ_j and ε_{ij} terms respectively. Hence a comparison of the values of σ^2_{u0} and σ^2_{e0} shows the relative importance of author (level 2) and estimate (level 1) effects in determining the variability of WTP values that is not explained by the fixed parameters in the model.

The parameter estimates for both σ^2_{u0} and σ^2_{e0} are greater than zero, suggesting that variability between estimates and between authors remains after controlling for the explanatory variables that were included in the fixed part of the model. Taking the ratio of these estimates suggests that approximately 9% of unexplained variation in elicited recreation value is associated with author effects. However, the calculation of *t*-statistics for each coefficient shows that, whilst statistically significant residual variation remains between estimates at level 1 ($t = 5.59$, $p < 0.001$), the effect of authorship at level 2 does not reach statistical significance ($t = 0.41$, $p > 0.05$). In other words, the multilevel analysis suggests that an author effect is present but is not statistically significant.

Although in conflict with the earlier findings from the conventional regression analysis, such a result accords with theoretical expectations that recreation values should not vary significantly according to study authorship. This provides a substantial (if on its own insufficient) support for the practice of placing monetary values upon preferences for non-market environmental goods. The author specific results are illustrated in Figure 13.1 where the value of the intercept value u_j estimated for each individual author is presented in rank order along with corresponding 95% confidence intervals. The figure shows that, in the multilevel analysis, studies by Hanley et al. are still predicted to give the highest recreation values and those by Willis et al. the lowest. However, the confidence intervals clearly overlap. This represents a reduction in variance from the situation observed in Tables 13.4 and 13.5 where estimates provided by Hanley et al. were found to be significantly different from those of other authors. The reduction of variance is due to the effects of the conservative estimation strategy implemented in Equation (13.5) where residuals converge towards the mean value. The contrast between Tables 13.4 and 13.5 and the findings of Table 13.6 provides a clear justification for the application of MLM techniques to meta-analysis studies.

The shrinkage illustrated by Figure 13.1 has interesting implications for the comparison of results between multilevel and non-multilevel models. The message from the multilevel model is that variation is present between authors but, because of the magnitude of the variance and the size of the sample, it cannot be said to be statistically significant. Hence we are making

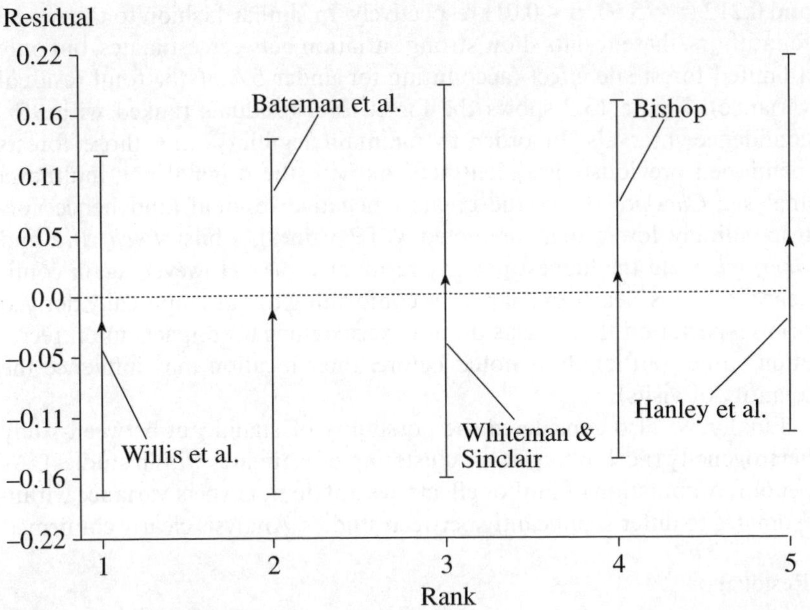

Figure 13.1 MLM author level residuals

a statement about the importance of context (in this case authorship) and composition (the remaining unexplained variation in between WTP estimates). The traditional regression approach used previously did the opposite; it told us little about the overall roles of context and composition, but it did highlight two authors with rather different patterns of responses from the rest of the sample. From this comparison, it is clear that, whilst the conclusions reached may be different from those of a conventional analysis, the multilevel approach is prudent if the intention of the analysis is to quantify whether there are overall contextual influences (in this case associated with different authors) on the measured outcome (recreation value).

The earlier conventional analyses also found evidence of a *Forest* (site) effect where recreation values for *Cheshire* were significantly lower than the rest of the sample, and those for *Loch Awe* and *Aberfoyle* were relatively higher (see Table 13.5). To test if any evidence of between-site heterogeneity remained after a multilevel approach was taken, the model presented in Table 13.6 was refitted, but this time authorship at level 2 was replaced by *Forest* identifiers. The fixed effect coefficient values and levels of significance were not found to differ greatly from the previous example and are hence not replicated here. However, in this case, the values of σ^2_{u0} (now for forests) and σ^2_{e0} (for value estimates) were estimated at 0.010 (t = 0.73, p > 0.05), and 0.212 (t = 5.63, $p < 0.01$) respectively. In similar fashion to the model for authors, these results show strong variation between estimates, but only a limited forest site effect (accounting for under 5% of the total residual variance). Figure 13.2 shows the forest level residuals ranked with 95% confidence intervals. In order to maintain legibility only those forests mentioned previously are identified. As with the original non-multilevel analysis, *Cheshire* shows the greatest negative residual (and hence correspondingly lower than predicted WTP values), whilst *Loch Awe* and *Aberfoyle* yield the highest positive residual values. However, again confidence intervals clearly overlap, thus conforming to our empirically derived prior expectation that forests do not exert significant impacts upon recreation values (although as noted before, their location may influence the quantity of visits).

Finally, we also considered the possibility of significant between-study heterogeneity (i.e. looking at the clustering of estimates within studies). As per our examination of author effects, we not do not expect variance within estimates to differ significantly between studies. Analysis clearly confirmed

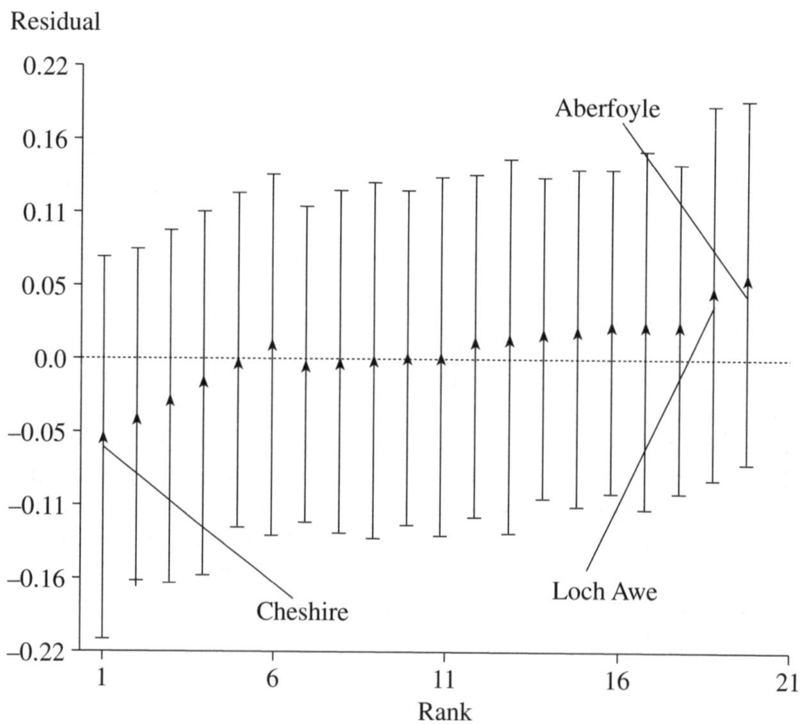

Figure 13.2 Forest level residuals

this expectation with values of σ^2_{u0} (between study variance) and σ^2_{e0} (for value estimates) estimated at 0.017 ($t = 0.55$, $p > 0.05$), and 0.216 ($t = 5.68$, $p < 0.01$) respectively.

5. DISCUSSION AND CONCLUSIONS

There are numerous routes through which benefit transfer and meta-analysis research may be taken forward. These include improvements in the conduct and reporting of new studies, the specific incorporation of benefit transfer and meta-analysis requirements within their design, and the reanalysis of past work. The present chapter goes some way towards highlighting a novel way in which this latter aim might be best realized. We have compared the application of traditional regression and novel MLM methodologies to meta-analyses of British woodland recreation values. While both sets of results generally conform well to expectations derived from either theoretical considerations or empirical regularities, our conventional regression findings suggest that certain authors and forests are associated with large recreation value residuals. However, the more sophisticated and conservative MLM approach shows that these residuals are not large enough (or are not based on a large enough sample size) to be differentiated from variation that might be expected by chance. In so doing it is only these MLM based models which conform in all respects to prior expectations, a finding which underscores the importance of adopting approaches which explicitly model the hierarchical nature of almost all meta-analysis datasets.

Here we have fitted only simple two level MLM models. More complex structures have not been implemented here for a number of reasons. No significant variation was observed between authors or survey site locations, and it is highly unlikely that a more detailed model hierarchy would have contradicted these findings. A second limitation to the use of more complex hierarchies concerns sample size; as models become more complicated there is an associated loss of degrees of freedom. In particular, the conservative estimation strategy used means that the presence of a small amount of level 2 variation in a simple two level model may be reduced to zero if a more complex structure is attempted. Whilst the dataset we have studied is comprehensive, it is a based on a sample of just 77 observations, and hence has somewhat limited power. The increased number of observations that would result from more studies being undertaken will allow a greater complexity of models to be fitted.

Although the essential ideas of multilevel models were developed over 20 years ago, it is only recently that improvements in computing power and advances in our understanding of effective model implementation have meant that their execution has become a practical proposition (Bull et al., 1998). We are currently on a wave of innovation as use spreads from the original developers to the wider research community. Having said that, the multilevel approach retains some of the limitations of more traditional quantitative techniques, as well as introducing new ones.

In the MLM models presented here, influences on recreation values are modelled more powerfully than traditional techniques allow, yet the random parameters can ultimately offer only limited insight into the reasons behind between-author and between-forest variations in outcome. Preferences for complex, non-market environmental goods such as open-access recreation involve a detailed interplay between a wide range of factors that are difficult to quantify and may be subject to random variation. This unpredictability will undoubtedly introduce uncertainty into any model, multilevel or not, developed to identify and predict the important influences on such preferences. However, whilst multilevel models cannot remove this uncertainty, they can allow it to be more richly quantified and accounted for, and hence allow for systematic factors to be assessed.

Finally, our MLM estimated meta-analysis has some clear messages for both policy makers and economists who work within the applied policy arena. As noted, our results conform well with prior theoretically and empirically derived expectations. However, these are not that value estimates will be invariant to choice of study methodology or analytical approach. Indeed, the reverse is true. For example, as predicted by considerations of incentive compatibility, we show that CV estimates of recreation value derived from an OE elicitation technique will be significantly lower than those obtained by a DC approach. Similarly, we show that TC values derived through inappropriate OLS estimators will be upwardly biased in comparison with those derived from maximum likelihood estimators or from CV studies using DC elicitation techniques. It is the responsibility of the economist to highlight these expected differences to the policy maker and to advise upon the most theoretically and methodologically appropriate approach to the issue at hand. That said, the absence of significant author or study level impacts within our MLM meta-analyses is encouraging, providing an argument against criticisms that, for example, certain authors produce unusually high or low valuation estimates. This analysis also has some specific messages for policy makers within the UK Forestry Commission. In particular, while some evidence for site effects was found in the conventionally estimated models reported in Table 13.5, these do not persist within the more sophisticated MLM analysis given in Table 13.6. As noted previously, this finding is in line with other research showing that, while visitor arrivals at UK woodlands are highly responsive to a variety of locational factors, they are somewhat less responsive to the facilities on offer at these sites (Brainard et al., 1999; 2001).[20] Given this, the onus upon woodland policy makers within the UK context appears to be upon using scarce resources to optimize site location rather than to extend the diversity of facilities within woodlands.

ACKNOWLEDGEMENTS

CSERGE is a designated research centre of the UK Economic and Social Research Council (ESRC) who also support the PEDM. The authors are grateful to Simon Gillam, Alastair Johnson and the UK Forestry Commission who provided further funding for this research.

NOTES

1. For reviews of the issues raised by benefit transfer applications see Brookshire and Neill (1992), OECD (1994), Pearce and Moran (1994), Bergland et al. (1995), Van den Bergh et al. (1997) and Desvousges et al. (1998).
2. Meta-analyses also face the problem that studies published in the available literature may overrepresent that subset of all studies which produce 'positive' or significant results if studies yielding 'negative' or non-significant findings tend not to be published.
3. Details of all of these estimates are given in Table A1 in Bateman et al. (2000).
4. As discussed subsequently, value estimates may also be 'cross-classified', e.g. where different authors conduct studies at the same, as well as differing, forest sites.
5. Markowski et al. (2001) clearly describe the weighting procedure used as follows: 'For these models we weight the data to reflect the "oversampling" of estimates associated with studies with a large number of observations relative to others with just a few or one observation. To do this, we first determine how many estimates (k_j) in the sample are associated with each study (j) to define a study weight. We then divide the data associated with each observation (dependent variable and explanatory variables) by the weights (k_j) for each study. Thus, rather than all observations having equal weights in the estimation, which is the case for the basic model, each study has an equal weight in this estimation for models of per-day and per-trip welfare estimates' (p. 12).
6. This decomposes into 14.7% of Scotland, 12.0% of Wales and 7.4% of England. However, this is still well below an EU average of about 25% of land area under forestry (FICGB, 1992).
7. Note that CV studies can be adapted to ask either WTP or willingness to accept compensation questions in respect of either gains or losses of the resource concerned (Mitchell and Carson, 1989), although only the WTP format was used in the studies concerned.
8. Further details of these studies are provided in Bateman et al. (2000).
9. For a discussion of ML estimators see Maddala (1983).
10. Allocation of estimates by forests and methods is as follows: 44 *CV* estimates across 20 forests; nine *ITCols* estimates across seven forests; seven *ITCml* estimates across seven forests; 17 *ZTC* estimates across 16 forests.
11. While the DC method is incentive compatible, whether or not it is in practice also demand revealing (i.e. produces unbiased estimates of true WTP) is an ongoing source of debate (Green et al., 1998; Carson et al., 1999).
12. Bateman et al. (1999a) use a reduced form of the model reported in Table 13.4 in their GIS based benefit transfer analysis of woodland recreation values.

13. In addition we have one further *Author* category *(Everett)* and one extra *Forest* study site *(Dalby)*.
14. Equation (A1) in Bateman et al. (2000) details such a model showing effects for individual forests.
15. By contrast the *Loch Awe* coefficient is positive (although not statistically significant) reflecting its somewhat remote and secluded location attracting a more 'dedicated' woodland user (as noted by Willis and Benson, 1989).
16. We initially develop this approach in Brouwer et al. (1999). However, this earlier analysis is restricted to CV studies alone, considers only one form of potential data hierarchy and is complicated by the necessity of drawing upon studies of diverse resources taken from a number of countries; factors which make interpretation of findings problematic. The present study examines a single resource within a single country but considers three potential data hierarchies (whilst also providing a fuller account of the MLM modelling structure).
17. If no two authors undertake a study in the same forest, then this may be extended to a three level hierarchy of WTP estimates (level 1) within forests (level 2) within authors (level 3). If multiple authors do study the same forests, then a more complex structure (known as cross-classified) exists wherein estimates (level 1) are nested within a cross-classified level (2) of forests and authors. Such a case is not considered here (although it is the subject of ongoing research by the authors), but the theory of cross-classified hierarchies is discussed in detail by Goldstein (1995).
18. An example might be an international dataset of value estimates nested within hundreds of study locations.
19. A limitation of IGLS for models with a binomial or Poisson distributed response variable (neither of which were used in the present application) is that is uses a method based on either marginal or penalized quasi-likelihood. This requires assumption of normally distributed variance above level one of the hierarchy.
20. This is not to suggest that site facilities are irrelevant in attracting visitors. However, as shown by Brainard et al., locational factors provide much stronger predictors of demand. In part this may be because virtually all UK sites provide the basic walking and recreational amenities which characterize woodlands visits and are thus relatively little differentiated in terms of further cogent attributes.

REFERENCES

Baaijens, S.R., Nijkamp, P., and Montfort, K.V. (1998) 'Explanatory meta-analysis for the comparison and transfer of regional tourism income multipliers', *Regional Studies*, **32** (9): 839–49.

Bateman, I.J. (1996) 'An economic comparison of forest recreation, timber and carbon fixing values with agriculture in Wales: a geographical information systems approach', Ph.D. Thesis, Department of Economics, University of Nottingham.

Bateman, I.J., Brainard, J.S., Garrod, G.D., and Lovett, A.A. (1999b) 'The impact of journey origin specification and other measurement assumptions upon individual travel cost estimates of consumer surplus: a geographical information systems analysis', *Regional Environmental Change*, **1** (1): 24–30.

Bateman, I.J., Garrod, G.D., Brainard, J.S., and Lovett, A.A. (1996) 'Measurement, valuation and estimation issues in the travel cost method: a geographical information systems approach', *Journal of Agricultural Economics*, **47** (2): 191–205.

Bateman, I.J., Jones, A.P., Nishikawa, N., and Brouwer, R. (2000) 'Benefits transfer in theory and practice: a review', *CSERGE Global Environmental Change*

Working Paper, Centre for Social and Economic Research on the Global Environment, University of East Anglia and University College London.

Bateman, I.J., and Langford, I.H. (1997) 'Budget constraint, temporal and ordering effects in contingent valuation studies', *Environment and Planning A*, **29** (7): 1215–28.

Bateman, I.J., Langford, I.H., Turner, R.K., Willis, K.G., and Garrod, G.D. (1995) 'Elicitation and truncation effects in contingent valuation studies', *Ecological Economics*, **12** (2):161–79.

Bateman, I.J., Lovett, A.A., and Brainard, J.S. (forthcoming) *Applied Environmental Economics: A GIS Approach to Cost Benefit Analysis*, Cambridge: Cambridge University Press.

Bateman, I.J., Lovett, A.A., and Brainard, J.S. (1999a) 'Developing a methodology for benefit transfers using geographical information systems: modeling demand for woodland recreation', *Regional Studies*, **33** (3): 191–205.

Benson, J.F., and Willis, K.G. (1990) 'The aggregate value of the non-priced recreation benefits of the Forestry Commission estate', *Report to the Forestry Commission*, Department of Town and County Planning, University of Newcastle upon Tyne.

Benson, J.F., and Willis, K.G. (1992) 'Valuing informal recreation on the Forestry Commission estate', *Bulletin 104*, Forestry Commission, Edinburgh.

Bergland, O., Magnussen, K., and Navrud, S. (1995) 'Benefit transfer: testing for accuracy and reliability', *Discussion Paper No. D-03/1995*, Agricultural University of Norway.

Bishop, K.D. (1992) 'Assessing the benefits of community forests: an evaluation of the recreational use benefits of two urban fringe woodlands', *Journal of Environmental Planning and Management*, **35** (1): 63–76.

Boadway, R., and Bruce, N. (1984) *Welfare Economics*, Oxford: Basil Blackwell.

Boyle, K.J., Bishop, R.C., and Welsh, M.P. (1985) 'Starting point bias in contingent valuation bidding games', *Land Economics*, **61**: 188–94.

Boyle, K.J., Poe, G.L., and Bergstrom, J. (1994) 'What do we know about groundwater values?: preliminary implications from a meta-analysis of contingent valuation studies', *American Journal of Agricultural Economics*, **76** (5): 1055–61.

Brainard, J.S., Bateman, I.J., and Lovett, A.A. (2001) 'Modelling demand for recreation in English woodlands', *Forestry*, **74** (5): 423–38.

Brainard, J.S., Lovett, A.A., and Bateman, I.J. (1999) 'Integrating geographical information systems into travel cost analysis and benefit transfer', *International Journal of Geographical Information Systems*, **13** (3): 227–46.

Brookshire, D.S., and Neill, H.R. (1992) 'Benefit transfers: conceptual and empirical issues', *Water Resources Research*, **28** (3): 651–5.

Brouwer, R., Langford, I.H., Bateman, I.J., and Turner, R.K. (1999) 'A meta-analysis of wetland contingent valuation studies', *Regional Environmental Change*, **1** (1): 47–57.

Brouwer, R., and Spaninks, F.A. (1999), 'The validity of environmental benefits transfer: further empirical testing', *Environmental and Resource Economics*, **14** (1): 95–117.

Bull, J.M., Riley, G.D., Rasbash, J., and Goldstein, H. (1998) *Parallel Implementation of a Multilevel Modelling Package*, Manchester: University of Manchester.

Button, K.J. (1995) 'Evaluation of transport externalities: what can we learn using meta-analysis?', *Regional Studies*, **29**: 507–17.

Button, K.J., and Kerr, J. (1996) 'Effectiveness of traffic restraint policies: a simple meta-regression analysis', *International Journal of Transport Economics*, **23**: 213–25.

Carson, R.T. Flores, N.E., Martin, K.M., and Wright, J.L. (1996) 'Contingent valuation and revealed preference methodologies: comparing the estimates for quasi-public goods', *Land Economics*, **72**: 80–99.

Carson, R.T., Groves, T., and Machina, M.J. (1999) 'Incentive and informational properties of preference questions', *Plenary Address, Ninth Annual Conference of the European Association of Environmental and Resource Economists (EAERE)*, Oslo, Norway, June 1999.

Desvousges, W.H., Johnson, F.R., and Banzaf, H.S. (1998) *Environmental Policy Analysis with Limited Information: Principles and Applications of the Transfer Method*, Cheltenham, UK and Lyme, USA: Edward Elgar.

Downing, M., and Ozuna, T. (1996) 'Testing the reliability of the benefit function transfer approach', *Journal of Environmental Economics and Management*, **30**: 316–22.

Espey, M., Espey, J., and Shaw, W.D. (1997) 'Price elasticity of residential demand for water: a meta-analysis', *Water Resources Research*, **33** (6): 1369–74.

Everett, R.D. (1979) 'The monetary value of the recreational benefits of wildlife', *Journal of Environmental Management*, **8**: 203–13.

Farquharson, R. (1969), *Theory of Voting*, New Haven: Yale University Press.

FICGB (Forestry Industry Committee of Great Britain) (1992) *The Forestry Industry Year-Book 1991–92*, London: FICGB.

Gibbard, A. (1973) 'Manipulation of voting schemes: a general result', *Econometrica* **41**: 587–601.

Glass, G.V. (1976) 'Primary, secondary and meta-analysis of research', *Educational Researcher*, **5** (10): 3–8.

Glass, G.V., McGaw, B., and Smith, M.L. (1981) *Meta-analysis in Social Research*, Beverley Hills, CA: Sage Publications.

Goldstein, H. (1995) *Multilevel Statistical Models* (2nd edn), London: Edward Arnold.

Grayson, A.J., Sidaway, R.M., and Thompson, F.P. (1975) 'Some aspects of recreation planning in the Forestry Commission', G.A.C. in Searle (ed.), *Recreational Economics and Analysis: Papers presented at the Symposium on Recreational Economics and Analysis, London Graduate School of Business Studies, January 1972*, Essex: Longman.

Green, D., Jacowitz, K.E., Kahneman, D., and McFadden, D. (1998) 'Referendum contingent valuation, anchoring, and willingness to pay for public goods', *Resource and Energy Economics*, **20** (2): 85–116.

Hanley, N.D. (1989) 'Valuing rural recreation benefits: an empirical comparison of two approaches', *Journal of Agricultural Economics*, **40** (3): 361–74.

Hanley, N.D., and Craig, S. (1991) 'Wilderness development decisions and the Krutilla-Fisher model: the case of Scotland's Flow Country', *Ecological Economics*, **4**: 145–64.

Hanley, N.D., and Ecotec Ltd (1991) *The Valuation of Environmental Effects: Stage Two Final Report*, Edinburgh: The Scottish Office Industry Department and Scottish Enterprise.

Hanley, N.D., and Munro, A. (1991) 'Design bias in contingent valuation studies: the impact of information', *Discussion Paper in Economics 91/13*, Department of Economics, University of Stirling.

Hanley, N.D., and Ruffell, R.J. (1991) 'Recreational use values of woodland features', *Report to the Forestry Commission*, University of Stirling.
HM Government (1995) *Environment Act 1995*, London: HMSO.
HM Treasury (1972) *Forestry in Great Britain: An Interdepartmental Cost/Benefit Study*, London: HMSO.
Hoehn, J.P., and Randall, A. (1987) 'A satisfactory benefit cost indicator from contingent valuation', *Journal of Environmental Economics and Management*, **14** (3): 226–47.
Hunter, J.E., Schmidt, F.L., and Jackson, G. (1982) *Advanced Meta-analysis: Quantitative Methods for Cumulating Research Findings Across Studies*, Beverly Hills, CA: Sage.
Just, R.E., Hueth, D.L., and Schmitz, A. (1982) *Applied Welfare Economics and Public Policy*, Englewood Cliffs, NJ: Prentice Hall.
Kirchhoff, S., Colby, B.G., and LaFrance, J.T. (1997) 'Evaluating the performance of benefit transfer: an empirical inquiry', *Journal of Environmental Economics and Management*, **33**: 75–93.
Krutilla, J.V., and Fisher, A.C. (1975) *The Economics of Natural Environments: Studies in the Valuation of Commodity and Amenity Resources*, Baltimore, MD: Johns Hopkins University Press (for Resources for the Future).
Lin, X. (1997) 'Variance component testing in generalised linear models with random effects', *Biometrika* **84**: 309–25.
Loomis, J.B. (1992) 'The evolution of a more rigorous approach to benefit transfer: benefit function transfer', *Water Resources Research*, **28** (3): 701–5.
Loomis, J.B., Roach, B., Ward, F., and Ready, R. (1995) 'Testing transferability of recreation demand models across regions: a study of Corps of Engineers reservoirs', *Water Resources Research*, **31**: 721–30.
Loomis, J.B., and White, D.S. (1996) 'Economic benefits of rare and endangered species: summary and meta-analysis', *Ecological Economics*, **18** (3): 197–206.
Maddala, G.S. (1983) *Limited-Dependent and Qualitative Variables in Econometrics*, Cambridge: Cambridge University Press.
Markowski, M.A., Boyle, K.J., Bishop, R.C., Larson, D.M., and Paterson, R.W. (2001) 'A cautionary note on interpreting meta analyses', unpublished paper, Industrial Economics Inc.
McCullagh, P., and Nelder, J.A. (1989) *Generalized Linear Models* (2nd edn), London: Chapman and Hall.
Mitchell, R.C., and Carson, R.T. (1989) *Using Surveys to Value Public Goods: The Contingent Valuation Method*, Washington DC: Resources for the Future.
Mrozek, J.R., and Taylor, L.O. (forthcoming) 'What determines the value of life? A meta-analysis, *Journal of Policy Analysis and Management*, in press.
NAO (National Audit Office) (1986) *Review of Forestry Commission Objectives and Achievements*, Report by the Comptroller and Auditor General, National Audit Office, London: HMSO.
Nelson, J.P. (1980) 'Airports and property values: a survey of recent evidence', *Journal of Transport Economics and Policy*, **19**, 37–52.
OECD (Organisation for Economic Co-operation and Development) (1994) *Project and Policy Appraisal: Integrating Economics and Environment*, Paris: OECD.
Pearce, D.W., and Moran, D. (1994) *The Economic Value of Biodiversity*, London: Earthscan.

Pearce, D.W., and Turner, R.K. (1990) *Economics of Natural Resources and the Environment*, Hemel Hempstead: Harvester Wheatsheaf.
Poe, G.L., Boyle, K.J., and Bergstrom, J.C. (2001) 'A preliminary meta analysis of contingent values for ground water revisited', in J.C. Bergstrom, K.J. Boyle, and Poe, G.L. (eds) *The Economic Value of Water Quality*, Cheltenham, UK and Northampton, MA, USA: Edward Elgar.
Rackham, O. (1976) *Trees and Woodland in the British Landscape*, London: Dent.
Rasbash. J., Browne, W., Goldstein, H., Yang, M., Plewis, I., Healy, M., Woodhouse, G., Draper, D., Langford, I., and Lewis, T. (2000) *A User's Guide to MlwinN: Version 2.1*, London: Institute of Education.
Roberts, K.J., Thompson, M.E., and Pawlyk, P.W. (1985) 'Contingent valuation of recreational diving at petroleum rigs, Gulf of Mexico', *Transactions of the American Fisheries Society*, **114**: 155–65.
Rosenberger, R.S., and Loomis, J.B. (2000) 'Using meta-analysis for benefit transfer: in-sample convergent validity tests of an outdoor recreation database', *Water Resources Research*, **36**(4): 1097–107.
Rowe, R.D., Schulze, W.D., and Breffle, W. (1996) 'A test for payment card biases', *Journal of Environmental Economics and Management*, **31**: 178–85.
Satterthwaite, M. (1975), 'Strategy-proofness and Arrow conditions: existence and correspondence theorems for voting procedures and welfare functions', *Journal of Economic Theory*, **10**: 187–217.
Schwartz, J. (1994) 'Air pollution and daily mortality: a review and a meta analysis', *Environmental Economics*, **64**: 36–52.
Shrestha, R.K., and Loomis, J.B. (2001) 'Testing a meta-analysis model for benefit transfer in international outdoor recreation', *Ecological Economics*, **39**: 67–83.
Skinner, C.J., Holt, D., and Smith, T.M.F. (1989) *Analysis of Complex Surveys*, Chichester, UK: Wiley.
Smith, V.K. (1989) 'Can we measure the economic value of environmental amenities?', *Southern Economic Journal*, **56**: 865–78.
Smith, V.K., and Huang, J.C. (1993) 'Hedonic models and air pollution: twenty five years and counting', *Environmental and Resource Economics*, **3**: 381–94.
Smith, V.K., and Huang, J.C. (1995) 'Can markets value air quality? A meta-analysis of hedonic property values models', *Journal of Political Economy*, **103**: 209–27.
Smith, V.K., and Kaoru, Y. (1990a) 'Signals or noise? Explaining the variation in recreation benefit estimates', *American Journal of Agricultural Economics*, May: 419–33.
Smith, V.K., and Kaoru, Y. (1990b) 'What have we learned since Hotelling's letter? A meta-analysis', *Economics Letters*, 32: 267–72.
Smith, V.K., and Osborne, L. (1996) 'Do contingent valuation estimates pass a "Scope" test? A meta-analysis', *Journal of Environmental Economics and Management*, **31**: 287–301.
Smith, V.K., and Pattanayak, S.K. (forthcoming) 'Is meta-analysis a Noah's Ark for non-market valuation?', *Environmental and Resource Economics*, in press.
Sturtevant, L.A., Johnson, F.R., and Desvousges, W.H. (1995) 'A meta-analysis of recreational fishing', *Triangle Economic Research*, Durham, NC.
Van den Bergh, J.C.J.M., Button, K.J., Nijkamp, P., and Pepping, G.C. (1997), *Meta-Analysis in Environmental Economics*, AH Dordrecht, the Netherlands: Kluwer Academic Publishers.
Van Houtven, G.L., Pattanayak, S.K., Pringle, C., and Yang, J.-C. (2001) 'Review and meta-analysis of water quality valuation studies', Draft Report, prepared for

US Environmental Protection Agency, Office of Water and Office of Policy, Economics, and Innovation, Washington, DC.

Walsh, R.G., Johnson, D.M., and McKean, J.R. (1990), 'Nonmarket values from two decades of research on recreation demand', in A. Link, and V.K. Smith (eds.), *Advances in Applied Micro-Economics*, Vol. 5: 167–93, Greenwich, CT: JAI Press.

Walsh, R.G., Johnson, D.M., and McKean, J.R. (1992) 'Benefit transfer of outdoor recreation demand studies, 1968–1988', *Water Resources Research*, **28** (3): 707–13.

Waters, W.G. (1993) 'Variations in the value of travel time savings: empirical studies and the values for road project evaluation', mimeo, cited in J.C.J.M. Van den Bergh, K.J. Button, P. Nijkamp, and G.C. Pepping (1997), *Meta-Analysis in Environmental Economics*, AH Dordrecht, The Netherlands: Kluwer Academic Publishers.

Weisbrod, B.A. (1964) 'Collective–consumption services of individual consumption goods', *Quarterly Journal of Economics*, **78**: 471–7.

Whiteman, A., and Sinclair, J. (1994) *The Costs and Benefits of Planting Three Community Forests: Forest of Mercia, Thames Chase and Great North Forest*, Policy Studies Division, Edinburgh: Forestry Commission.

Willis, K.G., and Benson, J.F. (1989) 'Values of user benefits of forest recreation: some further site surveys', *Report to the Forestry Commission*, Department of Town and County Planning. University of Newcastle upon Tyne.

Willis, K.G., Benson, J.F., and Whitby, M.C. (1988) 'Values of user benefits of forest recreation and wildlife', *Report to the Forestry Commission*, Department of Town and County Planning, University of Newcastle upon Tyne.

Willis, K.G., and Garrod, G.D. (1991) 'An individual travel cost method of evaluating forest recreation', *Journal of Agricultural Economics*, **42** (1): 33–41.

Wolf, F. (1986) *Meta-Analysis: Quantitative Methods for Research Synthesis*, Beverly Hills, CA: Sage.

Woodward, R.T., and Wui, Y.-S. (2001) 'The economic value of wetland services: a meta-analysis', *Ecological Economics*, **37**: 257–70

14. Individual-specific welfare measures for public goods: a latent class approach to residential customers of Yorkshire Water

Riccardo Scarpa, Kenneth G. Willis and Melinda Acutt

1. INTRODUCTION

As well as the provision of water as a private good for residential and business customers, water companies are responsible for management actions that affect the provision of public goods. This is well recognized and for this, as well as social policy reasons, the market operations of such companies are publicly regulated. Water customers pay a flat rate for water provision, either on property value or measured consumption. In the process of water provision, the management of water companies has discretion on how to achieve targets of water delivery and waste water disposal to satisfy demand, subject to legal minimum standards. In doing so, they also jointly provide certain levels of 'public goods', such as bathing water quality, water quality in rivers, risk of flood in case of piping malfunctions etc.

The supply of water delivery targets is compatible with a large variety of combinations of different levels of related public goods. Optimal supply level will depend on consumer preferences and willingness to pay for alternative levels of joint supply of the private/public good package. Such preferences cannot be derived from market transactions because customers cannot shop around for different levels of provisions of the public goods associated with water supply. An alternative way to investigate these preferences is via statements of choice.

Stated preference studies have recently established themselves as an important method of guiding public good provision in joint production processes. In the recent periodic price review in the UK, which will set the water tariff for 2004–09, a leading UK water company, Yorkshire Water, employed this approach to guide their management decisions in accordance with the preferences of the customers they serve. In this chapter we present the results of a portion of a much larger study. In that study a series of choice experiments was administered to a representative sample of Yorkshire Water residential customers. We focus on two of these choice experiments that address issues of preference for the quality of 'public good' aspects of waste water disposal and treatment.

The first choice experiment illustrated here (WW1) deals with the way customers trade off money with the percentage of area protected from sewage flooding (AF), the percentage of river length capable of supporting healthy fisheries and other aquatic life in the long term (RQ), and the number of businesses/households exposed to bad odour and flies (OF). The second experiment reported in this chapter (WW2) looks at how customers trade off money with the number of areas with waste water discharges designed to allow recreational activities on rivers (AM), and the standard of sewage works and disinfection designed to exceed government standards for bathing water (BB).

In this chapter we depart from the conventional way of analysing multinomial discrete choice responses via multinomial logit models and mixed logit models. The major focus of the analysis is an alternative characterization of preference heterogeneity via finite mixing (Provencher et al., 2002) or latent class analysis (Boxall and Adamowicz, 2002). This approach, perhaps less elegant and flexible than the continuous mixing allowed by mixed logit, is shown to have some appeal on the basis of ease of interpretation of the utility functions of each preference group, ease of computation, and type of results obtained. The main feature is that, instead of a continuum of taste intensities for each attribute of choice, it provides the preference structure for each of a small number – two to five – groups in the sample. Group identification is endogenous, although the number of groups is exogenously imposed, albeit statistically tested for.

On the basis of such preference estimates, we exploit the panel nature of the dataset to retrieve the distribution of part-worths (marginal willingness-to-pay values) for the individual in the sample, conditional on the individual sequence of observed choices in the choice experiment. This also departs from customary approaches in which the willingness-to-pay estimates are normally expressed as measures of central tendency of an a-priori distribution, such as mean or median value estimates with their computed standard errors. Instead, we compare and contrast the posterior kernel-smoothed distributions of these values estimated for each individual for a series of finite mixing models and for the mixed logit with normally distributed utility parameters.

In both samples we find statistical evidence in favour of the existence of four distinct preference groups. We argue that in some cases an immediate interpretation of the differences between groups is possible. While most preference structures in the groups are consistent with theoretical expectations in terms of signs, groups representing small fractions of the sample tend to show low significance of parameter estimates. Finally, the graphical representation of the distributions, of individual estimates of willingness-to-pay values for the attributes, show that while groups 2 and 3 latent class models (LCM) portray bi-modal WTP distributions, the group 4 latent class specification implies WTP distributions very similar to those produced by the normally distributed mixed logit.

The remainder of the chapter is organized as follows. Section 2 first provides a background to the representation of taste heterogeneity in finite and continuous preference mixture logit models; and then briefly discusses the subject of heterogeneity in logit-based random utility modelling. Section 3 documents the data sources; whilst Section 4 addresses the econometric issues. The results are presented and discussed in Section 5, and Section 6 draws some conclusions.

2. HETEROGENEITY IN RANDOM UTILITY-BASED MULTINOMIAL LOGIT MODELS

Taste Heterogeneity and Mixed Logit

The last decade has seen much attention paid to the development of alternative forms of modelling heterogeneity of preferences in discrete multinomial choice models based on random utility (Train, 2003). It is a fact of life that preferences dictating decision rules vary across both individuals and choices made by the same individual. Taste heterogeneity, as captured by mixed logit models (or random parameter logit), is often quite instructive in this context, and it virtually allows the researcher to approximate any preference structure (McFadden and Train, 2000). The notion that parameters of the utility function can vary according to continuous parametric distributions has greatly expanded the number of modelling assumptions available to researchers. Even the few limitations originally imposed by the relatively restrictive set of empirically tractable taste distributions has recently been overcome by more flexible forms that allow for censoring and bounding (Train and Sonnier, 2003). The underlying hypothesis in this modelling approach is a continuity of preferences over some range of parameter values.

Variance Heterogeneity and Heteroscedastic Logit

Even if preferences are fairly stable, decision contexts and respondent knowledge or cognitive ability may vary, thereby introducing sources of heterogeneity in observed choice. One example of this source is the effect of choice-complexity and respondent familiarity with the choice task on the scale parameter of the unobserved component of utility, as illustrated empirically by De Shazo and Fermo (2002). However, for those more inclined to think in terms of heteroscedasticity as the presence of covariates affecting the error variance, instead of the scale parameter one can make the error variance a function of covariates (e.g. Scarpa et al., 2003a). Either approach models heterogeneity affecting the spread of the noise or unobserved component (error) of utility in logit models. These models are normally called heteroscedastic logit, not to be confused with the Heteroscedastic Extreme Value model originally proposed by Bhat (1995). In this category of models a different scale parameter is fitted to each alternative in the set. One interesting recent example of heteroscedastic logit in the context of meta-design is the paper by Caussade et al. (2003), in which factors affecting the design of the choice-experiments are shown to have a systematic effect on the variance of the error term, along with individual-specific covariates.

Observed and Unobserved Taste Heterogeneity

From the researcher's perspective we find it quite useful to think of heterogeneity as observed and unobserved. When some individual-specific variables that the researcher can observe can be linked to systematic differences in choice behaviour, for example by creating interaction terms between attributes or alternatives with such individual-specific variables, then preference heterogeneity across individuals can be captured (Pollack and Wales, 1992).

On the other hand, when differences in taste for attributes are known to exist, but the available individual-specific variables cannot adequately capture this variability, then a generic form of heterogeneity of taste can be simply accommodated by mixed logit models, assuming that some attributes have taste parameters distributed according to some distributive law.

Of course, a single dataset can still display an amount of unobserved heterogeneity of taste, when unobserved heterogeneity is accounted for (Scarpa et al., 2001), and hybrid models accounting for individual-specific effects on the unobserved component of taste heterogeneity can be estimated, for example, by making the mean of a normally distributed parameter dependent upon some individual-specific variable (Nlogit version 3 allows for such a model, but the default application constrains standard deviations to be the same).

Continuous versus Finite Taste Heterogeneity

Mixed logit models assume heterogeneity to be continuous over the interval spanned by the assumed distribution for the varying taste parameters. For example, if no theoretical reason exists to limit the domain of a parameter value, one can assume a normal distribution. In that case the range of parameter values spans the real line and the values of the estimated mean and variance will dictate the probability with which these values are found in each segment of the line. A correlation structure can also be estimated. For example, if more than one parameter is normally distributed and there are reasons to believe that they are not independent, then the correlation structure can be estimated (Train, 1998). The structure of correlation can be informative for joint probability inference and segmentation of taste groups (Scarpa et al., 2003b).

However, the computational cost of mixed logit estimation is high, especially when parameters need to be bounded in their domain for theoretical reasons. Furthermore, some research questions are best answered through the identification of defined preference groups, with homogeneous preferences within the group. For example, from the perspective of a water company that wishes to optimize its management plan according to the preferences of its customers, the identification of such preference groups can be informative in allocating services accordingly.

This poses the practical query of identifying the size, number and preference structure of these distinct preference groups. This approach is sometimes referred to as finite mixing (Provencher et al., 2002) or latent class modelling (Swait, 1994). Although the latent class finite-mixing approach is well established theoretically (Heckman and Singer, 1984) and in the econometric application of count models, despite its relative merits it does not seem to be very popular in multinomial discrete choice models.

Recent applications include two travel cost revealed preference studies in recreational site choice (Provencher et al., 2002 and Shonkwiler and Shaw, 2003). Provencher et al. (2002) assume group membership to be conditional on individual characteristics and a serially correlated error structure across the sequence of one individual's choices. They conclude that there is evidence of time dependence across choices and that finite mixing (as they called it) is a convenient and intuitive alternative to mixed logit, especially in terms of computational cost. They find evidence for three separate preference groups.

Shonkwiler and Shaw (2003) also assume group membership to be conditional on individual characteristics, and observe how the two-group models they estimate display different marginal utilities of income. They suggest that this could be an elegant yet uncomplicated way to allow for non-linear preferences for money. This has implications in the valuation of attributes, which differ across groups. They also, as do we in this chapter, identify the potential use of posterior probabilities, although they do not seem to use them in the derivation of their welfare estimates.

Recent stated preference applications using latent class models (LCM) use a dataset on choice of road types in New Zealand and systematically contrast the merits of mixed logit with those of latent class modelling. Comparisons are carried out in terms of choice elasticities, distributions of predicted choice probabilities and changes in absolute choice shares. Based on the results from this dataset they conclude that no unambiguous recommendation can be made as to the superiority of either of the two approaches, although they find strong statistical support for the LCM approach with three preference groups.

Boxall and Adamowicz (2002) conduct a lucid investigation using factor analysis to determine the motivational determinants of trips to wilderness, and build individual specific factor loadings that are then used as determinants in the group membership equation. Their analysis supports the existence of four group preferences and a much richer interpretation than a conventional multinomial logit model. They do not contrast this approach with continuous taste heterogeneity models, such as mixed logit.

Scarpa et al. (2003a) use LCM analysis as an accessory to a more conventional conditional heterogeneity multinomial logit analysis of the choice of piglet breeds, in an effort to value an indigenous pig breed in Yucatan. They find evidence for two distinct preference groups, using membership equations including various individual specific variables.

As both theoretical and empirical evidence on the usefulness of finite mixing logit models is mounting, we observe that little attention has been devoted to one of its most promising features to inform decision makers. This is the identification of posterior distributions of attribute valuations. Such a feature is of particular interest in the context of motivating the collection of panel data on consumers' choice. The more numerous the panel, the sharper is the estimation of individual posterior statistics.

3. CHOICE EXPERIMENT DATA

In spring and summer 2002, as a part of a large-scale investigation into the preference structure of its customers, Yorkshire Water conducted a set of choice experiments. The aim was to characterize the preference for 15 different attributes related to water provision, here called service factors (SFs). As a result of focus-group activities and discussion with the management, these SFs were separated into five groups, giving rise to five separate choice experiments. The first three were mostly concerned with SFs of a private good nature, and are ignored here. In this study we are concerned with the two choice experiments that addressed attributes of the service that can be commonly interpreted as 'public goods'.

The first choice experiment, defined here as WW1, looked at four attributes: area flooding by sewage (AF); river quality (RQ); nuisance from odour and flies (OF); and cost of service (change in water bill payment). There were eight levels of payment expressed as increases or decreases on the current bill, while all other attributes were expressed at four levels. The design chosen was an orthogonal main effect factorial with a total of 32 profiles, which were split into sequences of four choices for each respondent.

The second choice experiment looked at three attributes: water amenities for recreation (AM); quality of bathing water (BB), and cost of service. There were seven levels of payment expressed as increases or decreases on the current bill, while all other attributes were expressed at three levels. The orthogonal main effect factorial of choice gave a total of 27 cards, which were also split into sequences of four choices for each respondent.

The survey instrument was tested in a pilot study and further refined as a consequence. It was finally administered face-to-face by personnel experienced in stated-preference questionnaires through a computer-assisted survey. A representative sample of 767 Yorkshire Water residential customers completed the sequence of choices in the first choice experiment for a total of 3,068 choices (sample WW1), and a representative sample of 777 residential customers completed the sequence for the second choice experiment with a total of 3,108 choices (sample WW2).

A full report on the study and the tested validity of the chosen experimental design are available to the interested reader (Scarpa and Willis, 2002; Willis and Scarpa, 2002).

4. ECONOMETRIC ISSUES

The derivation of the latent class logit model is based on a membership equation, and on a choice alternative equation, both of which turn out to have a convenient logit formulation when two independent Gumbel-distributed error components are used.

The membership equation explains the probabilistic assignment into a number of K groups, where K is exogenously defined and outside the space of estimable parameters. The choice probability equation explains the mechanics of probabilistic choice across alternatives based on a conventional random utility framework. For the sake of brevity, and to avoid undue repetition, we refer the reader to cited works for the details of the formal derivation. In this study, we have adopted the approach documented in Hensher and Greene (2003), which is conveniently applicable using Nlogit version 3.

In brief, our specification does not use any socio-economic covariate in the membership probability specification, which therefore assumes a semi-parametric format for the membership probabilities. The utility function for each of the three alternatives in each choice context is simply specified as a function of the attribute values.

The main focus of this study is to compare posterior marginal WTP for attributes conditional on the sequence of observed choices. We run this comparison across different group-sized latent class models (2, 3 and 4 LCM), and with the mixed logit specification with all attributes but cost distributed normally and zero off-diagonal covariance (MXL). The emphasis on posterior WTP estimate is justified on the basis of the interest that a water company has in identifying groups with specific public-good preferences and WTP amongst its customers, so as to better address and target management plans. In what follows, we describe in some detail the derivation of the individual WTP values from the LCM and MXL models.

Derivation of Posterior WTP Estimates from LCM Models

Consider a population with c preference groups (or classes) and a sequence of four observed choices per t individuals over J alternatives, including the status quo. Given a sequence of four choices by the same individual and conditional on belonging to a given preference group or class c, say for example class A, the joint logit probability of a sequence is:

$$P_{jt} \mid A = \prod_{t=1}^{4} \frac{\exp(\boldsymbol{\beta}_A' \mathbf{x}_t)}{\sum_{J(t)} \exp(\boldsymbol{\beta}_A' \mathbf{x}_{j(t)})} \tag{14.1}$$

With the individual probabilities of membership of a group c defined as Q_{tc} one can derive the unconditional probability by taking the expectation over all the c classes:

$$P_{jt} = \sum_{c=1}^{C} Q_{tc} \prod_{t=1}^{4} \frac{\exp(\boldsymbol{\beta}_c' \mathbf{x}_t)}{\sum_{J(t)} \exp(\boldsymbol{\beta}_c' \mathbf{x}_{j(t)})}, \tag{14.2}$$

where in this study the C = 2, 3, 4 and 5.

A posterior estimate of the individual-specific class probability can be obtained given the observed sequence of four choices and using the Bayes formula:

$$Q^*_{tc} = P_{jtc} \mid y_t, \mathbf{x}_t = \frac{Q_{tc}\prod_{t=1}^{4} \dfrac{\exp(\boldsymbol{\beta}_c'\mathbf{x}_t)}{\sum_{J(t)}\exp(\boldsymbol{\beta}_c'\mathbf{x}_{j(t)})}}{\sum_{c=1}^{C} Q_{tc}\prod_{t=1}^{4} \dfrac{\exp(\boldsymbol{\beta}_c'\mathbf{x}_t)}{\sum_{J(t)}\exp(\boldsymbol{\beta}_c'\mathbf{x}_{j(t)})}}, \tag{14.3}$$

where y_t and $\mathbf{x}_t$ are respectively the observed choices and the attributes of the alternatives in the choice set.

Given this set of individual-specific probabilities of membership in each preference group c, one can derive individual-specific posterior estimates of the marginal WTP as:

$$W\hat{T}P_t = \sum_{c=1}^{C} Q^*_{tc}\left(-\frac{\beta_c}{\gamma_c}\right), \tag{14.4}$$

where $\hat{\gamma}_c$ is the marginal utility of money.

Notice, however, that Nlogit version 3 allows you to store the values for the posterior individual parameter $\hat{\beta}_t = \Sigma_{c=1}^{C} Q^*_{tc}\beta_c$ by using the subcommand 'parameters' in the vector 'beta_i'. However, deriving

$$W\hat{T}P_t = \frac{\sum_{c=1}^{C} Q^*_{tc}\beta_c}{\sum_{c=1}^{C} Q^*_{tc}(-\gamma_c)} = \frac{\hat{\beta}_t}{-\hat{\gamma}_t} \tag{14.5}$$

is obviously incorrect. So this part was computed in Gauss.

Derivation of Posterior WTP Estimates from MXL Models

Train (2003, ch. 11) discusses the derivation of posterior means for normally distributed parameters of taste, conditional on observed choices in mixed logit models.

In our mixed logit specification, the marginal utility of income γ is fixed, so the distribution of estimates for the individual specific WTP for each attribute is given by the mean of the individual parameter distribution $\overline{\beta}_t$ divided by $-\gamma$, which is assumed to be fixed.

In general, $\overline{\beta}_t$ is to be found by taking the expectation of the parameter over the parameter distribution conditional on observed choices and parameter estimates:

$$\overline{\beta}_t = \int \beta \cdot h(\beta \mid y_t, \mathbf{x}_t, \theta) d\beta \tag{14.6}$$

By Bayes' rule:

$$h(\beta | y_t, x_t, \theta) = \frac{P(y_t | \mathbf{x}_t, \beta) g(\beta | \theta)}{P(y_t | \mathbf{x}_t, \theta)} = \frac{P(y_t | \mathbf{x}_t, \beta) g(\beta | \theta)}{\int P(y_t | \mathbf{x}_t, \beta) g(\beta | \theta)} \tag{14.7}$$

where $g(\beta|\theta)$ is the assumed distribution of the parameter in the entire population (in our case assumed to be normal, so $\theta = \{\mu, \sigma^2\}$). So:

$$\overline{\beta}_t = \int \beta \cdot h(\beta | y_t, x_t, \theta) d\beta = \frac{\int \beta P(y_t | \mathbf{x}_t, \beta) g(\beta | \theta) d\beta}{\int P(y_t | \mathbf{x}_t, \beta) g(\beta | \theta) d\beta} \tag{14.8}$$

Because of the non-closed form of these expressions, in practice one uses simulation methods. Posterior simulated estimates of $\overline{\beta}_t$ can be obtained in Nlogit version 3 for each individual by using the subcommand ';parameters' in the 'RPL' estimation routine and are automatically stored in the matrix 'beta_i'. The one used here were obtained using 100 Halton draws.

Number of Groups with Different Preferences

The number of groups with different preferences is not part of the maximization process from which the parameter estimates are derived. In other words it is outside the space of the estimable parameters. The conventional specification tests used for maximum likelihood estimates (likelihood ratio, Lagrange Multipliers and Wald tests) are not valid in this context because they do not satisfy the regularity conditions for a limiting chi-squared distribution under the null.

Resampling from the empirical distribution is feasible but very impractical because of the computational complexity it involves. As a guidance, some authors have used the Akaike information criterion: AIC $= -2 \times \ln L - \text{P}$, where $\ln L$ is the log-likelihood of the model at convergence, and P is the number of estimated parameters in the model. Others have suggested the Bayesian Information Criterion: BIC $= -\ln L + (P/2) \times \ln(N)$, where N is the number of respondents. Boxall and Adamowicz (2002) also used the Akaike Likelihood Ratio index, which we omit here, since the other two methods provide concordant conclusions. However, these criteria also fail some of the regularity conditions under the null for a valid test under the null (Leroux, 1992). The AIC is reported to over-estimate the number of groups,

Table 14.1 Tests for group numbers in latent class models

Choice experiment WW1			N = 767	
LCM groups	Parameters	Log-lik.	AIC	BIC
1	4	−2213.78	4429.55	2227.06
2	9	−2092.13	4188.26	2122.02
3	14	−2063.60	4133.20	2110.10
4	19	−2027.00	4062.00	2090.10
5	24	−2020.26	4050.52	2099.97
Choice experiment WW2			**N = 777**	
LCM groups	Parameters	Log-lik.	AIC	BIC
1	3	−2776.10	5554.21	2786.09
2	7	−2484.98	4973.96	2508.27
3	11	−2431.74	4869.47	2468.34
4	15	−2372.22	4752.43	2422.13
5	20	−2372.22	4754.43	2438.77

while the BIC does not do this, asymptotically, although in small sample sizes it tends to favour too few groups (McLachlan and Peel, 2000).

5. RESULTS AND DISCUSSION

For the sake of space we omit the presentation of all the model estimates. The testing for the number of preference groups is reported in Table 14.1 and it is consistent with the hypothesis that there are four distinct groups of preferences in the sample in each of the two choice experiments. Hence we only present the LCM estimate for four classes along with the more 'conventional' mixed logit model with normally distributed parameters. Such estimates are presented in Tables 14.2 and 14.3.

The descriptive statistics of the distribution of posterior WTP measures are reported in Tables 14.4 and 14.5. However, these distributions are best illustrated graphically by means of normal kernel densities in Figures 14.1–14.5, discussed below.

Preference Groups for WW1

Three attributes were investigated in this experiment. The attributes could either be improved by YW management from the status quo condition at an

Table 14.2 Model estimates for sample WW1 (asymptotic z-values in parentheses)

N = 767, choices = 3,068	Four-group LCM lnL = −2,027, Adj. R^2 = 0.397				MXL ln Sim.L = −2,164, Adj. R^2= 0.357	
	Group A	Group B	Group C	Group D	Mean	St. dev.
Area flooding (AF)	0.012 (12.21)	0.950 (1.58)	0.451 (1.32)	0.710 (1.13)	0.017 (10.67)	0.015 (4.36)
River quality (RQ)	0.062 (20.12)	6.192 (1.10)	1.311 (1.53)	2.730 (1.03)	0.114 (17.80)	0.081 (10.43)
Odour and Flies (OF)	−0.103 (−19.94)	−9.487 (−1.63)	−11.094 (−1.60)	−2.600 (−1.02)	−0.179 (−14.12)	0.099 (6.64)
Cost	−0.084 (−17.13)	−7.128 (−1.65)	−27.674 (−1.54)	2.267 (1.03)	−0.161 (−20.22)	n.a.
Group Probability	0.573 (24.68)	0.217 (9.98)	0.177 (9.04)	0.033 (3.88)		

Table 14.3 Model estimates for sample WW2 (asymptotic z-values in parentheses)

N = 777, choices = 3,108	Four-group LCM lnL = −2,752, Adj. R^2= 0.304				MXL ln Sim.L = −2,328, Adj. R^2= 0.317	
	Group A	Group B	Group C	Group D	Mean	St. dev.
Water amenities (AM)	0.451 (6.75)	0.166 (15.70)	0.010 (1.38)	−10.005 (0.00)	0.160 (11.15)	0.038 (15.54)
Bathing beaches (BB)	0.056 (6.82)	0.033 (23.50)	0.007 (7.73)	−0.211 (−4.23)	0.028 (14.11)	0.081 (13.13)
Cost	−0.704 (−7.29)	−0.039 (−3.415)	−0.216 (−17.93)	1.777 (3.50)	−0.305 (−20.56)	n.a.
Group Probability	0.350 (10.97)	0.284 (9.52)	0.294 (11.65)	0.072 (7.41)		

additional cost to customers; or they could be decreased at the advantage of a lower water bill for customers.

One attribute (RQ) was defined as 'the percentage of river length capable of supporting healthy fisheries and other aquatic life in the long term' and has the character of a pure public good. The other two were (AF) defined

Table 14.4 Statistics of the posterior distributions of WTP in the sample WW1

	Area flooding with sewage			
	LCM-2	LCM-3	LCM-4	MXL
Mean	0.1260	0.0356	0.1035	0.1036
St. dev.	0.0488	0.0990	0.0531	0.0327
Median	0.1687	0.1225	0.1103	0.1038
Kurtosis	−1.7127	−1.7550	25.3722	0.8207
	Water quality in rivers			
	LCM-2	LCM-3	LCM-4	MXL
Mean	0.5999	0.1964	0.5970	0.7085
St. dev.	0.1878	0.4153	0.2489	0.2845
Median	0.7642	0.5608	0.5760	0.7771
Kurtosis	−1.7127	−1.7550	18.3691	0.3625
	Nuisance from odour and flies			
	LCM-2	LCM-3	LCM-4	MXL
Mean	−0.9864	−0.8187	−1.0404	−1.1104
St. dev.	0.3393	0.4165	0.2954	0.2515
Median	−1.2832	−1.1842	−1.0287	−1.1734
Kurtosis	−1.7127	−1.7550	15.6647	4.7375

as 'percentage of areas protected from sewage escape in gardens, roads, paths and open areas' and (OF) 'number of households and businesses affected by odour and high numbers of flies from sewage treatment works'. Attributes AF and OF concern goods whose benefits are probably perceived by most respondents as accruing to other members of the collective, and are therefore special types of mixed public goods. For OF the expected sign for the taste parameter is negative for people who value improvement, as fewer houses affected means better quality.

The latent class analysis is consistent with the presence of four groups of preferences in the sample. The highest probability (57.33%) belongs to preference Group A, followed by preference Group B with 21.68%. Preference Groups C and D have 17.67% and 3.32% respectively.

Estimates for the taste parameters for attributes are all significantly different from zero at conventional levels only in Group A, the group with the largest probability. This group shows WTP estimates slightly larger but

Table 14.5 Statistics of the posterior distributions of WTP in the sample WW2

	Water amenities			
	LCM-2	LCM-3	LCM-4	MXL
Mean	0.4316	0.5705	2.4119	0.5155
St. dev.	0.4772	0.2140	1.7605	0.5815
Median	0.6764	0.5895	1.7713	0.5741
Kurtosis	1.1024	−1.5857	−1.1759	−0.4934
	Water quality in bathing beaches			
	LCM-2	LCM-3	LCM-4	MXL
Mean	0.0787	0.1062	0.3560	0.0945
St. dev.	0.0637	0.0482	0.2857	0.0961
Median	0.1114	0.1105	0.2323	0.1059
Kurtosis	1.1024	−1.5857	−1.2139	−0.6479

not dissimilar from those obtained by the conventional MNL model, except for the OF attribute for which this group seems to have a marginal valuation of £1.22, rather than £0.93.

Groups B and C have relatively high significance but they do not reach conventional significance levels. Group B has valuations practically identical to Group A, while the valuations in Group C are smaller by at least a factor of ten for AF and RQ, and less than half those for OF. This result is consistent with the existence of a small segment of customers (17.7%) with low values for these public goods. Group D has the smallest probability and its parameter estimates show lowest precision, so this group is ignored in the discussion.

Distribution of Posterior WTP Estimates for Area Flooding

As can be seen, the plot of the kernel estimates in Figure 14.1 shows the posterior WTP for each LCM model and for the MXL one. The two-group LCM (dashed line) displays a bi-modal distribution implying the existence of two groups, one with large and another with smaller WTPs. The three-group LCM (dotted line) is also bi-modal, but one modal value is negative, contrary to what one would expect, and altogether the distribution implies a much larger spread, with 0.41% of the respondents displaying negative WTPs for this attribute. The MXL posteriors (continuous line) and the four-group

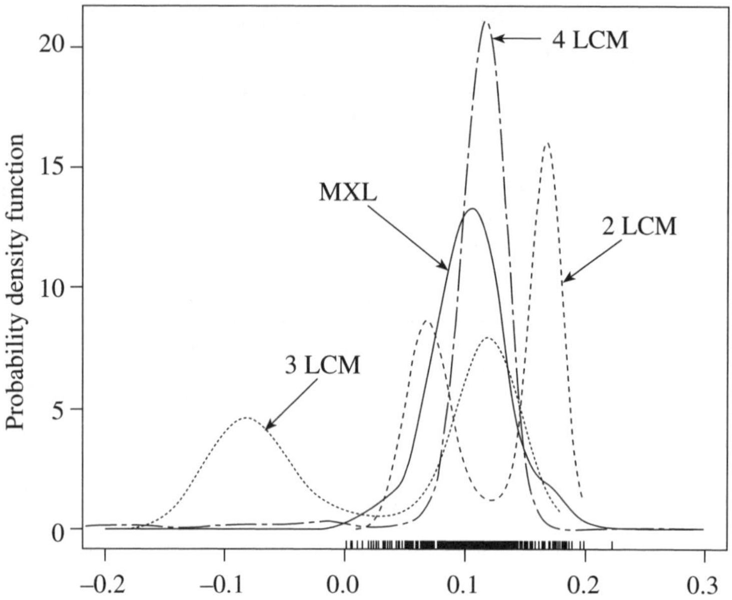

Figure 14.1 Individual WTP estimates for area flooding

LCM (dashed/dotted line) display similar one-peaked modal values, although the latter shows 4.56% of respondents with negative values.

Distribution of Posterior WTP Estimates for River Quality

Figure 14.2 reports similar plots but for the posterior distributions of WTP for river quality. Again, the dashed line of the two-group LCM displays a bi-modal distribution, implying the existence of two groups, one with large WTPs and another with WTPs centred round zero. The dotted line for the three-group LCM also implies a WTP distribution centred round zero with a much larger spread and 41% of individuals displaying negative WTPs. The MXL posteriors and the four-group LCM display similar one-peaked modal values, and both seem more consistent with a-priori expectations as they have much smaller portions of the densities with negative values.

Distribution of Posterior WTP Estimates for Odour and Flies

Figure 14.3 shows the plots of kernels smoothing for the WTP for the number of households exposed to nuisance from odour and flies. WTP is

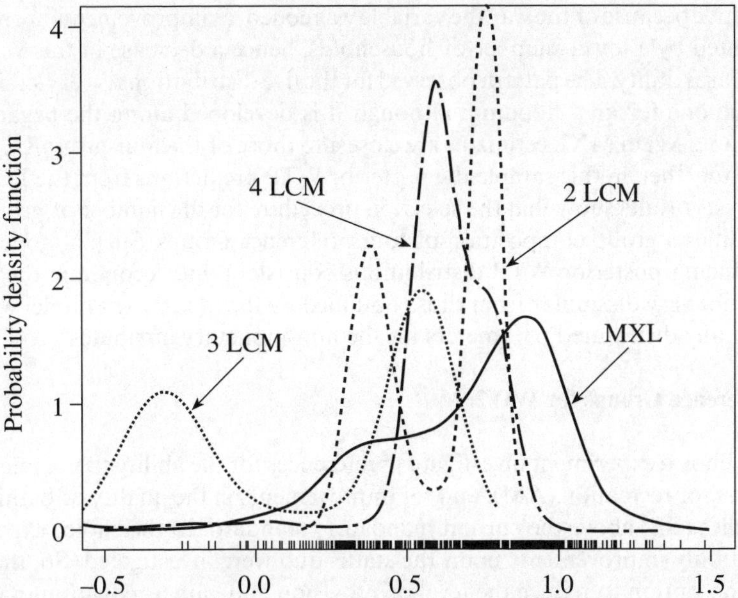

Figure 14.2 Individual WTP estimates for river quality

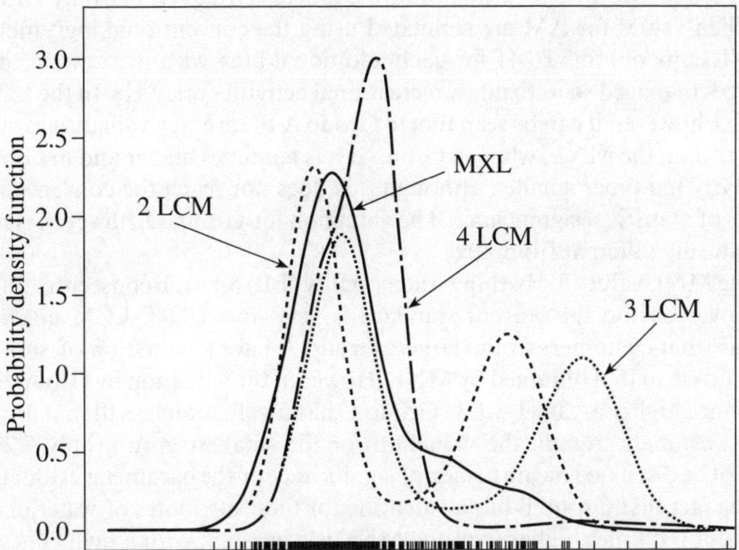

Figure 14.3 Individual WTP estimates for odour and flies

negative because of the way the variable was coded, as improvements are represented by a lower number of households, hence a decrease in this value increases utility. The pattern observed for the five distributions is very similar to the one for area flooding, although it is developed along the negative orthant. Again MXL estimates are closest to those of the four-group LCM.

Altogether, in this sample the posterior WTP predictions from the LCM analysis results show that the selection procedure for the number of groups identifies a group composition of four preference groups. Such a model is producing posterior WTP distributions consistent with economic theory and not very dissimilar from those obtained by the mixed logit model with normally distributed parameters for the non-monetary attributes.

Preference Groups for WW2

This choice experiment investigated preferences for the ability to use inland waters for recreation (AM), and for improvements in the quality of bathing beaches (BB) above the current mandatory standard. In the choice experiment only improvements upon the status quo were investigated. So, there was no option to reduce the level of provision and gain a reduction in the water bill in this case. The latent class estimation identified four distinct preference groups. Three have large probabilities (Group A 35.05%, Group B 28.41% and Group C 29.38%), while the fourth (Group D) has only 7.15%.

When values for AM are estimated using the conventional logit model (MNL) one obtains £0.41 for each additional area with waste water discharges managed so as to allow recreational activities on rivers. In the LCM results, however, it can be seen that in Group A the average valuation is 50% higher than the MNL, while in Group B it is ten times higher and in Group C nearly ten times smaller, although this does not reach the conventional levels of statistical significance. The valuation for Group D, however, is not statistically different from zero.

The MNL values for bathing water quality (BB) for each consecutive 50% improvement on the current standard is very low: £0.08. LCM analysis reveals that customers in the largest Group A have a valuation of similar magnitude to that obtained by MNL. However, the valuation by Group B is ten times higher at £0.83, while Group C has a valuation less than half the MNL estimate. Again, the valuation for the smallest group (only 7.2%) cannot be discussed owing to lack of significance of the parameter estimates.

The fact that Group B has a valuation for these attributes of water management ten times higher than the MNL is consistent with a high concern for amenity-related public good provision amongst a fraction of Yorkshire Water's residential customers. This group has a probability of 28.41%, nearly one-third of the sample. On the other hand, a similarly sized fraction (29.4%), represented by Group C, seem to value these goods much less, and such a result is consistent with a polarization of tastes, perhaps linked to diversity in use values from recreation.

Distribution of Posterior WTP Estimates for Water Quality of Bathing Beaches

Figure 14.4 shows the kernel smoothing plots of individual WTP for water quality of bathing beaches. As in all the other cases, the dashed and dotted lines of respectively the two-group and four-group LCM show a bi-modal distribution, the former with a much large peak, while the latter has two similar sized ones. Altogether they predict little variation in WTP values.

The dashed/dotted line for the four-group LCM WTP distributions and the continuous line for the mixed logit show a completely different picture. They both represent a much spread out distribution, with great variability. In particular, the four-group LCM shows a bi-modal distribution with a large fraction of respondents spread around £0.8 for each extra area 'with waste water discharges designed to allow recreational activities on rivers'. This group of customers may be keen recreationists, or people who care

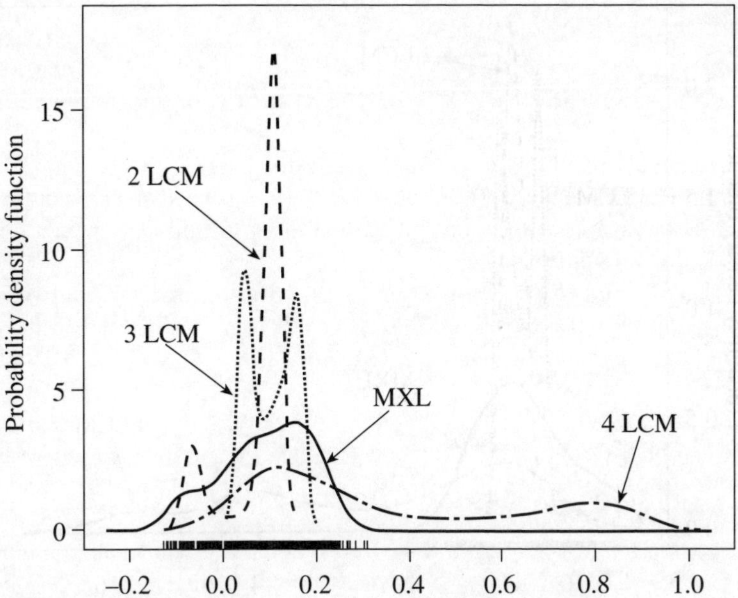

Figure 14.4 Individual WTP estimates for bathing beaches

strongly for the quality of water that the water company can provide for bathing.

Distribution of Posterior WTP Estimates for Water Amenities

A similar pattern is observed in Figure 14.5 for the plots for WTP for water amenities. The distributions of predicted posterior WTPs for two- and three-group LCM show a bi-modal and narrowly spread pattern, while those for the mixed logit and four-group LCM show a much more spread out distribution, only the latter, however, shows high densities of conspicuous values. This result would seem to indicate that care must be paid in selecting the adequate model when the purpose is the analysis of posterior WTP distributions. The choice of model can disguise some patterns that may be of interest to water managers, such as clear taste segmentation into separate preference groups, rather than a continuum of taste intensities.

In this case the statistical evidence from the log-likelihood values obtained in the analysis would seem to lend some support to the hypothesis that a finite group of four sets of preferences exists in the sample. The mixed logit assumption rests on the belief that taste attributes have a

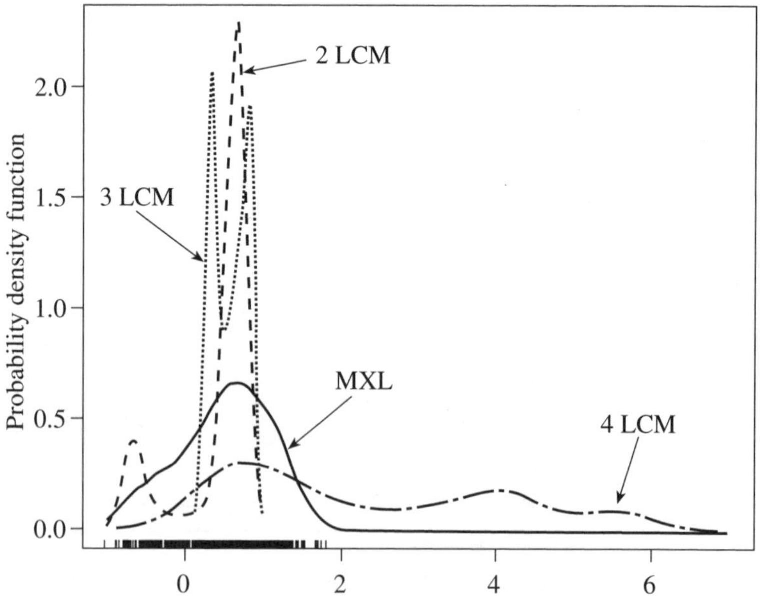

Figure 14.5 Individual WTP estimates for water amenities

specific continuous distribution, in our case the normal. There is no test that can be performed to compare LCM with MXL, and hence the choice of heterogeneity specification ultimately rests with the researcher and her beliefs. In our empirical case, the log-likelihood values are once in favour of the four-group LCM, in the WW1 sample, and once in favour of the MXL, in the WW2 sample. The LCM approach, however, may be desirable in some respects: it does not require distributional assumptions, the estimates are relatively easier to compute (no simulation methods are needed), and it is consistent with the existence of well-defined segments in the market for the public good. Finally, at least with respect to the posterior distribution of WTP values, LCM estimation seems to produce a richness of information similar to the mixed logit estimation.

6. CONCLUSIONS

This chapter explores alternative ways of modelling heterogeneity of tastes for attributes of a composite public good via choice experiments. It contrasts two advanced modelling techniques, the use of the mixed logit random parameter model with the use of latent class models, to explain water company customer choice; and to derive welfare estimates of changes in the levels of provision of a number of 'public goods' jointly produced as a function, in part, of changes to waste water treatment.

The mixed logit approach requires the analyst to specify a-priori a parameter distribution in the population (normal, log-normal, uniform, etc.), which is assumed to characterize the heterogeneity of preferences for that attribute. The choice of distribution, from which to report WTP estimates is then determined by whatever mixed logit model is perceived to have the best 'goodness-of-fit' statistics and theoretical consistency.

LCM do not require any assumptions about the mixing variable: in a sense LCMs 'let the data speak'. LCMs provide further insights into the data by identifying groups of customers who have high or low preferences for particular 'public goods'; and the share of water company customers that these potential purchasers represent. Such segmented information is potentially very useful to company managers for a wide range of purposes. The LCM analysis could be readily extended in order to assess the significance that customers' socio-economic characteristics, such as income or ethnicity, as well as attributes or SF levels have on choice.

There is no unambiguous test of the superiority of one approach (mixed logit or LCM) over the other. However, the LCM approach may offer insights into the heterogeneity of consumer preferences that are not readily identifiable through a traditional mixed logit random parameter model, especially when there are reasons to believe that these are clustered around certain values.

Finally, we focused on posterior estimates of welfare, in the form of the distribution of marginal willingness to pay values, rather than focusing on more conventional estimates of central tendency based on a-priori statistics. Distributions are obviously more informative than single values, and they should be pursued when possible. We would also argue that posterior measures display richer information because they are informed by a sequence of choices. Water companies intending to adequately characterize the preferences of their customer base should endeavour to collect panel data from representative samples. This chapter shows that, even with as few as four choices, posterior distributions can be usefully derived and studied.

REFERENCES

Bhat, C. (1995), 'A Heteroscedastic Extreme Value Model of Intercity Mode Choice', *Transportation Research B*, **29**, 471–83.

Bowman, A.W., and Azzalini, A. (1997), *Applied Smoothing Techniques for Data Analysis: The Kernel Approach with S-Plus Illustrations*, Oxford: Oxford University Press.

Boxall, P.C., and Adamowicz, V.L. (2002), 'Understanding Heterogeneous Preferences in Random Utility Models: The Use of Latent Class Analysis', *Environmental and Resource Economics*, **23** (4), 421–46.

Caussade, S., Juan de Dios, O., Rizzi, L.I., and Hensher, D.A. (2003), 'Assessing the Influence of Design Dimensions on Stated Choice Experiment Estimates', Manuscript, Department of Transport Engineering, Pontificia Universidad Católica de Chile Casilla 306, Código 105, Santiago.

De Shazo, J.R., and Fermo, G. (2001), 'Designing Choice Sets for Stated Preference Methods: The Effects of Complexity on Choice Consistency', *Journal of Environmental Economics and Management*, **44**, 123–43.

Greene, W.H. (2002), *Nlogit v. 3, Reference guide*, Econometric Software Inc.

Heckman, J.B., and Singer, F. (1984), 'Econometric Duration Analysis', *Journal of Econometrics*, **24**, 63–132.

Leroux, B.G. (1992), 'Consistent Estimation of Mixing Distribution', *Annal of Statistics*, **20**, 1350–60.

McFadden, D., and Train, K. (2000), 'Mixed MNL Models of Discrete Response', *Journal of Applied Econometrics*, **15**, 447–70.

McLachlan, G., and Peel, D. (2000), *Finite Mixture Models*, New York: John Wiley and Sons.

Pollack, R.A., and Wales, T.J. (1992), *Demand System Specification and Estimation*, New York: Oxford University Press.

Provencher, B., Barenklau, K., and Bishop, R.C. (2002), 'A Finite Mixture Logit Model of Recreational Angling with Serially Correlated Random Utility', *American Journal of Agricultural Economics*, November, 1066–75.

Scarpa, R., Drucker, A., Anderson, S., Ferraes-Ehuan, N., Gomez, V., Risopatron, C.R., and Rubio-Leonel, O. (2003a), 'Valuing Animal Genetic Resources in Peasant Economies: The Case of the Box Keken Creole Pig in Yucatan', *Ecological Economics*, **45** (3), 427–43.

Scarpa, R., Spalatro, F., and Canavari, M. (2003b), 'Investigating Preferences for Environment Friendly Production Practices', Eighth Joint Conference on Food, Agriculture and the Environment, Red Cedar Lake, Wisconsin, 25–8 August 2002, AgEcon Search Working Paper 03-3, available at http://agecon.lib.umn.edu/.

Scarpa, R., Philippidis, G., and Spalatro, F. (2001), 'Product-Country Images and Preference Heterogeneity for Mediterranean Food Products: A Random Utility Analysis'. Paper presented at the 75th conference of the Agricultural Economics Society, Harper Adams College, Newport, UK, 12 September 2001.

Scarpa, R., and Willis, K. (2002), 'Monte Carlo Experiments to Simulate Effectiveness of Experimental Designs in Residential SP Survey', Report to Yorkshire Water.

Shonkwiler, J.S., and Shaw, W.D. (2003), 'A Finite Mixture Approach to Analyzing Income Effects in Random Utility Models: Reservoir Recreation along the Columbia River', chapter 13 in *The New Economics of Outdoor Recreation*, Edited by N. Hanley, D. Shaw and R. Wright (eds), Cheltenham, UK and Northampton, MA, USA: Edward Elgar, pp. 242–68.

Swait, J. (1994), 'A Structural Equation Model of Latent Segmentation and Product Choice for Cross-sectional Revealed Preference Choice Data', *Journal of Retail and Consumer Services*, **1** (2), 77–89.

Train, K. (2003), *Discrete Choice Methods with Simulation*, Cambridge: Cambridge University Press.

Train, K., and Sonnier, G. (2003), 'Mixed Logit with Bounded Distribution of Part-worths', Working paper, Department of Economics, University of California, Berkeley.

Willis, K., and Scarpa, R. (2002), 'Yorkshire Water Customers' Utility & Willingness-To-Pay For Changes In Water Service Factor Levels: A Stated Choice Analysis', Report to Yorkshire Water.

15. Estimation of resource management objectives through empirical likelihood: can regulatory policies and economic optimization be reconciled?

Marita Laukkanen

Starting with Gordon's seminal paper (1954) economists have been concerned about open access to fisheries resulting in dissipation of economic rents. Economics literature has proposed sole owner fisheries management as an alternative that produces socially optimal harvest levels.[1] The declaration of 200-mile zones of extended fisheries jurisdiction in 1976 made explicit fisheries management reality, in that most important fisheries were brought under the authority of adjacent coastal nations. Management authority has generally been given to government agencies or intergovernmental organizations. While economists have been influential in introducing socioeconomic goals into fisheries management, much of real world fisheries policy continues to emphasize biological goals and short-term political considerations. From an economic point of view conservative concern for stock safety may result in building up stocks that are more than economically optimal. Stressing profits that are forgone during stock recovery, on the other hand, may mean conserving less than would be optimal.

Economic analysis of regulatory impact has largely focused on how regulations should be constructed in order to steer fisheries toward the rent maximizing ideal of sole owner management. Homans and Wilen (1997) point out that in practice virtually no fisheries operate under open access or sole owner management. They introduce a model of regulated open access resource use, where entry to the fishery is free but harvest is subject to regulations imposed by a management agency. They assume that the regulator chooses target harvest levels according to a safe stock concept, and estimate a regulator's quota rule. Their study focuses on describing industry and regulator behaviour, and leaves aside questions about whether the existing structures are economically efficient or which management alternatives would be optimal. Our focus in this chapter instead is on the efficiency of regulated open access resource use: We address the question of whether real world regulations in fact relate to the economic objective of rent maximization.

To provide an index of regulatory behaviour we estimate the implicit discount rate that is consistent with observed regulatory measures. The discount rate is obtained through studying quota choice in an economic optimization framework and econometrically estimating the first order conditions. We examine the North Pacific Halibut fishery as a specific example.[2] We assume that the regulator solves a dynamic optimization problem under uncertainty to maximize the expected present discounted value of rents. We estimate the regulator's objective function, including the discount rate that is consistent with our assumptions and available data. Our results show that a regulator holding rational expectations with respect to future prices and discounting future rents at a rate of 15 per cent would set quotas at about historical levels. Although the estimated discount rate is slightly higher than the 10 per cent social discount rate suggested by Arrow (1976), say, one can argue that the regulator's historical quota choices have in fact been close to socially optimal levels.

The study's objectives parallel those of Berck (1979), Fulton and Karp (1989), and Fernandez (1996). Berck estimates the discount rate inherent in private and public forest owners' decisions to cut timber. Fulton and Karp study how a public firm in the uranium industry balances different objectives in its output and exploration decisions. Fernandez examines how a public waste water treatment plant trades off cost minimization and pollution prevention. All of these problems involve estimating a dynamic model. Berck uses nonlinear least squares to recover the interest rate from a supply function that solves the timber entrepreneurs' intertemporal profit maximization problem. Fulton and Karp use two-stage least squares to recover parameters in a linear-quadratic optimal control model under uncertainty. Fernandez estimates a similar linear-quadratic model through maximum entropy.

Instead of the traditional techniques of two-stage least squares or method of moments, this study uses the maximum empirical likelihood (MEL) procedure proposed by Owen (1988, 1991), Qin and Lawless (1994), and Mittelhammer et al. (2000) to estimate the set of nonlinear stochastic first order conditions implied by the dynamic quota choice problem. The MEL is a new econometric estimation procedure that is well suited to estimating stochastic dynamic resource management problems. The MEL procedure provides an asymptotically efficient way to utilize the information in the moment equations implied by the first order conditions. In particular the MEL assigns optimal weights to the moment conditions included in the estimation criterion and thus effectively solves the problem of optimally combining estimating equations into an optimal estimating function estimator. Designed to work with small, incomplete data sets the MEL provides the same advantages as the maximum entropy approach used by Fernandez, but does not force the economic model into an entropy framework. The inference properties are in many ways analogous to parametric maximum likelihood methods.

The chapter is organized as follows. Section 2 states the regulator's optimization problem in a dynamic rent maximization framework and determines the optimal harvest level as a function of the discount rate. Section 3 describes data for the North Pacific halibut fishery. The econometric model is introduced in Section 4. The estimation procedure is summarized in Section 5. Section 6 presents the estimation results and examines the welfare implications of the regulatory programme. Section 7 concludes.

1. THE BIOECONOMIC MODEL

Halibut spawn during the winter months, with the peak of the activity occurring between December and February. The fishery is open to commercial harvest only outside the spawning season. The initial biomass at the outset of harvest and the amount of fish harvested determine the size of the spawning stock each season. The spawning stock in turn determines how the biomass evolves between seasons. Profits in each period depend on the harvest in that period and on the initial biomass which in turn is determined by past spawning stock levels. A bioeconomic model of a seasonal fishery best describes the halibut fishery. We use the model developed by Clark (1971) and employed by Clark (1972), Clark (1973), Spence and Starrett (1975), Levhari et al. (1981), Hannesson (1997) and others.

Formally, the size of the fish stock at the beginning of the fishing season in period t is X_t. The regulator sets a harvest quota Q_t prior to the commencement of harvest but after having observed the initial stock X_t. Harvesting then takes place. Once the quota has been reached the fishery is closed for the season. The stock left behind after harvest is referred to as the escapement S_t. Neglecting natural mortality during the fishing season, the relation between the initial stock X_t, the harvest quota Q_t, and the escapement level S_t is $X_t - Q_t = S_t$. The growth of the fish stock is a function of the escapement S_t. The escapement spawns at the end of the season and produces $F(S_t)$ recruits available to harvest in period $t + 1$ Recruitment to the stock is described by a discrete time version of the logistic growth model:

$$X_{t+1} = F(S_t) = aS_t - bS_t^2, \tag{15.1}$$

where a and b are biological growth parameters.

The prices p_t are stochastic. The regulator takes the prices as given and by assumption holds rational expectations with respect to future prices. The revenue R_t obtained from harvest Q_t in period t is

$$R_t = p_t Q_t = p_t(X_t - S_t). \tag{15.2}$$

The unit cost of harvest is c/x, where c is the unit cost of fishing effort and x the current stock level.[3] The total cost TC_t of harvesting the stock from the initial level X_t down to the escapement S_t equals

$$TC_t = \int_{S_t}^{X_t} \frac{c}{x} dx = c(\ln X_t - \ln S_t). \tag{15.3}$$

The period t net revenue to the fishery is $\pi_t = R_t - TC_t = p_t(X_t - S_t) - c(\ln X_t - \ln S_t)$. Given the information available at period t, the expected present value $E_t[J]$ of the stream of net revenues over time is

$$E_t[J] = E_t\left[\sum_{s=t}^{\infty}\left(\frac{1}{1+r}\right)^{s-t}\{p_s(X_s - S_s) - c(\ln X_s - \ln S_s)\}\right], \tag{15.4}$$

where r is the discount rate and $\{p_s\}$ the stochastic sequence of prices. The regulator sets the quota Q_t or equivalently the escapement S_t to maximize $E_t[J]$ subject to the stock dynamics $X_{t+1} = aS_t - bS_t^2$. The first order condition to the regulator's problem is

$$E_t\left\{p_t - \frac{c}{S_t} - \frac{1}{1+r}(a - 2bS_t)\left[p_{t+1} - \frac{c}{(aS_t - bS_t^2)}\right]\right\} = 0. \tag{15.5}$$

By assumption expectations are formed rationally. The expectation operator E_t then denotes both the mathematical conditional expectation and the regulator's subjective expectations as of date t.

2. DATA

We assembled data for the North Pacific halibut fishery from publications by the International Pacific Halibut Commission (IPHC).[4] The IPHC was established in 1923 by a convention between Canada and the United States as the first international agreement providing for the joint management of a marine resource. The first regulations enacted by the IPHC went into effect in 1932. Since then harvest quotas have been set by the IPHC annually. Data have been collected extensively throughout the entire regulatory period. Long time series thus exist on quota targets, annual harvests (catches), catch per unit of effort, prices and other economic variables. Quotas are published by the IPHC annually. A logbook programme has been in effect since the beginning of the regulatory programme to collect catch and effort statistics from fishermen. In addition information has been collected from fish processors to maintain accurate records of commercial catch.

We use data for the largest management area, referred to as Area 2, which includes waters off British Columbia and up to Cape Spencer in southeastern Alaska. The observations cover 42 years from 1935 to 1977. Following the 1976 declaration of 200 mile exclusive economic zones, Area 2 was in 1977 divided into separate Canadian and US waters, each with new management methods and data collection procedures. Since the data for Area 2 that pertain to years prior to and after 1977 are not compatible, we truncated the time series used in the econometric estimation in 1977.

We use biomass estimates from Quinn et al. (1985) as a measure of the beginning of the season stock X_t. Quinn et al. derived the biomass estimates using catch age and catch per unit of effort (CPUE) data, which were collected from logbook entries over the entire regulatory programme. The estimates were computed *ex post*, that is, catch age and CPUE data for year t were used to compute an estimate of exploitable biomass in year t. We assume that the estimates by Quinn et al. are unbiased representations of the estimates used by the regulatory authority for annual regulation decisions prior to the commencement of harvest. Quotas and harvests were obtained from a summary in Hoag et al. (1983). The report summarizes the quotas from IPHC regulation pamphlets for each year and compiles the catch records from fish processors and from logbooks of fishing vessels. Prices were obtained from a summary in the IPHC *Annual Report 1978*, Appendix 2. The prices are prices paid to the fishermen as reported by fish processors. Prices were deflated by a producer price index with base year 1982, provided by the United States Bureau of Labor Statistics and available at http://146.142.4.24/gi-bin/surveymos. Since no data are available for the unit cost of fishing effort, we were forced to treat the cost c as an unknown and unobservable parameter.

The quotas and realized harvests differ owing to delays in closing the fishery upon reaching the quota, cheating and measurement errors. Discrepancies of up to 37 per cent were observed. We computed two escapement measures in order to account for the disparities. The realized escapement denoted by S_t^R equals the difference between the initial biomass

Table 15.1 Summary statistics

Variable	Mean	Standard deviation	Min	Max
Stock, 1000 pounds	97 296	32 504	52 973	143 619
Quota, 1000 pounds	22 795	4 410	11 000	28 000
Harvest, 1000 pounds	23 728	7219	8 820	36 240
Realized escapement, 1000 pounds	73 568	27 596	33 130	116 190
Target escapement, 1000 pounds	73 807	28 737	34 563	117 119
Difference between quota and harvest, %	−5	13	−37	29
Price, dollars per 1000 pounds (deflated)	860	390	70	1700

and the realized harvest: $S_t^R = X_t - H_t$. The target escapement S_t^T equals the difference between the initial biomass and the quota target: $S_t^T = X_t - Q_t$. We constructed series of realized escapements and target escapements from the data on the biomass estimates, annual harvests and quotas. We use the realized escapements S_t^R to estimate the stock equation (15.1) and the target escapements S_t^T to estimate the first order condition (15.5). The stock equation (15.1) states a biological relationship between the realized escapement that actually spawns and the subsequent recruitment to the stock. The regulator chooses a target escapement level that satisfies (15.5) and sets the quota based on this target. Since the quota is implemented imperfectly, the realized escapement will in general differ from the target escapement.

Table 15.1 displays summary statistics for the data. Figure 15.1 shows the relation between the realized escapement and the initial stock in the

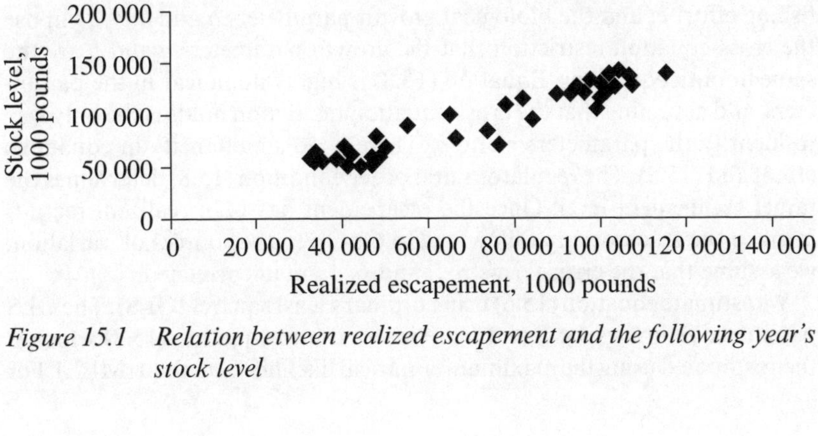

Figure 15.1 Relation between realized escapement and the following year's stock level

following year. The recruitment relation is consistent with the logistic growth specification. It is plausible that the recruitment levels have been on the increasing portion of the recruitment relation throughout the halibut programme.

3. THE ECONOMETRIC MODEL

The econometric model consists of the stock equation in (15.1) and the first order condition for the regulator's optimization problem in (15.5). Appending an additive error term, equation (15.1) becomes

$$X_{t+1} - aS_t + bS_t^2 = \eta_{t+1}. \tag{15.6}$$

The error term in the stock equation encompasses shocks in recruitment. In the econometric estimation of the first order condition in (15.5) we interpret the terms

$$p_t - \frac{c}{S_t} - \frac{1}{1+r}(a - 2bS_t)\left[p_{t+1} - \frac{c}{(aS_t - bS_t^2)}\right] = \varepsilon_{t+1} \tag{15.7}$$

as disturbances arising from mistakes made by the regulator in choosing the optimal escapement target. The first order conditions (15.5) arising from the regulator's present value maximization problem imply

$$E_t\left\{p_t - \frac{c}{S_t} - \frac{1}{1+r}(a - 2bS_t)\left[p_{t+1} - \frac{c}{(aS_t - bS_t^2)}\right]\right\} = E_t[\varepsilon_{t+1}] = 0. \tag{15.8}$$

The parameters to be estimated are the discount rate r, the unit cost of fishing effort c, and the biological growth parameters a and b. We impose the cross-equation restriction that the growth parameters a and b are the same in both equations. Equation (15.8) is highly nonlinear in the parameters, and assuming that the cross-equation restriction holds is the only way to identify the parameters r and c. There is no simultaneity in equations (15.6) and (15.8). The regulator's first order condition (15.8) determines the target escapement level. Once the escapement has been realized, recruitment to the stock occurs following (15.6). Given the sources of variation, we assume that the error terms η_{t+1} and ε_{t+1} are uncorrelated.

We estimate equation (15.6) using ordinary least squares (OLS). The OLS parameter estimates for a and b are inserted into equation (15.8) which is then estimated using the maximum empirical likelihood method (MEL). For comparison we also report parameter estimates obtained through maximum entropy empirical likelihood (MEEL), generalized method of moments (GMM) and nonlinear two-stage least squares (NL2SLS).

4. ESTIMATION

The traditional approach to estimating moment conditions are the generalized method of moments and nonlinear two-stage least squares. The maximum empirical likelihood method of estimation (see Owen, 1988, 1991; Qin and Lawless, 1994; and Mittelhammer et al., 2000) provides a new way to use the information represented by moment conditions such as the first order conditions to the regulator's programme. Since the MEL is not widely known, we next briefly outline the estimation procedure.[5]

The MEL estimates are obtained by assigning the maximum probability possible to the sample outcome actually observed, subject to the information provided by the moment equations. The moment equations depend in a nonlinear way on the observed variables and the unknown parameters. They link the data, the population distribution and the parameters.

Consider now an M dimensional vector of instrumental variables $\mathbf{z}_t$ that are in the regulator's information set at time t and included in the data. Assume that the $\mathbf{z}_t$ and ε_{t+1} have finite second moments. The moment equations (15.8) imply the population orthogonality conditions

$$E\left\{\left[\left[p_t - \frac{c}{S_t} - \frac{1}{1+r}(a - 2bS_t)\right]\left[p_{t+1} - \frac{c}{(aS_t - bS_t^2)}\right]\right]\mathbf{z}_t\right\}$$
$$= E[\boldsymbol{h}(p_t, p_{t+1}, S_t, \mathbf{z}_t, r, c)] = 0. \quad (15.9)$$

The orthogonality conditions (15.9) can be interpreted as the expectation of the M dimensional unbiased vector estimating function $\boldsymbol{h}(p_t, p_{t+1}, S_t, \mathbf{z}_t, r, c)$.

The potential set of instrumental variables for our problem includes p_t, S_{t-1}^T, S_{t-2}^T, X_t, X_{t-1}, S_{t-1}^R and S_{t-2}^R. In many estimation problems the choice of which of the potential instrumental variables to include in the estimation is ad hoc. In the present problem the potential instrumental variables are highly correlated with each other, with most of the correlation coefficients close to one (Table 15.2). The choice of instruments to include in the estimation is challenging in that some of the potential instruments may provide little or no additional information. The MEL provides a basis for weighing the information added by the instrumental variables. It is thus a useful method to estimate the problem at hand. By assigning optimal

Table 15.2 Correlation matrix for the model variables

ρ	S_t^T	p_t	S_{t-1}^T	S_{t-2}^T	X_t	X_{t-1}	S_{t-1}^R	S_{t-2}^R
S_t^T	1.000							
p_t	−0.497	1.000						
S_{t-1}^T	0.983	−0.486	1.000					
S_{t-2}^T	0.936	−0.466	0.983	1.000				
X_t	0.996	−0.565	0.978	0.931	1.000			
X_{t-1}	0.983	−0.543	0.996	0.979	0.985	1.000		
S_{t-1}^R	0.970	−0.458	0.995	0.986	0.964	0.991	1.000	
S_{t-2}^R	0.915	−0.438	0.970	0.995	0.909	0.964	0.977	1.000

weights to each equation the MEL procedure combines the information in the orthogonality equations into an optimal estimating function estimator. Further advantages of the MEL procedure are that (i) it is nonparametric in errors, (ii) it can easily be applied to nonlinear systems, (iii) it works well with small, incomplete data sets and (iv) it does not require restrictions on parameters to estimate ill-posed or underdefined problems.

The information in the unbiased estimating functions (15.9) combined with the concept of empirical likelihood defines an empirical likelihood function for (r, c). Maximizing the empirical likelihood function with respect to the parameters yields the maximum empirical likelihood (MEL) estimates. The estimation procedure begins with the definition of a joint empirical probability distribution $\Pi_{t=1}^T v_t$ for sample observations that is supported by the sample data. Parameter v_t denotes the probability of observing the tth sample outcome $\{p_t, p_{t+1}, S_t, \mathbf{z}_t\}$. In order to obtain an empirical likelihood function in terms of (r, c) the v_t are first chosen to maximize $\Pi_{t=1}^T v_t$, or equivalently $\Sigma_{t=1}^T \ln(v_t)$, subject to the moment equations (15.9). The parameters (r, c) enter the empirical likelihood function through the moment equations that constrain the maximization problem. Using the empirical probabilities v_t the moment constraints (15.9) can be represented empirically as the $(M \times 1)$ vector equation

$$\sum_{t=1}^{T} v_t \boldsymbol{h}(p_t, p_{t+1}, S_t, \mathbf{z}_t, r, c) = \sum_{t=1}^{T} v_t \left\{ \left[p_t - \frac{c}{S_t} - \frac{1}{1+r}(a - 2bS_t) \left[p_{t+1} - \frac{c}{(aS_t - bS_t^2)} \right] \right] \mathbf{z}_t \right\} = 0. \quad (15.10)$$

Since the v_t's represent a probability distribution, the maximization problem is subject to the additional constraints $\Sigma_{t=1}^T$ and $v_t > 0 \;\; \forall\, t$. The probability vector $\boldsymbol{v}$ that assigns maximum probability to observing the actual sample outcome and the Lagrange multipliers associated with the constrained maximization problem are first solved as functions of (r, c). The optimal values for $\boldsymbol{v}$ found through the maximization are then substituted back into $\Sigma_{t=1}^{T} \ln(v_t)$ which now defines a concentrated or profile empirical likelihood function in terms of (r, c). Parallel to the parametric maximum likelihood procedure, the maximum empirical likelihood (MEL) estimates of (r, c) are found by maximizing the concentrated empirical log-likelihood function

$$\ln[\mathrm{L}_{\mathrm{EL}}(r, c)] \equiv \max_{\boldsymbol{v}} \left[\sum_{t=1}^{T} \ln(v_t) \text{ s.t. } \sum_{t=1}^{T} v_t \boldsymbol{h}(p_t, p_{t+1}, S_t, \mathbf{z}_t, r, c) = 0 \right. \\ \left. \text{and } \sum_{t=1}^{T} v_t = 1 \right] \tag{15.11}$$

with respect to (r, c). The solution to the optimization problem must be found numerically. We used the NSolve procedure in Mathematica 3.0 for the computation. Further details of the estimation procedure are available from the author upon request.

5. ESTIMATION RESULTS

Table 15.3 presents the MEL estimation results of the model parameters. The table also reports parameter estimates obtained through maximum entropy-based empirical likelihood (MEEL), generalized method of moments (GMM) and nonlinear two-stage least squares (NL2SLS). The MEEL estimates were computed to compare the MEL results with those of another nonparametric likelihood approach. The MEEL method can be readily applied to a set of estimating functions, and it uses an estimation criterion that is similar to the MEL criterion (see for example Golan and Judge, 1996; Mittelhammer et al., 2000). The MEEL procedure minimizes the weighted average discrepancies between the logarithms of the estimated probabilities v_t and empirical frequency weights T^{-1}. Data based probability estimates are used as weights. The MEL criterion can be expressed in a similar form but with the empirical frequency weights T^{-1} weighing the discrepancies. The GMM and NL2SLS methods were used to compare the MEL results with those of traditional methods. The GMM method suggested by Hansen (1982) and Hansen and Singleton (1982) and the nonlinear two-stage least squares of Amemiya (1974, 1977) are the mainstay methods for estimating sets of moment conditions. Differing from the MEL and MEEL methods which assign optimal weights to the moment equations,

Table 15.3 Estimation results

Method	Parameter				
	a	*b*	*r*	*c*	Vector of weights on the moment constraints in MEL/MEEL estimation[1]
OLS	1.5395	$2.5935*10^{-6}$	–	–	–
MEL	–	–	0.15	6704	{0.0006, −4.3, 0.0019, 0.0024, −0.0023, 0.0014, 0.0015}
MEEL	–	–	0.19	21 945	{0.0002, −2.5, 0.0013, −0.0016, −0.0014, 0.0011, 0.0008}
GMM	–	–	0.38	17 591	–
NL2SLS	–	–	0.40	11 720	–

Note: [1]The weights refer to the moment equations that include p_t, S^T_{t-1}, S^T_{t-2}, X_t, X_{t-1}, S^R_{t-1} and S^R_{t-2} as instruments, respectively.

the GMM method uses the estimated variance of the moments as the metric. The NL2SLS approach uses the identity matrix.

The signs of all the parameter estimates are as expected and the magnitudes are reasonable. The estimates of the key parameter *r* obtained through the four estimation techniques differ slightly. The empirical likelihood based MEL and MEEL methods yield estimates that are close to each other. The GMM and NL2SLS methods yield somewhat higher estimates of *r*. The GMM and NL2SLS estimates are also close to each other. While similar in magnitude, the results for parameter *c* obtained through the four estimation techniques differ more markedly.[6] The methods use different criterion functions to solve the highly nonlinear estimation problem. It is not surprising that the estimates differ. The MEL and MEEL criteria both maximize the empirical likelihood of obtaining the sample outcome actually observed but they weigh sample information differently. The GMM and NL2SLS methods set the sample versions of the orthogonality conditions close to zero but again use a different metric.

While there is considerable controversy on what is the proper social rate of discount, the 10 per cent rate suggested by Arrow (1976) provides a widely used benchmark. The MEL estimate of *r* implies a discount rate of 15 per cent. This means that a fishery manager who is aiming at maximizing the expected present value of the fishery and discounting the future at the rate of 15 per cent would set harvests at about historical levels. The MEEL estimate implies a discount rate of 19 per cent. The estimated discount rates exceed the social discount rates commonly suggested for resource management, although the disparities could be considered small for a risky resource industry such as fishing. The results indicate that historical regulatory behaviour is closer to the sole owner optimum than economists' concern about misguided fisheries management based on biological objectives would allow us to believe. With implied discount rates of 38 per cent and 40 per cent, the GMM and NL2SLS results render a more pessimistic view of regulatory behaviour. The traditional estimates give rise to the interpretation that the regulator is conserving the halibut stocks at less than would be economically optimal. However, accounting for the fact that fisheries problems are characterized by discount rates as high as infinity, corresponding to unregulated open access (see for example Clark, 1990), the disparities between the empirical likelihood based estimates and those obtained through traditional methods are relatively small.

The estimated biological parameters imply an equilibrium biomass level of 208 million pounds in the absence of harvest. The maximum sustainable physical yield occurs at half of this level, at a biomass of 104 million pounds and a yield of 28 million pounds. Apart from the years 1953–60, the target escapement has been below the escapement producing the maximum sustainable yield. This implies modest stock conservation goals as seen from the biological standpoint. We continue to entertain the hypothesis of present value maximization and turn to the welfare implications of making regulatory decisions based on the rates of discount indicated by our analysis. We solved for the optimal escapement and annual profits at the average price and the benchmark social discount rate of 10 per cent as well as the estimated discount rates. The MEL estimate of the cost parameter c and the benchmark social rate of discount of 10 per cent imply a socially optimal escapement level of 99.8 million pounds and annual profits of \$22.5 million. The estimated discount rate of 15 per cent implies an optimal escapement of 91.5 million pounds and annual profits of \$22.1 million. Biological overfishing in terms of target escapements below the maximum sustainable yield level is optimal at discount rates exceeding 7.5 per cent. In our example the disparity between the estimated discount rate and the benchmark social discount rate is relatively minor. The MEEL results have similar implications. The benchmark 10 per cent discount rate and the MEEL estimate of c imply an optimal escapement of 109 million pounds and annual profits of \$19.1 million. The estimated discount rate of 19 per cent implies an optimal escapement of 97.5 million pounds and annual profits of \$18.6. Based on these results one can argue that historical harvest decisions have been close to the socially optimal harvest levels. For the GMM estimates the disparities are larger, with annual profits of \$20 million and \$16 million corresponding to the benchmark discount rate of 10 per cent and the estimated discount rate of 38 per cent. The NL2SLS estimates lead to annual profits of $21.4 million at the 10 per cent discount rate and $16.4 at the estimated rate of 40 per cent.

A discount rate that exceeds the benchmark social rate of discount could be explained by incomplete control of future stocks. A high level of uncertainty characterizes the evolution of fish resources. In particular, fleets from outside the authority of the commission members have had access to the halibut fishery. Japanese fleets intercepted the fishery prior to 1952 when Japan agreed to abstain from fishing halibut along the coast of North America under the Convention between Canada, Japan, and the United States that established the North Pacific Fisheries Commission (INPFC) (IPHC Technical Report No. 16).[7] Incidental catch taken by fishermen targeting other species is also outside the commission's authority. Migrations of halibut do not seem to provide a reason for heavy discounting since the direction of migration is mainly from Area 3 to Area 2 (Hoag et al., 1983). The relatively high rates of discount implied by the GMM and NL2SLS results could also be interpreted as indicating that economic factors are not taken into consideration in regulatory decisions and that an alternative model would more accurately describe regulatory behaviour.[8]

6. CONCLUSION

This study has moved beyond static analysis of regulated open access resource use to analyse dynamic regulatory decisions with available data. The study set out to provide an index of the efficiency of regulatory decisions that allows comparisons between historical regulatory policy and socially optimal harvest levels. It was posited that the regulator sets the target harvest levels, or quotas, to maximize the expected present value of the stream of rents from the fishery. The discount rate consistent with historical target harvest levels was estimated to provide an index of regulatory behaviour. We found that the regulator was implicitly discounting the future at a somewhat higher rate than that proposed by Arrow as a social discount rate. However, the disparities were relatively small and could be explained by uncertainty characterizing the future of the fish stock and control of the fishery. The welfare implications of using a discount rate exceeding the one suggested by Arrow were minor for the MEL and MEEL estimates but more noticeable for the GMM and NL2SLS estimates.

We formulated and solved the dynamic estimation problem using the MEL method. The MEL proves to be a feasible alternative to traditional estimation. The procedure allows the recovery of meaningful information from sets of first order conditions for a dynamic programming problem of the kind that frequently appears in natural resource management. The MEL procedure assigns optimal weights to the estimation equations. This property effectively solves the problem of how to weigh the potential instrumental variables in the estimation and hence provides an advantage over traditional methods. The MEL estimates were similar to the estimates obtained through the MEEL method which also assigns optimal weights to the estimation equations but uses a maximum entropy framework.

A number of questions require further study and elaboration. We only studied the efficiency of the regulator's harvest decisions in terms of the time path of the quotas and the resulting stock recruitment. We did not address capacity choices in the fishery. It would be of interest to analyse investment in both the fish stock and fleet capacity over time. While we conclude that the time path of the quotas set by the regulator was close to the socially optimal harvest programme, open access under quota regulation could result in overinvestment and dissipation of economic rents. A total quota provides a way to achieve target stock levels, but open access to a fishery has been shown to attract excessive fishing effort. Actual season lengths in the halibut fishery have fallen to just a few days each year. The extremely short season indicates a race for harvest that is likely to be motored by overinvestment in fishing capacity.[9] Another topic for future study would be to allow the discount rate to vary in order to study how environmental fluctuations and changes in the economic environment or the state of the fishing industry affect regulatory behaviour. In our analysis the discount rate was by assumption constant over time. Periods of slow economic growth or high unemployment may result in the regulator emphasizing current profits over expected gains in the long run. The exclusion of Japanese vessels in 1952 may have increased the weight given to stock conservation and future profits. Finally, it would be of interest to explicitly account for fluctuations in recruitment and imperfectly implemented management measures.

Another limitation of this study is that we treat the unit cost of fishing as a parameter. Since no data are available for the measure, estimating the cost was the only way to recover the discount rate.

NOTES

The study has benefited enormously from ongoing discussions with George Judge and Larry Karp. All remaining errors are the author's. Financial support from the S.V. Ciriacy-Wantrup Fellowship and the Yrjö Jahnsson Foundation is gratefully acknowledged.

1. Early examples of such studies include Scott (1955), Turvey and Wiseman (1957), and Crutchfield and Zellner (1962).

2. Homans and Wilen (1997) also studied the Pacific Halibut fishery.
3. The cost function applies if the unit cost of fishing effort is constant and the catch per unit of effort is proportional to the size of the stock available for harvest. The approximation is widely used in fisheries economics.
4. Homans and Wilen (1997) also relied on these data.
5. The exposition follows Mittelhammer et al. (2000).
6. While more detailed in many other respects, the descriptive static model of Homans and Wilen (1997) does not include a discount rate. The closest equivalent to our cost parameter in their model would be the efficient cost of fishing effort, or variable cost divided by the catchability coefficient. The cost estimates we obtained are somewhat smaller but similar in magnitude to those in Homans and Wilen.
7. In 1962 the INPFC allowed the Japanese to harvest in the Bering Sea. The area falls outside regulatory Area 2 investigated here.
8. One possibility would be a model assuming solely biological objectives in regulatory decision making such as the one described by Homans and Wilen (1997). Another possible hypothesis we might entertain to describe the motivations of a regulatory authority would be that of rent seeking behaviour.
9. IPHC, http://www.iphc.washington.edu/halcom/commerc/updates.htm.

REFERENCES

Amemiya, T. (1974), 'The Nonlinear Two-stage Least Squares Estimator', *Journal of Econometrics*, **2**, 105–10.

Amemiya, T. (1977), 'The Maximum Likelihood and Nonlinear Three-stage Least Squares Estimator in the General Nonlinear Simultaneous Equations Model', *Econometrica*, **45**, 955–68.

Arrow, K.J. (1976), 'The Rate of Discount for Long-term Public Investment', in H. Ashley, R. Rudman and C. Whipple (eds), *Energy and the Environment*, New York: Pergamon Press.

Berck, P. (1979), 'The Economics of Timber: a Renewable Resource in the Long Run', *Bell Journal of Economics*, **10**, 447–62.

Clark, C.W. (1971), 'Economically Optimal Policies for the Utilization of Biologically Renewable Resources', *Mathematical Biosciences*, **12**, 245–60.

Clark, C.W. (1972), 'The Dynamics of Commercially Exploited Animal Populations', *Mathematical Biosciences*, **13**, 149–64.

Clark, C.W. (1973), 'Profit Maximization and the Extinction of Animal Species', *Journal of Political Economy*, **81**, 950–61.

Clark, C.W. (1990), *Mathematical Bioeconomics*, New York: Wiley.

Crutchfield, J., and Zellner, A. (1962), 'Economic Aspects of the Pacific Halibut Fishery', *U.S. Department of Interior, Fishery Industrial Research*, Washington, DC.

Fernandez, L. (1996), 'Estimation of Wastewater Treatment Objectives through Maximum Entropy', *Journal of Environmental Economics and Management*, **32**, 293–308.

Fulton, M., and Karp, L. (1989), 'Estimating the Objectives of a Public Firm in a Natural Resource Industry', *Journal of Environmental Economics and Management*, **16**, 268–87.

Golan, A., and Judge, G. (1996), 'A Maximum Entropy Approach to Empirical Likelihood Estimation and Inference', Giannini Foundation Working Paper, University of California.

Gordon, H.S. (1954), 'The Economic Theory of a Common Property Resource: The Fishery', *Journal of Political Economy*, **62**, 124–42.

Hannesson, R. (1997), 'Fishing as a Supergame', *Journal of Environmental Economics and Management*, **32**, 309–22.

Hansen, L.P. (1982), 'Large Sample Properties of Method of Moments Estimators', *Econometrica*, **50**, 1029–54.

Hansen, L.P., and Singleton, K. (1982), 'Generalized Instrumental Variables Estimation of Nonlinear Rational Expectations Models', *Econometrica*, **50**, 213–24.

Hoag, S.H, Myhre, R.J., St-Pierre, G., and McCaughran, D.A. (1983), 'The Pacific Halibut Resource and Fishery in Regulatory Area 2. I. Management and Biology', International Pacific Halibut Commission Scientific Report No. 67.

Homans, F.R., and Wilen, J.E. (1997), 'A Model of Regulated Open Access Resource Use', *Journal of Environmental Economics and Management*, **32**, 1–21.

International Pacific Halibut Commission (1978), *Annual Report 1978*.

Levhari, D., Michener, R., and Mirman, L.J. (1981), 'Dynamic Programming Models of Fishing: Competition', *American Economic Review*, **71**, 649–61.

Mittelhammer, R.C., Judge, G.G., and Miller, D.J. (2000), *Econometric Foundations*, New York: Cambridge University Press.

Owen, A. (1988), 'Empirical Likelihood Ratio Confidence Intervals for a Single Functional', *Biometrika*, **75**, 237–49.

Owen, A. (1991), 'Empirical Likelihood for Linear Models', *The Annals of Statistics*, **19**, 1725–47.

Qin, J., and Lawless, J. (1994), 'Empirical Likelihood and General Estimating Equations', *The Annals of Statistics*, **22**, 300–25.

Quinn, T., Deriso, R., and Hoag, S. (1985), 'Methods of Population Assessment of Pacific Halibut', International Pacific Halibut Commission Scientific Report No. 72.

Scott, S. (1955), 'The Fishery: The Objectives of Sole Ownership', *Journal of Political Economy*, **63**, 116–24.

Spence, M., and Starrett, D. (1975), 'Most Rapid Approach Paths in Accumulation Problems', *International Economic Review*, **16**, 388–403.

Turvey, R., and Wiseman, J. (eds) (1957), *The Economics of Fisheries*, Rome: FAO.

16. Examining the Environmental Kuznets Curve: what can Kernel estimation say?

Salvatore Di Falco

1. INTRODUCTION

The relation between economic development and environmental quality in the last ten years has captured a lot of attention in the scientific community. Today it is one of the most lively research lines in Environmental and Resource Economics. In fact after some seminal papers, for instance: Shafik and Bandyopadhyay (1992), Grossman and Krueger (1991, 1993, 1995), Panayotou (1993), Saldon and Song (1994), an increasing amount of this literature has flourished around the so-called Environmental Kuznets Curve hypothesis (EKC, hereafter), and this is likely to continue for some time. The EKC is an empirical finding which relates environmental degradation, captured by some environmental quality indicators, and per capita income levels. The hypothesized functional relation between these two variables is concave. Therefore, environmental degradation will initially increase and after a 'peak' in a successive stage decrease as the level of income increases. In other words, after a first stage in which economic development is harmful to the environment, there exists a stage in which higher levels of per capita income are positively correlated with an improvement in environmental quality. So, richer and greener is not only to be hoped for, it is also to be expected, and it is possible to 'grow out' of some environmental problems. The simple (or simplistic?) policy implication is that, as stated by Beckerman (1992), 'the best way for countries to reach low levels of environmental degradation is to become richer'. This idea of income determinism has been strongly criticized by several authors (e.g., Arrow et al., 1995) and more attention has been devoted to identifying whether the EKC hypothesis does or does not hold for those environmental quality indicators, and in finding the empirical arguments which may explain what the driving forces are behind the inverted U shape. Other authors have focused on the analytical side of the story by providing economic models and specifying under which assumptions or conditions these models might explain an EKC path (see, among others, the models by Salden and Song, 1995; John and Pecchenino, 1994; John et al., 1995; McConnell, 1997; Byrne, 1997; Stokey, 1998; Ansuategi et al., 1996). Surprisingly, less attention has been paid to the econometric and methodological problems arising from the quantity and quality of the data. Stern et al. (1996) pointed out that environmental data are 'patchy in coverage, and poor in quality' and that 'there are a number of simultaneity issues that make identification of alternative structures difficult if not impossible within a single equation OLS framework'. Furthermore one should consider the sources of heteroscedasticity in the context of cross-sectional regressions of grouped data. Therefore, if heteroscedasticity is present, a GLS regression should be estimated. Cole et al. (1997) addressed in their analysis the problems inherent in the reliability of the estimated turning points of the EKC. They also addressed the feedback from environmental degradation to economic growth, 'which would lead to simultaneity bias in the estimation'. Xepapadeas and Amri (1998) used univariate and ordered probit models and showed that the probability of getting an acceptable environmental quality in a country increases as it attains a higher state of economic development.[1] Recently, Taskin and Zaim (2000) have suggested the use of non-parametric tools to test the existence of EKC behaviour. This approach should be more suitable than a parametric one because of its flexibility. In non-parametric econometrics one does not have to specify an a priori functional form but, rather, let data determine the relation between variables. This chapter focuses on similar issues, and its purposes are to provide:

1. a critical review of the EKC literature;
2. a standard econometric analysis using Italian data, in order to test the existence of an EKC in Italy;
3. an alternative applied approach based upon non-parametric econometrics on the same dataset;
4. a comparison of the results of the different econometric procedures.

2. THE EKC LITERATURE: A BRIEF REVIEW

In the existing literature a number of theoretical and empirical explanations of the EKC have been provided. The link between income and demand for environmental quality, structural economic changes, trade, technology, policies and regulations are all consistent with the quadratic behaviour of some environmental degradation indicators. This section will provide a brief resume of the large body of literature on the driving forces behind the EKC hypothesis.

2.1 The Link between Income and Demand for Environmental Quality

This argument starts from the hypothesis that environmental quality is, basically, a 'luxury' good. When people attain a certain level of income per capita, they are willing to consider the quality of their environment as a need to be satisfied. As underlined by Beckerman (1974): 'the richer class are the largest part of the demand for environmental quality'. It turns out that if the income elasticity of the demand for environmental quality is quite 'reactive' then the increase in the level of per capita income should lead to a significant increase in the demand for environmental quality. This increase in the demand for environmental quality will be transformed 'into a higher realised level of quality, as both public and private institutions and organisations respond to political and market forces' (Antle and Heidebrink, 1995). Earlier, the link between the demand for environmental quality and income was confirmed in 1971 by Vernon Ruttan in his presidential speech to the American Agricultural Economic Association: 'in relatively high income economies the income elasticity related to sustenance is low and declines as income continues to rise, while the income elasticity of demand for more effective disposal of residuals and for environmental amenities is high and continues to rise. This is in sharp contrast to the situation in poor countries where the income elasticity of demand is high for sustenance and low for environmental amenities'. John and Pecchenino (1994), John et al. (1995) and Jones and Manuelli (1995) adopt the Overlapping Generations (OLG) framework to analyse the case in which the current generation considers its welfare affected by pollution, so the externality is partly internalized. Others (e.g. Saldon and Song, 1995; López, 1994; Stokey, 1998) adopt the infinitely lived households framework, in which perfect altruism is assumed, and any intergenerational conflict is ignored to capture the same empirical behaviour. All these models attempt to produce the EKC, irrespective of whether they consider different sources of pollution (production or consumption), or different restrictions about preferences or technology, or use the same assumptions (addivity or homotheticity of preferences). McConnell (1997) presents a simple static model to show the role of the income elasticity of demand for environmental quality in the EKC. This static model is 'essentially an amalgam of models from literature' with three variants: the first model has an additive utility function, the second has non-additive preferences, and in the third pollution reduces output. The role of the income elasticity of demand for environmental quality, which is theoretically one of the driving forces of the EKC hypothesis, can be mitigated. In fact preferences that are equivalent to a high income elasticity can be diminished by other factors (such as low marginal effectiveness of either abatement or the effect of pollution on output). From McConnell's work on the connection between the aggregate EKC and individual evaluation, it turns out that the role of 'preferences consistent with a positive income elasticity of demand for environmental quality are neither necessary nor sufficient for the EKC. Increasing pollution may occur with increasing income but preferences that would imply both a high income elasticity of demand for environmental quality and decreasing pollution may occur simultaneously with preferences that put lower values on pollution reduction as income rises'. So the positive income elasticity for environmental quality that is found regularly in the contingent valuation method literature does not confirm a reduction in pollution in the theoretical microeconomic framework.

2.2 The Structural Hypothesis

Another driving force to an EKC path is the structural one. This hypothesis emphasizes Rostow's idea that structural transformations are features of the growth process. These transformations are inherent in the shift in the sectoral composition of economic activity. So, in a growth process, the economy is transformed from being agricultural (resources intensive) to being industrial (pollution intensive). Then the economy may move further to a model of growth based upon the services sector (technology intensive, less pollutant activity etc.). This kind of pattern can explain the non-monotonic relationship between environmental degradation and per capita income. Therefore it suggests that economic growth can lead to an improvement in environmental quality. Hettige et al. (1992), using a dataset composed of 80 countries from 1960 up to 1988, have found evidence of the importance of differences in the structure of production for toxic manufacturing emissions. Suri and Chapman (1998) estimate that the relationship between the share of manufacturing in GDP and environmental degradation is positively significant. De Bruyn (1997), applying the decomposition analysis developed by Grossman and Krueger (1991), found instead no evidence for the hypothesis that structural changes explained the reduction in SO_2 emissions in developed countries during the 1980s. The attribution method used by Stern (1998) showed that 'though input and output mix are statistically significant they make only a small contribution to changes in global emissions' of SO_2. However, the acceptance of the structural hypothesis as an argument which supports the EKC implies (probably) acceptance of the idea that all countries experience the same development stages and the same structural transition. Those stages of economic development are a deterministic process. As stated by Unruh and Moomaw (1998), 'it is not certain whether stages of economic growth are a deterministic process that all countries must pass through, or a description of the development of countries in the 19th and 20th centuries that may or may not be repeated in the future. This question is important because much of the EKC literature explicitly assumes that the emissions and income data for many countries can be reduced to a single pollution-GDP development trajectory'. Anyway, this driving force, even if quite reasonable and appealing from a theoretical point of view, has no strong empirical confirmation. Of course the availability of more disaggregated sectoral data may improve the econometric performance and highlight more clearly whether or not structural change affects significantly the downward sloping part of the EKC.

2.3 International Trade

Some of the EKC empirical studies included trade intensity or openness variables in the estimation. In fact it is recognized that international trade may well affect environmental quality, but whether this is in principle a positive or a negative effect is controversial. Removing borders and more open trade policies should improve the circulation of technologies with less impact and strengthen the property rights system. But by the same token, a trade liberalization programme may encourage the movement of environmental hazardous waste or it could induce an increase in the scale of production or a market expansion. This would lead to more pressure on environmental resources and emission of some pollutants might experience a sharp increase. These topics have been discussed in one of the first papers on the relationship between environmental degradation and economic development: Grossman and Krueger (1991). In their analysis of the environmental impact of the North American Free Trade Agreement (NAFTA) they argued that in order to assess this relationship one must take account of three different mechanisms that interact between trade and resources depletion or pollution: changes in the scale of production, in its composition, and in technology. As the direction of the effects is quite ambiguous, it is not possible, theoretically, to establish an a priori net effect on the environment.[2] In their empirical analysis they found evidence that economic growth may 'alleviate pollution problems'. This depends on whether or not a country has reached a certain level of income per capita. In a nutshell, there is a direct effect of trade on environmental quality which can be positive or negative and an indirect effect through income, which empirically appears to be positive. The Grossman and Krueger conclusion looks more connected to the latter, thus it is dealing with the environmental effect of economic growth rather than purely trade. Hettige et al. (1992) find evidence that toxic intensity increases sharply the more closed an economy is to international trade.

This should confirm the working of comparative advantages theory: 'more open economies have had higher growth rates of labour intensive assembly which are also relatively low in toxic intensity. Highly protected economies have had more rapid growth of capital-intensive smokestack sector'. Again, Grossman and Krueger (1995) observed that the environmental quality improvement, captured by the downward sloping part of the EKC, could occur 'because as countries develop, they cease to produce certain pollution intensive goods and begin instead to import these from other countries with less restrictive environmental protection laws'. However, the authors conclude that such trade is quantitatively modest and its impact cannot explain the reduction of pollution.[3] Another argument which supports a positive relationship between openness and environmental quality is that suggested by Shafik and Bandyopadhyay (1992). They argued that openness of the economic system may lead to an increase of the level of competition among firms. This will induce an increase of investments in new technologies, that 'embodies cleaner process [of production] to meet the higher environmental standard of technology exporting countries'. Nonetheless, in the same vein, one may argue that the competition process is a complex one. Firms may face competition, if is feasible, which lowers prices and so may not invest in new (cleaner) technologies. Or, if they cannot act on the price side, they may well be induced to augment the scale of production. So competition, *per se*, can have more than one effect on environmental quality. This kind of issue cannot be analysed without considering market structure.[4] Suri and Chapman (1998) present an econometric quantification of the interaction of trade in manufactured goods with the growth environment relationship, explicitly considering trade between countries of goods that embody pollution. They find that exports of manufactured goods by industrialized countries has been an important factor in producing the upward portion of the EKC, and their imports have contributed to the downward slope.

2.4 Other Driving Forces

In the previous subsections I reviewed the most popular theoretical explanation of the parabolic empirical pattern of the EKC. Other authors have also argued 'in favour' of other variables. For example, technology and R&D have been regarded as one possible determinant of an environmental quality improvement, because more technology may imply a more efficient use of resources or availability of a new, and cleaner, production technique or new opportunities for abatement. Opschoor (1990) casts doubts about this kind of explanation and considers the long run effect: 'once technological improvement in resources use and/or abatement opportunity has been exhausted or has become too expensive, further income growth will result in net environmental degradation'. This would imply that the relationship should not be a quadratic function with a negative coefficient of the squared term, but a cubic one. In other words, instead of having a U inverted shape, if we consider a longer time span, the relation could be an N shaped one. This has been foreseen by Pezzey (1989), and found at least in some studies for some pollutants.[5]

Komen et al. (1997), analysing a dataset composed of 19 OECD countries, found that income elasticity with respect to public research and development funding for environmental protection is positive. Given this result, these variables are expected to increase as income increases. This may explain why, for industrialized countries and some pollutants, the EKC appears to be negatively sloped. As stated in the introduction to this chapter, the 'simple' (or simplistic?) policy implication derived by Beckerman (1992) has been strongly criticized (see next section). And, it is increasingly recognized that environmental policies may play an important role in the EKC pattern. First, policies are possible driving forces. Hence, the downward sloping segment may be the result of the implementation of specific environmental regulations.[6] Second, policies may have an impact on the determination of the turning point and the corresponding environmental degradation value, as pointed out by Panayotou (1997), who found evidence that a better environmental policy results in a lower EKC. Finally, Torras and Boyce (1998) investigate the role of a more equitable power distribution in the society. They find that this may enhance the influence on policy 'of those who bear the costs of pollution, relative to the influence of those who benefit from pollution-generating economic activities'. Magnani (2000) investigates the role of income distribution. She finds that 'moments of the income distribution function other than the mean may be important for the emergence of a virtuous path of sustainable growth in high-income countries'. Table 16.1, adapted from Barbier (1997), summarizes the empirical evidence in support of the EKC for SO_2 and CO.

Table 16.1 Empirical evidence on the EKC

Environmental degradation indicator	U inverted shape (EKC)	Decreasing
SO_2	S, GK1, GK2, SS, P1, CRB, P2,	CJM
CO	SS, CRB	CJM

Notes: Key to studies: CJM = Carson et al. (1997), CRB = Cole et al. (1997), GK1 = Grossman and Krueger (1993), GK2 = Grossman and Krueger (1995), S = Shafik (1994), P1 = Panayotou (1995), P2 = Panayotou (1997), SS = Selden and Song (1994).

3. CRITIQUES

What is emerging from the previous analysis is that it is not really clear what is the 'true' reason is behind the EKC hypothesis. This, probably, is itself a critique, which can be addressed in this framework. But in this debate some researchers have proposed other attacks. From the theoretical point of view, Rothman (1998) argues about the production based approach and the consumption based approach: 'most environmental degradation can be traced to the behaviour of the consumer either directly through activity like the disposal of garbage or the use of cars, or indirectly through the production activities undertaken to satisfy them'. Further, if a shift in the production pattern has not been accompanied by a shift in the consumption pattern, two conclusions follow: (1) environmental effects due to the composition effect are being displaced from one country to another rather than reduced, and (2) this means that reducing the environmental impact will not be available to the latest developing countries, because there will be no countries coming up behind them where environmentally intensive activities can be located. An important contribution that may put into perspective the EKC hypotheses is the one of Arrow et al. (1995). In this work, they observe that the relationship has been 'shown to apply to a selected set of pollutants only'. It has been found just for 'pollutants involving local short term costs' and 'not for the accumulation of stocks of waste or for pollutant involving long term and more dispersed costs' nor for the stock of natural resources. Moreover the EKC does not take account of the fact that a 'reduction in one pollutant in one country may involve increases in other pollutants in the same country or transfers of pollutants to other countries' and does not give any information about ecological sustainability (intragenerational and intergenerational). Arrow et al., suggest resilience as an ecological concept and that carrying capacity should be adopted as index (and not a single pollutant). They conclude that economic growth, far from being a panacea for environmental quality, is not even the main issue: 'what matters is the content of growth – the composition of inputs (including environmental inputs) and outputs (including waste products). This content is determined, among other things, by the economic institutions within which human activities are conducted'. Finally, Stern (1998) and Stern et al. (1996) synthesise a number of economic critiques, after observing that even if data appear to confirm the EKC hypothesis of individual countries, this does not imply that more growth may be good for the global environment. The econometric critiques are as follows:

(a) *Unidirectional causality* This assumes unidirectional causality from growth to environmental quality and the reversibility of environmental change. Therefore, there is no feedback from the state of the environment to economic growth, and environmental damage is reversible. This assumption implies that a single equation specification does not consider the side-effects of a damaged environment on economic production possibilities frontier.

(b) *Asymptotic behaviour* Following the thermodynamics laws, resources use implies production of waste. So regressions that enable levels of indicators to become zero or negative are usually inappropriate. Anyway, one way to restrict this value is to take the logarithm of the dependent variable.

(c) *Concentration versus emissions analysis* In the EKC literature, it is possible to find that studies sometimes use concentration of the pollutant and sometimes emissions as the environmental degradation indicator. In this study the choice is driven by data availability and homogeneity. Moreover in a general macro framework, emissions are probably better measures than concentrations. First, emissions reflect the sources of pollution and allows us to capture its composition (e.g. whether the SO_2 comes mainly from the use of cars or residential heating). Second, concentrations are more relevant if one wants to study the effects on human health of pollution in urban areas. As 'societies tends to go through a process of increasing and then falling urban population densities and concentration as they develop' (Stern, 1992), the concentration of pollutant is likely to go through a similar pattern. So 'declining ambient concentrations of pollutant do not mean necessarily that the overall pollution burden is declining'. Third, concentrations may not reflect the pollution produced in situ and may well be affected by the weather conditions.

(d) *Isolation* The interpretation of particular EKCs in isolation from EKCs for other environmental problems may give a partial and misleading picture of the actual state of the environment.

4. DATA AND VARIABLES INFORMATION

To illustrate the econometric issues of this chapter a cross-section dataset based upon observations on the Italian provinces in 1990 is used. The dependent variable is per capita emissions of sulphur dioxide (SO_2) for the first estimation and carbon oxides (CO) for the second. The source is Ente per le nuove technologie (ENEA) (see Cirillo et al., 1996). These are two of the most common environmental degradation indicators and they are widely used in the EKC framework. They often exhibit a U inverted relation when regressed against income per capita (see Table 16.1). SO_2 and CO are found in significant quantities in cities and other densely populated areas. The former affects the welfare of citizens because of its connection with lung damage and other respiratory illnesses, plus it contributes to ecosystem acidification. It is one of the agents relevant in acid rain and in soil acidification. It is produced mainly by energy use, the burning of fuels, automobiles' exhaust, certain chemical manufacturers and certain economic activities. The latter is produced mainly from car gases and combustion in general. It has been found that after a certain length of time of exposure it can be harmful for both the heart and the brain.[7] The independent variable is per capita income, and the source is the 'Istituto G. Tagliacarne' in Rome (Italy). In the dataset I have found three outliers. A dummy variable has been added in both estimations in order to properly consider these outliers. The econometric software used in this paper is R.

5. THE PARAMETRIC ESTIMATION

The estimation is based upon a standard OLS over a cross-sectional dataset. The EKC model is the following:

$$E_i = \beta_0 + \beta_1 X_i + \beta_2 X_i^2 + e_i$$

where, on the left-hand side, *E* represents environmental degradation. In this study *E* is sulphur dioxide emissions per capita and carbon monoxide emissions per capita. On the right-hand side, *X* is income per capita (also represented squared), plus the intercept and the error term. All the variables are in logarithms. A reduced form model is used in order to get the direct, or net effect, of the level of per capita income on emissions, to avoid possible sources of multicollinearity, and to deal with data scarcity at a disaggregated level. Moreover, as one of the purposes of this study is to compare output from a standard parametric estimation with a non-parametric estimation, the latter being a 'one to one' graphical analysis the choice is constrained. The result of the estimation for SO_2 is:

$$\underset{}{SO_2} = \underset{(46.378)}{-130.708} + \underset{(21.781)}{60.114X} - \underset{(2.555)}{6.926X^2}$$

the figures in parentheses are the standard errors. In Table 16.2, other relevant econometric information is reported. From the result it is clear that the overall fit of the estimated equation is significant. The individual significance of the coefficients is very high; in fact it is possible to reject the null hypothesis $\beta_j = 0$ at the 1% confidence level. The signs of the coefficients are consistent with the hypothesized U inverted behaviour and the coefficient of determination gave a noticeable goodness of fit.

Now let me consider the carbon monoxide case. The estimation results are:

$$CO = -168.8265 + 79.6031X - 9.3412X^2$$
$$(49.39) \qquad (23.4682) \qquad (2.7536)$$

Again, the figures in parentheses are the standard errors. In Table 16.3, the other relevant econometric information is available. The overall fit of the estimated CO equation is significant, and the coefficient of determination

Table 16.2 Testing and diagnostics for SO_2

Variables	*t*-values	P-prob
Constant	−2.818	0.00608**
Per capita income	2.760	0.00717**
Per capita income squared	−2.710	0.00822**

$R^2 = 0.4387$ Adjusted $R^2 = 0.4177$, F Test = 20.84 ***
Mean (Y value) −0.360808; Var (Y value) 0.127753
Mean (X value) 4.2965; Standard deviations (X value) 0.12158
Minimum −0.62239
Maximum 0.82137
Significance Codes: 0 = ***, 0.001 = **, 0.01 = *
RESET test: F(1, 79) = 0.89403 [0.41131]

Table 16.3 Testing and diagnostics for CO

Variables	*t*-values	P-prob
Constant	−3.379	0.001127**
Per capita income	3.392	0.001081**
Per capita income squared	−3.391	0.001079**

$R^2 = 0.2135$ Adjusted $R^2 = 0.184$ F Test = 7.239 ***
Mean (Y value) 0.579162; Var (Y value) 0.103922
Mean (X value) 4.2965; Standard deviations (X value) 0.12158
Minimum −0.63994
Maximum 0.94331
Significance Codes: 0 = ***, 0.001 = **, 0.01 = *
RESET test: F(1, 79) = 6.6993 [0.0021]

gives an acceptable goodness of fit (0.21, for just one explanatory variable). The individual significance of the coefficients is very high. In fact it is possible to reject the null hypothesis $\beta_j = 0$ at the 1% confidence level. The signs of the coefficients are consistent with the hypothesized U inverted behaviour.

6. NON-PARAMETRIC ESTIMATION

Recently, Taskin and Zaim (2000) used a non-parametric Kernel regression in order to estimate an unknown conditional mean of environmental efficiency and 'let data determine the exact form of relationship between efficiency and income variables'. In this kind of analysis one observes data $\{(X_i Y_i)\}_{i=1}^{n}$ and attempts to estimate $m(x) := E(Y_i | X_i = x)$ where Y is a univariate response and X a vector of covariates. Undoubtedly, one of the most useful and attractive feature of this methodology is flexibility. Therefore, 'it gives predictions of observations to be made without reference to a fixed parametric model'. Moreover 'It provides a tool for finding spurious observations by studying the influence of isolated points' and 'it constitutes a flexible method of substituting for missing values or interpolating between adjacent X-values'.[8] In this section the result of non-parametric estimation is presented and compared to parametric estimation. When using non-parametric tools two decisions are important: the smoothing technique and the bandwidth selection, as stated by Silverman (1986): 'The overriding problems are the choice of what method to use in any given practical context and, given that a particular method is used, how to choose the various parameter needed by the method'. In this work we use a popular estimator, the Kernel Nadaraya Watson, and the optimal bandwidth has been computed by the HCV method (see Hardle, 1990, for a rigorous exposition). The two decisions are not separate, and the accuracy of the Kernel smoothers depends on the Kernel k and the bandwidth selection. The graphical outputs are shown in Figures 16.1 and 16.2.

Applying the two different procedures confirms the EKC hypothesis for the datasheet at hand. Both parametric and non-parametric econometrics offers the U inverted shape for both pollutants. Anyway, it is worth looking closer at the estimated values of the turning points and the corresponding level of environmental degradation. They are respectively the x value and the y value corresponding to the maximum value of the curve. Panayotou (1997) defines the latter as an 'environmental price'. In fact, it is the maximum quantity of pollution one country must receive in order to get an improvement of the environmental quality through, in this case, economic

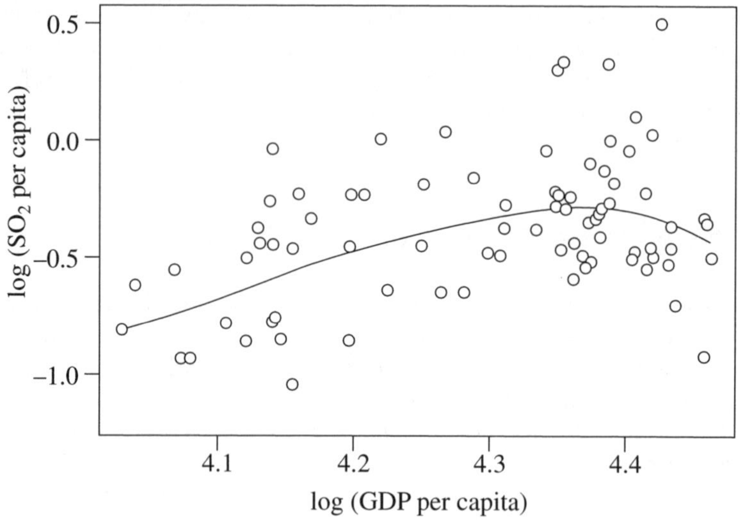

Figure 16.1 SO_2 non-parametric estimation

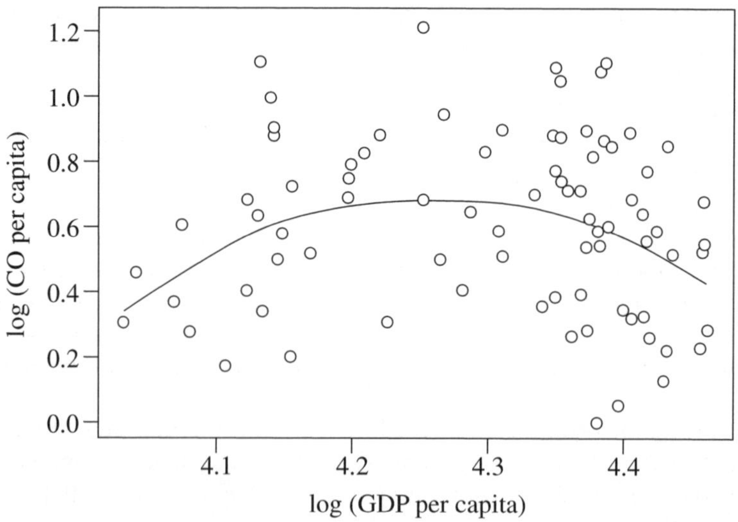

Figure 16.2 CO non-parametric estimation

development. Following Barbier (1997), EKC turning points analysis may provide some important information because:

- they allow us to consider if the estimated per capita level falls within or outside the dataset income range;
- they shed light on the stability of the turning points, thus assessing reliability of estimates. Tables 16.4 and 16.5 report the values for these estimations.

It has been observed that for most of the existing EKC studies per capita income levels of less developed countries are far to the left of their estimated peaks (Barbier, 1997). This does not happen in the analysis presented in this chapter. In fact, Italy is a developed country and data fall within quite a small range. Hence, there are none of the clustered data characterizing the world database.

However, Tables 16.4 and 16.5 highlight another important feature of the estimated turning points. Comparing parametric and non-parametric estimations, it turns out that the values of the non-parametric approach estimates lower turning points and corresponding environmental degradation values. In order to test the significance of this difference one could plot a confidence interval using non-parametric estimates and check if the parametric function belongs to this interval.[9] However, by graphical and numerical inspection alone it is possible to note that the two procedures

Table 16.4 Parametric estimation results

Turning points comparison	Parametric estimation	Non-parametric estimation
SO_2	4.39	4.36
CO	4.26	4.24

Note: Please note that all values are in log terms.

Table 16.5 Non-parametric estimation results

Environmental degradation comparison	Parametric estimation	Non-parametric estimation
SO_2	−0.837	−0.273
CO	0.762	0.0702

Note: Please note that all values are in log terms.

differ noticeably in the location of the turning point. For income per capita this has been identified around the 2.5% difference for SO_2, and around 2.1% for CO. The difference becomes big when one compares the associated environmental degradation values. The difference there is around 65% for SO_2, and around 50% for CO. Such a difference might highlight a low stability of these values, and be very dangerous for ecological thresholds, and the environment may be harmed with serious consequences in the long run.

CONCLUDING REMARKS

In this chapter, after a critical review of the literature, I have tested the EKC hypothesis using Italian data for two of the most common environmental air degradation indicators: sulphur dioxide and carbon oxides. Applying parametric and non-parametric regression, it was found that both tools confirm the EKC hypothesis. So there exists, for the data at hand, a Kuznets Curve between environmental degradation and economic development, but substantial differences have been found for the estimated turning points and the corresponding level of environmental degradation. Therefore, this divergence, detected by comparing parametric and non-parametric tools, may indicate the existence of a bias, which impacts seriously on the estimates. More generally, it should be noted that the explanatory power of the analysis is scanty, given that per capita income is heterogeneous in its magnitude, thus it is affected by a lot of other factors (e.g. economic structure, technology) for which data are not available yet. More research effort should be devoted to the control of estimates for other variables and possibly inserting the time dimension, in order that something about technology and other possible driving forces may be inferred. It implies that the use of policy recommendations from this framework may not be reliable. In fact it is not possible to specify a threshold level of per capita income and environmental degradation beyond which there would be an improvement in environmental condition. After these improvements, the EKC framework could be used more effectively and could answer more questions than it has raised, as well as having the main merit that it has reawakened interest in the side-effects of economic development.

NOTES

An earlier version of this chapter has appeared as 'Environmental Quality and Economic Development. An Economic Analysis', in *Economia delle Fonti d'Energia e dell' Ambiente*, no.1, (2002). The author is grateful to Phoebe Koundouri, Luigi De' Paoli and the anonymous referee. The usual disclaimer applies.

1. Therefore, testing how a qualitative variable reflecting the state of the environment (e.g. whether acceptable or not) is related to another that reflects the state of economic development (e.g. countries classified as low or middle or high income).
2. At least for the scale effect, if the nature of economic activity does not change, it should display a negative correlation between environmental quality and trade. The effect of trade liberalization on the composition of the economic activity, on the other hand, is quite ambiguous. In fact, with more openness comparative advantages theory would apply, and if the advantage arises from differences in environmental regulations: 'each country then will tend to specialize more completely in the activities that its government does not regulate strictly, and will shift out of production in industries where the local costs of pollution abatement are relatively great' (Grossman and Krueger, 1991). But, on the other hand if the source of comparative advantage are natural resources and technology, the net effect on the environment will depend upon whether 'pollution intensive expands or contracts in the country that on average has the more stringent pollution controls'. Finally, concerning the technique, it applies the usual, reasonable, assumption that modern technologies are cleaner than the old one. So more openness would imply that these new technologies must be made available to other countries as well.
3. We do not consider explicitly the interaction with eco dumping.
4. It should be noted that recognizing the links between environmental degradation and competition, though an interesting issue, may be rather a difficult exercise empirically. This is due to definitions and measurement of the two phenomena, but also because of data availability and aggregation.
5. For instance, Moomaw and Unruh (1997) for carbon dioxide, Grossman and Krueger (1995) for total coliforms, Shafik (1994) for faecal coliforms.
6. De Bruyn (1997) found that regulations are particularly significant when coupled with an international agreement.
7. Wark and Warner (1983).
8. Hardle (1990), pp. 6–7.
9. This point has been made by the reefree.

REFERENCES

Ansuategi, A., Barbier, E., and Perrings, C. (1996), 'The Environmental Kuznets Curve, between Theory and Practice', USF workshop Economic Modelling of Sustainable Development: Free University, Amsterdam, November.

Antle, J.M., and Heidebrink, G. (1995), 'Environment and Development: Theory and International Evidence', *Economic Development and Cultural Change*, **43** (3).

Arrow, K., Bolin, B., Costanza, R., Dasgupta, P., Folke, C., Holling, C.S., Jansson, B.-O., Levin, S., Maler, K.-G., Perrings, C., and Pimentel, D. (1995), 'Economic Growth, Carrying Capacity, and the Environment', *Science*, **268**.

Barbier, E. (1997), 'Introduction to the Environmental Kuznets Curve', Special issue, *Environment and Development Economics*, **2** (4).

Beckerman, W. (1974), *In Defense of Economic Growth*, London: Jonathan Cape.

Beckerman, W. (1992), 'Economic Growth and the Environment: Whose Growth? Whose Environment?', *World Development*, **20**.

Byrne, M.M. (1997), 'Is Growth a Dirty Word? Pollution, Abatement, and Endogenous Growth', *Journal of Development Economics*, **54**.

Cirillo, M.C., De Lauretis, R., and Del Ciello, R. (1996), 'Review Study on European Urban Emission Inventories', Report to the European Environmental Agency from the centre of air emissions.

Cole, M., Rayner, A.J., and Bates, J.M. (1997), 'The Environmental Kuznets Curve: An Empirical Analysis', *Environment and Development Economics*, **2** (40).
de Bruyn, S.M. (1997), 'Explaining the Environmental Kuznets Curve: Structural Change and International Agreements in Reducing Sulphur Emissions', *Environment and Development Economics*, **2** (40).
de Bruyn, S.M., and Opschoor, J.B. (1997), 'Development in the Throughput – Income Relationship: Theoretical and Empirical Observations', *Ecological Economics*, **20**.
Di Falco, S. (2002), 'Environmental Quality and Economic Development. An Econometric Analysis', *Economia delle Fonti d'Energia e dell'Ambiente*, no. 1.
Galeotti, M., and Lanza, A. (1999), 'Desperately Seeking (Environmental) Kuznets Curve', Fondazione Eni Enrico Mattei, NOTA DI LAVORO 2.99.
Grossman, G.M., and Krueger, A.B. (1991), 'Environmental Impact of a North American Free Trade Agreement', *NBER Working Paper*, no. 3914.
Grossman, G.M., and Krueger, A.B. (1993), 'Environmental Impact of a North American Free Trade Agreement', in P. Gaber (ed.), *The US Mexico Free Trade Agreement*, Cambridge, MA: MIT Press.
Grossman, G.M., and Krueger, A.B. (1995), 'Economic Growth and the Environment', *Quarterly Journal of Economics*, **110** (2).
Hardle, W. (1990), *Applied Non Parametric Regression*, Cambridge: Cambridge University Press.
Hettige, H., Lucas, R.E.B., and Wheeler, D. (1992), 'The Toxic Intensity of Industrial Production: Global Patterns, Trends, and Trade Policy', *American Economic Review*, **82**.
John, A., and Pecchenino, R. (1994), 'An Overlapping Generations Model of Growth and the Environment', *Economic Journal*, **104**.
John, A., Pecchenino, R., Schimmelpfennig, D., and Schreft, S. (1995), 'Shortlived Agents and the Long-lived Environment', *Journal of Public Economics*, **58**.
Jones, L.E., and Manuelli, R. (1995), 'A Positive Model of Growth and Pollution Control', *NBER Working Paper*, no. 5205.
Kaufmann, R.K. (1998), 'The Determinants of Atmospheric SO_2 Concentrations: Reconsidering the Environmental Kuznets Curve', *Ecological Economics*, **25**.
Komen, M., Gerking, S., and Folmer, H. (1997), 'Income and Environmental R & D: Empirical Evidence from OECD Countries', *Environment and Development Economics*, **2** (4).
List, J.A., and Gallet, C.A. (1999), 'The Environmental Kuznets Curve: Does One Size Fit All?', *Ecological Economics*, **31**.
López, R. (1994), 'The Environment as a Factor of Production: The Effects of Economic Growth and Trade Liberalization', *Journal of Environmental Economics and Management*, **27**.
Magnani, E. (2000), 'The Environmental Kuznets Curve, Environmental Protection and Income Distribution', *Ecological Economics*, **32**.
McConnell, K.E. (1997), 'Income and the Demand for Environmental Quality', *Environment and Development Economics*, **2** (4).
Moomaw, W.R., and Unruh, G.C. (1997), 'Are Environmental Kuznets Curve Misleading Us? The Case of CO_2', *Environment and Development Economics*, **2** (4).
Opschoor, J.B. (1990), 'Ecologische duurzameeconomischeontwikkeling: eentheoretish idée en een weerbarstige praktijk', in P. Nijkamp and H. Verbruggen (eds),

Het Netherlands milieu in Europese ruimte: preadviezen van de Koninklijke vereniging voor staathuishoudkunde, Leiden: Stenfert Kroese.

Panayotou, T. (1993), *Empirical Tests and Policy Analysis of Environmental Degradation at Different Stages of Economic Development*, Working Paper no. 238, Technology and Employment Programme, Geneva: International Labour Office.

Panayotou, T. (1995), 'Environmental Degradation at Different Stages of Economic Development', in I. Ahmed and J.A. Doeleman (eds), *Beyond Rio: The Environmental Crisis and Livelihood in the Third World*, London: Macmillan Press.

Panayotou, T. (1997), 'Demystifying the Environmental Kuznets Curve: Turning a Black Box to a Policy Tool', *Environment and Development Economics*, **2** (40).

Pezzey, J. (1989), *Economic Analysis of Sustainable Growth and Sustainable Development*, Environment Department Working paper no. 15, Washington, DC: The World Bank.

Rothman, D.S. (1998), 'Environmental Kuznets Curves – Real Progress or Passing the Buck? A Case for Consumption Based Approach', *Ecological Economics*, **25**.

Ruttan, V.W. (1971), 'Technology and Environment', *American Journal of Agricultural Economics*, **53**.

Selden, T.M., and Song, D. (1994), 'Environmental Quality and Development: Is There a Kuznets Curve for Air Pollution?', *Journal of Environmental Economics and Management*, **27**.

Selden, T.M., and Song, D. (1995), 'Neoclassical Growth, the J Curve for Abatement and the Inverted U Curve for Pollution', *Journal of Environmental Economics and Environmental Management*, **29**.

Shafik, N. (1994), 'Economic Development and Environmental Quality: An Econometric Analysis', *Oxford Economic Papers*, **46**, 757–73.

Shafik, N., and Bandyopadhyay, S. (1992), *Economic Growth and Environmental Quality: Time Series and Cross-Country Evidence*, Background Paper for the World Development Report 1992, Washington, DC: The World Bank.

Stern, D. (1992), 'Population Distribution in an Ethno-ideologically Divided City: The Case of Jerusalem', *Urban Geography*, **13**.

Stern, D., Common, M.S., and Barbier, E. (1996), 'Economic Growth and Environmental Degradation: The Environmental Kuznets Curve and Sustainable Development', *World Development*, **24** (7).

Stern, D.I. (1998), 'Progress on the Environmental Kuznets Curve?', *Environment and Development Economics*.

Stokey, N.L. (1998), 'Are there Limits to Growth?', *International Economic Review*, **39**.

Suri, V., and Chapman, D. (1998), 'Economic Growth, Trade and Energy: Implications for the Environmental Kuznets Curve', *Ecological Economics*, **25**.

Taskin, F., and Zaim, O. (2000), 'Searching for a Kuznets Curve in Environmental Efficiency using Kernel Estimation', *Economic Letters*, **68**.

Torras, M., and Boyce, J.K. (1998), 'Income Inequality and Pollution; A Reassessment of the Environmental Kuznets Curve', *Ecological Economics*, **25**.

Unruh, G.C. and Moomaw, W.R. (1998), 'An Alternative Analysis of Apparent EKC Transitions', *Ecological Economics*, **25**.

Wark, J., and Warner, D. (eds) (1983), *Air Pollution, its Origin and Control*, London: Harper & Row.

Xepapadeas, A., and Amri, E. (1998), 'Some Empirical Indications of the Relationship between Environmental Quality and Economic Development', *Environmental and Resources Economics*, **11**.

Index